T0329842

Economizing Mind, 1870–2015

Economizing Mind, 1870–2015: When Economics and Psychology Met ... or Didn't

Annual Supplement to Volume 48
History of Political Economy

Edited by Marina Bianchi and Neil De Marchi

Duke University Press
Durham and London 2016

Contents

Introduction   1
MARINA BIANCHI AND NEIL DE MARCHI

Letts Calculate: Moral Accounting in the Victorian Period   16
HARRO MAAS

War of the Ghosts: Marshall, Veblen, and Bartlett   44
SIMON J. COOK AND TIZIANA FORESTI

Economics and Psychology: Why the Great Divide?   71
CRAUFURD D. GOODWIN

Behaviorism and Control in the History of Economics
and Psychology   170
JOSÉ EDWARDS

Implementation Rationality: The Nexus of Psychology and Economics
at the RAND Logistics Systems Laboratory, 1956–1966   198
JUDY L. KLEIN

Psychology Fails to Trump the Multiyear, Structural Development Plan:
Albert Hirschman's Largely Frustrated Efforts to Place the "Ability to
Make and Carry Out Development Decisions" at the Center of the
Development Economics of the Late 1950s and the 1960s   226
NEIL DE MARCHI

Measuring the Economizing Mind in the 1940s and 1950s:
The Mosteller-Nogee and Davidson-Suppes-Siegel Experiments
to Measure the Utility of Money   239
IVAN MOSCATI

The Sidney Siegel Tradition: The Divergence of Behavioral
and Experimental Economics at the End of the 1980s   270
ANDREJ SVORENČÍK

The Economics of Motivations:
Tibor Scitovsky and Daniel Berlyne   295
MARINA BIANCHI

Theoretical Behaviorism, Economic Theory, and Choice   316
JOHN STADDON

Contributors   332

Index   335

Introduction

Marina Bianchi and Neil De Marchi

Over much of the past half century, sporadic attention has been given to the possible links between economics and psychology, though recently there has been a steady rise in the numbers of both psychologists and economists interested in behavioral economics. From both disciplines have come behavioral challenges to the strong version of rational choice thinking. And, along with them, have come challenges to the challengers to relate their observations to mathematical models, as favored by economists (Camerer 1999), and to explain how people come to make the choices that they do.

This recent trend is not part of what we set out to examine, though the one essay in the volume by a laboratory psychologist, John Staddon, offers a methodological reflection on a particular form of behavioral economics, prospect theory. For the rest, the focus is historical, which is to say that we wish first and foremost to identify and shed light on different contexts and episodes involving contact between the two disciplines, and on the questions that either spurred or were raised by such contact.

Correspondence may be addressed to Marina Bianchi, Department of Economics and Law, University of Cassino, Via S. Angelo, 03043 Cassino, Italy 03043 (e-mail: marina.bianchi @unicas.it); or to Neil De Marchi, Duke University (e-mail: demarchi@econ.duke.edu). The editors wish to thank all the participants at the *HOPE* conference, "Economizing Mind, 1870–2015: When Economics and Psychology Met . . . or Didn't," held at Duke University in April 2015. Special thanks to Jeff Biddle, for his many interventions and thoughtful suggestions throughout that conference. Finally, thanks also to all the anonymous referees of earlier versions of the essays.

History of Political Economy 48 (annual suppl.) DOI 10.1215/00182702-3619214

As with any history, context and contemporaries' perceptions are all important. How did such contacts as occurred come about? What seemed at stake to those involved? How did they view their options at the time? If challenge of one sort or another colored the interaction, in what terms was it couched? And how was it resolved? Or, was it not resolved but simply dropped? Then why? Was it perhaps dropped but only temporarily, to be taken up at a later date, maybe in modified form? And so on. One more disclosure, superfluous though it may be: in a single volume we cannot aspire to completeness. Yet even if selectively, the reader will discover unexpected threads (or the lack thereof) clarifying the identities of and connections between the two disciplines.

We begin with a novel focus on the widespread use in the Victorian era of diaries, daily planners, and the like, as aids to good decision making. As Harro Maas makes clear, good here connotes both sensible but also morally responsible. Benjamin Franklin, a most assiduous eighteenth-century user of diaries and planners and, more important, a publisher of almanacs, thought of his way to structure decision making as a sort of moral algebra. Good decision making is part of being an ordered, responsible person—thus, again, "good" in both senses.

A version of Franklin's method was famously applied by Charles Darwin in trying to decide whether he should marry his cousin Emma Wedgwood. It was adopted by the heroine of George Eliot's *Middlemarch*. And, Maas reminds us, the economist William Stanley Jevons, in Sydney, used it in weighing whether, when offered the post of head assayer at the Melbourne Mint, he should accept the offer and the higher income it would bring. That would enable him comfortably to fulfill his obligations to his younger siblings back in England, but would postpone his personal wish to return to London to study economics.

In most cases the Franklin method was closely linked to a diary or planner, and these typically included blank sheets useful for setting out the pros and cons of a pending decision. Indeed, so widespread was the use of diaries and planners, and so important was their auxiliary role in clarifying and improving choices, that Maas speaks of there being an "economy of the self" or of "self-accounting" that rested squarely on these simple aids.

Interestingly, Jevons also went beyond this. He invoked the theories of the mid-nineteenth-century psychologist-physiologist Alexander Bain to convey that keeping a diary or planner was not just a sensible and worthy practice but was the way our minds actually work. In other words, what was a "moral" aid became for Jevons also a psychological given.

This extra step taken by Jevons made Jeremy Bentham's pleasure-pain calculus an integral part of personhood, one in which the pendulum naturally moves in the direction of pleasure. A comparable motion may be observed in markets (though with "gain" replacing "pleasure") and is reflected in the numbers, graphs, indexes, and so forth that are used to convey what is going on in them.

Jevons's conflation was gratuitous, and some decades later, as shown by Craufurd Goodwin in this volume, it became a target of the institutionalist economist Wesley Clair Mitchell, who blamed Jeremy Bentham for the simplistic framework that had come to dominate economic theory: consumers and businessmen treated as just two sorts of rational actor; pleasure and profit made interchangeable, as was pain and loss, in both cases the dollar serving as the unit of sensation.

Simon Cook and Tiziana Foresti provide a detailed account of the relationship between economics and the tradition of experimental psychology established at Cambridge University. This is a complex history and one scarcely addressed by historians of psychology or economics, but which contains threads that link three different approaches to the scientific study of society: those of the economists Alfred Marshall and Thorstein Veblen, and that of the early social psychology of F. A. Bartlett, appointed director of the Cambridge Psychology Laboratory in 1922.

Although this Cambridge tradition is commonly considered to have begun only at the very end of the nineteenth century, Cook and Foresti have uncovered an earlier tradition that, though not experimental, incorporated a common model of the human mind.

This model, whose ultimate source was Herbert Spencer, included hierarchical, accumulative, and comprehensive aspects of the evolution of the nervous system: *hierarchical*, in that it distinguished higher levels from lower, the former being more evolved, so more recent and more complex, and exercising control, or inhibiting the older and simpler lower levels; *accumulative*, in that evolution adds new levels while not removing the older; and *comprehensive*, in that it explains the operation of all levels in the same manner.

Cook and Foresti suggest that this model was held by both Marshall and the Cambridge psychologist W. H. R. Rivers. The scientific psychology of Herbert Spencer formed part of a recently established Moral Sciences Tripos in the 1860s, where Marshall encountered it. Rivers learned it from the great neurologist Hughlings Jackson, an ardent disciple of Spencer.

The common model allowed for differences. Thus Marshall conceived of the evolution of new mental tendencies and instincts in a linear progressive way, while Rivers emphasized the potential for conflict between new and old tendencies, new and old instincts.

For Rivers, indeed, when new behaviors are incompatible with old routines, the older are not just put aside, as Marshall suggested happens with old habits. Rivers made of old instincts a repository that he dubbed the unconscious. Rivers is known for his insistence that shell-shocked soldiers in World War I tap into their unconscious and confront their worst dreams and hidden memories, if they were to be restored. Bartlett, for his part, though influenced by Rivers, focused on the interaction between various fixed and stable human instincts.

Tracing differences and links in Cambridge, Cook and Foresti also identify cross-Atlantic congruences (note: not direct influences). Chief among these for their purposes here is that between Alfred Marshall and the American economist Thorstein Veblen. Veblen took his understanding of habits from the psychologist William James, but he elaborated on it in a way all his own, insisting that habits establish efficient routines for individuals and, on the social level, release communities from having constantly to redefine and reorganize social roles and shared values. Veblen's notion of habit is different from that of Marshall and rests their different conceptions of the relationship between habit and instinct, a conception that Veblen took mainly from William McDougall. Cook and Foresti also explore how this difference had a real impact on Veblen's and Marshall's respective social philosophies.

A second transatlantic congruence, though of a different sort and not mentioned by Cook and Foresti, may be that between William McDougall, who later moved from Cambridge to Harvard and then to Duke University, and Wesley Clair Mitchell (for whom see Goodwin's essay). Mitchell aligned himself with McDougall's characterization of consumers as lazy, influenced by habit, whim, fashion, and so forth, and careless about prices: a far cry from the rational behavior supposed in economic theory.

Craufurd Goodwin notes that, even if economics and psychology acquired their identities at about the same time and in contexts that might have given rise to an open and shared universe of concerns and of ways to go about addressing them, on the whole this did not happen. We might think of this in the following terms (not Goodwin's): with the roles of "parent" disciplines themselves and their place in university curricula still open—think anthropology and moral philosophy in relation to both economics and psychology in Cambridge, England—the progeny bumped into each other but then went their separate ways.

As to why this state of affairs has persisted, Goodwin offers a three-stage approach to an answer. In stage 1 he lists four hypotheses, applicable more especially, though not only, to the situation in the United States.

Under *methodology* falls the fact that economists adopted a conveniently few postulates of human behavior even if they were empirically false, because they undergirded the theory of the competitive market system. Think here (again, not Goodwin's example) of the wonderfully tidy theoretical result in economics that every competitive market equilibrium is a Pareto optimum, and vice versa. Psychology, by contrast, became increasingly unwieldy as one after another relevant variable, many of them not subject to measurement, had to be added to the list forming a more complete empirical account of behavior.

Under *ideological commitment* Goodwin notes the long utilitarian tradition in economics, going back to the eighteenth century. The marginal revolution of the 1870s in economics, he notes, reaffirmed the stability of utilitarian values while suggesting that they might be measured and thus treated mathematically. This was difficult in psychology for the reason already noted—multiple, unmeasurable variables—to which evolution only added further complications.

Under *national identity* or cultural history Goodwin refers to the belief, held in the United States by all social classes, that there is something unique about the American psyche that was essential to national identity. The implication was that the American psyche should never be thought of as something that could be manipulated or controlled, as psychologists, and not economists, seemed inclined to do.

Finally, under *accidents of history*, Goodwin considers random strategic events in one discipline or the other—a new laboratory here or a widely influential textbook there—that affected the position of one of the two disciplines in the social sciences or in relation to the sciences generally.

Not surprisingly, in stage 2 Goodwin concludes that all four hypotheses probably have something to contribute. But he also narrows the focus, elaborating under methodology five ways in which economics and psychology *might* have proceeded (but did not) in the decades of the late nineteenth and the early twentieth centuries.

Finally, in stage 3, and to test the hypotheses and counterfactuals outlined in the first two stages, Goodwin introduces the results of a comprehensive literature review he undertook, covering articles from all the leading international journals, economic, psychological, and a few more general in nature, plus reflective books, including major textbooks, from 1890 through 1939, to see in the views of outspoken representatives just how and how closely and well the two disciplines might have collaborated at various stages within this time span. The result is an extraordinary assemblage of test materials.

Goodwin's massive labor yields a rich lode of impressions and possibilities. To complement it, however, some focused case studies are included in the volume. These precisely define issues between the two disciplines or of episodes in which collaboration was consciously sought, in some cases with outside funding, and sometimes with spectacular success.

We begin with the essay by José Edwards, who argues that, unless great care is exercised, events may be improperly interpreted to encourage a fit between our two disciplines where there was nothing of the sort. Edwards's target is historians of economics but also advocates of behavioral economics. Some of these historians and advocates, too eager Edwards finds, have claimed that behavioral psychology entered economics as early as the revealed preference revolution in the 1930s. This, they allege, is the case even with the mastermind of that revolution, Paul Samuelson: witness Samuelson's admiration for the physicist Percy Bridgman. But, Edwards objects, Bridgman was a functionalist, not at all the same thing as a behavioral psychologist, and not tending, like behavioral psychologists, to control.

Edwards has a case, though psychologists who knew Skinner would caution that he did not try to change motivations (e.g., the desire to eat) but sought to condition the way they are expressed (see Staddon 2016). Perhaps this comes closer to the recent vogue for the nudge version of behavioral economics (see Thaler and Sunstein 2008), where direct manipulation is avoided by subtly redefining options for the consumer.

Ivan Moscati and Andrej Svorenčík, in separate contributions, address early experimentation by economists. In our view, the history here is made more instructive when these two essays are juxtaposed or combined, as we shall treat them here.

Moscati explores the relation between economics and psychology in the 1940s and 1950s by investigating the origin, content, and influence on economic analysis of two experiments on individual decision making. The experimenters observed participants' preferences between gambles where small amounts of money were at stake. The experiments could be understood as a way to measure the utility of money, hence, in principle as an indirect test of expected utility theory.

It became apparent that real people can and do distort probabilities; they also become confused when facing gambles with complicated odds. Interestingly, the experimenters acknowledged these as "disturbing causes" but were inclined to think that the experimental record offered weak support to the expected utility theory. The researchers involved were Frederick Mosteller and Philip Nogee, in one instance, and Donald Davidson, Patrick Suppes, and Sidney Siegel, in the other, though they consulted and had to persuade leading economists and statistical theorists of their method and purpose. They viewed their work as allowing for expected utility theory to be falsified, whereas the paradoxes identified by Maurice Allais in France did not allow for such falsification.

Andrej Svorenčík also explores experimentation in economics and psychology but moves the narrative to the second half of the 1980s and early 1990s. This short period saw a rapid acceptance of experimentation in economics, manifested in the number of experimental papers published in leading journals, the large range of topics explored systematically through economic experiments, the emergence of an experimental economics community and its institutionalization, and the emergence of a new site for economics research to be done, the economics laboratory (Svorenčík 2015).

This period also witnessed the formation of a distinct group of behavioral economists—a mixed community of psychologists, decision scientists, and (predominantly) economists—with an agenda, however, set by the joint work in the 1970s of the cognitive psychologists Daniel Kahneman and Amos Tversky (Heukelom 2014).

Experimental economists and cognitive psychologists shared an interest in experimentation, but, not surprisingly, methodological differences quickly came to the fore, much as Moscati observed of experiments undertaken earlier, only now on a much larger scale and against the backdrop of a growing body of behavioral "anomalies" and their apparent robustness in a market setting.

Svorenčík lays out these differences under three heads: whether to include monetary payments in economic experiments as a way to exercise better control over subjects' motivations; whether to include learning (desirable to ascertain whether anomalies disappear, and whether there are different rates of disappearance for different anomalies), an issue that worried experimenters of both disciplines; and whether deception should be excluded from experiments (the practice of deception being not uncommon in experimental psychology).

These procedural differences, especially the first and the third, had been at issue since Sidney Siegel's work in the 1950s, and when the Sloan and Russell Sage Foundations in the late 1980s decided to fund work in behavioral economics, lack of agreement between economists and psychologists on experimental procedures eventually derailed the initiative.

Differences continued to exist between experimental economists, led on the one side, to name just two prominent proponents, by Vernon Smith and Charles Plott, who would like to see more attention given to market behavior and to ways of enriching economic theory to incorporate such anomalies as appear to persist. On the other side were Tversky (when he was alive) and Kahneman, since the 1970s joined by many experimentally inclined behavioral economists, who focus on anomalies but use experimental methods that admit what Sidney Siegel, when he was alive, eschewed.

Judy Klein examines an instance of genuine and successful collaboration between psychologists and economists in the Logistic Systems Laboratory at the RAND Corporation in Santa Monica, California, from 1956 to 1966. Over the decade analyzed by Klein, economists and experimental psychologists joined forces to conduct game simulations with Air Force personnel on optimal operational decision rules that would be implemented by all levels of personnel in the Air Force. These simulation experiments were structured by four separate laboratory problems: optimal inventory control, missile squadron maintenance, management structures based on weapon systems, and maintenance at a complex combat base.

For the efficient implementation of optimal decision rules, Klein coins the term *implementation rationality*. Her concept, which builds on Herbert Simon's notion of procedural rationality, is intended to show that, as with procedural rationality, implementation rationality shifts the economist's focus from a substantively optimal outcome to a problem-solving process, in this case ensuring effective *implementation* on the part of the client, here the US Air Force.

To clarify the context within which this collaboration was made possible, Klein documents two previous instances of RAND economists and experimental psychologists working as separate disciplines. One, started in 1954, involved economists in the RAND Logistics Department devising a new approach to stocking spare parts for US bomber aircraft based overseas. The optimizing problem was to design kits to minimize stockouts of parts likely to ground bombers and which, in the event of war, would have to be flown out. Their solution was demonstratively more efficient than the previous stocking practice, but there was resistance in the

Air Force to implementing the new plan, which differed from its customary (and preferred) practice.

But where to turn? The answer was provided by psychologists at RAND, working, as they did from 1951 to 1956, in their own laboratory, the Systems Research Laboratory, where there were no economists. In this laboratory, human behavior was the focus and held instructive lessons for successfully implementing optimized Air Force operations. Klein explores in this context how the psychologists approached instructing crews of "spotters" to identify rapidly and accurately breaches of US air space by Soviet bombers.

Two innovations proved crucial. One was to use computer-driven simulations. The second was to treat crews as organic wholes and to view them as "organisms" to be "grown." The program was a huge success. Spotters improved, the stress of failure notwithstanding, and quickly learned to distinguish "important" from "unimportant" tracks on their radar screens. By 1954 the group had created a training manual, and the Air Force commissioned RAND to install the system in all 150 of its US radar bases. Toward the end of 1956, moreover, this RAND training unit was spun off under a new name and became a fully incorporated independent entity. At this point RAND bequeathed the simulation laboratory facilities and many of the RAND staff psychologists to the newly formed Logistics Systems Laboratory, giving rise to the collaboration that Klein documents.

Neil De Marchi focuses on development economics immediately after World War II, when supposed expert advisers, usually "foreign" to the country or region being assisted with development, were inclined (with World Bank and USAID influence and financial backing) to devise integrated (internally consistent and comprehensive), multiyear plans to combat "backwardness." The prevailing understanding was that backwardness was due to certain "obstacles"—summarized as shortages or "gaps," specifically inadequate domestic savings and foreign exchange. Remove those obstacles, so the thinking went, and development would follow. Plans, therefore, whatever their specific emphasis—"balanced growth" across all sectors, investments to secure import substitution, and so on— were tailored to address the supposed obstacles or causes of backwardness, basically, the domestic savings gap and the foreign exchange gap. Consistency and coherence in a plan required that a single test be applied to all potential investments. The marginal rate of return was chosen.

The economist Albert Hirschman dissented from this whole approach. He focused on the need for local administrators to be bold in the face of difficulties whose form and timing were unpredictable but which would occur as projects were implemented. With good data rarely available, and the form and timing difficulties not predictable, Hirschman deemed estimating rates of return an exercise in futility. The basic need, as Hirschman saw it, was for a widespread prodevelopment mind-set and especially for decision-taking ability among the officials responsible for implementing development efforts. In particular, he urged, these persons should be confident enough to address difficulties squarely, with boldness and with the conviction that they can be mastered and overcome, that a *bias for hope*—the title he chose for one of his books—would prevail.

At base, then, Hirschman saw the development problem as one of *mind*. And he borrowed selectively from psychologists of human behavior to bolster his case, especially Orval Hobart Mowrer and Leon Festinger. Mowrer had observed subjects with a fear of stress, learning to overcome it by directly confronting their fear. Festinger noticed that some of his subjects, when faced with a reality that contradicted their beliefs, were willing to adapt their beliefs. The relevance Hirschman saw in this outcome was that it challenged a tendency he observed in Latin Americans to believe that success in overcoming backwardness was beyond them. Why couldn't a change similar to what Festinger observed be instilled in development administrators, difficulties in implementing projects notwithstanding?

Hirschman was effectively dismissed, probably for reasons having nothing to do with his attempt to engage psychology, though that was central in what the mainstream among development economists rejected. The 1959 review by a prominent proplanning economist of Hirschman's *Strategy of Economic Development* (recently published) found Hirschman's emphasis on mind a dubious placing of faith in an "elusive" variable.

This was ironic in the light of the psychologists' success in the spotter training project at RAND and already published accounts of that success. The project drew out increased group performance under stress. That was not quite the same as decision making, but it was close enough that anyone knowing of the RAND psychologists' success might have been expected to ask whether this might be a way to train local administrators in developing countries to overcome unpredictable difficulties. That did not happen.

Marina Bianchi focuses on another instance of economics and psychology coming together eventually. She discusses the economist Tibor Scitovsky, whose *Joyless Economy: The Psychology of Human Satisfaction* (1976) was either ignored or heavily criticized when it first appeared. Critics did not know what to make of his borrowings from the psychophysiologist D. E. Berlyne or the application of them to explain what Scitovsky suggested was the condition of consumers in advanced economies. This Scitovsky characterized as one in which consumers, having grown rich, become habituated to salving boredom with easy come–easy go "fixes" in the form of comforts that scarcely last beyond the consumption of them. More disruptive, however, was the effect of this condition of unskilled consumption on the poor, poorly educated, and unemployable, possibly causing them to express their frustrations in violence to themselves or toward society.

A second edition of The *Joyless Economy* appeared in 1992, this time to much more positive reviews and even selective acclaim. Berlyne's psychological work remained at the book's core. Bianchi elaborates on Berlyne's terminology and arguments, which are often misrepresented as having to do, in particular, with finding the optimal amount of stimulation and resulting pleasure—neither too much nor too little. In fact, Berlyne's "discovery" was the role that variables of change—novelty, surprise, complexity, for example—play in motivating people. It was this theory of motivation that Scitovsky embraced fully and made the basis of his distinction between comfort, the satisfaction that comes from our bodily needs, and pleasure, the satisfaction that comes from the pursuit of activities that are intrinsically rewarding. Bianchi notes, too, a recent growing body of research by experimental psychologists on the determinants of aesthetic preferences and curiosity that again focus on analyzing those activities that carry the potential to generate sustained pleasure, by exciting interest, and a desire to explore new challenges.

The upshot is a fresh take on the human condition and the components of the good life that addresses the call of some advocates of the new behavioral economics, but with a new attention paid to the dynamics of motivations and their implications for economics in terms of creative endeavor and positive enjoyment.

John Staddon, who, as we pointed out earlier, is the only laboratory psychologist to be represented here, contributes a deeper sense of what it would mean to have sustained collaboration between our two disciplines. To start with, if economists had laboratories, that would not necessarily do much, if anything, to bridge the disciplinary gaps.

As a way to substantiate that assertion, it will serve if we simply paraphrase Staddon's own discussion. To begin with pigeons (or other laboratory animals), for example, they "choose" according to a cumulative effect, or "CE" model. In this model, for every situation there is a repertoire of possible responses: think pecks for payoff food, right and left levers to choose from, and a variety of preset regimens. The "strength" of each possible response for laboratory animals is the cumulated payoff probability for that response, biased by a prior probability. Staddon stresses that it is the absolute value that counts: laboratory animals and birds arrive at very stable patterns but, unlike humans, do not follow an average.

This CE model of "choice" is very different from human choice in a whole slew of ways. (1) People, but not animals, have a stock of wealth that affects the value they put on current payoffs (as Daniel Bernoulli noticed long ago). (2) There is no animal equivalent to "loss." (3) Individual differences are common in human groups, but close to 100 percent of animal subjects give the same result as all the others in a specific situation. (4) Animal choices are stable, whereas humans learn from experience and may even switch from one pole to its opposite, for example, from risk aversion to risk seeking.

With points (3) and (4) in mind, it is unsurprising that, when Kahneman and Tversky, in the eyes of many of the founders of the recent behavioral economics revolution, explored their own answers to various questions and then checked with groups of human subjects, inconsistencies across time and between individuals were prominent (see Heukelom 2014; and Svorenčík, this volume).

One version of human choice in new behavioral economics is so-called prospect theory. Staddon notes that prospect theory, meant to be a replacement for standard utility theory, is itself a hybrid. There is a "front end" or "editing" process that precedes evaluation and involves the cognitive processes that identify the problem to be evaluated in the second phase of the choice process.

"Editing," Staddon notes, is "not defined in any calculable way." Various labels have been suggested—framing, combination, segregation, isolation—but when one or another of these specific processes is invoked, why it has been chosen, and how it works, remains unspecified. As a result, prospect theory is "essentially" data classification. It allows us to spell out various possible ways in which questions and evaluations may be asked and made, but it is not a predictive model of human choice. Rather than rely on some form of utility theory to explain economic behavior, Staddon concludes, future research might better examine the historical and cultural factors that determine people's choice repertoires and explore in depth how and why they choose as they do.

Closing Word

Perhaps the most striking instance of a collaboration between economists and psychologists in the papers collected here is that dating from 1956 at the RAND Corporation, as discussed by Judy Klein.

How unique was it? Quite, we suspect, for several reasons. Both groups, though working in separate laboratories at RAND, were clients of the US Air Force, and client satisfaction and continued funding was a common concern. Related to this, a pressing need was acknowledged by one party—the economists—who faced an implementation crisis: their optimizations of Air Force operations were resisted in practice by Air Force personnel. Third, the psychologists, from a different research laboratory, just happened to have a tried and proven innovative training program, written up as a manual, and which had been so successful that the RAND Systems Research Laboratory that generated it, late in 1956, was spun off as a fully incorporated entity. This program seemed just what the economists needed.

How many examples like this are to be found in the essays above? Neil De Marchi suggests that the same RAND training manual might have changed the face of development economics at the time. However, this was not likely, since there was no felt need to change on the part of leading economists, especially not from planning to something as "elusive" as a capacity to take decisions. Nor were they under funding pressure even to consider changing.

A not dissimilar reaction among economists was registered when the first edition of Tibor Scitovsky's *The Joyless Economy* appeared. Marina Bianchi documents the majority sense that Scitovsky's borrowings from modern psycho-psychological research were not needed, hence gratuitous.

Some at least of such resistances can be traced to the long history noted by Craufurd Goodwin of basic methodological differences marking the two disciplines. Economists have long been given to making spare hypotheses, not necessarily empirically grounded, and processing these into tight models of optimal choosing by subjects, the modeling being carried out analytically, geometrically, or mathematically—at any rate deductively. By contrast, psychologists have tended to experiment, which turns up multitudes of observed behaviors, all of which have some claim to be explained. This inductive (or piecemeal) approach generates many psychologies but relatively few attempted generalizations.

The essays by Ivan Moscati and Andrej Svorenčík highlight modern variants of the methodological divergence just noted. For the last six decades and more, though especially since the 1970s, economic theorists and, latterly, experimental economists have drawn on the expertise of psychologists in conducting experiments. On the whole, however, they have also strongly resisted the use of hypothetical questions, the lack of real money payoffs associated with subjects' choices, and the use of deception by experimenters—that is, common elements in psychological experiments. Moreover, distinct traditions of experimentation are now favored or shunned within the still-small community of experimental economists and within the larger and growing community of behavioral economists.

And misunderstandings still abound. José Edwards, for example, identifies misreadings of "behavioral" as a cause for mistaken historical readings and current differences among behavioral economists. John Staddon, himself a psychologist, weighs in with a whole series of reasons why the prospect theory introduced by Tversky and Kahneman as an improvement on traditional economic modeling of choice must be imbibed critically.

Yet, despite these persisting differences in aims and methods, it is striking that each discipline, for much of the past century and more, has been aware of, drawn on, complained about, shunned, and at the same time welcomed the other. In these encounters there was more involved than a comparison of methods and tools. Foundational issues were also being decided. These emerged even before the two disciplines took scientific shape. As Harro Maas makes clear in his account of the use in the Victorian era (and before) of diaries and planners, these were accessories to good decision making, good here meaning well thought through and morally to be approved. At a different level, Cook and Foresti document how different models of mind translated into different views of society. In the late nineteenth century such concerns were part of debates about the meaning of rationality and individual freedom, the role of motivations and incentives, the ordering of social interactions and the emergence of norms and, ultimately, the very nature of utility, pleasure/satisfaction, and well-being. It seems fair to say that, while the problem of human choice and its consequences remains a focus of inquiry in both disciplines, psychologists and economists will find themselves in dialogue and probably in experimentally generated entanglement.

References

Camerer, C. 1999. "Behavioral Economics: Reunifying Psychology and Economics." *Proceedings of the National Academy of Sciences of the United States of America* 9 (19): 10575–577.

Heukelom, F. 2014. *Behavioral Economics: A History*. Cambridge: Cambridge University Press.

Kahneman, D., and A. Tversky. 1979. "Prospect Theory: An Analysis of Decision under Risk." *Econometrica* 47 (2): 263–91.

Staddon, J. E. R. 2016. *Adaptive Behavior and Learning*. 2nd ed. Cambridge: Cambridge University Press.

Svorenčík, A. 2015. "The Experimental Turn: A History of Experimental Economics." PhD diss., University of Utrecht.

Thaler, R., and C. R. Sunstein. 2008. *Nudge: Improving Decisions about Health, Wealth, and Happiness*. New Haven, Conn.: Yale University Press.

Letts Calculate: Moral Accounting in the Victorian Period

Harro Maas

> A diary. Dies. Hodie. How queer to read some of the entries in the journal!
> Here are the records of dinners eaten, and gone the way of flesh.
> —William Makepeace Thackeray, "On Letts's Diary" (1861)

Max Weber famously argued that the "foundations" of economics were not to be found in the complexities of the human mind, scrutinized by means of laboratory experiments, but in history. Weber responded to investigations in German industrial psychology and related attempts in Britain to derive the marginalist principles of utility theory from psychophysics. According to Weber, it was useless to ground utility theory on the so-called Weber-Fechner law; instead, marginalism emerged as a historical reality from specific historical circumstances.

For Weber, these circumstances were tied to a commercial society in which "principles of commercial bookkeeping" made people act "rationally." The only thing the economist needed to assume was "the merchant's soul." Just as a merchant was able to numerically rank the "intensity" of his

Correspondence may be addressed to Harro Maas, Centre Walras-Pareto, University of Lausanne, Bâtiment Géopolis, 1015 Lausanne, Switzerland; e-mail: harro.maas@unil.ch. Earlier versions of this article were presented at workshops at the Wissenschaftskolleg in Berlin and Sciences Po in Paris, and at the *HOPE* annual conference at Duke from which this final version emerged. I would like to thank the organizers and participants of these workshops, especially Wendy Espeland, Martin Gireaudeau, Marina Bianchi, and Neil De Marchi, for their comments. Further thanks go to Emmanuel Didier, Tiago Mata, Chris Starmer, and Bob Sugden for their encouragements at various stages in the gestation of this essay, and to the referees of this journal.

History of Political Economy 48 (annual suppl.) DOI 10.1215/00182702-3619226

needs, so did the economist theorize on the "increasingly true assumption" that "everyone [was] to shape his conduct towards his environment exclusively according to the principles of commercial bookkeeping—and, in *this* sense, 'rationally'" (Weber 1975, 32–33).[1]

Weber was not the first or the last to connect principles of commercial bookkeeping to rational and orderly conduct (Carruthers and Espeland 1991; Coquery, Menant, and Weber 2006). Already in 1711 Richard Steele wrote in the *Guardian* that someone was not so much a "very fine gentleman" because of his table conversation but because he was able to keep the books (Deringer 2012). Keeping the books increasingly came to be seen as a way to control and regulate not only one's business but also one's personal and family life. The reference to a "very fine gentleman" shows the moral connotations of personal accounting practices. Indeed, the notion that came into fashion in those days to refer to the systematics of someone's behavior was one's "moral economy," a notion that nicely captures an economic-financial and moral meaning while leaving in the middle whether it is a quality of the instruments used, a quality of the individual, or a characteristic of the infrastructure that encompasses both.[2]

Contemporary economists and psychologists who link accounting principles to rational conduct do so to argue that the human mind itself functions on accounting principles, leaving aside the social and material infrastructure that in Weber's view were all important. In a well-known article the behavioral economist Richard Thaler (1999) takes up Daniel Kahneman and Amos Tversky's notion of mental accounting (see also Thaler 1985). Starting from "basic" psychological principles that conceptualize human decision makers as "pleasure machines," he argues that simple experiments show the systematic limits in rational decision making, because humans, as in traditional household accounts, incorrectly sort their decisions in uncommunicating boxes, thus violating principles of rational choice theory. Thaler (1999) writes: "Mental accounting is the set of cognitive operations used by individuals and households to organize,

---

1. That it would be wrong to uniquely identify the use of moral accounting practices with the rise of capitalism in Western Europe can be seen from the use of such practices elsewhere. On Chinese ledgers of merit and demerit, see, e.g., Brokaw 1991.

2. This meaning clearly differs from that of E. P. Thompson's influential 1971 article, where it referred to an economy of provision as opposed to the free market, but it is not so far off the meaning that can be found in Lorraine Daston's 1995 essay on the moral economy of science. It steers away from being a matter of individual psychology, which in any case would have been anachronistic for the eighteenth century. For recent usages of "moral economy" along the lines of Thompson, see, e.g., Fassin 2009, 2012.

evaluate, and keep track of financial operations." The cognitive psychologists Gerd Gigerenzer and Peter Todd take issue with Benjamin Franklin's so-called moral algebra to argue against contemporary rational choice theory from a perspective orthogonal to Kahneman and Tversky. Just like Thaler, however, they identify what was essentially an accounting aid in decision making with a theory of the functioning of the human mind that they subsequently criticize. Neither Steele nor Franklin referred to "cognitive operations" but to a social and material practice. Weber located the shift from practice to mind historically, when individuals increasingly started shaping their behavior according to the rules of accounting.

The historical moment of this quid pro quo can be located in William Stanley Jevons's exposition of his theory of pleasure and pain in *The Theory of Political Economy* (1871), when he refers to Alexander Bain's *Emotions and the Will* of 1859 and, more precisely, though without explicit reference, to Bain's analysis of the usefulness of Franklin's moral algebra in improving our decision making. In Jevons's hands, an accounting procedure became a theory of mental deliberation in which arguments pro and con transform into numbers that sway, like a pendulum, the price lists in the market.

Much has been written on the presence of marginalist principles before the so-called marginalist revolution in the last quarter of the nineteenth century. Limiting myself to the Victorian context, no political economist before Jevons considered a view of man driven by pleasure and pain (a view most easily found in the work of James Mill and John Stuart Mill, who embraced Jeremy Bentham and associationist psychology) linked to price formation in the market. Neither does the evidence listed in the introduction of Jevons's *Theory of Political Economy* give reason to do so. "The private-account books, the great ledgers of merchants and bankers and public offices, the share lists, price lists, bank returns, monetary intelligence, Custom house and other Government returns" may be evidence that will turn economics into an "exact mathematical science" (Jevons [1871] 2013, 11) but does not point to a theory that singles out the "feelings" of individual minds as driving the prices in the market.

We may take Weber's idea that accounting tools made people increasingly behave as accountants as a cue that bridges the gap between evidence and theory. In what follows I first explore how the intrusion of accounting practices into the private sphere in the Victorian period made individuals act as accountants who linked their decisions to their wealth, especially when this concerned their most consequential decisions in life. I then investigate how Victorian accounting practices were received in the work of Bain, George Eliot, and Jevons. I concentrate on one tool for improving decision making, Franklin's moral algebra. In conclusion, I briefly return to contemporary analogies in economics and psychology between accounting practices and mental deliberation.

Family Fortunes

Recent scholarship has highlighted the importance of accounting practices in shaping everyday life in the Victorian period (e.g., Creaton 2001; Hopwood 1994; Miller 1992; Miller and O'Leary 1987; Walker and Llewellyn 2000). Peter Miller (1994, 1) detailed the different channels through which accounting practices "infiltrated" all aspects of everyday family life and how accounting became "intrinsic to, and constitutive of social relations." The original engraving of the feuilleton version of Charles Dickens's *Dombey and Son* can serve as an example. The rise and downfall of Dombey is visualized as a carousel of diaries, account books, ledgers and journals, and a house of cards that turns accounting instruments—instruments of control, accuracy, and certainty—into their exact opposite: a gamble that left Dombey at the mercy of Fortuna's wheel. Neglecting his daughter, Florence, for his son, the engraving tells us that Dombey never got his ledgers properly balanced (see figure 1). *Dombey and Son*, written midway through the nineteenth century, was a feuilleton about the rise and fall of family fortunes, in the private and public sphere, moral and financial. Bankruptcy, as Dickens knew from personal experience, was not just a financial but also a moral disaster. Being listed in the yellow pages of the *Gazette* ended in what Barbara Weiss, with a wink to Thomas Carlyle, called the "hell of the English." As Weiss (1986, 39) shows, the persons listed ranged across all mercantile occupations, from manufacturers and shipowners to cheesemongers and line drapers, next to financial scoundrels like Augustus Melmotte in Anthony Trollope's *The Way We Live Now*. A bankruptcy destroyed one's life and reputation. Accounting tools could prevent one's financial and moral downfall.

Systems of accounting included simple lists of incomes and expenditures in waste-books and journals as well as double-entry bookkeeping. William Kitchiner's *Housekeeper's Ledger* of 1824 matched in complexity George Wilson's *Comprehensive Method of Bookkeeping* of 1823 that

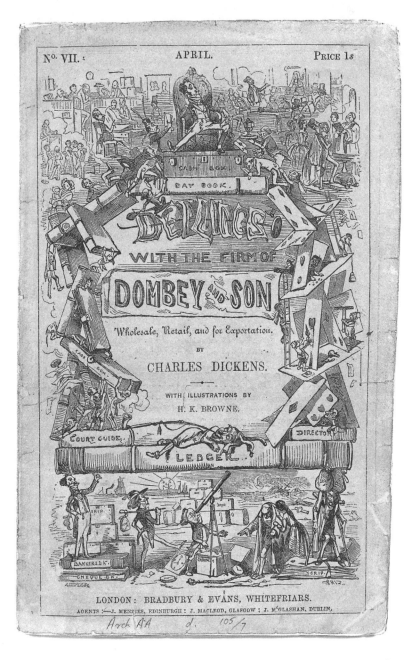

Figure 1. Original cover design for the feuilleton version of *Dombey and Son*. Arch. ΛΛ d105T/P (no. 7 April). Bodleian Library, Oxford.

explained the use of daybooks, journals, ledgers, and other devices. Control was an important function of accounting systems. A household diary for 1831 included a page that specified laundry lists in two columns, one of which was to be handed to the maid and the other served to check the returns. The simple categories of a journal gave an idea of expenditure patterns and where the money went on a weekly or monthly basis.

Keeping the books had clear moral implications for someone's personal life and for the household's social status. Household accounts were an aid in learning to know one's needs, but also in learning to restrain expenditures. Knowing one's needs and controlling them were two sides of the same coin. The usefulness of a journal depended on the accuracy of its user—and on the diligence with which "sundries" were written down and checked. In the first decades of the nineteenth century, manuals were published for young married (or to be married) women that explained in detail what books to keep and how. Indeed, the moral esteem (and their value as a marriage partner) of middle-class women increasingly hinged on their capabilities to manage domestic accounting systems. In *Martin Chuzzlewit* Dickens (1844, 359) tells of "prudent Cherry," one of the daughters with which Mr. Pecksniff was "blessed," sitting at a "little table white as driven snow, before the kitchen fire, making up accounts!" The "neat maiden," "pen in her hand," and "calculating look addressed towards the ceiling," is checking "the housekeeping expenditure."

Manuals warned women to exert restraint in expenditures, for which purpose the regular keeping of accounts was an important check and antidote. Keeping the books served purposes of "efficiency" or "economizing" (both expressions can be found at the time). Eighteenth-century debates on luxury consumption were centered on its moral implications. But morality was inevitably connected with uncertainties about work and income flows in an environment that became increasingly governed by the law of the market. "Mrs. Lavish," who indulged in "conspicuous consumption" (an expression also regularly found around 1850), and "Mrs. Liberal," who did not care to keep control of her servants, threatened to bring family fortunes to ruins. They were contrasted with the prudent housewife, who kept a good eye on the balance between income and expenditures and who made sure savings would withstand the wheel of Fortune. Thus, the "prudent economy" of the family became an emblem not just of a well-managed household but of a person's moral character, a person's ability to control the self. An instrument to exert self-control was a diary—what we nowadays would call a daily planner.

Almanacs and Daily Planners

According to Philippe Lejeune (2009, 51), "The diary, like writing itself, was born of the needs of commerce and administration." A good example of a diary that moved from the commercial to the private sphere is *Letts's*. Its full title was *Letts's Diary or Bills Due Book and an Almanack*. John Letts launched the original diary in 1797 to meet the increased need among merchants for a device to record the "movements of stock and to control their businesses," and it soon became sold in the thousands to individuals for private use.[3] Diaries such as *Letts's* had almanacs as their historical predecessors. Customers could ask the binder to interleaf their almanacs with blank pages for additional notes.

Though the seventeenth century is commonly seen as the heyday of the almanac (Capp 1979; Perkins 1996), total almanac sales over the eighteenth century rose into the millions and trumped sales of the Bible (McCarthy 2013; see also Stowell 1977). In the eighteenth century, Benjamin Franklin was better known as the editor and publisher of *Poor Richard's Almanack* (from 1748 continued as *Poor Richard Improved*) than for his work as a scientist or politician. His almanac was renowned for its proverbs and wisecracks ("time is money"), but was also bought for its practical information. Franklin, rightly or wrongly considered by Weber as the embodiment of the Protestant ethic (Weber 2002; see also Kolko 1961 and Tolles 1947), published his almanac from 1733 to 1758, with sales that averaged ten thousand pieces a year. The almanac was cheap, portable, and compact and came to be considered a vital personal accessory. "A person without an almanac is somewhat like a ship without a compass; he never knows what to do, nor when to do it" (McCarthy 2013). Almanacs gave rule and structure to personal lives. George Washington wrote on every page of his blank pages "where & how my time is spent." In the nineteenth century, publishers started substituting for the blank pages preprinted lined and columned pages indicating the days of the week, enabling the combination of financial and other note taking. This innovation also meant that someone could now look forward and plan ahead.

---

3. In 1870 Letts, Son & Co. converted to a limited liability company to raise working capital for its vastly expanding diary business. Unfortunately for Thomas Letts, who had taken over the business from his father, John, in 1835, nothing came to nothing. Profits did not materialize, and the business went into liquidation in 1885. By then Charles Letts, Thomas's son, had already set up his own stationery business that flourishes still today. See Rebecca Steinitz (2001) for an excellent discussion of Letts's marketing strategies and, more pertinent for this article, Letts's importance in creating prefabricated "social spaces for the Self." See also Steinitz 2011.

Letts's Diary was only one of the many daily planners that became merchandised in the Victorian period. There was *The Ladies Pocket Book, The Law and Commercial Daily Rememberancer, The Housekeeper's Diary, Beeching's Annual Diary, The Methodist Diary*, and many more titles, some of them short-lived, others, such as *Beeching's*, as widely distributed as *Letts's*.[4] It was the favorite of George Eliot's companion in life, George Henry Lewes. Next to such preprinted diaries there were so-called blank books (Eliot's choice) that were used for similar diaristic purposes and that by themselves governed an impressive commercial market. By the mid-nineteenth century, a Boston publisher of blank books ranked as one of the city's two highest taxpayers (McCarthy 2013).

How widely daily planners were used in Victorian Britain can be gauged from one of William Makepeace Thackeray's New Year's sermons, originally published in *Cornhill Magazine* in 1861, which was without much ado titled "On Letts's Diary." *Letts's Diary*, Thackeray explains, consisted "of two pages, ruled with faint lines for memoranda, for every week, and a ruled account at the end, for the twelve months from January to December," where revenues and expenses could be registered. The two ruled pages contained columns in pounds, shillings, and pence so that the diary could serve as a waste-book. Dates for payment of insurances, and other important dates, such as the self-advertisement to renew purchase at the end of the year, were preprinted.

The Diary as Ephemeris and Précis

Thackeray discussed the kinds of entries that could be found in a diary and the many good intentions with which their owners filled its pages (intentions that of course would not materialize). These good intentions addressed different aspects of life: financial, social, and personal, mostly pointing to the gospel of efficiency and improvement. "I hope, sir, you will be 'a better man,' as they say, in '62 than in this moribund '61, whose career of life is just coming to its terminus. A better man in purse? In body? In soul's health? Amen, good sir, in all" (Thackeray [1861] 1907). Striking is Thackeray's emphasis on the diary's promise to improve its user "in all" aspects of human life. The diary did not merely serve to register appointments, payments, and daily events but to improve the self. Yet, with the

---

4. See Steinitz 2001 for an analysis of the different versions of *Letts's Diary* that were merchandized over the nineteenth century. By the 1860s Letts produced fifty-five different versions that were "identified by number rather than title" (Steinitz 2001, 164).

exception of the evaluative statements at the close of the year, intentions were remarkably absent from these daily planners. Rather, they were used to register one's doings in a matter-of-fact way.

Introductions to almanacs contained sample entries, and the general opinion was that these entries were so highly predictable and made in such a standardized fashion that they were made fun of, as Thackeray did with the entries of his supposed readership in *Letts's Diary*.[5] Its introduction shows its relation to the management of one's moral economy. The diary's "real value" extended well beyond the recording of financial and business transactions—the "stock and business" that came to be moved and controlled was one's complete personal life.

> Use your Diary, we say, with the *utmost familiarity and confidence*; conceal nothing from its pages, nor suffer any other eye than your own to scan them. No matter how rudely expressed, or roughly written or with what material, let nothing escape you that may be of the slightest value hereafter, even though it be but to form a simple link in the daily chain of common transactions. If you receive a trivial Commission, a Diary can be more safely entrusted with it, than your vanished memory, and one word is often a sufficient memorandum to render it intelligible. . . . You expend or obtain a sum of money, which, however small, will not harm you to register, although no further use be made of the entry. An appointment, a notice or any other circumstance of promise or expectancy should be committed in its pages with equal fidelity.

Striking is the appeal to be comprehensive and faithful. The "daily chain of common transactions" could be interpreted to pertain only to financial and business transactions (as witnessed from the reference to sums of money), but clearly one's inner and social life was at stake as well: an appointment, a notice, a promise, all should be noted "with equal fidelity." The user should trust his or her most personal thoughts and reflections to its pages.

> Nay, even your Thoughts upon very many incidents, that are passing; for a valuable suggestion will often occur to the mind once, and be for ever lost if not then secured. Do not care if the miscellaneous character of its appreciation should render the Volume a little unsightly. . . . Not a

---

5. Although introductions taught individuals how to use the diary, surviving records show how users adapted diaries to their own purposes, writing outside reserved spaces or replacing preprinted instructions and indications with their own. See especially Lejeune 2009.

solitary fact contained is thereby prejudiced. If from any Accident, Sickness or Neglect you have discontinued its use or availed yourself of it but fitfully, heed not the gap or irregularity; your Perseverance will be rewarded and your Negligence passed over without a single comment.

By striving to completeness, the diarist would become an orderly person in full mastery of his or her own "wants and practices" and capable of acting efficiently.

Let *this* be the Rule! *Undeviating*! Before you lie down to sleep, or before you leave your dressing room in the morning, or if you prefer at any other fixed hour, daily (one of the foregoing will usually prove the best). Read over the Entries of the Past Day to provide against any omission, and then those of tomorrow (if there be any) to arrange your time in the most advantageous manner.

Thus, first almanacs and then diaries were used for many purposes. They served to mark time and to keep track of one's activities, and they were also used to track one's income and expenses. In contrast with autobiographical writing in which the author targets an external readership,[6] these diary notes were not made with such an audience in mind; they served personal purposes, which sometimes became apparent only to the diarist himself or herself through his or her persistence in taking notes day by day, over the years. In short, the diary functioned as an ephemeris that was not registering the movements of the heavenly bodies—nature's economy—or, as in the case of the physiocrats, the social economy, in their *Ephémérides du citoyen*, but the economy of the self.[7] Void of judgment or reflection, the entries, piling up day after day, week after week, year after year, summarized their makers, being, rather than making, a moral account of their owners.

When leafing through the diary, its users were presented with—in Molly McCarthy's felicitous term—an "abbreviated self." At the end of the year, users calculated the balance of their wealth, sometimes transferring the result to next year's diary. The introduction to *Letts's*

6. A good example is Marcus Aurelius's well-studied *Meditations*, sometimes considered the beginning of the autobiographical genre. Written by the Roman emperor, or rather by his secretary, in Greek, Aurelius's meditations clearly addressed an outside audience. The meditations are unspecified in space and time, thus conveying a universal idea, rather than time-bound facts. See Lejeune 2009.

7. The full title of Franklin's almanac for 1852 was *Poor Richard Improved: Being an Almanack and Ephemeris of the Motions of the Sun and the Moon.*

recommended summarizing all the transactions (financial, social, personal) listed daily in the ruled account at the end of the diary. Hence, the ideal user of a diary was to become an accountant, using the diary to give a précis of his or her private, social, and financial life.[8] The diary served, in Mary Poovey's (2002, 32) words, to establish "what I am" and "what I am worth."

Becoming a Writer

Let me now examine how two Victorians, George Eliot and William Stanley Jevons, made use of their diaries. Eliot, nom de plume of Mary Ann Evans (1819–1880), started as a translator, editor, and journalist for the *Westminster Review* but was to become one of the most important novelists of the Victorian period. Jevons (1835–1883) is known to the readership of this journal as one of the so-called marginalist revolutionaries who introduced the calculus and the idea of the utility-maximizing agent to economics. Both Eliot and Jevons serve here as exemplars for a common practice of moral accounting that they examined in their writings.

From 1849 onward Eliot recorded in blank books the books she read, her inabilities to work, her financial rewards, and the pains of rejections and revisions. Her entries were made in a factual, "bareboned" style (Millim 2013). Eliot's local and time-bound entries enabled her to retrace and evaluate her achievements daily and to assess her persona as a professional writer (Millim 2013). A sequence of entries for October 1862 reads as follows:

18. An Unfruitful week. Only at p. 45 of Part VII [of *Romola*]
20. Wrote nothing because of indisposition. Began "Il Principe."
22. Received £180 from Blackwood for Adam Bede. 6/-ed.
24. Only at p. 51, having rejected a chapter which I had begun, and determined to defer it to the next part.

Anne-Marie Millim (2013, 69) emphasizes how Eliot's "countless bareboned entries" show themselves "relatively resistant to analysis" if only

---

8. I take the notion of précis from Andrew Mendelsohn (2011), who examines how meteorological records and medical diagnoses in eighteenth-century France were combined and synthesized into a summary (précis) of the state of health of France. Drawing the annual balance from one's diary can be seen as taking a précis of one's personal life.

because of their "immense number and lack of explicit confession."[9] However, for this manner of note taking, it is not the singular note but their regularity and repetitiveness that give them their significance.[10] Their number changes these entries into a factual account of the self that enabled Eliot to make her evaluative statements at the end of each year, which were as a rule accompanied by a statement of her annual earnings (which increased spectacularly over the years).

31 [December 1862] Last day of the kind old year. Clear and pleasantly mild. At p. 58 of my 9th Part which I think will be the dullest that has yet to come. Yesterday a pleasant message from Mr. Hannay about Romola.

We have had many blessings this year—opportunities which have enabled us to acquire an abundant independence, the satisfactory progress of our two eldest boys, various grounds of happiness in our work, and ever growing happiness in each other. I hope with trembling that the coming year may yield as comforting a retrospect: with trembling, because my work is not yet done. Besides the finishing of Romola, we have to think of Thornie's passing his final examination, and, in case of success, his going out to India: of Bertie leaving Hofwyl: and of our finding a new residence. G.'s health has been very variable and frequently infirm. I have had more than my average amount of comfortable health until this last month in which I have been constantly ailing and my work has suffered proportionately.

From the words with which she closed her diary for 1877, we can see how matters of fact that may resist our analysis served Eliot's purpose of self-accounting well:

9. In his *History of Sexuality* and subsequent work, Michel Foucault examined diaristic practices from the standpoint of its confessional (Christian) history. Though related, the diaristic practice I examine here is, as Anne-Marie Millim notes, almost void of explicit confessions.

10. In one of the first studies on English diaries, Robert Fothergill (1974, 12) writes that Eliot's blank books "consist mainly of notes on her reading and on her health," and so she does not come into the orbit of the "geniuses" of diary writing, such as "Pepys, Boswell, Haydon, Kilvert, Barbellion." Fothergill's characterization of such diaries as the "heart" of the genre misapprehends the work done by Eliot in her time-bound entries. Rather than ignore the financial and repetitious entries in diaries or downplay their importance, Millim argues that it is the interconnectedness of personal, moral, and financial concerns that matters; keeping a diary was a process of moral accounting, of what Millim (2013, 69, 87) refers to as "emotional accounting" or "emotional management" that was instrumental in constructing and maintaining a diligent and efficient persona.

Today I say a final farewell to this little book which is the only record I have made of my personal life for sixteen years and more. I have often been helped by looking back in it to compare former with actual states of despondency from bad health or other apparent causes. In this way a past despondency has turned to present hopefulness. . . . I shall record no more in this book, because I am going to keep a more business-like diary. Here ends 1877.

For this more "business-like" diary, she chose *Beeching's Annual Diary*, Lewes's favorite. *Beeching's* preprinted pages enabled her to more easily plan ahead and to record her financial affairs more systematically. Eliot left no diary for 1878, the year of Lewes's unexpected death, and continued her entries in much the same style in *Beeching's* when she resumed the year after.

Choosing a Destiny in Life

Next to *Beeching's*, just such a more businesslike diary was *Letts's*, the diary used by Jevons. Only the diaries he kept in his early twenties are preserved, and it is not known, though it seems unlikely, whether he kept similar diaries after his return to London from Sydney in 1859. Jevons (1835–1883) was a Unitarian from Liverpool, whose father's iron-trading business went bankrupt in the aftermath of the Great Railway crisis of 1845. This forced the family to move from Liverpool to Manchester. Shortly after, his mother, daughter of the banker William Roscoe of Liverpool (whose banking business had gone broke in the aftermath of the Napoleonic Wars), died, and his eldest brother, Roscoe, turned insane.

Thomas Jevons retained sufficient means to send Stanley and his brother Herbert to London to study at University College. But when Stanley Jevons had finished his bachelor's degree in mathematics and chemistry and was offered the extremely well-paid job as one of the two gold assayers at the Sydney Mint, his father pushed hard to make him accept the offer. For the rest of his life, Jevons financially supported two of his sisters. For a youngster of middle-class family descent like Jevons, to become a rule-governed, accountable person was an ideal for very practical reasons that related to family setbacks and long-term family commitments.

So how did Jevons use his diary? Did he live up to the high standards set by the diary's introduction? I discuss two exhibits. The first (figure 2) is taken from *Letts's Diary* for 1855. We see Jevons's entries for the first

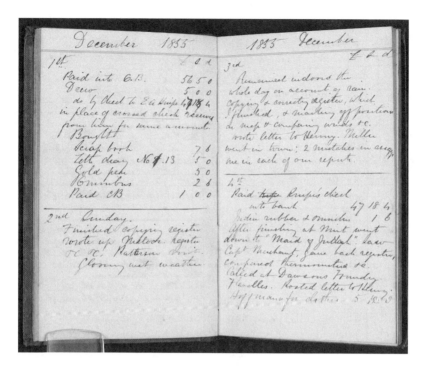

Figure 2. Page from Jevons's diary for 1855, JA 6/4/2. Copyright of The University of Manchester.

four days of December. By this time Jevons, aged nineteen, had settled down in Sydney as one of the two gold assayers for its newly established mint. Jevons wrote down the month at the top of the page and then drew two dividing lines for the days of the week. After taking notes for one day, he drew a line to commence the next. He did the same for the next two days, thus, as a rule, writing notes for four days on two pages.

The first of December shows some financial transactions and payments made (among others for *Letts's Diary* for the coming year, for the omnibus that he regularly took to the mint, and a substantial money transfer to his family in Great Britain). On the second, he copied from a meteorological register that he borrowed from the captain of the *Maid of Judah*, the same ship that had brought him to Sydney. He mentioned a visit and made a note on the weather. On the morning of December third, he finished "copying and correcting" the meteorological register (elsewhere in the diary he noted that he was displeased with its quality) and started marking the data on a map for comparison purposes. He also made a remark on mistakes he found in assaying reports of himself and Charles Miller, the second assayer to the mint. On the fourth Jevons returned the meteorological register to Isaac Merchant, captain of the *Maid of Judah*, read the thermometer, called at a merchant's shop, and posted a letter to pay for cloths. The entries are stated with a rough indication of the time of day when they were written (morning, afternoon, evening).

This exhibit enables us to reconstruct in great detail Jevons's life over these four days: payments and social, scientific, and work activities. But for Jevons it did more than track his steps. Recording that he had borrowed the meteorological register entailed the promise to hand it back, which he did two days later. Recording he had not finished copying meant there was more to do—which had to be finished before the ship sailed again. Noticing mistakes made at work entailed the wish to improve. Paying a check into the bank fulfilled a promissory note of the first of December. The diary moderated his social, financial, professional, and intellectual life. It sequenced his actions through time. It showed him who he was through what he did. His actions implied norms that are not stated or logically inferred. But they were entailed in his actions. Sending money home, paying a debt, returning a borrowed register, marking mistakes, paying for clothing: such matters of fact display him as a diligent person to be trusted and whom he himself could trust.

The second exhibit is taken from the final page of Jevons's diary for 1858 and marks a dramatic moment in his life (see figure 3). He uses space reserved for November but dates the entry December 3. Jevons gives an account of his wealth for that year, how it changed compared with the previous year, and then he starts reasoning on how long he could live on his wealth, thus opening the possibility of moving back to London to study political economy at University College. He speculates on other sources of income (including the share of his inheritance—his father died while he was in Australia). To return to London to study political economy was an important and uncertain step to make, even though Jevons had always planned to stay in Sydney for only a limited period. But he had just received an offer to become head of assaying at the newly established mint in Melbourne, which would raise his annual income from roughly £800 to £2,000. This was not an offer to simply put aside, as he had financial commitments to his siblings. Clearly, however, accepting it would prevent him from pursuing his studies in political economy, which had increasingly

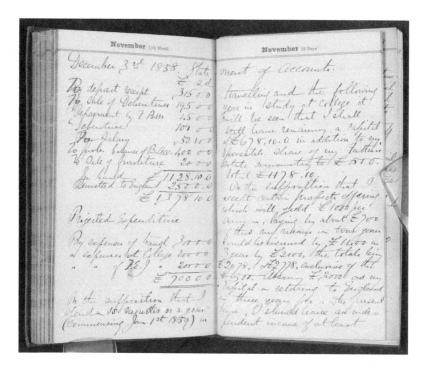

Figure 3. JA Jevons's statement of accounts for 1858 6/4/2. Copyright of the University of Manchester.

moved to the center of his attention. Thus, recording the balance of his wealth was an important step in assessing future options. It enabled him to put this complex and life-changing decision into perspective.

These two exhibits show how the diary enabled Jevons to manage his personal life. Going through his diary, he was able to construct a balance of his accounts—moral, financial, and social—which helped him decide to reject the offer to become the first gold assayer at the Melbourne mint, and to risk leaving his job as a gold assayer in Sydney to return to England to follow his intellectual interests and study political economy. The diary helped him define a new purpose in life. Stemming from a middle-class family whose father suffered a bankruptcy, with financial commitments to his siblings, Jevons's decision to pursue his own education was an uncertain and risky step to make. His diary enabled him to weigh the risks and to balance the pros and cons.

Franklin's Moral Algebra

In previous sections I probed the Victorian's use of accounting tools in the social and private sphere. Household accounts were widely used to regulate and control family expenses. Almanacs and merchant accounting tools transformed into daily planners that served to improve the self along several dimensions, financial, social, personal. Improving decision making fenced off uncertainty in the market by strengthening one's moral character. Moral accounting was not a property of the mind but a tool-based practice with normative consequences for one's personal life.

Halfway through the nineteenth century, the use of accounting tools as moral organizers was theorized by Bain in *The Emotions and the Will* (1859).[11] The book was the second and final volume of Bain's attempt to merge the principles of associationist psychology with physiological explanations of the mind, the preceding volume having addressed, as its title stated, "the senses and the intellect." In these two volumes Bain aimed to show how an individual's physiological infrastructure enabled the emergent higher functions of the mind to evolve into a unified whole, though it suggested rather than demonstrated these connections. Bain's magnum opus lacked the physiological reductionism stated two decades later in Thomas Huxley's 1874 essay in the *Fortnightly Review*, "On the Hypothesis That Animals Are Automata," and fit rather the renewed and intense interest in Baruch Spinoza's *Ethica* in midcentury Britain. Translated by Eliot, the *Ethica* was important for her own novelistic writing, but also for the psychological investigations of Lewes, Herbert Spencer, and others.

It has been observed, nonetheless, that Bain's volumes were, on the one hand, highly modern, almost laying the foundation for the format of present-day psychology textbooks. He started with an exposition of the nervous system that then served as the groundwork for an investigation of the higher functions of the mind. He also made excursions into areas that, from a modern perspective, have little bearing on an investigation of the functioning of the mind proper. Equally, he moves between sustained synthetic descriptions and normative suggestions to improve the mind's functioning.

One issue at stake was the extent to which human deliberation could be analyzed in terms of reflex action (as Huxley maintained) or was dependent on willpower. For Bain, willpower was not a given but could be

11. I quote from the second edition of 1865.

trained. Accounting tools could serve as training aids to counteract the weakness of the will. Following the associationist tradition of Hartley, and of the Mills, Bain analyzed deliberation as a complex voluntary act in which motives of varying strength join or oppose one another. At their root, these motives could be retraced to feelings of pleasure and pain. Because their strength could vary over time, so might the outcome of a deliberation. This could have the effect that men were "liable to hasty decision on the one hand, and protracted indecision on the other" (420), and it was a quality of the "well-trained intellect" to estimate the time and thought necessary to come to a well-balanced decision.

Bain gave the example of a decision between "a life of liberty with small means, and a life of constraint with considerable affluence," where the allowance of a sufficient amount of time to pass would enable the mind to "survey and estimate" all the "*pros* and *cons*" to arrive at a well-balanced decision (423). For most men, however, it was "no easy matter" to "retain in the mind the just values of all the opposing considerations, so as to have, at the instant of closing the account, a true sum on either side" (424). Because the mind, left to itself, "may leave us at the mercy" of our last impressions, Bain (1865, 426) recommended "the method of recording and summing up the separate decisions" used in business. Bain then quoted at length the famous letter of September 19, 1772, that the "great genius of prudential calculation" Benjamin Franklin had sent to Joseph Priestley, "in which he recommends the use, in daily-life questions, of the artificial methods practised in money accounts" (424):

> To get over this [the uncertainty that perplexes us in decisions of great difficulty], my Way is, to divide half a Sheet of Paper by a Line into two Columns, writing over the one Pro, and over the other Con. Then during three or four Days Consideration I put down under the different Heads short Hints of the different Motives that at different Times occur to me for or against the Measure. When I have thus got them all together in one View, I endeavour to estimate their respective Weights; and where I find two, one on each side, that seem equal, I strike them both out: If I find a Reason pro equal to some two Reasons con, I strike out the three. If I judge some two Reasons con equal to some three Reasons pro, I strike out the five; and thus proceeding I find at length where the Ballance lies; and if after a Day or two of farther Consideration nothing new that is of Importance occurs on either side, I come to a Determination accordingly.

Franklin continued that if he thus has "the whole" before him, he can "judge better, and am less likely to take a rash Step; and in fact I have found great Advantage from this kind of Equation, in what may be called Moral or Prudential Algebra" (Bell and Labaree 1956).

Nowadays, Franklin's method is perhaps best known from its use by Charles Darwin in making up his mind to marry his cousin Emma Wedgwood. Gigerenzer and Thomas Sturm (2012) quote from Franklin's letter to his nephew of April 8, 1779, in which he described the procedure in almost identical words as in his letter to Priestley, finishing in a jest that "if you do not learn it, I apprehend you will never be married." Gigerenzer and Sturm (and earlier Gigerenzer and Todd [1999]) consider the arguments Franklin adds on either side of the balance sheets as "cues" for uncertain prospects, thus moving Franklin's balance of arguments from moral space to probability space. Bain is not concerned with uncertain prospects, however, but with temporizing decision making to prevent choices being driven by immediate emotions instead of calm deliberation. His recommended mode is almost copied from the introduction to *Letts's Diary*: every evening recording the impressions of the day, and by allowing a fixed amount of time to pass by, to average out "casual or accidental biasses" (426).

> What I should suggest is that every evening we record the impression of the day, or put down the side which preponderates according to the balance of motives passing through the mind in the course of that day; and that this record should be continued during the whole period that the deliberation lasts. It would happen that in some days we feel more acutely the pressure of the motives on one side than on others; the preponderance being liable to be reversed from day to day in a question where the total of pleasures and pains is very nearly equal. But by allowing a lapse of time we should reduce the casual or accidental biasses to a general average, and at the end of the period we have only to sum up the records of the days, and see which has the majority. (426)

Instead of giving weight to individual arguments, Bain puts weight on the "general average" of motives:

> If we found such a result as twenty to eleven or nineteen to twelve, our decision would probably be a safe one, while fifteen to sixteen would of course be indecisive, but also of value as showing that no great blunder would be likely to arise in either course. The essence of this procedure

lies in its taking account of all the states of mind that we pass through in reference to the opposing questions, and therefore the judgment should be deferred until we have described a complete cycle in this respect. (426)

As examples of the kinds of deliberations in which these auxiliaries could be particularly useful, Bain mentioned "the choice of a profession, the change of one's country by emigration, the undertaking of an extensive work which we cannot get back from, the contracting of the irrevocable tie of domestic life." In all such cases, the "feelings of the moment should be resisted by the machinery of the intelligence" to ensure a balanced decision. "In discussing the choice of profession, we must look at it through all variety of seasons, circumstances, and states of body and mind, and this cannot be done in a day," because of the untrustworthiness of the mind and the "advantage" of having considerations in front of us, which would fall "out of sight" otherwise (427).

In Bain's description (and in Franklin's), the balance of motives recorded daily harnessed the mind against overhasty or emotionally prompted decisions. The purpose was to come to a *reasoned decision*, one that would not be biased by immediate emotions or myopia. But the mind could not be trusted to resist the emotions on its own account; it needed instruments in support. Bain's "machinery of the intelligence" was not simply seated in the brain but dependent on "auxiliary instruments," the material infrastructure of moral accounting.

Balancing Pleasures and Pains

Around midcentury, Bain was the towering philosopher of mind, and it is small wonder that both Jevons and Eliot (who knew Bain well) invoked his theory of mind in their examination of human deliberation. Jevons did so in *The Theory of Political Economy*, Eliot in her novels, especially *Middlemarch*. While Bain's use of Franklin's moral algebra was clearly normative, both Jevons and Eliot shifted to a naturalistic analysis in which the instrument as an aid in decision making vanished from view. Both Jevons and Eliot were highly interested in the physiological basis of human conduct (White 1994; Maas 2005a, 2005b). Only recently returned from Australia, Jevons famously remarked to his brother Herbert at the beginning of the 1860s that he was "reading up the *Nervous System*," a plausible reference to Marshall Hall's *Memoirs of the Nervous System*

(Black and Könekamp 1981, 120; White 1994). Jevons was almost literally matched by Eliot at the end of the 1870s, when she writes in her diary that she is "reading Bain on the Nervous mechanism" while finishing George Henry Lewes's multivolume work on psychology *Problems of Life and Mind* on which he had be working when Eliot wrote *Middlemarch*.[12] Commentators such as Henry James complained that Eliot tried too hard "to recommend herself to a scientific audience" in her novelistic writing (quoted in Myers 1984, 192; see also Shuttleworth 1984 and Rylance 2000).

Jevons, for his part, superimposed Bain's use of Franklin's algebra on a physiological reading of Bentham's theory of pleasure and pain. The second chapter of *The Theory of Political Economy* opens with an exposition and then simplification of Bentham's theory. Jevons then reinterprets Franklin's algebra as not being about balancing arguments to come to a reasoned decision but being about the balancing of quantities of pleasures and pains themselves, keeping, so to speak, the weight Franklin attributed to his respective arguments while suppressing their substance. For Franklin, the weight followed from the importance of arguments; for Jevons, the weight became a property of the feelings themselves. In the process, a procedure for regulating deliberation became a mechanism driving our behavior.

We can see the change immediately following on the introduction of Bentham's springs of human action. "We may treat pleasure and pain as positive and negative quantities are treated in algebra. The algebraic sum of a series of pleasures and pains will be obtained by adding the pleasures together and the pains together, and then striking the balance by subtracting the smaller amount from the greater. Our object will always be to maximize the resulting sum in the direction of pleasure, which we may fairly call the positive direction" (32).

"Adding the pleasures together and the pains together" and then "striking the balance" describes a procedure not so different from Franklin's, except that pleasures and pains replace arguments. Jevons still describes a procedure, performed by a subject (will) on these pleasures and pains. "Striking the balance" is further described as maximizing pleasures over pains, which is a procedure that has to be performed. Jevons continues quoting from Bain's *Emotions and the Will*, which "exactly expresses the opposition of pleasure and pain," the one, more or less, neutralizing the other, as "acids" can neutralize one another (33).

---

12. Entry of Tuesday, March 25, 1879, in Eliot 2000, 167.

Following the Mills, Bain did not question that we are "uniformly put in motion" by "some variety of pleasure or pain," but "time, careful training, one's own observations and reflections" ensure that our feelings of pleasure and pain become "checked" by our will and intellect (428–29). Indeed, John Stuart Mill's struggles with Bentham's felicific calculus turned on the issue that not all pleasures or pains are of the same kind and so cannot be properly weighed against one another; pushpin was not as good as poetry. This meant that the will had to be harnessed against the drive of our immediate feelings. Bain recommended Franklin's method to that end, or his own similar method. Both Bain and Franklin emphasized the mind's untrustworthiness and the necessity of collecting all considerations before coming to a decision. Earlier, Jevons avoided the complexity of our feelings altogether by restricting himself to the "lowest rank of feelings" that were incomparable to humanity's higher motives, but nevertheless the only feelings the economist had to deal with. By excluding the "power and authority" of the higher motives for action, Jevons exchanged a balance of arguments for a balancing process of pleasures and pains. Thus, in contrast to Bain and Franklin, Jevons did not consider the paper and pencil balancing method he described as an auxiliary to improve the mind's deliberation process. Rather, this method described the mind's own functioning. Instead of being a sustained process of collecting and comparing considerations over time to come to a balanced decision, pleasures and pains are instantaneously weighed against one another to sway the decision in the direction of pleasure.

"This Is the Question"

Darwin headed his list of pros and cons involved in the decision to marry Emma Wedgwood with "This is the question." He followed Franklin's advice, to check the emotions in life-changing decisions by an extended process of sustained deliberation, but adapted the method to his own wishes. Rather than a list of pros and cons, we find his considerations to marry or not to marry not all consistently listed, and neither did he give them explicit weights (he may have done so mentally). The decision to marry follows as a proof, QED. We do not know if his decision indeed followed from his considerations that seem to have been listed over time ("better than a dog anyway" was added afterward), or was a decision driven by emotions after all.

Whether such life-changing decisions were made intuitively, driven by immediate feelings of pleasure and pain, or followed on a balance of arguments was tested by Eliot in *Middlemarch*. Her protagonist, Dorothea Brooke, serves as stellar example. In an overly hasty and ill-considered decision, the young woman decides to marry the much older Edward Casaubon in hopes of contributing to the social good, but finds herself imprisoned in the loveless Lowick estate where Casaubon works on his dead-end project to find the key to all mythologies. Casaubon's jealousy of his much younger relative Will Ladislaw, who openly worships Dorothea, makes him decide to add a codicil to his will that disinherits Dorothea if she ever marries the man. His jealousy seems misplaced, however, because after his death, Dorothea's faithfulness to her husband is unabated. Only later does Dorothea become aware of her deep affection for Ladislaw when she unexpectedly finds him in the company of Rosamond, the unhappy wife of *Middlemarch*'s new and young physician Tertius Lydgate (who is persistently frustrated by the older generation of physicians in his efforts to bring medical treatment in *Middlemarch* up to modern standards). But Dorothea refuses to admit the thought of an engagement, in part because of social considerations, in part because of the social goals she hopes to reach with the aid of her inheritance from her late husband.

Dorothea allows Ladislaw a farewell meeting. Awaiting his appearance, she leafs through her "particular little heap of books on political economy and kindred matters" for advice on how best to use her fortune for the social good, but they fail to shed much light. When Ladislaw enters, they express their mutual feelings, but also acknowledge the impossibility of an engagement. They part with what should be a final and definitive good-bye. Dorothea's marriage to Casaubon had been motivated by her wish to put her own life to the purpose of the greater good, which proved to be a flawed project. Even after his death, she had chosen to respect his testament, thus securing the moral esteem of the small gossiping *Middlemarch* community—to the annoyance of Rosamond, who rightly guessed Dorothea held feelings for Ladislaw but wrongly supposed that she had made them known to him. This convoluted set of motives was present at this most decisive moment of her life. Yet it was not a carefully crafted algebra of reasons but her most immediate emotion that swayed the balance. "In an instant," and in marked contrast with Franklin's and Bain's advice, Dorothea changed her mind on this life-changing decision. "'Oh, I cannot bear it—my heart will break' said Dorothea, starting from her seat, the flood of her young passion bearing down all the obstructions which had kept her silent—the great tears rising and falling in an instant: 'I don't mind about poverty—I hate my wealth'" (Eliot 1986, 800–801).

William Myers (1984, 184) argues that Eliot developed in *Middlemarch* a complex web of relations between her characters that cannot be disposed of in a utilitarian bookkeeping exercise. But he forgot that at this most decisive moment of Dorothea's life, it was the avoidance of the greater pain that swayed the balance. By making Dorothea—as in a reflex—move away from her greater pain, Eliot made her no longer follow external, abstract, and socially accepted motives, but the deepest and most immediate source of value—selfish love. Yet no one at the time would have made such a decision without considering the consequences for their wealth, and Eliot was too keen an observer of her times to ignore the omnipresence of such calculated decisions. In the split second that Dorothea stirs from her chair (a detail Eliot added to the first draft), she calculates and fixes her needs to the price lists in the market; in tears and out of breath she promises Ladislaw to be a prudent wife: "'We could live quite well on my own fortune—it is too much—of seven hundred a-year—I want so little— no new clothes— and I will learn what everything costs'" (Eliot 1986, 801).

Conclusion

Franklin's procedure to improve decision making, especially for difficult and consequential ones like marriage or change of occupation, was part of a widespread practice of diaristic note taking (made popular by Franklin himself), in which people drew a yearly balance of their lives at the end of what we now call daily planners. Early in the second half of the nineteenth century, Bain incorporated Franklin's moral algebra in *The Emotions and the Will*. Bain suggested the use of Franklin's moral algebra, or cognate personal accounting practices, as a check to hasty decisions prompted by our emotions. Reason needed to be educated. Bain's suggestion was tested by Eliot in her "study of provincial life"—*Middlemarch*— to show that important decisions may be taken in an emotional reflex, rather than in a process of sustained deliberation. The human mind can very well take care of its own, if emotions stand to reason. Jevons takes Eliot's reevaluation of the human frame one decisive step farther, however, by washing out the difference between reason and emotions altogether. There is nothing moving the mind except feelings of pleasure and pain, the balance of which decides what action will follow. In Jevons's hands, Bain's version of Franklin's moral algebra became a theory of mind, in which arguments are reduced to numbers that sway, like a pendulum, the price lists in the market.

In the introduction to *The Theory of Political Economy*, Jevons ([1871] 2013, 11) argued that all the data are available to turn economics into an exact science. "There is not a clerk nor book-keeper in the country who is not engaged in recording numerical facts for the economist. The private-account books, the great ledgers of merchants and bankers and public offices, the share lists, price lists, bank returns, monetary intelligence, Custom-house and other Government returns, are all full of the kind of numerical data required to render Economics an exact mathematical science." There is nothing in this list of account books that suggests or requires a connection between accounting data and a theory of mind, a theory in which feelings of pleasure and pain sway the price lists in the markets. Neither energetics nor psychophysics will establish this connection. A culture in which individuals are immersed in accounting practices might. In this essay I have examined how, in such a culture, agency became theorized in terms of accounting tools. Tools to regulate and control private conduct informed a theory of the economic agent, who came to be seen as mimicking such tools in his mental deliberations.

When Jevons identified arguments with feelings, and feelings with numbers, he came to consider the future in numbers as well. Rather than think about deliberation on the future in terms of a balance of arguments that bear on a person's character, Jevons started to consider the future as events that needed to be weighted according to their probability of occurrence. When there is uncertainty in decisions, we "must reduce our estimate of any feeling in the ratio of the numbers expressing the probability of its occurrence." We do not make these adjustments consciously. Rather, "almost unconsciously we make calculations of this kind more or less accurately in all the ordinary affairs of life" (36). Franklin and Bain used accounting methods so that uncertain decisions would not be made in haste and on the basis of immediate emotions. For Jevons, balancing pleasures and pains no longer checked the emotions; rather, it expressed the way the mind gravitates, unconsciously, to its preferred course of action. In Jevons's theory of pleasure and pain, the establishment of a moral self is exchanged for a self that estimates future causes of action in terms of risk and uncertainty. Moral deliberation turns into an assessment of uncertain prospects.

Weber considered the image of rational man, following the principles of accounting in its deliberations, as a historical reality. Jevons naturalized this image based on the idea that mental accounting is hardwired in the brain. This image survives in present-day encounters between economics and psychology. Whether in the hands of a Gigerenzer or a Thaler, when comparisons are drawn between accounting principles and mental deliberation, deliberation is considered to follow the principles of accounting and, in behavioral economics, subsequently criticized for not standing up well in the comparison. Such comparisons no longer consider accounting principles as tools to support a mind falling short of perfection.

References

Aurelius, Marcus. 1997. *Meditations*. Hertfordshire, U.K.: Wordsworth Classics.

Bain, Alexander. (1855) 1864. *The Senses and the Intellect*. London: Longman, Green, Longman, Roberts and Green.

———. (1859) 1865. *The Emotions and the Will*. London: Longmans, Green and Co.

Bell, Whitfield J., Jr., and Leonard W. Labaree, eds. 1956. *Mr. Franklin: A Selection from His Personal Letters*. New Haven, Conn.: Yale University Press.

Black, R. D. C., and R. Könekamp. 1981. *Papers and Correspondence of William Stanley Jevons*. Vol. 7. London: Macmillan

Brokaw, C. J. 1991. *The Ledgers of Merit and Demerit: Social Change and Moral Order in Late Imperial China*. Princeton, N.J.: Princeton University Press.

Capp, Bernard. 1979. *English Almanacs, 1500–1800: Astrology and the Popular Press*. Ithaca, N.Y.: Cornell University Press.

Carruthers, Bruce G., and Wendy N. Espeland. 1991. "Accounting for Rationality: Double-Entry Bookkeeping and the Rhetoric of Economic Rationality." *American Journal of Sociology* 97 (1): 31–69.

Coquery, Natacha, François Menant, and Florence Weber. 2006. *Écrire, compter, mesurer: Vers une histoire des rationalités pratiques*. Paris: Editions ENS.

Creaton, Heather, ed. 2001. *Victorian Diaries: The Daily Lives of Victorian Men and Women*. London: Mitchell Beazley.

Daston, Lorraine. 1995. "The Moral Economy of Science." *Osiris* 10:2–24.

Deringer, William Peter. 2012. "Calculated Values: The Politics and Epistemology of Economic Numbers, 1688–1738." PhD diss., Princeton University.

Dickens, Charles. 1844. *Martin Chuzzlewit*. London: Chapman and Hall.

Eliot, George. (1871–72) 1986. *Middlemarch*. Edited by David Carroll. Oxford: Clarendon Press.

———. 2000. *The Journals of George Eliot*. Edited by Margaret Harris and Judith Johnston. Cambridge: Cambridge University Press.

Fassin, Didier. 2009. "Les économies morales revisitées." *Annales. Histoire, Sciences Sociales* 64 (6): 1237–66.

———. 2012. "Compassion and Repression: The Moral Economy of Immigration Policies in France." *Cultural Anthropology* 20 (3): 362–87.

Fothergill, Robert A. 1974. *Private Chronicles: A Study of English Diaries*. Toronto: Oxford University Press.

Foucault, Michel. 1984. *Le souci de soi*. Vol. 3 of *Histoire de la sexualité*. Paris: Gallimard.

Gigerenzer, Gerd, and Peter M. Todd. 1999. *Simple Heuristics That Make Us Smart*. Oxford: Oxford University Press.

Gigerenzer, Gerd, and Thomas Sturm. 2012. "How (Far) Can Rationality Be Naturalized?" *Synthese* 187 (1): 243–68.

Hopwood, Anthony G. 1994. "Accounting and Everyday Life: An Introduction." *Accounting, Organizations and Society* 19 (3): 299–301.

Jevons, William Stanley. (1871) 2013. *The Theory of Political Economy*. London: Palgrave Macmillan.

Kitchiner, William. 1824. *The Housekeeper's Ledger and the Elements of Domestic Economy, to Which Is Added Tom Thrifty's Essay on the Pleasure of Early Rising*. London: Hurst, Robinson and Co.

Kolko, Gabriel. 1961. "Max Weber on America: Theory and Evidence." *History and Theory* 1 (3): 243–60.

Lejeune, Philippe. 2009. *On Diary*. Edited by Jeremy D. Popkin and Julie Rak. Translated by Katherine Durnin. Manoa: University of Hawaii Press.

Maas, Harro. 2005a. *William Stanley Jevons and the Making of Modern Economics*. New York: Cambridge University Press.

———. 2005b. "Jevons, Mill, and the Private Laboratory of the Mind." *Manchester School* 73 (5): 620–49.

McCarthy, M. A. 2013. *The Accidental Diarist: A History of the Daliy Planner in America*. Chicago: University of Chigaco Press.

Mendelsohn, J. Andrew. 2011. "The World on a Page: Making a General Observation in the Eighteenth Century." In *Histories of Scientific Observation*, edited by Lorraine Daston and Elizabeth Lunbeck, 396–420. Chicago: University of Chicago Press.

Miller, Peter. 1992. "Accounting and Objectivity: The Invention of Calculating Selves and Calculable Spaces." *Annals of Scholarship* 9 (1–2): 61–86.

Miller, Peter, and Ted O'Leary. 1987. "Accounting and the Construction of the Governable Person." *Accounting, Organizations and Society* 12 (3): 235–65.

Millim, Anne-Marie. 2013. *The Victorian Diary: Authorship and Emotional Labour*. Farnham: Ashgate.

Myers, William. 1984. *The Teaching of George Eliot*. Leicester: Leicester University Press.

Perkins, Maureen. 1996. *Visions of the Future: Almanacs, Time, and Cultural Change, 1775–1870*. Oxford: Clarendon Press.

Poovey, Mary. 2002. "Writing about Finance in Victorian England: Disclosure and Secrecy in the Culture of Investment." *Victorian Studies* 45 (1): 17–41.

Rylance, Rick. 2000. *Victorian Psychology and British Culture, 1850–1880*. Oxford: Oxford University Press.

Shuttleworth, Sally. 1984. *George Eliot and Nineteenth-Century Science: The Make-Believe of a Beginning*. Cambridge: Cambridge University Press.

Steinitz, Rebecca. 2001. "Social Spaces for the Self: Organizing Experience in the Nineteenth- Century British Printed Diary." *Auto/Biography Studies* 16 (2): 161–74.

————. 2011. *Time, Space, and Gender in the Nineteenth-Century British Diary*. London: Palgrave Macmillan.

Stowell, Marion Barber. 1977. *Early American Almanacs*. New York: Burt Franklin.

Thackeray, William Makepeace. (1861) 1907. "On Letts's Diary." In *Roundabout Papers: And Denis Duval*. No. 18. London: Macmillan and Company.

Thaler, Richard H. 1985. "Mental Accounting and Consumer Choice." *Marketing Science* 4 (3): 199–214.

————. 1999. "Mental Accounting Matters." *Journal of Behavioral Decision Making* 12 (3): 183–206.

Thompson, E. P. 1971. "The Moral Economy of the English Crowd in the Eighteenth Century." *Past and Present* 50:76–136.

Tolles, F. B. 1947. "Benjamin Franklin's Business Mentors: The Philadelphia Quaker Merchants." *William and Mary Quarterly: A Magazine of Early American History* 4 (1): 60–69.

Walker, S. P. 1998. "How to Secure Your Husband's Esteem: Accounting and Private Patriarchy in the British Middle Class Household during the Nineteenth Century." *Accounting, Organizations and Society* 23 (5–6): 485–514.

Walker, S P., and Llewellyn. 2000. "Accounting at Home: Some Interdisciplinary Perspectives." *Accounting, Auditings & Accountability Journal* 13 (4): 125–49.

Weber, M. 1975. "Marginal Utility Theory and 'The Fundamental Law of Psychophysics.'" Translated by L. Schneider. *Social Science Quarterly* 56 (1): 21–36.

————. 2002. *The Protestant Ethic and the Spirit of Capitalism: And Other Writings*. London: Penguin.

Weiss, B. 1986. *The Hell of the English: Bankruptcy and the Victorian Novel*. Lewisburg, Penn.: Bucknell University Press.

White, Michael V. 1994. "The Moment of Richard Jennings: The Production of Jevons's Marginalist Economic Agent." In *Natural Images in Economic Thought: "Markets Read in Tooth and Claw,"* edited by Philip Mirowski, 197–230. Cambridge: Cambridge University Press.

War of the Ghosts: Marshall, Veblen, and Bartlett

Simon J. Cook and Tiziana Foresti

"The War of the Ghosts" is a Chinook story, recorded and translated by Franz Boas (1901, 182–86), and subsequently used in a famous psychology experiment by Sir Frederic Bartlett (1886–1969), the great twentieth-century Cambridge psychologist. Here is how Bartlett presented the tale in his report of 1920:

> In *The War of the Ghosts* . . . two young Indians are seal hunting, when they are accosted by warriors from a canoe, who ask them to help in a fight which is about to take place. One of the Indians agrees, and goes with them. In the fight he hears somebody say: "That young Indian has been hit," but he feels no hurt. He merely remarks casually: "Oh, they are ghosts." He goes back home, tells his friends, lights a fire, and the next morning at sunrise falls down: "something black came from his mouth. He was dead." (Bartlett 1920, 37)[1]

Correspondence may be addressed to Simon J. Cook at simonjohncook@gmail.com or to Tiziana Foresti, Baffi Carefin Centre for Applied Research on International Markets, Banking, Finance and Regulation, Bocconi University, Milan; e-mail: tiziana.foresti@unibocconi.it. An earlier version of this article was presented at the Duke conference on psychology and economics. We are grateful for the comments of the participants, in particular the questions of Judy Klein and Ivan Moscati. We are also much indebted to an anonymous referee for some acute observations on the relationship between the thought of Veblen and Bartlett.

1. In the introduction to his collection of tales, Boas (1901, 5) explains that he had two of them—of which one was "The War of the Ghosts"—repeated three and a half years later to check the accuracy of his informant, Charles Cultee. Bartlett does not mention this, but we may

History of Political Economy 48 (annual suppl.) DOI 10.1215/00182702-3619238

Bartlett's experimental subjects were students and teachers at his university. They read the original story and, after a set interval, repeated it, sometimes to others who in turn repeated it, and so on. The experiment revealed the removal of the mysterious from the story and a gradual process of familiarization of both details and basic narrative. For example, familiar words were frequently substituted for unfamiliar: "canoe" became "boat," "paddling" became "rowing," and so on. More strikingly, in "every one of the series of reproductions all mention of ghosts drops out almost immediately, and this in spite of the fact that ghosts appear in the original title." Further modifications followed, for, without the ghosts, the painless wound and strange death are left "in the air." Over a series of reproductions the story was thus reconstructed; for example, by the ninth reproduction a real arrow from another point in the story was said to have hit the Indian, causing an ultimately fatal wound.

Bartlett's experiment appears to have undergone a similar fate in the telling. Today it is widely discussed (we even found a "reenactment" on YouTube in which a ten-year-old girl recalls the story "The Gift of a Cow Tail Switch") and invariably presented as a celebrated contribution to the psychology of memory. More involved accounts typically explain that Bartlett was investigating the effect of mental schema on participants' recall.[2] These contemporary storytellers are psychologists of one kind or another, and their presentations mold the experiment to the disciplinarily familiar while occluding the mysterious. In retellings Bartlett presented his experiment as an exercise in psychology, but he presented it originally as a contribution to the study of cultural diffusion. One finds "Some Experiments on the Reproduction of Folk-Stories" in the March 1920 issue of *Folk-Lore*, sandwiched between the presidential address to the

---

surmise that he found this initial repetition a useful check for his own purposes. Bartlett (1920, 35n) states that the version of the tale that he used for his experiment was "slightly adapted" from the translation by Boas, but does not elaborate. Comparison shows Bartlett to have censored the description of the death of the Indian at the end of the tale, which in Boas's 1891 version reads, "Something black came out of his mouth and blood came out of his anus. His face became contorted. He was dead" (184); and in the 1894 version, "Blood came out of his mouth, and something black came out of his anus. It was like salad berries" (186).

2. Bartlett began his career with the conviction that there was little psychology that was not social psychology, a position still clearly discernible in his classic *Remembering* (1954; see, e.g., 243), which also presented "The War of the Ghosts" experiment, and from which almost all accounts of this experiment are drawn, and which was written after Bartlett, in the 1920s, had derived from Henry Head the idea of an individual mental schema. By the late 1950s, however, Bartlett appears to have largely discarded his concerns with the cultural and social dimensions of psychology (see Bruno 2000, xv).

Folk-Lore Society delivered by A. C. Haddon, reader of ethnology at the University of Cambridge, and a paper titled "The Concept of 'Soul-Substance' in New Guinea and Melanesia," by W. H. R. Rivers.[3]

The intellectual historian can learn much from Bartlett's experiment and also its subsequent fate. The past, they say, is a foreign country, but Bartlett showed how memory assimilates the foreign to the domestic, remaking the past in the image of the present. Disciplinary histories are prone to this sort of occlusion and transformation, and the rational reconstructions of historians of economics particularly so. But the fate of Bartlett's experiment illustrates that historians of economics are by no means the only makers of disciplinary memory ensnared by the perilous temptations of anachronism. Historians of economics interested in the historical relation of their discipline to another must be wary, not only of the memories of economists, but also of the received views as to the history of other disciplines. As our introductory discussion demonstrates, our own article is a case in point. To even begin to discuss certain aspects of the historical relationship between economics and the tradition of psychology associated with Cambridge University, we have had to bring into view much that has hitherto been overlooked in the history of that latter tradition.

Our primary point of reference is the tradition of experimental psychology associated with early twentieth-century Cambridge, England. But while this tradition is (and following Bartlett) conventionally held to begin only at the very end of the nineteenth century, we have traced its antecedents to an earlier generation who, while not engaging in experiments, nevertheless subscribed to a broadly similar model of the working of the human mind. By way of a reconstruction of the history of this tradition, we have attempted to explore its relation to three different approaches to the scientific study of society: those of the economists Alfred Marshall and Thorstein Veblen, and the early diffusionist anthropology, or social psychology, of Bartlett.

On the face of it, our discussion is unsatisfactory, for nowhere do we find a straightforward connection between the experimental psychology of Cambridge and the history of economics. Marshall's early psychological studies certainly influenced his subsequent economic work, but the former does not initiate so much as anticipate (and that only partially) the

---

3. Nor was this a flash in Bartlett's psychological pan. The December issue of *Folk-Lore* carried a second essay, "Psychology in Relation to the Popular Story," in which Bartlett criticized the treatment of the folktale (be it by James George Frazer or by Sigmund Freud) as an expression of individual psychology.

later psychological tradition developed by the likes of Bartlett. Veblen's model of the mind was, on the whole, much closer to that of Bartlett, yet it was mainly (not wholly) arrived at independently. And while the young Bartlett clearly saw Cambridge psychology as the key to a new science of man, what he had in mind was an anthropological study of primitive culture, not an economic study of modern trade and industry.

Our inquiry thus brings into view a somewhat messy picture, at least from the perspective of the history of economics. But lack of neat intellectual borders and direct connections need not suggest a misdirected historical gaze; reality is messy, and it is (or should be) the overly simple disciplinary history that is prima facie suspect. Behind the discordant appearances our article traces a fairly straightforward development, whereby a new model of the mind, grounded initially in physiology but increasingly focused on the behavioral manifestations of mental tendencies, fed into, and was also driven by, some extremely important attempts to understand those interactions of human beings that give rise to social and economic life. That our emerging psychology of mental tendency was at one time connected to modern economic actions and another time with primitive culture is a sign of the richness of this psychological tradition, as well as of the contingent and somewhat arbitrary nature of modern disciplinary divisions. But the proof of the pudding is in the eating. What we hope to have shown, by the end of this article, is that by establishing the path that leads from Marshall to Bartlett in Cambridge, we thereby lay the groundwork for a comparison of the theoretical systems of Marshall and Veblen.

A Shared Psychological Model?

Bartlett (1936, 41) was inclined to date the beginning of modern psychology in Cambridge to 1893. This was the year that Rivers was appointed by Michael Foster, the Cambridge professor of physiology, to teach the physiology of the special senses. Before 1893 was to Bartlett a sort of philosophical prehistory. Thus James Ward's celebrated *Encyclopaedia Britannica* article, "Psychology" (1886), set out "a system based upon principles never intended to be within the reach of experimental verification or examination" (Bartlett 1937, 97). And before Ward, Bartlett did not look, which is why he found it puzzling that Bartlett first entered the Cambridge Psychological Laboratory in 1909 as an undergraduate studying not the natural but the moral sciences. In fact, the Reverend John Grote had introduced psychology to a fairly new Moral Sciences Tripos in the late 1850s, with the intention of forging an alliance with the disciples of J. S. Mill in opposition to Oxford's "theological relativism" (Cook 2005). This was how, in the late 1860s, a young moral scientist named Alfred Marshall came to study both idealist philosophy and the scientific psychology of Herbert Spencer. Marshall did not engage in laboratory experiment, but the physiological ground of his psychology was similar to that of Rivers.

The evolutionary model of the human nervous system held by both Marshall and Rivers is hierarchical, accumulative, and comprehensive. Its ultimate source was Spencer. The model is hierarchical, in that higher levels (more evolved, so more recent and more complex) control (or inhibit) the lower (older and more simple) levels; accumulative, in that evolution adds new levels but does not remove the older; and comprehensive, in that it explains the operation of all levels in the same way (or, as the later Cambridge psychologists would put it: intelligence is not different in kind from instinct). Marshall took this evolutionary model directly from Spencer; Rivers learned it from the great neurologist Hughlings Jackson, an ardent disciple of Spencer.[4] Here is how the historian of science Anne Harrington (1987, 210) describes Jackson's integration of the doctrine of reflex action and Spencer's evolutionary system:

> The nervous system had evolved over time into a pyramid of sensory-motor ganglia of ever-increasing complexity, heterogeneity, and flexibility. The lower, more rigid, and less specialized (automatic) centers represented comparatively early evolutionary acquisitions, whereas the higher, more flexible, and specialized (voluntary) centers had evolved at a later stage. The very highest and most differentiated levels of cortical activity, those associated in human beings with conscious experience, operated according to the same physical laws governing activities in the more basic, homogenous levels of the spinal cord.

This captures the evolutionary and comprehensive elements of the model. We can look to Rivers (1920, 31) to supply a brief comment on the hierarchical dimension:

> It is now recognised that the activity of every functional unit of the nervous system is of two kinds. Every unit forms part of a hierarchy in which it controls lower, and is itself controlled by higher, elements of the hierarchy.

---

4. As Robert Young (1970, 198) observes, "There is hardly a single matter of principle or detail for which [Jackson] does not at some point cite Spencer as source, inspiration, or authority."

Compare this last quotation with the following footnote in Marshall's *Principles of Economics*:

> There is probably something like an organized bureaucracy of the local nerve centres: the medulla, the spinal axis, and the larger ganglia generally acting the part of provincial authorities, and being able after a time to regulate the district and village authorities without troubling the supreme government. Very likely they send up messages as to what is going on: but if nothing much out of the way has happened, these are very little attended to. (bk. 4, chap. 9, n. 107)

Incidentally, such political metaphor is rare in Marshall's prose. From his mature perspective the key significance of such a hierarchical structure was the efficient operation it facilitated in an uncertain world: leaving routine work to the lower centers allows higher centers to attend to unprecedented and difficult situations thrown up by the environment—a division of labor and system of management applicable to economic organizations as well as individual organisms (Raffaelli 2003).

So much for common ground; in what way did the psychological thinking of Marshall and Rivers diverge? An illuminating approach here is through Rivers's late work, *Instinct and the Unconscious* (1920). In light of the accumulative nature of the shared model of the mind, Rivers asks an obvious question: what happens if new behaviors are incompatible with old routines? The question arises because the accumulative nature of development makes forgetting problematic: reflection shows that evolution requires active suppression of incompatible older tendencies. Rivers therefore posits a storehouse in which old and unusable instincts are placed; this is the unconscious—a sort of organic wastebasket that is never emptied. Marshall had not thought to make a place for the discarded flotsam of our less-developed selves. Rivers, or so it might seem, shows how easily the dog can be revealed beneath the skin of Marshall's serenely progressive psychological model.

Nevertheless, if we push Marshall's model in this way, we are likely to end up with a rather different notion of the unconscious. Marshall's primary case of a behavioral tendency is a habit, and he adopts Spencer's Lamarckian idea that an instinct can be formed through the inheritance of acquired habits. But Rivers sets up his model in terms of instincts, and his point of reference here is William McDougall's massively influential *Introduction to Social Psychology* (1908). Although best known today for his controversial Harvard lectures and his establishment of psychology at

Duke University, McDougall began as a younger contemporary of Rivers at St. Johns College, Cambridge. For McDougall (1908, 43), as also for Rivers (and Veblen and Bartlett), instincts are primary: "Habits are in a sense derived from, and secondary to, instincts. . . . they are formed only in the service of the instincts." Furthermore, the same limited set of instincts is found "in men of all races now living on the earth" (McDougall 1908, 19–20). Instincts are indeed the product of evolution, but for the entirety of human history they can be regarded as fixed in number and stable in nature.[5] This means that any conflict between old and new instincts is less about the "savage" than about the beast within: human tendencies bang up against—and are on occasion overthrown by—animal instincts developed when we were still in the trees, or even the water. Ultimately, there is no reason why a similar clash of instincts could not be generated out of Marshall's model. But in terms of a clash between old and new, Marshall's focus on habits is likely to generate a conception of nervous breakdown associated less with primordial terrors than with the kind of junk found in a grandparent's attic.[6]

The more general point here is that the new instinct psychology did not so much overthrow Marshall's psychological model as introduce potentially far-reaching modifications. But the instinct model was itself capable of very different developments. In terms of the history of Cambridge thought, Rivers's account of the unconscious constitutes an interesting turning point: a halfway house between the old and new behavioral models of the mind. Rivers's great protégé in psychology was Bartlett (McDougall being too headstrong to become anyone's disciple). Much of Bartlett's early work can be read as an imposition of order on the not always fully baked mixtures of psychology and ethnology cooked up by his mentor in the last years of his life. Bartlett never explicitly rejected Rivers's notion of the unconscious, but he wasted little time on it. What Bartlett did pick up on was Rivers's insight that there might be a conflict between different instincts. But in place of Rivers's concern with a conflict between new and old, between the human and the animal within, one keystone of Bartlett's

5. McDougall (1908, 20) adds that the same set of instincts "played the same essential part in the minds of the primitive human stock, or stocks, and in the pre-human ancestors that bridged the great gap in the evolutionary series between man and the animal world."

6. Marshall simply did not concern himself with the potential conflict of mental habits. Like many of his contemporaries, he related "nervous breakdown" among the intelligentsia to the overworking of one particular organ, the brain, and advocated the balanced exercise of all parts of the body, the brain included. See Cook 2009, chap. 3.

early psychological thought became the idea that any instance of human behavior is the product of more than one instinct, the chief task of the social psychologist becoming the arrangement of instincts and the analysis of their mutual interactions. We can thus identify a three-step progression of the Cambridge psychological model: Marshall conceives of the evolution of new mental tendencies; Rivers notes the potential for conflict between new and old tendencies; and Bartlett declares that the relevant interaction is between various fixed and stable human instincts.

With Veblen in North America we see a quite different development of instinct psychology, in which the relationship between habits and instincts is at the heart of the understanding of both individual and social behavior. Veblen's system has its roots in his engagement with the works of Charles Darwin, Immanuel Kant, and William James, with the latter's *Principles of Psychology* (1890) being a key initial psychological resource.[7] It was from James that Veblen derived his understanding of habit, which was always for him the fundamental psychological concept. Habit, for Veblen, establishes efficient routines for individuals, relieving them from the necessity of attending to all details of everyday life. On the social level, habit works to release the community from the constant effort of reorganizing and redefining social roles and shared values. Habit is thus an inherently conservative force, invariably lagging behind the most recent environmental developments. But Veblen further takes from James the notion of habit as a form of systematization from experience and identifies habits of thought behind each distinct scientific explanatory pattern, thereby arriving at an account of scientific progress in terms of the evolution of habits (Foresti 2004). By and large, Veblen's conception of habit is actually quite close to that of Marshall. Nevertheless, while Marshall is clear on the role of habit as a routine that conserves the attention of the individual mind, his conception of social custom as the external manifestation of habit and his understanding of the role of habit in the development of science are, rather, implicit features of his thinking, requiring careful exegesis to bring them properly to light.[8]

---

7. In confirmation of the significance of James's enduring influence on Veblen, we find James's *Psychology* (1900) and *Pragmatism* (1907) among the readings that Veblen assigned in his course Economic Factors of Civilization at the University of Missouri in 1910–17. The list also included Jacques Loeb's *Comparative Physiology of the Brain and Comparative Psychology* (1900) and *Mechanistic Conception of Life: Biological Essays* (1912), and William McDougall's *Introduction to Social Psychology* (1908) (Joseph Dorfman Collection, box 69).

8. For such exegesis, see, e.g., Cook 2009, chaps. 6–7.

James was also a crucial resource for McDougall (see, e.g., 1908, 23–24; 1921, 286), and Veblen evidently read and engaged with McDougall's *Introduction to Social Psychology* soon after its publication in 1908. The result was Veblen's adoption of a new language of instinct while retaining habit as the fundamental concept. Veblen concurred with McDougall's idea of instincts as primary, with habits serving instincts. Furthermore, he accepted (albeit with some modification) McDougall's contention that habits can modify instinctual behavior. This latter contention was, for both men, the key to avoiding the biological determinism that might seem to follow from adopting the idea of the primacy of instincts; it allowed for what (anachronistically) we might call a "cultural influence" and was in line with James's own philosophical position on nature and free will. But the end result, at least for Veblen, was a unique vision of the interplay between environment, habits, and instincts. Where Marshall emphasized the evolution of new habits, and Bartlett the relationship between different instincts, Veblen looks to the different ways in which environmental variation modifies instinctive behavior, thereby engendering new habits. But Veblen also seeks to understand the contingent social factors that determine whether new habits displace old ones; that is to say, on the social level, Veblen investigates the very possibility of institutional change.

Alfred Marshall

Marshall's early psychological project was undertaken in the first years of his association with the Cambridge moral sciences and for the few years before he dedicated himself to political economy. The kernel of his project is set out in two manuscripts, "Ferrier's Proposition One" and "Ye Machine," which are dated to 1868 and were read at consecutive meetings of the Grote Club, the weekly gathering of those involved in the moral sciences. In "Ferrier's Proposition One" Marshall argues that self-consciousness cannot be explained in terms of a physiological model; in "Ye Machine" he sets out a two-level model of those elements of mental life that can. The project as a whole thus accomplishes Grote's looked-for reconciliation of Cambridge idealist philosophy with metropolitan scientific psychology.

Just how Marshall conceived of the relationship between self-consciousness and the mechanical mind is contentious.[9] Indeed, a prefatory

9. For an exchange over Marshall's dualism, that is, the extent to which his physicalist model of the brain was complemented by a notion of self-consciousness as an active force in the world, see Raffaelli 2012 and Cook 2012.

note to the second essay shows that Marshall felt that his ideas had been misunderstood from the beginning. Here he clarifies that at the last meeting of the Grote Club he had intended to identify self-consciousness as the gateway between physiological phenomena and conscious experience. "My eye supplies me with the affection," he now explains, and "my self-consciousness turns the affection into a conscious affection or feeling, and by the aid of memory enables me to perceive differences between feelings" (quoted in Raffaelli 1994, 69). The implication is that the mechanical model subsequently outlined in the second paper describes mental operations of which an organism may not be conscious. But as argued at length elsewhere (Cook 2009), Marshall's subsequent writings, beginning with his notes on G. W. F. Hegel's *Philosophy of History* in the early 1870s but continuing through to various statements in *Principles of Economics*, point to a further conception of self-consciousness as a potential spring of human action, capable of overriding the behavioral tendencies of the body and, as such, providing the ground of human free will and moral choice.

Marshall's mechanical model is an attempt to extend the physiological notion of the reflex arc to the higher (if not the very highest) mental actions. The hallmark of his model is a two-level structure. The lower level consists of various mental connections that allow an organism to respond automatically to an environmental stimulus. When a novel situation is encountered, the organism responds randomly; successful (or at least nonfatal) responses are repeated, thereby becoming habits, and acquired habits are passed on to offspring, eventually becoming instincts. Marshall suggests that here is an explanation of both animal behavior and evolution. But humans have somehow evolved a whole new kind of mental circuit—a sort of subroutine that allows a quite different response to the unprecedented: rather than throw out a random response, the lower-level circuits pause and the upper circuit begins to picture possible outcomes of different actions, thereby generating a "deliberated" response to novelty. The implication is that where animal evolution is a matter of random chance and natural selection, human development is potentially driven by planning and prudent investment.

From a philosophical perspective there is substantial divergence between Marshall's conception of the mind and that of both Veblen and the later Cambridge psychologists. McDougall, the pioneer of the new instinct psychology, is explicit that the Spencerian idea of compound reflex action is insufficient as a definition of instinct. In addition to a mechanical process in the nervous system, he argues, instinct always includes a psychic component: "Every instance of instinctive behaviour involves a knowing of some thing or object, a feeling in regard to it, and a striving towards or away from that object" (McDougall 1908, 26).[10] In a sense, of course, this is just a bringing together of the two parts of Marshall's project. In a symposium of 1910 titled "Instinct and Intelligence," the Cambridge psychologist C. S. Myers put the new position succinctly: rather than two modes of mental activity, instinct and intelligence are simply two viewpoints on mental behavior. From the outside, explained Myers (1910, 209), behavior appears instinctive—"characterised by mechanism"; from the standpoint of individual experience, the same behavior appears intelligent—"characterised by finalism."[11] Self-consciousness and physiological reflex have become but two sides of the same coin.

One could argue, then, that what we have here is a philosophical disagreement with little or no substantial psychological significance; but this, we think, would be only partly correct. Certainly, the *combined* activities of self-consciousness and (physiological) instinct in Marshall's model generate something rather like the mental instinct of McDougall and Myers. Indeed, there is clearly a parallel of sorts between Marshall's conception of self-consciousness as a potential agency and the insistence of Myers and the other proponents of instinct psychology that instincts may be modified through experience. Thus McDougall (1908, 269–70) echoes both Marshall and Mill when he suggests that "reason and intelligent foresight modifies profoundly the operation of all the instincts, and is especially apt to modify and work against the play of the reproductive and parental instincts."[12] Nevertheless, the fact that mechanical action and self-consciousness are separate in Marshall's model means that much human activity may be purely automatic (or, as Myers might say, "reflex") and even the highest deliberation may be carried out without conscious awareness. Furthermore, where McDougall and Myers would insist that purposeful action is found in animals (even in wasps), Marshall suggests that even primitive humans do not possess self-consciousness.

10. McDougall identified the emotional part of the instinct as its "central part." This association of instinct and emotion would be important for Rivers, whose theory of the unconscious, developed through his work with "shell shocked soldiers," would have made little sense unless suppressed instincts were regarded as emotionally charged.

11. Myers (1910, 212) describes the flight of the moth toward a lamp as a reflex and not an instinct, for "no amount of experience alters the reaction."

12. Cf. "Civilization in every one of its aspects is a struggle against the animal instincts" and "the conduct of human creatures is more or less influenced by foresight of consequences, and by impulses superior to mere animal instincts; and they do not, therefore, propagate like swine" (Mill [1848] 1965, 367, 157).

From the viewpoint of the later Cambridge psychologists, Marshall might be said to have smuggled an older opposition between instinct and intelligence into his Spencerian evolutionary model. Of course, there is no reason why we should evaluate Marshall's model from this rather than some other intellectual viewpoint. From the perspective of Grote's project for the Cambridge moral sciences, Marshall succeeded in marrying Spencer's psychology and Cambridge idealist philosophy. Through his historical studies of the early 1870s, Marshall himself came to think of this opposition in terms of primitive and modern humans (Cook 2013a). Marshall's archetypal primitives are not nomadic hunter-gatherers but peasants, who inhabit a village governed in all respects by time-bound custom. The villagers are not self-conscious and do not deliberate about the future; they just do what they do because their fathers and grandfathers did the same before them. Human history is the scene of a gradual emergence of self-consciousness (the advent of Christianity is identified as a turning point) as well as the increasing utilization of the higher mechanical circuit (Christianity supposedly fosters a new habit of reflecting on possible consequences prior to acting). The moral dimension of this historicism should not be missed: in contrast to the primitive, who remains part of the natural world, the modern overcomes animal tendencies and assumes responsibility for the future.

Marshall's contrast of primitive and modern underlines his vision of the mind in modern society as active, individuating, and ultimately creative. His economic theory is crafted specifically for a modern society, but his reform of economic doctrines can be expressed as a conviction that the older political economists had conceived the modern working class as if they were primitives—governed purely by animal tendencies and incapable of restraining their instinctual passions for the sake of an imagined future.[13] Like many of his academic liberal colleagues, Marshall believed not only that working-class individuals of his day were more responsible than their parents and grandparents but also that continued education (both formal, through schools and colleges, and informal, through market participation and industrial training) would make them even more like modern gentlemen. The upshot was that economics had to be remade as a moral rather than a natural science, appropriate for a progressive society of self-conscious deliberating agents.

---

13. Marshall put this differently: perceiving in his predecessors a problematic inheritance, deriving from the physiocrats and, ultimately, ancient Roman philosophy of law, which identified the existing state of society with the natural order. In other words, the older political economy had been formed around an ancient conceptual inheritance that lacked insight into the moral world. See Marshall [1890] 1961, 1:507–8, 756n2; and also Cook 2009, 204–6.

Marshall's conception of the distinctive character of the modern mind influenced his economic thought in a few basic ways. To begin with, already in the 1870s Marshall was suggesting that a responsible citizenry would dedicate higher wages to educating their children rather than raising more of them. Combined with the idea that an educated worker was a more efficient worker, this line of thought undermined the old "wages fund" theory by suggesting that, in time, a higher wage bill would more than pay for itself. In later years, this same line of thought led Marshall to what has been described as an evolutionary vision of industrial production (Raffaelli 2003), in which new machinery embodying technological innovations calls forth new and more skilled mental behaviors and, in general, fosters plasticity of mental routines among the working class. But at the same time, Marshall consistently emphasized the importance of forward-looking deliberation and creative thought over mere mental routine. From this perspective, his most fundamental move in the remaking of economic science was simply to shift emphasis from production to the market as the primary site of economic activity. But while the market fosters deliberation, foresight, and choice among all consumers, Marshall valued above all the entrepreneurial spirit of the modern business person, which manifested itself at the meeting point of productive and market activity, and worked creatively to bridge the gap between present and future (Cook 2007).

Thorstein Veblen

In 1898 Veblen launched his challenge to neoclassical economics with "Why Is Economics Not an Evolutionary Science?"[14] Here he linked the advent of evolutionary-institutional economics to the acquisition of the new analytical tools associated with recent advances in the science of humanity. What he had in mind is indicated by the quotation from George Vacher de Lapouge's "Fundamental Laws of Anthropo-sociology" (1897), which opened Veblen's essay, and according to which anthropology was destined to revolutionize the political and social sciences, just as bacteriology had done in medicine.

Lapouge, generally an important source for Veblen, had introduced a taxonomy of ethnic groups on the basis of the cephalic index that, in his view, provided an indication of different mental capabilities.[15] As such,

14. As is well known, Veblen introduced to the discipline the expression "evolutionary economics."

15. On the many references to Lapouge in Veblen's works, see Maccabelli 2008; and Foresti 2014.

Lapouge is a spokesperson for that great sea change in social thought that began in the early 1880s and which was associated with the toppling of comparative philology from its throne: the establishment of anthropology and archaeology at the vanguard of the social sciences, a new biological identification of ethnicity independent of language, and a revolution in the understanding of prehistoric society (Cook 2014). As we argue, Marshall stood on one side of this historiographical revolution, Veblen (as also McDougall, Rivers, and Bartlett) on the other.

Historiographical rupture goes hand in hand with philosophical divergence, at least with regard to the thought of Marshall and Veblen. This is not to identify any inherent philosophical dimension to the intellectual revolution of the 1880s. Certainly, Marshall's insistence on the gulf between primitive and modern humans did not sit comfortably with the new scientific idea of race, with its inevitable suggestion of fixed identities throughout history (modern Frenchmen recognizing themselves in the ancient Celts depicted in *Asterix*, to give a twentieth-century illustration). But then, and as against Enlightenment preoccupations with the contrast of modern Europe with ancient Rome, earlier nineteenth-century comparative philology had already introduced the idea of enduring (barbarian) ethnic identities. So Marshall's blending of idealist philosophy with the kind of comparative social history advanced in the 1860s and 1870s by Henry Maine and E. A. Freeman, the roots of which lay in comparative philology, was fairly idiosyncratic. In fact, and as already suggested above, Marshall's synthesis of idealism with other branches of moral science (both physicalist and philological) was the product of a fairly local context, namely, Grote's determination to combat Oxford theological relativism by forging an alliance with metropolitan radicals. But if there was no intrinsic connection between a vision of history built on comparative philology and an idealist philosophy, the actual combination of the two in Marshall's historical thought generated ideas of primitive society and the path into modernity quite removed from anything that Veblen would subscribe to.

But psychology cannot be entirely dismissed from this picture. In "Why Is Economics Not an Evolutionary Science?" Veblen made it clear that the acquisition of a new psychological model constituted one of the main fronts of his campaign. In this essay Veblen ([1898] 1990, 57) refers to Marshall as a spokesman of the "old generation" of economists. In his later article "The Preconceptions of Economic Science" (1900), in which Veblen introduced to the discipline the expression "neoclassical economics" (Aspromourgos 1986), he explicitly holds up Marshall's *Principles of Economics* as "the best work that is being done under the guidance of the classical antecedents" (Veblen [1900] 1990, 171).[16] Intriguingly, Veblen identified the old psychology at the basis of English economics with an account of the mind and actions of *homo economicus*. Such psychology, he complained, treated the human as "an isolated, definitive human datum, in stable equilibrium except for the buffets of the impinging forces that displace him in one direction or another" (Veblen [1898] 1990, 73). As a more acceptable alternative, Veblen looked to a conception of the human individual as "a coherent structure of propensities and habits which seeks realization and expression in an unfolding activity" (74).[17] But we have already noted that Marshall's conception of habit was not only foundational to his psychology but had much in common with what Veblen derived from James. For sure, Veblen rejected Marshall's Lamarckian derivation of instincts from inherited habits, holding rather that habits arise to serve instincts. But if this disagreement is real, and has substantial implications, it hardly corresponds to Veblen's contrast of old and new psychological models.

Nevertheless, a key difference between Marshall and Veblen can be expressed in terms of their different conceptions of the relationship between habit and instinct. Veblen derives from James the idea that humans are characterized by a number of instincts greater than the other animal species and, more importantly, that instincts can be modified by experience and habit and controlled by mind. But his most mature treatment of the relation between instinct and habit, *The Instinct of Workman-*

---

16. In the United States, the coming of marginalism largely succeeded in "healing the rift" between adherents of classical economics and their critics that had opened up in 1885, when, on the initiative of German-trained economists, the American Economic Association had been founded (Ross 1991, chap. 6; Yonay 1998, chap. 2). For the adherents to the "old school," Marshall's *Principles of Economics* represented the reconciliation of the development of marginal utility with the old classical tradition; for the "new schoolers," Marshall's work offered them analytical tools better suited than historicism to supplant the classical paradigm (Dorfman 1969, vol. 3).

17. Veblen was far from alone in emphasizing the gap between the new psychology and the old. A rather similar contrast is to be found in the writings of McDougall, who characterized the subject of the older psychology as essentially a Lockean tabula rasa, the one-dimensionality of which had been exacerbated by being put through the mangle of Benthamism. There are differences of course, in emphasis, detail, and shrillness of rhetoric. Where Veblen associated the old psychology with economics and emphasized the reactive nature of economic man, McDougall identified the root social philosophy as utilitarianism (which he consistently conflated with psychological hedonism; see, e.g., McDougall 1908, 8; 1921, 333), the great error of which, he declared, was a failure to acknowledge innate differences between different individuals and races. And where Veblen adopts the measured tone of the philosophical inquirer, McDougall, at least when touching on the iniquities of Victorian social philosophy, is both strident and vehement in the cause of social science, moral progress, and civilization.

ship and the State of Industrial Arts ([1914] 1964), bears the clear imprint of McDougall's 1908 *Introduction*.

For McDougall, we recall, instincts are not mere reflexes but mental processes, and as such consist of three parts: the cognitive, the affective, and the conative. The "afferent part," the "central part," and the "motor or efferent part" correspond to the cognitive, the affective, and the conative parts, respectively, of the instinctive process (McDougall 1908, chap. 2). An object triggers a sense response that is elaborated at the nervous or neuronal level, and this represents the afferent part of the instinctive process. The distribution of the nervous impulses modifies the working of human organs and gives rise to an emotional excitement (i.e., the central part of the instinctive process) from which the action, indeed, results (i.e., the conative part). According to McDougall, human action can be the result of the interaction of different instinctive dispositions. In his view, the cognitive and the conative parts of the instinctive disposition are liable to modification and alteration by repetition and experience, but the central part (i.e., the emotional excitement) remains unchanged. For McDougall, habit, understood as an acquired mode of activity, can become a source of motive or action, but habit is secondary to instinct. In his own words: "For, in the absence of instincts, no thought and no action could ever be achieved or repeated, and so no habits of thought or action could be formed. Habits are formed only in the service of instincts" (43). While insisting that emotional excitement, the "central part," remained fixed, McDougall allowed for the modification of the other two parts of the instinctive process through experience. This position avoids biological determinism (as does also, albeit in a different manner, Marshall's interplay of mechanical habit and self-consciousness).

In 1914 Veblen endorsed McDougall's view of habit as an acquired and transmissible character. In Veblen's view, instincts are a set of basic drives or ends of human action but, unlike tropism, instinctive behavior involves consciousness and intelligence.[18] Instinct sets the goal of human behavior, but the way in which the goal is accomplished requires intelligence. In other words, instinctive behavior is the result of the adaptation of instinct to specific environmental circumstances. As Veblen ([1914] 1964, 38) put

---

18. Veblen draws from Jacques Loeb's *Comparative Physiology of the Brain and Comparative Psychology* (1900) the distinction between tropism and instinct. Tropism is a blind response to a certain stimulus and requires a nervous complexity inferior to that of instinct. Veblen met Loeb during his stay at the University of Chicago in 1892–1904 (see Hodgson 2004, 128–29). Tropism, for Veblen, is clearly akin to what reflex is for McDougall.

it, "All instinctive behaviour is subject to development and hence to modification by habit." Nevertheless, Veblen specifies that the range of habituation concerns "the sequence of acts by which [the] end is to be approached" (38). In line with McDougall, Veblen was maintaining that only the conative part of the instinctive behavior was subject to modification by habit. In his own words: "Men take thought, but the human spirit, that is to say the racial endowment of instinctive proclivities, decides what they shall take thought of, and how and to what effect" (6).

When all three factors—historiographical, philosophical, and psychological—are placed together, the results are two very different pictures of the evolution of human society. Marshall's position reflects that early stage in the reception of Darwinism in which it was widely assumed that the continuous evolution of nature has witnessed the development of human nature itself. For Marshall, the primitive human mind is devoid of self-consciousness and is characterized by a small set of unchanging habits, while primitive society is entirely governed by customs, which are assumed to be but the external manifestation of individual mental habits. In theory, environmental divergence can produce enormous variation, even leading within some generations to divergence in the instinctual endowment of different populations (think H. G. Wells's Morlocks and Eloi). But a straight path from primitive to modern is given by the supposed unfolding of self-consciousness in history, which works to liberate the mechanical mind and foster a habit of deliberation. Veblen's position reflects a more mature Darwinism, in which it is taken as given that human instincts are universal to the species. Variation of habit, then, is always in reference to the same set of basic instincts; so while habits may evolve, and also accumulate, their potential divergence is much more limited than with Marshall. What is more, with no hint of Marshall's metaphysical notions of the emergence of self-consciousness in history, Veblen provides a uniform explanation of environmental promotion or inhibition of instincts throughout history with no suggestion of inherent difference between primitive and modern minds. At the same time, Veblen's conception of the modification of instinct by habit allows him to avoid the trap of biological determinism (Rutherford 1998; Asso and Fiorito 2004).

At the heart of Veblen's evolutionary economics is the notion of an institution as the social form of established habits. Institutions are social forms of routinized behavior, the established habits that arise as environmental variation calls forth new modifications of instinctive behavior. Broadly speaking, Veblen's vision of social evolution is as follows: under the impulse of their instincts, individuals develop habits of life, which are methods of dealing with the material means of life; habits of life give rise to habits of thought, which, through social enforcement, become institutions (Brette 2003). Instincts thus form the starting point of the process and also a stable point of reference throughout, but the social dynamic is all about the relationship between environmental variation and changing habits, that is, institutions. The development of institutions *is* the development of society. Veblen further argues that present institutions act on our habitual view of things, thereby altering or fortifying a viewpoint or a mental attitude handed down from the past. Thus, institutions are products of past processes, are adapted to past circumstances, and are therefore never in full accord with the requirements of the present. By the very nature of the case, selective adaptation can never catch up with the progressively changing situation in which a community finds itself at any given time (Veblen [1899] 2009, chap. 8).

Of course, Veblen famously argued that some institutions are more obsolete than others. In *Theory of the Leisure Class* (1899), he suggested that a fundamental social division had occurred very early in human history. In the first instance, this was a division between those who gathered and those who hunted, which later manifested itself in the distinction between farmers and soldiers. More generally, this is a division of labor between those who work and those who engage in "exploit," that is, predatory behavior, which emerges hand in hand with a systematized form of private property. The emergence of the "leisure class" both fosters a new cultural outlook, in which work is looked down on as unworthy drudgery while predatory exploit is deemed honorable, while in modern industrial society also insulating one particular section of society—the leisure class—from the environmental changes in the form of economic forces that drive the process of adjustment between institutions and environment. The habits of life and thought of the leisure class are unresponsive to environmental changes, and "the office of the leisure class in social evolution is to retard the movement and to conserve what is obsolescent" (Veblen [1899] 2009, 131).

Veblen's historical account of the emergence of the leisure class neatly illustrates some distinctive features of his evolutionary thought. His starting point is a universal instinct of workmanship, which is accompanied by an intrinsic, "quasi-aesthetic" sense of economic merit that deems inefficiency distasteful, be it in the gathering of edible berries or the crafting of some modern piece of scientific machinery. The instinct of workmanship is thus set against the traditional assumption that "economic man" is averse to labor—no animal, Veblen points out, has an intrinsic disinclination to perform those exertions on which rests its survival. But Veblen now explains the origination of that conventional distaste for work that has been incorporated into the psychology of *homo economicus*. As human society moved out of the lowest stages of "savagery," a natural division between hunting and gathering connected with an emerging need for defense against predation to generate a basic division of social labor between (lower status) gatherers and makers and (higher status) warriors and hunters. A conventional disdain for industry characterizes the culture of those who concern themselves with exploit rather than with arts and crafts, and so new habits of thought are established that modify the instinctual behavior of this new social grouping. If we now shift our gaze back to Cambridge, we find an account of the role of instinct in the division of primitive labor that, while bearing a family resemblance to Veblen's vision, is also marked by fundamental differences.

Frederic C. Bartlett

Bartlett's early experimental study of the transmission of folktales formed part of a wider study of the psychology of cultural diffusion, itself a direct offshoot of the 1898 Cambridge Torres Strait expedition. Led by A. C. Haddon, this anthropological expedition had included, in addition to Rivers, the two men destined to become the leading lights of Edwardian psychology—Myers and McDougall. The immediate wake of the expedition saw the establishment in Cambridge of a new psychological laboratory, headed by Myers, and a new board of anthropology, which brought Rivers and Haddon together with traditional scholars, such as the classical archaeologist William Ridgeway and the Anglo-Saxonist H. M. Chadwick. The early institutional histories of psychology and anthropology in Cambridge are thus closely intertwined.[19] And out of this meeting of anthropological minds a new social theory began to emerge: in place of older accounts of the evolution of particular social forms, attention now shifted to the inter-

19. McDougall and Rivers were two of the founding members of the British Psychological Society in 1901, with Myers becoming its secretary in 1904 and McDougall his deputy. All three of these members of the Torres Straits expedition served on the society's management committee. Both Myers and McDougall were closely involved in the establishment of the *British Journal of Psychology* in 1904, which was first coedited by Rivers and James Ward, then from 1911 by Rivers and Myers, and then until 1924 by Myers alone.

action of social groups and the diffusion of culture (Cook 2016).[20] *Psychology and Primitive Culture* (1923), Bartlett's first book (which includes an extensive discussion of the folktale), was an attempt to provide the psychological underpinnings of this new social theory.

Here is the wider intellectual context of Bartlett's revision of instinct psychology described above in the first section—his revision of Rivers's account of conflict between old and new instincts to a focus on the relationship between different existing human tendencies. We now see that Bartlett's intent was to move beyond evolutionary models in both psychology and sociology. As he stated his position in "Psychology of Culture Contact," "The main, if not the only, general condition of mental and social development is that the individual or the group should come into contact with other individuals or other groups" (Bartlett 1926, 765).

What we first encountered as a mere modification of Marshall's model of the mind turns out to support a rejection of some of Marshall's key social and historical presuppositions. Take, for example, his assumption that primitive society is simple, which supports the idea that primitive custom is merely an externalization of fixed mental habits and that social development is driven by psychological progress. Bartlett's starting point is that tension between different but universal human instincts generates cultural specialization even in primitive society. For example, primitive ceremonial ritual is found to be dominated by fear, while curiosity generates the folktale, with each sphere excluding manifestations of the opposing instinct.[21] But cultural spheres generate social groups (the practitioners and the followers or audience of witchcraft, of storytelling, etc.), and such groups come to exist independent of the original instinct (the force of which is always transitory). This is fundamental: "Social control now passes partially outside the bounds of the psychological activity involved and becomes directly exercised by custom, institution, and tradition"

---

20. Three key moments in the establishment of a new diffusionist social perspective that provided the context of Bartlett's early work may be identified: in *The Origin of Tragedy* (1910), Ridgeway argued that Athenian tragedy arose out of a fusion of native (Pelasgian) funeral rituals and intruding (Achaean) lays for dead heroes; Chadwick followed up in *The Heroic Age* (1912) with an explanation of the origins of English individualism in the encounter between the Roman Empire and the premigration Continental tribes; while already in 1911, Rivers announced his "conversion" to diffusionism in his presidential address to the anthropology section of the British Association, where he recounted how he had come to see that the marriage customs he had recorded in his 1908 expedition to Melanesia were not, after all, the product of social evolution but had rather come about "under the influence of the blending of peoples" (494).

21. Thus Bartlett explains taboo, hitherto treated as a primitive institution without modern parallel, as but an early expression of the principle of specialization.

(Bartlett 1927, 103). Social custom is thus brought into view as distinct from psychological tendency (be it habit or instinct) yet a factor in the determination of individual conduct. Bartlett thus recognizes the autonomy of the social and takes into account the influence of group membership on individual conduct (which brings us back to the kinds of insights Bartlett was looking for in his "War of the Ghosts" experiment).

For Marshall, the purpose of history is to create modern individuals, that is, self-conscious and self-determining moral agents.[22] Like Veblen, and also like Rivers and McDougall, who had actually encountered so-called primitives in the field, Bartlett has no time for the idea that individuality is absent in "savage society."[23] Over and over again, the later Cambridge psychologists insist that the distance between primitive and modern minds is much less than between ordinary people (of whatever time and place) and the "man of science."[24] But Bartlett, as we have just shown, insists that the individual's conduct is everywhere partly determined by the social groups of which the individual is a member: the psychological subject is never simply an individual but always an individual who is a member of a range of social groups. What differences can be found between primitive and modern individuals relate largely to the massive intensification of specialization—and consequent proliferation of social groups—in modern society. Given the diffusionist thesis that development (both mental and social) follows from the contact of groups, their greatly increased

22. This is to pass over Marshall's ideas on the relationship between individuals and modern groups, in particular what he referred to as "economic nations." For discussion of this aspect of Marshall's thought (which is rooted in his idealist philosophical ideas and, as such, quite distinct from the thinking of Bartlett—if not, perhaps, so very far removed from that of McDougall), see Cook 2011 and 2013a.

23. See on this especially McDougall [1920] 1927, 72 (emphasis added): "Many facts of savage behaviour forbid us to accept the extreme view that denies them individual self-consciousness—individual names, private property . . . [and so on; all of which] reveals clearly enough to the unbiased *observer in the field* the effective presence of individual self-consciousness in the savage mind."

24. These criticisms were invariably directed at the French philosopher Lucien Lévy-Bruhl (whose idea of a collective, prelogical "primitive mentality" had been picked up by the Cambridge classicists Jane Harrison and Francis Cornford, the great opponents of Ridgeway). In rebutting this position McDougall ([1920] 1927, 75–76) insists that "the interval . . . between the modern man of scientific culture and the average citizen of our modern states is far greater than that between the latter and the savage," while Bartlett (1923, 284) points out that the antithesis drawn is invariably "not between the primitive man and the ordinary member of a modern social group, but between the former and the scientific expert at work within his own field." Bartlett's point that like was not being contrasted with like would be elaborated by the social anthropologist E. E. Evans-Pritchard (1934); on the latter, see also Douglas 1980, 32–33.

quantity in the modern world provides a ready explanation for the apparently rapid pace of modern mental and social development.

What were the implications of Bartlett's social psychology for the study of modern economics in Cambridge? This is an extremely difficult question to address because there was so little intellectual contact. Economics had been granted its own faculty, and hence institutional autonomy, back in 1903, when our ethnological psychologists were still writing up their notes from Torres Strait. The product of Cambridge anthropology, the new social theory of diffusionism was from the start developed in relation to primitive and ancient societies, and of course Marshall had regarded primitive economics as almost a contradiction in terms. Furthermore, the traditional scholars associated with the new board of anthropology, Ridgeway and Chadwick, pioneered the study of society through literature, arguing that it was possible to build up a picture of the social world of early Greece and migration-age northern Europe through careful reading of, respectively, Homer and *Beowulf.* Bartlett's early focus on the folk story is fully in keeping with an anthropological gaze directed at literary (or oral) culture rather than economic activity. It is true that Bartlett presented *Psychology and Primitive Culture* as an introductory step intended to lead to a social psychology of modern culture; but Rivers's untimely death in 1922, Bronisław Malinowski's functionalism and successful bid for Rockefeller funding, and the dubious version of diffusionism propagated by Grafton Eliot Smith and William Perry all worked to bring Bartlett's research program to a premature end. Cambridge social psychology might well have been on a collision course with Marshall's modern economics, but if this was so, the former ground to a halt before any direct challenge could be made.

Nevertheless, the later Cambridge psychologists did make some forays into the world of modern industry. Indeed, Myers left the Cambridge Psychological Laboratory (that he, more than anyone, was responsible for establishing) to head the new National Institute of Industrial Psychology, which he founded with H. J. Welch in 1921. His writings on this subject (Myers 1920, 1929), as also the occasional paper on industrial psychology by Bartlett (see, e.g., 1943, 1947, 1948), are enlightening. A primary concern throughout is the efficiency of work and related problems of fatigue; the discussions of which are reminiscent of Marshall's vision of production as an interplay between mechanical innovation and the training of new human habits, albeit with a great deal of experimental data and hands-on observation thrown in. This similarity is of course testimony to the underlying physiological basis of all the psychological models surveyed here.

But these essays also point clearly to divergence from Marshall's psychology of the modern mind. The emphasis is always on the ordinary worker and the role of the group, never on the entrepreneurial spirit. No doubt such differences reflect a changed economic and political climate. But their conceptual roots are clear. Bartlett's very idea of a science of social psychology directs attention to the modern industrial group and away from the exceptional individual; it is no accident that the one discussion of modern industry in his 1923 book concerns trade union representatives and collective bargaining.[25] Leadership, for these early twentieth-century British psychologists, is a question of authority, to be analyzed in terms of such fundamental social instincts as dominance, submission, and suggestibility.[26] Finding creative solutions to problems—"thinking outside the box," as the mind-numbing contemporary cliché has it—has no place in their conception of modern industrial leadership. This is the immediate intellectual price paid for discarding Marshall's preposterous metaphysics and his related (and deeply politically incorrect) faith in the superiority of the modern over the primitive. For the similarity of modern and primitive minds has been established by pushing down the former no less than elevating the latter. Theirs is a world in which the businessperson is seen less as a creative entrepreneur than as a bankroller of the manipulation of social and material reality, reliant on scientific experts in the workplace and the propaganda of modern advertising in the market.

Conclusion

We have set out some parts of a complex tapestry in the history of thought, making no claim to completeness of narrative. Even at the heart of our story, the tradition of instinct psychology itself, we find an unresolved puzzle. Three of the key figures in the establishment of experimental psychology in England traveled together to the Torres Strait Islands on what was undoubtedly a defining moment in their professional as well as per-

---

25. Bartlett's one foray into the modern world in his 1923 book explains the breaking of contracts agreed on by trade union negotiators. The conduct of the union representative, he argues, is modified in different ways as he moves between the union and the group of negotiators that includes the bosses. See Bartlett 1923, 258–61.

26. Bartlett (1923, 41n3) informs us: "Dr Myers points out to me that Rivers eventually treated suggestibility as the most fundamental social instinct possessing the three forms of sympathy, imitation and intuition."

sonal lives. And yet the relationship between McDougall, who soon left Cambridge (moving, via Oxford and Harvard, to Duke), and his colleagues remains obscure. It seems clear that personal relations were, at least at times, strained. Having left Cambridge, McDougall wrote one of the most popular psychological works of the twentieth century, which in North America rapidly became the standard reference for instinct psychology. But the reception of McDougall's *Introduction to Social Psychology* in Cambridge is hard to fathom, or at least has not been studied. For example, Rivers's debt to McDougall in his 1920 study of *Instinct and the Unconscious* is evident, but implicit.

Yet putting scholarly caution aside, some points of interest do already suggest themselves. It is striking to observe the clear steps by which the various developments of our psychological model bring into view an autonomous conception of the social, only for it to almost immediately vanish from sight. With Marshall we have an implicit correlation between the fixed habits of a stable population and the social customs that govern that community. With Veblen, an evolutionary connection between mental habits and social institutions is made explicit, and indeed placed at the center of economic analysis. Furthermore, Veblen is clear that such institutions can exert a conservative hold over the minds of individuals. Bartlett takes this last point a step farther, insisting that the social group, while arising out of individual instincts, soon assumes an independent existence that henceforth constitutes an additional tendency—a cultural tendency—influencing the conduct of individuals. What is particularly interesting here is to see how Bartlett, moving beyond evolutionary thinking, derives an autonomous social sphere from a psychological reformulation of that fundamental economic idea of the division of labor, with early specialization now explained as arising out of the separation of the spheres of influence of potentially conflicting instincts (such as fear and curiosity).

In terms of the history of economic thought our investigation seems, again, at once both illuminating and puzzling. While Veblen claimed instinct theory as a novel foundation for his evolutionary-institutional economics and emphasized only that side of Marshall's model of the mind that had its roots in hedonistic psychology, we have discovered much common ground between their respective models of the mind. Our investigation of the emergence and dissemination of instinct theory in Cambridge and in the United States thus leaves us with some unexpected questions about the relationship between heterodox and orthodox economics at the beginning of the twentieth century.

References

Aspromourgos, T. 1986. "On the Origins of the Term 'Neoclassical.'" *Cambridge Journal of Economics* 10 (3): 265–70.

Asso, P. F., and L. Fiorito. 2004. "Human Nature and Economic Institutions: Instinct Psychology, Behaviorism, and the Development of American Institutionalism." *Journal of the History of Economic Thought* 26 (4): 445–77.

Bartlett, F. C. 1920. "Some Experiments on the Reproduction of Folk-Stories." *Folk-Lore: A Quarterly Review of Myth, Tradition, Institution, and Custom* 31 (1): 30–47.

———. 1923. *Psychology and Primitive Culture.* Cambridge: Cambridge University Press.

———. 1926. "Psychology of Culture Contact." In *Encyclopaedia Britannica*, 13th ed., 1:765–71. London: Encyclopaedia Britannica.

———. 1927. *Psychology and the Soldier.* Cambridge: Cambridge University Press.

———. 1936. "Frederic Charles Bartlett." In *A History of Psychology in Autobiography*, edited by C. Murchison, 3:39–52. Worcester, Mass.: Clark University Press.

———. 1937. "Cambridge, England, 1887–1937." *American Journal of Psychology* 50:97–110.

———. 1943. "Fatigue following Highly Skilled Work." *Proceedings of the Royal Society B* 131 (864): 247–57.

———. 1947. "The Task of the Operator in Machine Work." *Bulletin for Industrial Psychology and Personnel Practice* 3 (1): 3–12.

———. 1948. "Men, Machines, and Productivity." *Occupational Psychology* 22:190–96.

———. 1954. *Remembering: A Study in Experimental and Social Psychology.* Cambridge: Cambridge University Press.

Boas, F. 1901. "Kathlamet Texts." *Bulletin of the Bureau of American Ethnology.* Washington, D.C.: Government Printing Office.

Brette, O. 2003. "Thorstein Veblen's Theory of Institutional Change: Beyond Technological Determinism." *European Journal of the History of Economic Thought* 10 (3): 455–77.

Bruno, J. 2000. Foreword to *Bartlett, Culture, and Cognition*, edited by Akiko Saito, xii–xvi. Hong Kong: Psychology Press.

Chadwick, H. M. 1912. *The Heroic Age.* Cambridge: Cambridge University Press.

Cook, S. J. 2005. "Minds, Machines, and Economic Agents: Cambridge Receptions of Boole and Babbage." *Studies in History and Philosophy of Science Part A* 26 (2): 331–50.

———. 2007. "Poetry, Faith, and Chivalry: Alfred Marshall's Response to Modern Socialism." *History of Economics Review* 48:20–38.

———. 2009. *The Intellectual Foundations of Alfred Marshall's Economic Science: A Rounded Globe of Knowledge.* Cambridge: Cambridge University Press.

———. 2011. "The History of Nations." In *Marshall and Marshallians on Industrial Economics*, edited by Simon Cook and Tiziano Raffaelli, 67–85. London: Routledge.

———. 2012. "On Marshall's Idealism." *European Journal of the History of Economic Thought* 19 (1): 109–14.

———. 2013a. "From Ancients and Moderns to Geography and Anthropology: The Meaning of History in the Thought of Smith, Marx, and Marshall." *History of Political Economy* 45 (2): 311–43.

———. 2013b. "Race and Nation in Marshall's Histories." *European Journal of the History of Economic Thought* 20 (6): 940–56.

———. 2014. "The Making of the English: English History, British Identity, Aryan Villages, 1870–1914." *Journal of the History of Ideas* 75 (4): 629–49.

———. 2016. "The Tragedy of Cambridge Anthropology: Edwardian Historical Thought and the Contact of Peoples." *History of European Ideas.* doi:10.1080/019 16599.2016.1147196.

Dorfman, J. 1969. *The Economic Mind in American Civilization.* 5 vols. New York: Augustus M. Kelley.

———. Collection, Columbia University Rare Book and Manuscript Library, New York.

Douglas, M. 1980. *Evans-Pritchard.* Glasgow: Fontana Paperbacks.

Evans-Pritchard, E. E. 1934. "Lévy-Bruhl's Theory of Primitive Mentality." *Bulletin of the Faculty of Arts* (Cairo) 2:1–36.

Foresti, T. 2004. "Between Darwin and Kant· Veblen's Theory of Causality." *International Review of Sociology—Revue Internationale de Sociologie* 14 (3): 399–411.

———. 2014. "Thorstein Veblen on the Intellectual Pre-eminence of Jews: Beyond the Myth of Veblen's 'Social Marginality.'" *Research in the History of Economic Thought and Methodology* 32:63–81.

Harrington, Anne. 1987. *Medicine, Mind, and the Double Brain: A Study in Nineteenth-Century Thought.* Princeton, N.J.: Princeton University Press.

Hodgson, G. M. 2004. *The Evolution of Institutional Economics: Agency, Structure, and Darwinism in American Institutionalism.* London: Routledge.

Maccabelli, T. 2008. "Social Anthropology in Economic Literature at the End of the Nineteenth Century: Eugenic and Racial Explanations of Inequality." *American Journal of Economics and Sociology* 67 (3): 481–525.

Marshall, A. (1890) 1961. *Principles of Economics.* 9th (variorum) ed. London: Macmillan.

McDougall, W. 1908. *An Introduction to Social Psychology.* London: Methuen.

———. 1921. "The Use and Abuse of Instinct in Social Psychology." *Journal of Abnormal Psychology and Social Psychology* 16:285–333.

———. (1920) 1927. *The Group Mind: A Sketch of the Principles of Collective Psychology with Some Attempt to Apply Them to the Interpretation of National Life and Character.* Cambridge: Cambridge University Press.

Mill, J. S. (1848) 1965. *Principles of Political Economy with Some of Their Applications to Social Philosophy.* Vol. 2 of the *Collected Works of John Stuart Mill.* Toronto: University of Toronto Press.

Myers, C. S. 1910. "Instinct and Intelligence." *British Journal of Psychology* 3:209–18.

————. 1920. *Mind and Work: The Psychological Factors in Industry and Commerce*. London: University of London Press.

————, ed. 1929. *Industrial Psychology*. London: Oxford University Press.

Raffaelli, T., ed. 1994. "Marshall's Early Philosophical Writings." *Research in the History of Economic Thought and Methodology*. 4 (archival supplement):51–158.

————. 2003. *Marshall's Evolutionary Economics*. London: Routledge.

————. 2012. "On Marshall's Alleged Idealism." *European Journal of the History of Economic Thought* 19 (1): 99–108.

Ridgeway, W. 1910. *The Origin of Tragedy: With Special Reference to the Greek Tragedians*. Cambridge: University Press.

Rivers, W. H. R. 1911. "Presidential Address." In *Report of the Eightieth Meeting of the British Association*, 490–99. London: John Murray.

————. 1920. *Instinct and the Unconscious*. Cambridge: Cambridge University Press.

Ross, D. 1991. *The Origins of American Social Science*. Cambridge: Cambridge University Press.

Rutherford, M. 1998. "Veblen's Evolutionary Programme: A Promise Unfulfilled." *Cambridge Journal of Economics* 22 (4): 463–77.

Veblen, T. B. (1898) 1990. "Why Is Economics Not an Evolutionary Science?" In *The Place of Science in Modern Civilization*, 56–81. New Brunswick, N.J.: Transaction.

————. (1899) 2009. *The Theory of the Leisure Class*. Oxford: Oxford University Press.

————. (1900) 1990. "The Preconceptions of Economic Science." In *The Place of Science in Modern Civilization*, 148–79. New Brunswick, N.J.: Transaction.

————. (1914) 1964. *The Instinct of Workmanship and the State of Industrial Arts*. New York: Augustus M. Kelley.

Ward, J. 1886. "Psychology." In *Encyclopaedia Britannica*, 37–85. 9th ed. London: Encyclopaedia Britannica.

Yonay, Y. P. 1998. *The Struggle over the Soul of Economics: Institutionalist and Neoclassical Economists in America between the Wars*. Princeton, N.J.: Princeton University Press.

Young, R. M. 1970. *Mind, Brain, and Adaptation in the Nineteenth Century*. Oxford: Clarendon Press.

Economics and Psychology:
Why the Great Divide?

Craufurd D. Goodwin

The motivating question in this article is why economics and psychology, two disciplines that gained professional status during the second half of the nineteenth century and that addressed many of the same questions, failed to come together and cooperate over most of their history and, until recently, went their separate ways, both in rather bad humor. In the nineteenth century they broke away from the mother discipline of moral philosophy to seek their own identity, and each sought to understand how humans acted and interacted together. But for the most part they took different approaches to these questions and looked for answers independent of the other.

The article begins by suggesting several hypotheses to explain this picture that relate variously to methodology, ideology, cultural history, and strategic decisions. The bulk of this article tests these hypotheses from an examination of the early literature of economics and psychology in the English-speaking world, from the 1890s until the outbreak of World War II in 1939. Through the miracle of JSTOR relevant articles and reviews have been identified in the main journals of the two disciplines: the *American Economic Review*, the *American Journal of Psychology*, *Annals of the American Academy of Political and Social Science*, the *Economic Journal*, *Economica*, the *Journal of Political Economy*, the *New Republic*, the *Quarterly Journal of Economics*, and *Political Science Quarterly*. In some cases this search also led to an examination of books. These

History of Political Economy 48 (annual suppl.) DOI 10.1215/00182702-3619250

materials tell the story of events mainly in the United States. They have been examined before and have yielded important contributions to the history of economics, including rational reconstructions of the struggles between contending giants in the discipline over turning points in theory such as the moves toward and away from institutionalism (Coats 1976; Rutherford 2011; Asso and Fiorito 2004), the ordinal and revealed preference revolutions (Hands 2010; Giocoli 2003), and whether to accept the behavioral principles embedded in Milton Friedman's famous 1935 article on methodology (Lewin 1996). Some studies have speculated, rather wistfully, about where economics might have gone if it had selected a different path (Bruni and Sugden 2007). The objective here is more humble: to examine how and why the contending disciplines interacted and went their separate ways.

The first, methodological, hypothesis to explain this separation is that economists adopted, and held tightly to, certain postulates of human behavior, regardless of evidence of their incompleteness and even falsity, because these were central to the emerging market theory on which their whole picture of a competitive economic system rested. To have done anything else would have brought the whole theoretical structure tumbling down. This approach by the economists may also be seen as an application of the principle of Occam's razor: when formulating a scientific explanation, the simpler the better, and in particular the fewer assumptions the better. The simplifying assumption of economic rationality, that actors behave consciously to maximize what they like and minimize what they dislike, made possible the construction of uncomplicated models that often yielded helpful predictions that were useful in practice. But this assumption also opened the way for critics. By contrast, the models in the new discipline of psychology grew increasingly more complex over the period examined here, with more and more variables proposed for consideration, many of them not subject to measurement.

The second hypothesis, closely related to the first, is that the ideological commitment of most economists going back to the eighteenth century was to a utilitarian tradition associated with Thomas Hobbes and Adam Smith, and even with the ancient Greeks, that made cooperation difficult with psychologists, who had commitments especially to modern evolution theory. The economists' tradition was strengthened by their "marginal revolution" of the 1870s that suggested that relatively stable utilitarian values might be measured and treated mathematically. The skeptical questioning by psychologists of any simple explanation of human action such as utilitarianism, and their demands for an open mind, was a second reason why the two disciplines found cooperation difficult.

The third hypothesis that may help explain why economics and psychology went their separate ways is that economics more than psychology resonated to a widely held view in American culture, among all social classes, that the existing American psyche was something precious and unique. It was central to national identity, was the result of events and forces that went back to the earliest settlement, and made Americans exceptional and distinct from other nationalities. The implication of this cultural belief was that the American psyche should never be treated with disrespect or thought of as something that could be manipulated, as psychologists seemed wont to do. By contrast, the utilitarian foundation of economics was supportive of this cultural tradition.

The final hypothesis is that the long detachment of economics from psychology was simply the result of random strategic decisions made within the two disciplines, accidents of history, as it were. It will perhaps be no surprise to discover that all these hypotheses help us find an answer to our overriding question.

1. Contrasting Disciplinary Strategies

The social sciences had their origins in the moral philosophy of the eighteenth century, but by the nineteenth their purpose was as much didactic as analytical. In economics the goal of most political economists was primarily to instruct economic actors about how to behave in markets and even in economic aspects of their personal lives: how much to save and how many children to have; always to eschew monopolies of all kinds, to defend property rights, to encourage free trade, and to protect "sound" money. Political economy offered a body of doctrine that could guide humans in relations with each other, in family, in friendships, in markets, and in politics. A change in emphasis that took place during the second half of the nineteenth century was away from such normative thinking to positive thinking, away from ex cathedra positions about how to behave in a market or in relations with other people to a deepened understanding of how markets actually work and how people respond to different stimuli in their lives.

To accomplish their different goals, both economics and psychology were determined to achieve the status of the sciences and to move away from inclusion in the "less rigorous" humanities. The steps taken by these two fields had some things in common. In the English-speaking world each field came to revere an important leader at a prestigious university to whom they might look for guidance: Alfred Marshall in economics at Cambridge and William James in psychology at Harvard. Both of these men wrote massive textbooks in 1890 and established professional associations that helped define their fields for decades. They each trained cadres of students to provide leadership for the professional growth to come. And they both worked hard to establish a college curriculum and publication outlets for research: the *American Journal of Psychology* in 1887 (Dallenbach 1937) and the *Economic Journal* in 1890.

But in their scientific research the two fields took very different roads as they moved forward (Fay 1939). Perhaps the greatest difference came in methodology. For both, there were at least five alternative ways to proceed. First, they could use deductive methods to model reality, paying little attention to the facts of the economy or of the psyche. Second, they could use the inductive method of gathering historical evidence to discover generalizations. Third, they could gather contemporary evidence, from experimentation or other methods, to suggest laws of wide applicability. Fourth, they could become clinical scientists working directly with clients: government and private firms in the case of economics, patients in psychology, where in the process of selling their services they could discover generalizations for their sciences. Finally, they could remain closely associated with philosophy and explore issues remote from economics or psychology raised in a wide range of other literatures, especially history, religion, and political theory. For some years the main quarrels in economics and psychology concerned which of these paths to take.

Many economists, spurred on by the marginal revolution of the 1870s, concluded that the first alternative was the best, to construct increasingly complex deductive models based on plausible assumptions about human behavior discovered from introspection and when possible expressed in simple mathematical form. Economists could observe the predictions that followed from the models and reject those models that did not predict well. For the postulates they employed in their models, the economists went back to the utilitarianism of Hobbes, Smith, and Jeremy Bentham in the eighteenth century, softened somewhat by John Stuart Mill in his textbook of 1848. The essence of the doctrine was that humans were, for the most part, hedonists and could be counted on to think carefully and rationally about choices open to them and decisions they must make; they preferred more to less, had reasonably stable preferences, and would optimize the allocation of resources under their control for their own benefit. These marginal economists discerned from their models that free trade was most efficient no matter what the economic system and that security of property was essential to preserve the incentives at the root of competitive markets—essentially the same lessons set forth by their classical predecessors but now expressed more explicitly. They welcomed the important side effect that a competitive market system promised personal freedom and autonomy in most things and a small role for government.

Many of the controversies in the early decades of the consolidation of a deductive orthodoxy in economics involved rejection of the second and third methodological alternatives, economic history in the second case and what would be known as institutionalism in the third. The fourth alternative of looking to interactions with clients for reliable data and theory seemed inconsistent with modern notions of science. The final alternative of reaching out to a wider literature suggested a move away from rigor and a return to debates over such distasteful topics as socialism and the redistribution of income and wealth. Orthodox "marginal utility economics," as it came to be called, grew steadily stronger over the half century examined here, with only a few economic historians nipping at its heels. Institutionalism, oriented to contemporary inductive studies, engaged a substantial part of the profession until technical innovations in orthodox economics and other factors weakened its position. Participation of prominent institutionalists in the New Deal of the 1930s helped discredit the close engagement of economists in government, and the growth of business schools made it possible to push business economics into another part of the academic landscape. Continued pursuit of a literary economics, popular in the nineteenth century, became increasingly difficult as the subject became steadily more impregnable to the amateur.

The early history of psychology had many parallels to that of economics. The subject was usually taught by refugees from philosophy who, before their migration, had specialized in ethics, logic, aesthetics, religion, or metaphysics, and who, like William James, moved slowly and reluctantly away from a broad eclectic orientation. In their efforts to become respectably scientific, some psychologists moved methodologically toward biology and medicine, especially physiology and anatomy. John Dewey, whose textbook in psychology in 1887 was of a new kind, described what had gone before in this way: "Rash speculation, immature and crude generalization, unfounded assertion of individual opinion as scientific fact, this has been too often presented as physiological psychology"

(207). The new physiological psychologists were convinced that progress in their discipline lay in the laboratory. The presumption was that to understand human behavior, it was necessary first to know more about the brain. The main tension in the early years of professionalization was between the "old" eclectic psychologists, based still in philosophy, and a "new" community of experimentalists, some with their early training in Germany with Wilhelm Wundt at Leipzig, and in America with G. Stanley Hall at Johns Hopkins and E. B. Titchener at the University of Wisconsin. A second tension in the evolving discipline was between the experimentalists and the clinicians, who generalized from their experiences with individual patients to explain human behavior. The most prominent of these were Sigmund Freud and Carl Jung.

The struggle of psychology for recognition and resources as it eased away from philosophy was a slow one. A survey of the discipline in 1890 tells a sad tale (Jastrow et al. 1890). At the University of Wisconsin the library was so weak that the faculty had to open their own book collections to students, and for laboratories they had to go to the physiology department. At the University of Nebraska the curriculum was still listed under philosophy, and the main goal was the training of secondary school teachers. At Columbia the redoubtable Nicholas Murray Butler, chair of philosophy, reported that a separate department of psychology would be created "in the near future," while at Harvard William James and Josiah Royce, the two professors, were busy buying the first laboratory equipment. Looking at this survey, it seems that by 1890 the norm for professors was the teaching of two courses located in a philosophy department with only primitive lab equipment. Hall and Titchener (1921) reported that after they began publishing the *American Journal of Psychology* in 1887, with the intention of encouraging experimental psychology, they found that there was not enough good material of that kind to fill the pages, and reluctantly they had to encourage submission of the kind of eclectic offerings that they were attempting to supplant.

When we compare these two disciplines at the turn of the twentieth century according to the five development paths open to them, we see that very different choices were made. Economics was heavily committed to the first path of deductive models. To psychology this path seemed absurd. Why would you assume behavior when your objective was to understand it? The second alternative, of learning from historical evidence, was taken seriously in economics as a contender but was judged trivial in psychology. The third alternative, to learn from contemporary evidence, was taken seriously in both disciplines, but techniques to accomplish it were different. In economics the institutionalists advocated close engagement with current affairs, while in psychology high hopes were raised mainly about what could be achieved in the laboratory. The fourth alternative was controversial in both fields. There were those who expected much to be learned from interaction with clients and patients, but there were critics who predicted intellectual corruption and serious loss of rigor. In the case of the fifth alternative, those who considered themselves on the modern frontiers of their subject in both disciplines saw a move away from open-ended philosophical and literary inquiry as critical to a move forward, away from antiquated and discredited procedures.

There were still some important areas of overlap, as well as areas where if more overlap had occurred, there might have been impressive progress in both disciplines. For example, there was attention in both subjects to the early history of utilitarianism, undoubtedly to reflect on the origins of marginal utility theory as well as its current usefulness. Adam Smith's *Theory of Moral Sentiments* interested scholars in both disciplines, as did the work of Thomas Hobbes and Thomas Robert Malthus. Reasons for the focus in economics on pleasure and pain as overpowering motivating forces were discussed often in psychology (e.g., Ward 1893; Marshall 1894; Mavor 1894; Luckey 1895; Sutherland 1898; and V. F. Moore 1899). The two disciplines had a strong mutual interest in Jeremy Bentham, who, they discovered, had also turned to introspection as a way to understand human behavior. Economists took from Bentham that human nature was immutable. Psychologists, however, informed by the evolution theory of the second half of the nineteenth century, interpreted Bentham to suggest that the character of hedonism changed over time with the struggle for survival.

During the 1890s the thought occurred to a number of social scientists, especially sociologists, that a satisfactory allocation of responsibilities had not yet been agreed on among the disciplines and should thus be considered carefully. The Columbia sociologist Franklin Giddings suggested in 1895 that sociology and psychology might perhaps be thought of as "realistic and concrete" and therefore "fundamental" social sciences (Giddings 1895a). These yielded reliable data from which the "hypothetical and deductive" social sciences like economics might then specify their postulates, construct their models, and make their predictions. If the deductive sciences neglected the foundational ones, they would become stagnant and unable to predict successfully and would become, as economics was then said to be, stalled within an anachronistic utilitarian picture of human behavior contrived by theorists of another age like Bentham and Malthus. Giddings claimed that the foundational sciences had discovered in recent years at least as much cooperative spirit among humans as competition, and the deductive economists needed to take this into account. The Chicago sociologist Albion Small agreed with Giddings and argued for "an organic concept of society" as a device for keeping all the social sciences truly descriptive and out of the dead end into which economics had moved. "The proposition, 'society is organic,' is an attempt to assert in the briefest form a most obvious truth. Instead of committing sociologists to some mystical hypothesis, it is the truism from which sociologists make their departure in social observation" (Small 1895, 88).

The Brown University sociologist Lester Ward, the first president of the American Sociological Association, claimed that a society that took its guidance from "biological" economics rather than from a "social" or "psychological" economics would, contrary to what modern economists thought, increase waste rather than efficiency by ignoring the opportunities for cooperation among men. Monopoly and other nefarious market practices could not be reduced simply by competition. A psychological approach allowed for planning, "foresight," and "design." The benefits of laissez-faire as seen by this evolutionist were much exaggerated. In a word, take advice directly from Malthus's first *Essay on Population* (chapter 1) by explaining that

> Nature's way of sowing seed is to leave it to the wind, the water, the birds and animals. The greater part falls in a mass close to the parent plant, and is shaded out or crowded to death by its own abundance. . . . The most of these even never attain maturity, and only the most highly favored live to continue the race. To meet this enormous waste, correspondingly enormous quantities of seed are produced. Such is nature's economy. . . .
>
> A close analysis shows that the fundamental distinction between the animal and the human method is that *the environment transforms the animal, while man transforms the environment.* (Ward 1893, 80–81)

Sociology and psychology had yielded valuable insights that if carried farther in economics, Ward claimed, might have done much to enrich the discipline. For example, Ward rejected the economists' "biological" conception of capital as an accumulation of physical goods. Instead, most capital should be seen as psychological, what we now call "human capital." "The sum total of human arts constitutes man's material civilization, and it is this that chiefly distinguishes him from the rest of nature. But the arts are the exclusive product of mind. They are the means through which intelligence utilizes the materials and forces of nature. And as all economics rests primarily on production it seems to follow that a science of economics must have a psychological basis" (81).

Another insight from sociologists and psychologists in their early years that, if taken in the right spirit, might have borne fruit in economics, was the use of games as a metaphor for human interaction. For example, the psychologist Alfred A. Cleveland in a thirty-nine-page article with an extensive bibliography studied "the psychology of the game of chess" to trace the stages in the development of a chess player and to interpret this progress in psychological terms. "The game of chess has not been confined to any particular age, race, country, or class. It is without doubt one of the oldest, if not the oldest, of the intellectual pastimes, and it is the game of skill *par excellence*" (Cleveland 1907, 269–70). When he drew his findings together, including those from questionnaires submitted to chess players, Cleveland attempted to relate them to contemporary findings on human instincts: "In summary we may say of chess as a form of human play that in the first place it is a contest, and, as such, it appeals to the fundamental fighting instinct, the instinct which in every normal individual impels him to measure his skill with that of others. In the second place chess offers its devotees opportunity to exercise their ingenuity in the solution of problems and puzzles, a form of pleasure that may well rest upon that general interest in the unknown which at one time must have had the greatest survival value. It would seem further, that intellectual activity is indulged in for the pleasure which such activity gives in itself, and sport of this kind is, perhaps, an expression of the general play instinct" (272–73).

Why was chess so ubiquitous in human societies? Cleveland answered that it responded to certain instincts that ensured survival in the evolutionary process: "In common with a multitude of other games and sports, it appeals to the fundamental instinct of combat, in a way that is direct and at the same time exempt from the anti-social features that are inherent in actual physical combat. Here lies a large share of its attractiveness, and its capacity for stirring emotion. It takes hold upon those suppressed survivals of savage impulse (if we are to credit the savage alone with a first-hand liking for a contest) which in their modified exercise have been shown to be so large a factor in adult sport" (271). Cleveland examined various aspects of contemporary chess play: simultaneous games, blindfold games, and others, and he marveled at the feats of memory they demonstrated. He analyzed types of play using William Stanley Jevons's *Lessons in Logic* (1905) as a guide. But Cleveland does not make the jump from chess to market interactions.

Not as many economists attended to the potential overlap between economics and psychology as did the psychologists. One who did was Sidney Sherwood, a Princeton graduate with a law degree from Columbia who went on to a PhD in economics from Johns Hopkins and afterward an appointment to the Hopkins faculty. He was an associate professor when he died after a farm accident at the age of forty-one in 1902. In 1897 he entered the discussion over contrasting methodologies in the two disciplines with an article titled "The Philosophical Basis of Economics: A Word to the Sociologists," in which, like the sociologists, he looked for an agreed hierarchy among the social sciences. For Sherwood, the main question was whether the current relationship between economics and psychology was appropriate as the psychologists framed it. Did the two overlap? Did each one supplement or impede the other? Did one clearly dominate the other? In contrast to what the sociologists and psychologists had proposed, he insisted that economics as the science of choice must be considered the mother social science. The destiny of economics was to carry its distinctive message to the other social sciences like an imperial conqueror. "The fundamental and general science of man's activities, therefore, is economics. Economic science, if it would fill out its legitimate scope, must follow the workings of the economic law into all the lines of man's choice and into the formation and change of all social institutions. The self-conscious, self-willing individual is the unit of investigation. Social causation must be traced along lines of psychical not physical forces. Society itself is the creation of choice and choice is always essentially economic. In other words society must be studied primarily in its relation to the individual mind—not in its relation to the physical cosmos" (Sherwood 1897, 58–59).

Economics did use data from the other social sciences, Sherwood said, psychical indeed but of distinctive character and relevant only to the models that economists found useful in understanding choice. "Science, then, to get any basis for itself must recognize the reality of its primary judgments, likewise psychical facts" (60). Like psychologists, economists were interested in the psychical world, but they needed to explore those aspects of that world that were relevant to their own concerns. They could not simply turn to the other social sciences and work with their data alone. "We are perfectly aware of these psychical realities in the midst of which we live,—public opinion, law, custom, social institutions, traditional morality, courtesy of friendship and of business, customary prices—facts all—intangible creations of the minds of members of society. The student of political and economic science must likewise get this practical grasp of the fact that these things which make society are psychical forces and no less real than the physical" (64). Economists must never forget that understanding of the human psyche was as important to their science as the sciences of the physical world. An economist "studies the relations of the individual regarding the satisfaction of his wants, in utilizing himself, society, and nature. The traditional economics has dealt little with the individual's economic utilization of himself" (66). The main point that Sherwood stressed was that while all the social sciences required psychical data, the kind that economists must have were of a particular sort so as to understand the choice process. The other social sciences used psychical data mainly to understand the behavior of humans in groups; the economist's focus was on the individual, and mainly as a consumer. "Always and everywhere the individual stands alone. The kernel of his life is in himself. . . . All consumption resolves itself into appropriation by the individual of goods fitted for his use. Consumption is a psychical act and as such belongs to the individual" (69).

Perhaps to strengthen his case with biologist readers, Sherwood said that marginal utility economics should be seen as the equivalent of evolutionary biology. "The general economic law—the pursuit of the greatest utility with the least sacrifice—is simply the psychical form of the law of evolution—the survival of the fittest. . . . Utility is the subjective name for fitness, and fitness is the objective name for utility" (71). Sherwood had no difficulty in concluding that marginal utility could explain phenomena traditionally the province of other fields with a simplicity and universality that should be welcomed:

> All forms of want, aesthetic, ethical, physical, are commensurable as motives in the individual mind. The term want is generic and applies to all human desires. The corresponding term utility is also generic and applies to all things capable of supplying want. This is the plain fact of life. Our science must recognize it. . . . The direction of social change depends thus upon the utilitarian choices of individuals, and these choices are in their last analysis economic choices. In other words the

economic law—greatest utility with least sacrifice—is the generic law of human activity, both that which is directed to preserve the status [quo?] and that which aims at social evolution. . . . The universality of the principle of utility as the determinant in human choice has been established. Utility has likewise been identified with the generic law of economic life. (72–73)

Sherwood argued that in what he called "the psychical sciences" there needed to be a master paradigm (not his word) that economics had provided with its theory of choice. "My claim is that such a science must explain all the conscious activities of men by reducing them to terms of the motives and choices of the individual consciousness. My further claim is that economics is pre-eminently the science fitted to hold this place" (76). The founder of this master social science that encompassed, together with economics, also sociology, psychology, and political science was Adam Smith. He built the first bridge between economics and psychology.

In the "Wealth of Nations" we have already reached a recognition of a general science of economics which systematizes the laws underlying the economic activities both of individuals and of the state. Furthermore, this general science is conceived by Smith as studying the operation of the motives of individuals in leading to the activities of individuals and of societies. Society and all social activities are treated as resting on ultimate bases of individual thought, choice, and deed. Smith and his followers studied mankind as made up of individual units. Social groupings were secondary, not primary. (86)

Sherwood recognized very early what Frank Knight recognized decades later, that deductive economics would be deeply threatened if laboratory studies of human behavior by psychologists were to make accurate predictions of how humans behave. If everything were determined biologically, what good was a science of choice? "So soon as the individual man comes to be looked on as an automaton moved solely by the forces of matter, the significance of these activities which seem to be initiated by the free will of men is lost. The bonds which unite men in society are regarded in the light of physical forces" (87).

As I have shown, in the 1890s leaders in the new disciplines of sociology and psychology reached out to economics rather tentatively, and patronizingly. The response they received, from Sidney Sherwood at least, was something of a rebuff, that the role of economics was far more than to manipulate the data that others in these two disciplines would collect. Indeed, economics was the true mother social science and had little to benefit from the kinds of data it might receive from others. One who attempted to improve the atmosphere of this discussion and build more bridges among the social sciences was Simon Nelson Patten, the first professor of political economy of the Wharton School at the University of Pennsylvania. Patten argued that the establishment of a community among the social sciences where all were of an equal status was essential for scientific progress. A narrow focus by any one of these disciplines acting alone necessarily obscured aspects of human behavior critical to advances in human welfare. The notion of an economic man was a caricature that should no longer be taken seriously: "The economic man of Ricardo is a deductive concept. It is the man we see, stripped of many of his vital attributes" (Patten 1888, 687).

Inattention to the full psychology of humans, Patten claimed, blinded economists to opportunities for constructive public policy and left them rushing to catch up. "The American people are adjusting their political ideas to their economic and social environment, and are beginning to see more closely that a reasonable activity on the part of the state is not detrimental to the harmonious development of each individual" (690). He gave examples. One was the consequences of the neglect of the relationship between the consumption of what we call today "merit goods" and the progress of civilization. "With the higher civilization of man comes a greater desire for less exclusive commodities, the demand for which allows a better adjustment of man to nature and thus increases the efficiency of labor" (689). A second example was the relationship between the moral climate of a society and its interest rates. "The rate of interest is largely determined by the esteem in which the future is held. The development of the moral nature greatly increases the regard for future welfare, and this increases the amount of capital which will be accumulated at a given rate of interest. The effect of the lower rate of interest would therefore be counteracted by the greater esteem in which the future is held, and the growth of capital would be as large as before" (689).

The most practical suggestion that Patten made for bringing the two disciplines together, drawn perhaps from his readings in psychology, was to shift attention in economics from the production of wealth to its consumption, from what he called study of a "pain economy" and the costs of production to a "pleasure economy," meaning welfare actually achieved through consumption. The quality of life depended undoubtedly on the number of goods and services actually produced, but also on how these goods were then converted into utility by consumers (what he called the translation of pain into pleasure) and thus determined welfare. Since so much attention had been devoted to the production side of the economy, more might now be accomplished by attending to consumption. He suggested that a balanced understanding of economic history could best be achieved by examining the progress of efficient consumption as well as efficient production. For this, study of such social institutions as monopolies and laws of inheritance was necessary, and the skills of the psychologist must be employed.

> When the tendencies were strong in economics to seek a physical basis for all economic theories, he was forced to become a physicist, and even an agricultural chemist, in order that he might determine the principles which regulate the production of wealth on its physical side. Of recent years a strong tendency has arisen to lay stress upon the subjective side of economics and hence the economist has become a psychologist and has investigated many psychological problems which have been neglected by psychologists with metaphysical tendencies. (Patten 1892, 129)

In some of these studies on the demand side, Patten said, economists had moved ahead of old-style psychologists, and with the new-style laboratory-based psychology, opportunities had opened up for exciting new forms of cooperation. "Out of all this has come a new method of psychological investigation and the formulation of laws that throw new light upon some old problems, the solution of which was not possible by accepted methods" (129). Looking ahead to the study of incentives and what would be known as externalities, he suggested that "morality" be strengthened by directing a "surplus of pleasure" to "right actions" and a "surplus of pain" to "evil" ones. But to do this successfully it was necessary to understand the behavior of social groups, which was the specialty of the newly emerging subdiscipline of social psychology, as well as the mental processes of individuals within groups. The characteristics of moral pleasures had been especially neglected by economists. "The progress of civilization tends to enlarge these harmonious groups of pleasures, but, as yet much less in size than those of pain" (136).

Patten criticized social scientists of all kinds for neglecting the study of consumption. He chastised sociologists and psychologists for not following the advice he gave them and for staying out of touch with the progress made in economics through the study of markets.

The traditional psychology is the creation of a group of skeptical idealists. In the endeavor to get unity and simplicity, they have thrown out all
the complex forms of thought that do not fit their theory. Nature, atoms
and other objects have been eliminated and the universe is so emaciated
that its only content is a single series of ideas. If these skeptical idealists
cannot find a place for the objective world or any proof of the existence
of other minds, still less can they find a basis in their psychology for the
social relations which grow up between men. (Patten 1896, 435)

He was just as critical of the sociologists for their enthusiasm about laboratory-based psychology, for their

acceptance of the narrow dogma of the sceptics that the individual
mind has no phenomena but the chemistry of its ideas. Such a psychology must be discarded before a solid basis for sociology can be found.
When a more complex concept of the mind is worked out in which
other elements of human nature are on equal footing with the sensory
ideas, there will be no need of such hybrid concepts as minds above
minds or a social will above that of individuals. (4)

Patten's advice to the economists was that they should pay more attention to the environment in which consumption occurred. The complex
constraints of a pleasure economy are quite as important as the actual
consumption of goods and services. "Thus we see that the home, the family and society are environment ideas. They are due to the place relations,
which the early types of pleasure economy created, and are changed and
developed with the changes it has undergone. To these common pleasures
the different forms of control are due. Men subordinate themselves to
external conditions or to other men, so that they can participate more fully
in the enjoyments of a pleasure economy" (16). Patten urged economists
to follow up insights from psychologists and sociologists to strengthen
their understanding of an economy based fundamentally on a utilitarian
foundation but with complexities understood best by psychologists.

The community of professional economists did not often take direct
issue with Patten, but they did not line up behind him either. He was
viewed more as someone to be tolerated. A. C. Pigou (1903) was mildly
complimentary. Henry Seager of Columbia University and the author of a
popular textbook in economics reviewed favorably Patten's achievements
to 1902. He noted especially Patten's courage in engaging so enthusiastically in interdisciplinary controversy. "Professor Patten has seemed open
to the charge of turning his back on his chosen specialty to embroil

himself with sociologists, psychologists, historians and other quarrelsome persons" (Seager 1902, 75). But this, Seager thought, was unfair. He noted that Patten's forays into other disciplines were no more welcome there than they were among his economist colleagues: "He proposed an explanation of the nature and laws of growth of the mental mechanism which caused psychologists at first to gasp and then to clamor against the daring invader" (75). Seager called for sympathetic attention to Patten's ideas because, although unfamiliar, they were important to both of the disciplines he sought to bring together.

> His successive tilts with sociologists, psychologists and historians were undertaken in the conscious endeavor to enlarge the scope of economic speculation. Only when it is clearly perceived what he was driving at in these seemingly uneconomic excursions can the significance of his latest work be understood. . . . An original thinker, such as Professor Patten is universally conceded to be, should be welcomed in any field and requires no excuse for venturing where he pleases so long as his efforts are constructively directed. (76–77)

Seager suggested that Patten's early life in rural midwestern America, followed by postgraduate study in Germany, had made him naturally critical of orthodox economics. "If, as Professor Patten came to believe, even ideas, beliefs and modes of reasoning are changed by local conditions, the old associational psychology and the old utilitarian ethics are no longer adequate bases for economics. Inspired by this conviction he set about formulating new psychological principles in order to show how previously unobserved properties of mind act as social forces in shaping human progress" (78). Seager saw Patten's "principal service" to economics to be "helping others to break away from traditional distinctions and accepted theories. It opens a wide field for thought and study and perhaps not its least merit is that it leaves the reader persuaded that while the field is undoubtedly there, much the larger part of it is still open" (91).

Patten had at least as many critics as admirers. The Yale economist Arthur T. Hadley thought Patten's efforts through excursions into other disciplines like psychology to make economics a "dynamic" science simply misguided. "It may be true that Jevons's solution of the problem of value was a purely statical one, and that there is room for a wider 'dynamic' treatment of the subject. But if an author seems to secure this wider treatment by abandoning rigidity of analysis, he makes a step backward instead of forward" (Hadley 1892, 563). Others were even less charitable.

Lionel D. Edie, writing in 1925 shortly after Patten's death, saw little of long-term value.

> The younger generation of economists will derive much of inspiration from Patten's brilliant phrases and contrasts, but they are bound to realize after all that the most that Patten accomplished was to throw out stimulating suggestions and to state new problems. He did not by any means arrive at concrete answers to the outstanding new problems of the science. He indicated pathways of needed research, but did not travel over them himself. Economists will read Patten chiefly because he is a great guide and introduction to the real research studies which need to follow. (Edie 1925, 303–4)

It is worth noting that there was no discernible difference among those economists who commented on Patten's engagement with psychology between those on the ideological left and those on the right. On the left, Alvin Johnson, later a founder of the New School in New York, was delighted with Patten's "vigorous independence of thought," and in 1902 he wrote of Patten's latest book: "Iconoclastic in the extreme, it attacks and overthrows many accepted doctrines of economic theory. Yet its general effect is rather to supplement and complete current theory than to displace it or destroy it" (313). Johnson gave an example of how Patten, through his study of human motivations, had helped demonstrate the value of thinking about a "pleasure" rather than a "pain" economy. "Labor, even in the final hour, is not normally painful to the normal man. Where the laborer is virtual slave, toil may be so prolonged as to become painful" (314). From the right, B. M. Anderson Jr. (1913, 123), one of the most committed Austrians in America, writing just before World War I, compared Patten's latest article to the work of the mildly rebellious current generation of modernist painters known as "post-impressionists": "The first reading of Professor Patten's essay leaves one gasping. Surely this is post-impressionism in economics! Where is the unity? What is the drift? Brilliant and startling notions abound, but how are they related to each other?"

Yet Anderson was sympathetic to Patten's efforts to introduce dynamic elements and psychology into economics. He wondered only what it all amounted to. "Professor Patten would reject the theories which make distribution depend on natural law or 'static' law. He would introduce the elements of struggle, monopoly, legal changes, changes in education, in morals, in standards of consumption; 'distribution is thus complex, following no one law'" (126). Anderson concluded graciously: "Few men read what Professor Patten writes without changing their opinions on the points discussed—not necessarily changing them in the direction that Professor Patten indicates, but none the less changing them" (129; see also Ely 1900). It may have been unfortunate that for at least two decades Patten was seen as the main standard-bearer for inclusion of more psychology in economics. Since so many considered him no more than a well-meaning and sometimes stimulating maverick, the question of psychology's usefulness was not treated with the seriousness that it deserved.

2. Critiques from Psychology of Marginal Utility: Instincts, Habits, William James, William McDougall, and Behaviorism

Patten's appeal for inclusion of psychology in economics was relatively genteel and polite, calling for the enrichment of orthodox political economy, and certainly not its replacement by something else. He wanted dynamic elements to be added to the existing static ones and more attention paid to consumption. By the turn of the century, however, more strident critiques of the use of marginal utility by economists could be heard within psychology. These did not suggest, as Patten had done, that orthodox economics could simply be straightened out and strengthened by sympathetic psychologists. Now the demand was for marginal utility to be removed from economics root and branch. The new critics argued that the picture of the rational actor soberly making choices among technologies and consumer goods was simply absurd. All the psychological research to date had shown something else. Because of this attitude among some leading psychologists, their whole discipline came to be seen by economists as radical, hostile, and disrespectful. There were four phases in the evolution of psychology in this confrontational role.

The first phase consisted of prominent figures in the psychology community taking up seriously the way economists portrayed economic behavior. They found that the differences from the approach of psychologists had much to do with how the two disciplines viewed evolution theory. Marshall might say that "*natura non facit saltum*," but to the psychologists it seemed that his theory implied that nature did not move at all. In equilibrium a kind of stasis was established that evolutionists believed never occurred. They claimed that Charles Darwin, T. H. Huxley, Herbert Spencer, and Alfred Russel Wallace had demonstrated that the forces driving changes in human behavior were always in flux, and equilibrium was a fantasy. In this tradition William James made "instincts" an essential part of his portrayal of the human mind. Others had discussed instincts before him, especially in the 1870s when there was a surge of interest, but he was the first to give them "a place in the very frontline of human life" (James Rowland Angell in 1911, quoted in Donnelly 1992, 263). In his 1890 textbook James provided a succinct definition: "Instinct is usually defined as the faculty of acting in such a way as to produce certain ends, without foresight of the ends, and without previous education in the performance" (quoted in Donnelly 1992, 272). He also provided a list of instincts he could discern that included resentment, sympathy, shyness, modesty, emulation, and imitation (273). It would be hard to think of a list of forces driving human action, without foresight or forethought, more likely to be perceived as inconsistent with a society based on rational action. Instincts operated without consciousness and could not play much of a role at all in a society of rational actors: "Reflexes grade into instincts, with reflexes generally affecting our own bodies and instincts affecting the outside world," said James (273). However, James was a pluralist, and he did not ascribe all behavior to instincts.

The psychologist who pointed out most forcefully the extent to which instinct theory threatened the rational actor model upon which the economists depended was William McDougall (1871–1938). By the time he entered the fray with economists, he was well into a most distinguished career as Reader in Psychology at Oxford, professor at Harvard in 1920, successor to William James, and finally professor at the new Duke University from 1927, where he built the psychology department from scratch. McDougall's main contribution was to claim that the economists' approach to behavior was fundamentally inconsistent with modern evolutionary theory that showed living things, including humans, responding through time to changing challenges, with those who made the right choices, in most cases by instinct, winning the struggle for survival. The determinants of human behavior, he said, had little to do with rational choice and much to do with inherited "instincts," nonrational forces that evolved through time and incorporated the results of past evolutionary struggles. He offered a more detailed definition of an instinct than James, as "an inherited or innate psycho-physical disposition which determines its possessor to pay attention to objects of a certain class, to experience an emotional excitement of a particular quality upon perceiving such an object, and to act in regard to it in a particular manner, or, at least, to experience an impulse to such action" (quoted in Donnelly 1992, 285). Instincts incorporated the cultural norms of a society, including economic ones. These, according to Jean-Baptiste Lamarck, could be passed on from one generation to another.

The first full explanation of McDougall's position on instincts came in his textbook *An Introduction to Social Psychology* (1908). As Frank A. Pattie (1939, 304) wrote in an obituary of McDougall,

> In this book McDougall sought to lay a firm foundation for the social sciences to replace the ad hoc psychologies previously concocted by many writers in this field. This firm foundation he believed to be the theory of instincts and their derivatives, the sentiments. In his [later work] *Outline of Psychology* (1923) he carried this theory farther and named it, after a suggestion of Percy Nunn, the hormic theory. This theory states that purposive striving is the most fundamental category of psychology, and that the springs of purposive activity are the instincts. The instincts are inborn dispositions, which cannot be defined by reference either to definite stimuli or to bodily movements, but only by the kind of change in the situation which their activity brings about or, when introspection is possible, by the specific accompanying emotional quality. The ascription of a specific emotion to each of the human instincts is one of the most original but at the same time one of the most questionable points in McDougall's system.

After his 1908 book McDougall was widely accepted as one of the founders of the new field of social psychology, and what he wrote about instincts was taken very seriously. His list of instincts and related emotions in 1908 was summarized by a reviewer as seven pairs: "(1) The instinct of flight and the emotion of fear. . . . (2) The instinct of repulsion and the emotion of disgust. (3) The instinct of curiosity and the emotion of wonder. (4) The instinct of pugnacity and the emotion of anger. (5) The instinct of self-abasement (or subjection) and the emotion of subjection. (6) The instinct of self-assertion (or self-display) and the emotion of elation. (7) The parental instinct and the tender emotion" (Leuba 1909, 286). Increasingly McDougall used the terms *propensity* and *inherited tendency* instead of *instinct*, but his critique of the rational actor remained strong and clear. Utilitarian behavior had not been eliminated from McDougall's thinking, but thanks to his textbook, students now could go from their economics class to their psychology class and see that the picture of the human actor was quite different in one from the other. While

McDougall seemed to reject the ideas about behavior he found in Smith's *Wealth of Nations*, there are indications that he approved of *The Theory of Moral Sentiments* even though he modified Smith's metaphors a little. McDougall wrote of people seeing themselves as parading before a "gallery of spectators" rather than the "impartial spectator," as Smith put it.

McDougall's reputation within the profession of psychology continued to grow as he developed his instinct theory (Ginsberg 1924). But at the same time, he was criticized for excursions into international relations and American racial policy where he had no special qualifications and where his conclusions were deeply controversial. He claimed that there should be no such thing as "universal ethics." Ethics depended on the circumstances. In this respect his views on eugenics were clear. One unsympathetic reviewer of his book *Ethics and Some Modern World Problems* (1924) reported that "the application of universalist principles on a large scale would result, he thinks, in a terrific increase of population, in the rapid preponderance of peoples of lower cultures and lower standards of life, in miscegenation and the ultimate swamping of the white race" (Ginsberg 1925, 99). There were others as well who thought he had led social psychology into a dead end. A young psychologist, Henry C. Link, wrote in 1921 that

> it is impossible to see to what practical result McDougall's list of instincts can lead. McDougall's confessed purpose is to make a contribution to the Social Sciences by analyzing the dynamic and determinative factors in human nature. However, he has left us with a mosaic of facts which are connected only in a schematic way. Beginning with a handful of supposedly specific, but in actuality hopelessly vague causes, he has left us with an infinitude of results, all obvious but all more or less irrelevant. (141)

Link wrote again in 1922, in a fragment published from his recent dissertation at Yale, that McDougall made claims for instinct theory that could not be sustained. "There is no questioning the fact that instincts are fundamental and determining factors in the organism and in society. But our knowledge of the instincts is by no means such as to warrant any wholesale speculation, far less any scientific certainty about the individual and social values to which they give rise" (Link 1922, 4).

Link wrote that while McDougall had set out to establish a firm foundation for the social sciences, he had led them, instead, toward a method of "psychological rationalism" that was fully as unsatisfactory as what he wished to replace. "McDougall's account of instinct-values can be so comprehensive and at the same time of such little significance from a scientific point of view. Another writer could start either with half as many or with twice as many instincts as McDougall and attribute to them the values of society with equal plausibility and equal futility" (8–9). Link regretted that some economists, thinking perhaps of Thorstein Veblen, had been misled into believing that instinct psychologists had found the true explanation for human behavior in the market.

> It is absurd for economists to believe that they can translate their study of economics from the field of conjecture to the field of science by borrowing a set of ready-made instincts from psychology. We can imagine Thorndike, Watson, McDougall and a few others trying to agree on a classification of instincts as the axioms of economics! We may agree empirically upon the uniformity and strength of the sex instinct. But what relation has this instinct to the marginal desirability of a second, third, or fourth wife? (16)

The Cornell economist and institutionalist leader Morris Copeland (1924, 128) agreed with Link in 1924 that no matter how plausible instincts were as determining human behavior, they were hopelessly difficult to pin down (on the mounting critique of instincts, see Rutherford 2011, 97, 99, 102, 120).

H. W. Wright, reviewing the whole field of psychology in 1937, reported that in the view of another psychologist, F. C. Bartlett, "'social psychology had a brilliant beginning when William McDougall wrote his *Introduction to Social Psychology*, but since then it seems to have made very little advance.' For this static condition he finds McDougall's book, despite its originality and value, largely to blame, since by its emphasis on instinct in social behavior it led to a long period of fruitless controversy in the field of social psychology between instinct psychologies and psychologies of every other kind" (49). But while this dispute was carried on in psychology, the importance and progress of social psychology and instinct were still claimed from time to time in economics. For example, a session on the relevance of instinct theory to economics was held at the 1919 annual meeting of the American Economic Association with the main paper "The Psychological Basis for the Economic Interpretation of History" by the distinguished sociologist William F. Ogburn (1919). The Princeton economist Frank A. Fetter (1919, 306) remarked at the session that "conventional economics is still utilitarian and rationalistic, whereas the authoritative psychology of today is volitional and gives a much larger place to impulses and instincts. I need not in this company restate my own position, which has long been favorable to the psychological conception."

The notion of habit, although like instinct with a long history in the nineteenth century, came along soon after the attention to instinct among psychologists, and it gave new strength to the claim that much human behavior was not the consequence of rational calculation. The Cornell psychologist B. R. Andrews (1903, 121–22), in a review of the literature up to 1903, defined the term as follows: "A habit, from the standpoint of psychology, is a more or less fixed way of thinking, willing, or feeling acquired through previous repetition of a mental experience . . . habit in itself lies outside consciousness. It implies simply an accustomed way of reacting. . . . Habit is the mode of mental functioning when repeated processes are in mind. . . . habit is the way consciousness runs its course when familiar processes are experienced." Graham Wallas, a British political scientist at the London School of Economics, was one of the first to urge that habit as well as instinct be taken seriously throughout the social sciences. He wrote in his influential book *Human Nature in Politics* (1908) that "most of the political opinions of most men are the result, not of reasoning tested by experience, but of unconscious or half-conscious inference fixed by habit" (quoted in Williamson 1909, 697). In an article in the *American Economic Review* in 1924, Lawrence Frank, a Columbia graduate, suggested that the study of habits could "emancipate" not only economists but all the social sciences from too narrow a focus on "an autonomous, rationally volitional being." He himself integrated habits into a theory of the business cycle (Rutherford 2011, 239–40). By the 1930s discussion of habit had shifted from the question of whether the concept threatened the vision of the rational actor to the practical matter of whether learning theory could help people break their bad habits (Dunlap 1932).

For those economists who objected to the bodies of doctrine in psychology that suggested much human behavior was determined not by rational calculation but by some sort of automatic response, the approach of many psychologists by the 1920s known as "behaviorists" was the last straw. John Watson of Johns Hopkins University, one of the leaders of the movement, described it in an often-cited manifesto of 1913 as follows: "Psychology as the behaviorist views it is a purely objective experimental branch of natural science. Its theoretical goal is the prediction and control of behavior. Introspection forms no essential part of its methods, nor is the scientific value of its data dependent upon the readiness with which they lend themselves to interpretation in terms of consciousness" (158). This definition, of course, contained instruction mainly about what behaviorism was not; it left open the question of what it might become. One author who attempted to pull this subject together in 1924 saw McDougall as the inspiration by making the case that much human action took place beyond consciousness (Roback 1924). But the behaviorists went beyond McDougall, whose contribution was to trace behavior to evolutionary struggles that resulted in forces that were survival characteristics. Curt Rosenow, a behaviorist at the University of Kansas, pointed out that he and his colleagues emphasized all the physiological characteristics of humans: "All of us who sympathize with Behaviorism at all are attracted by its emphasis on the study of behavior as a biological phenomenon and by its frank recognition of the sterility of the study of the states of consciousness" (Rosenow 1925, 233; Ogden 1933). Behaviorism suggested that psychology should move away from cultural anthropology and sociology, where instincts and habits might be discovered, to laboratories where the biological determinants of behavior could be perceived. This would move psychology out of the humanities and perhaps even out of the social sciences. This outcome was entirely to be desired, said the behaviorists. H. W. Chase said that if psychology was to contribute to the solution of the great economic problems that had been raised by the war, it must become truly scientific. "To be scientific, students of social problems need to base their work not on the laws of biology or economics, but on the laws of human behavior. And, further, human behavior throughout its whole extent must be conceived in scientific terms; as uniform and as discoverable only by adequately controlled investigation" (Chase 1917, 228). However, as one critic of behaviorism put it: "Inasmuch as ethics, jurisprudence, medicine, religion and the social sciences are written in terms of subjectivism, behaviorism is incompatible with them. If psychology is to be conceived in terms of behavior, it must lose all contact with these fields" (Hunter 1923, 467). Despite this view, of course, behaviorism did inevitably raise questions of ethics and personal responsibility. So long as your behavior was determined by your physicochemical makeup, how practical was it to think of modifying this behavior for the social good or assigning responsibility to the perpetrator for antisocial acts?

For those economists who observed the growth of behaviorism from afar, it must have been somewhat confusing, as there was no single paradigm to which all subscribed. Katherine Williams, a psychologist at Radcliffe College, in a long review article on the rise of behaviorism, found "a multitude of behaviorisms" to confuse the observer. She described the behaviorists as a quarrelsome and undisciplined bunch. The behaviorist "hastens to seize the behaviorist banner and in the act of grasping it pauses to say that of course this does not mean allegiance to anybody or to anybody's ideas" (Williams 1931, 337). She discovered unanimity among the behaviorists only in rejection of other factions among the psychologists such as the mentalists and the introspectionists (358). For the most part, there was discord. The only technical point where one could be confident of agreement was a minor one about "sensation." "They merely agree that the essence of sensation is to be sought in the discriminative aspect of response" (358). Some behaviorists rejected instincts altogether as determining causes of behavior; others admitted them altogether. Some saw learning as the acquisition of conditioned reflexes; others did not. They did agree from the beginning that the physicochemical makeup of humanity was a most critical matter for study, and that self-conscious introspection could be ignored.

3. Critiques of Marginal Utility from within Economics: Thorstein Veblen and Rexford Tugwell

A few economists as early as the nineteenth century were aware of critiques of the rational actor coming from psychologists like William James and William McDougall. However, these critiques must have seemed rather mild and neither challenging nor threatening. That changed in 1899 when Thorstein Veblen published *The Theory of the Leisure Class* followed by *The Theory of Business Enterprise* (1904) and a stream of other works such as an article in the *Journal of Political Economy* in 1909 titled "The Limitations of Marginal Utility" (Veblen 1909; also Veblen 1914). These works must not have seemed a great surprise to any psychologists well-read in their own literature. Even the terms used by Veblen and the titles given to his list of instincts appeared to have been taken directly from McDougall. But in contrast to the psychologists who, for the most part, did not turn their study of instincts and habits directly against economics, Veblen did. Now economists had to confront the psychologists' ideas coming from one of their own young stars. Some of the early readers of Veblen were stimulated and even complimentary about his accomplishments, while remaining puzzled. Thomas Nixon Carver (1905, 141) began his review of the second book: "The reader of this work is likely to be reminded of what Socrates said of the work of Heraclitus the obscure, viz. that 'what he understood of it was excellent, and he had no doubt that what he did not understand was equally good; but the book required an expert swimmer'" (see also Day 1901).

The earlier critiques of the rational actor by psychologists had not been directed at economics in general or price theory in particular. Mainly they were internal to psychology with sideways glances at the economists. Veblen, by contrast through his intimacy with economics, could aim his barbs directly at the heart of modern economics, not only its core theory but its policy implications and cultural values as well. Moreover, by implication he showed little of the respect normally given to senior figures in the field. Veblen's portrayals of humans interacting in markets are filled with pictures of unreasoning decision making and unconscious responses to various stimuli, some with deep genetic origins and others with contemporary roots that he explained anthropologically. Moreover, the picture he painted was of instability without equilibrium even in the background. Instincts and habits were always changing, and so human behavior was always in evolution. If all of Veblen's comments were taken into account, there was not much left of the rational actor. Instead, markets were seen to be governed on both sides by actors who were pushed and pulled by the instinct of workmanship, the instinct of emulation, the pugnacious bent, idle curiosity, and numerous other forces over which they had little control.

This psycho-economic approach taken by Veblen and his institutional compatriots was not politically revolutionary. Indeed, for the most part they disliked Karl Marx, and they saw the forces bringing change in the economy as powerful, capable of bringing change on their own, and not often in need of outside assistance. "Planning" was often the most radical intervention they were prepared to contemplate. They were not confident that "progress" was inevitable or that humans could make it move faster. In an article on the history of economics in 1900, Veblen claimed that neoclassical economics was fundamentally misleading on this point. "The two main canons of truth on which the science proceeded and with which the inquiry is here concerned, were: (a) a hedonistic-associational psychology, and (b) an uncritical conviction that there is a meliorative trend in the course of events, apart from the conscious ends of the individual members of the community" (242). He argued that the new psychology undermined the two most important preconceptions in modern economics, natural rights and laissez-faire.

The natural-rights preconception begins to fall away as soon as the hedonistic mechanics have been seriously tampered with. . . . The mechanics of natural liberty—that assumed constitution of things by force of which the free hedonistic play of the laws of nature across the open field of individual choice is sure to reach the right outcome—is the hedonistic psychology; and the passing of the doctrine of natural rights and natural liberty, whether as a premise or as a dogma, therefore coincides with the passing of that mechanics of conduct on the validity of which the theoretical acceptance of the dogma depends. (246)

The old psychology of universal self-interest was doomed, Veblen wrote, and would not be around for much longer. "The later psychology is biological, as contrasted with the metaphysical psychology of hedonism. . . . While hedonism seeks the causal determinant of conduct in the (probable) outcome of action, the later conception seeks this determinant in the complex of propensities that constitutes man a functioning agent, that is to say, a personality. Instead of pleasure ultimately determining what human conduct shall be, the tropismatic propensities that eventuate in conduct ultimately determine what shall be pleasurable" (247–48). Veblen regretted that "economic conduct still continues to be somewhat mysterious to the economists; and they are forced to content themselves with adumbrations whenever the discussion touches this central, substantial fact" (268). He concluded with a characteristically patronizing remark. "All of this, of course, is intended to convey no dispraise of the work done, nor in any way to disparage the theories which the passing generation of economists have elaborated or the really great and admirable body of knowledge which they have brought under the hand of the science; but only to indicate the direction in which the inquiry in its later phases—not always with full consciousness—is shifting as regards its categories and its point of view" (268).

When reviewing Veblen's contributions in 1937, still deep in the Great Depression, John R. Hobson (1937, 139) wrote: "Veblen, as soon as he had passed through an early phase of philosophic study, betook himself to anthropology as the seed bed of social psychology." There he discovered the root of the failure of modern economics to solve the great problems of the day. "To present economic man as a rational being, calculating and regulating all his activities in terms of conscious costs and satisfactions, falsifies the actual situation, for it requires the suppression of facts and activities which intimately interfere with the hedonist calculus. The recent failure of economic forecasts is manifestly due to this policy of intellectual separation" (140). Hobson said that Veblen's main achievement had been to introduce instincts and habits into economic analysis: "His high claim to intellectual distinction, his main service to social science, lay in his insistence upon interpreting social institutions and their values in terms of an instinct-habit psychology which gave a main determinant place to economic activities and needs" (143). If anyone looked for the guilty party in confronting orthodox economics with challenges from psychology, Hobson made clear that Veblen was the culprit.

Veblen soon acquired a following in the economics profession and in the wider public. But the obscurity of his writing style and his strange use of words caused some careful readers to have doubts and others to throw up their hands. One representative reviewer concluded: "He has given us some interesting reading viewed as a cynical comment on modern life, and has made some contribution to the study of social survivals, but the title of his book is a misnomer, because it is not a satisfactory theory of the leisure class" (Lindsay 1900, 141). Before long, some Veblenites narrowed their focus to the concept of marginal utility alone, and this caught the attention of conventional theorists. One Veblen sympathizer, E. H. Downey (1910, 255) from the University of Missouri, writing in the *Journal of Political Economy*, explained Veblen's critique of orthodoxy: "The objection to all this is its want of verisimilitude, and that in two respects. (1) It assigns too large a place to reflective choice as an element in human conduct, and (2) it misconceives the basis of choice. . . . Habit, not calculation, governs the greater part of all our acts." Downey even quoted McDougall to the effect that "mankind is only a little bit reasonable and to a great extent unintelligently moved in quite unreasonable ways" (255). It seemed that Downey had picked up some of Veblen's sarcasm: "Quite irrespective of its psychological inadequacy, the marginal-utility theory falls short of practical usefulness. It does not solve concrete problems of price, but only translates them into a jargon hard to be understood" (263). Habits were again suggested as the best predictors of human action. "The behavior of men can be neither predicted nor understood apart from their habitual modes of thought and from the institutional situation in which they act. It is not surprising, therefore, that a century and a quarter of diligent research into 'labor-pain,' 'abstinence,' 'marginal utility,' and the like, should have contributed substantially nothing to 'the increase and diffusion of knowledge among men'" (268).

By the 1920s direct attacks on marginal utility analysis were frequent and prominent within the economics profession. Two of the most pointed essays during this decade were by Rexford Tugwell of Columbia University, one the lead article in an issue of the *Journal of Political Economy* in 1922 and the other a chapter in his collected volume *The Trend of Economics* (1924). Tugwell, who in a decade would become one of the most influential members of President Franklin Roosevelt's "brains trust," already demonstrated considerable rhetorical skill. These were scholarly essays with a well-developed argument including a thorough review of the literature. Tugwell studied at the University of Pennsylvania and was influenced by Simon Nelson Patten. Like Patten, he found that orthodox economic theory "fails to take advised and realistic account of human nature" (Tugwell 1922, 317). Economic theorists seemed resolutely determined to ignore the results of recent research that had come from the laboratories of respectable psychologists.

> Economics is admitted to have a conception of human nature; but the root of the trouble seems to lie exactly in the fact that it is a conception— or, perhaps more accurately, a preconception. Its critics feel it to be inexact, unreal and without documentation or careful description; advanced, possibly, a step beyond the rigid classical *homo economicus* in the thinking of the marginalists or corrected classicists of today, but still lacking the complex and irrational features of the human figure beginning to be bodied [*sic*] forth in the laboratories of the present generation of psychologists. (317)

Tugwell applauded the advances being made by the psychologists James, Watson, and Edward L. Thorndike, and by the economists Wesley Clair Mitchell and Leo Wolman (see below), and he criticized prominent "orthodox" economists for their timidity and their reluctance to abandon an out-of-date psychology; none had had the courage to write a textbook that included modern psychology such as that of McDougall (1924, 406). It was sad to report that even "W. C. Mitchell seems almost to have approximated this attitude when he characterized modern psychology as a 'dark, subjective realm' which a man without a lantern had better leave unexplored" (Tugwell 1922, 321). Tugwell could not name any modern economist except Patten who was willing to incorporate the study of human nature into economics so as to "explain human conduct": "Throughout his long career as teacher and writer he has been insistently emphasizing the dependence of economics on psychology" (325). It was hard to explain why economists had been so hesitant, since "so far, it can be said, economics never has had an entirely adequate theory of choices" (320).

Tugwell worried that perhaps the notoriety of Freud and psychoanalysis had misled economists about what might be learned from psychology: "From the attitude of many economists one might gather that the study of the mind is a region of superstition or at best of pseudo-science, which men had best avoid in the interest of finding more fruitful and less metaphysical fields of endeavor elsewhere. This is naïve and is ungenerous to the eminent psychologists of the present generation and to some, like William James, of the past" (331). Tugwell suggested that a reconstruction of marginal economics from a psychological perspective might help answer questions that were more than two centuries old, such as those raised by Bernard de Mandeville and Adam Smith over the relationships among sympathy, philanthropy, and self-interest. Such a reconsideration should include a new look at marginal productivity theory: "It does not seem so remarkable that the classically trained should be so reluctant to admit this new-appearing specter of human nature. It calls into question immediately the whole justification for the distribution of income" (339).

Tugwell's collection of essays in 1924 was intended to show that the "trend of economics" was toward institutionalism and greater cooperation with psychology. These familiar critiques of orthodoxy were expressed by Mitchell, Copeland, J. M. Clark, Paul Douglas, Sumner Slichter, George Soule, and A. B. Wolfe. Some attempt at balance was achieved by allowing Frank Knight to explain his skepticism about the potential contribution of psychology; he was supported by Raymond Bye, an assistant professor at the University of Pennsylvania. Bye felt confident that improvements in price theory, accomplished already in response to criticisms, made further attempts to incorporate psychology unnecessary: "The crude cost doctrines of the classicists and the extreme hedonistic marginal utility analysis of the subjective economists are giving way to a more objective representation of the forces of supply and demand freed from faulty psychology" (quoted in Tugwell 1924, 298).

A. B. Wolfe (1924, 472) offered a vigorous response to Knight and Bye and the "American Psychological School" overall that included the "psychic income" economics of Frank Fetter and the "counting house" economics of Irving Fisher. "The notion that economics, to be scientific, must discard any attempt to study psychological motivation is born of fatigue over the endless disquisitions on value and valuation which the 'psychological' economists, especially certain Americans [Fetter and Fisher?], inflicted upon us as long as we could stand it" (462). No responsible economist should have any choice but to stay in touch with developments in psychology. "This means that the scientific economist must be cognizant enough of the general results of psychological research to be able to interpret his data in the light of present psychological knowledge. Especially must he be familiar with social psychology" (465). Wolfe indicted modern economists for ignoring psychology and thereby failing to address the main questions before them. "Classicism and marginalism fail to meet present demands, not only because they afford practically no theory of the origin and stimulation of demand and because they have neglected a scientific study of consumption, but much more broadly speaking because they do not give us a realistic theory, that is a theory which explains economic life as it actually is and one based on an adequate (statistical and genetic) method" (467).

4 Human Relations during the Great War: Frank Tannenbaum, Carleton Parker, and Leo Wolman

The terrible conflict of 1914–18 was so destructive, futile, and unreasonable that it raised very pointedly the issue of whether economics and psychology should not work more closely together to understand and reduce human tensions and prevent such catastrophes in the future. The question was explored along three fronts. First, the war seemed to exacerbate struggles at home and abroad that at times threatened rebellion or even revolution. In particular, relations between capital and labor became extraordinarily tense, under pressure from inflation, shortages, and the military draft. It had to be asked whether labor strife would continue into peacetime. Conventional economics could not do much to explain or resolve the strikes, walkouts, and other acts of defiance in the labor market that threatened not only the war effort but social stability thereafter. The sense of crisis in industrial relations led to work in several disciplines (e.g., Guggenheim 1915; Hopkins 1916; Speek 1917; and Ogburn 1920). A number of younger economists insisted that there must be ways in which social psychology could help explain and alleviate these problems. These economists were closely associated with, and sympathetic to, organized labor, but they were not themselves radical politically. They brought to studies of the labor market their own broad personal experience and a sense of urgency that was unusual and distinctive. They also brought some serious study of social psychology. The three most prominent were Frank Tannenbaum, Carleton Parker, and Leo Wolman.

Tannenbaum found in the labor movement features that could be seen in other special-interest groups, but also some distinctive and unconventional aspects that should, he said, be taken into account when designing policy. "The psychology of the labor movement, like that of any other group activity, is complex and overlapping in motives, interests and ideals. In addition to the psychical factors characteristic of all group behavior, such as imitation, emulation, the craving for conspicuousness, leadership and personal expression, organized labor exhibits a few very specific features without which it would not be the vital force in the world that it is" (Tannenbaum 1920, 169). The modern worker, he observed, was perforce a wanderer looking always for a new job as the old one closed down, and because of this mobility the worker had little bargaining power. It was not just that many of the new factory workers were disoriented and still adjusting from being uprooted from the farm; their new lives seemed without any security forever. "The industrial revolution has torn the worker from his moorings and set his body adrift. But a drifting body tends to carry with it a restless mind. . . . Life for the wage earners is more hazardous, existence more precarious, their work and habits more unsettled and change more constant; all of these have their influence upon the mind of the workers" (169). War only added to the tensions that were endemic during all industrialization.

> Instability means lack of regularity for the individual and for society as a whole, it means constant friction, constant danger, constant upsetting of old standards, and the increasing difficulty of creating new ones. The older agricultural economy which the industrial revolution has upset, was that lent itself to the growth of custom, habit and tradition. . . . Ours is above all a dynamic age—and it is dynamic not only in terms of new mechanical processes but in terms of new relationships, which these new processes enforce upon society. All of these forces compel a revaluation of accepted values and contribute both to the agitation of the mind and the discomfort of the body. (170)

Thus the dynamic conditions of the modern economy, exacerbated in wartime, were bound to create dangerous labor-management conflict. "The wandering temper and habit, the dynamic character of our civilization and the greater imaginative equality determine the general background for the development of the peculiar manifestation of the worker's psychology" (171).

Tannenbaum's interpretation of labor market conditions sounds very much like that of Veblen, with terms taken directly from McDougall, for example: "With the average worker—conservative and radical—it is an instinctive resistance against suppression of the freedom for play, for interest, for creativeness. For all men are in their own spontaneous way artists and creators and the curse of the machine is that it standardizes thought and kills it, that it standardizes emotion and destroys it, that it standardizes the artistic sense and annihilates it" (171). Without suggesting an alternative to the present system, Tannenbaum called for reconsidering industrialization, with particular attention paid to the battered psyche of the worker. Failure to do so would lead to increasing tensions and ultimately violent confrontation: "The present system is not only bad, but is kept so by the perfidy and selfishness of the powers who are benefiting by it. It adds to the discontent of the workers a belief in the villainous character of the capitalists as a class—a conviction that adds contempt to hatred" (172).

In the years immediately after the Great War, the economist who made the strongest case for the infusion of psychology into economics was Carleton Parker, a heroic young academic on the faculty first of the University of California, Berkeley, and then at the University of Washington in Seattle. Like Tannenbaum and Wolman, Parker worked closely with organized labor and immersed himself in the circumstances of industrial conflict and the conditions of the poor. Also like Tannenbaum, he was a reformer, but not a revolutionary. He understood and appreciated the competitive market system, but found it deeply flawed. He read widely in the literature of economics and social psychology and felt confident that he could achieve a resolution between the two disciplines so as to find a solution to labor problems. Walter Lippmann, who had been fascinated by psychology since his college days (see below) and admired all three of these young men, arranged a tour of eastern universities for Parker to make his case. In the 1918 supplement to the *American Economic Review*, Parker demonstrated what he saw to be the potential benefits of reconciliation between the two disciplines and the difficulties in bringing it about. He described the mounting tensions in industrial relations in Seattle and the "delinquency of modern economics" when pressed for a solution. "Our conventional economics today analyzes no phase of industrialism nor the wage relationship, nor citizenship in pecuniary society, in a manner to offer a key to such distressing and complex problems as this" (Parker 1918, 213). The reason why was obvious. "We economists speculate little on human motives. We are not curious about the great basis of fact which dynamic and behavioristic psychology has gathered to illustrate the instinct stimulus to human activity. Most of us are not interested to think of what a psychologically full or satisfying life is. We are not curious to know what a great school of behavior analysis called the Freudian has been built around the human instincts" (214).

Parker found few contributions from economists to understanding the psychology of markets. "Noteworthy exceptions are the remarkable series of Veblen books, the articles and criticisms by Mitchell, Fisher, and Patten, and the significant small book by Taussig entitled *Inventors and Money-Makers*" (214). Within psychology Parker could identify twenty-five "economic psychologists" with whom economists might collaborate: "Each one of these has contributed criticism touching the springs of human activity of which no economic theorist can afford to plead ignorance. The stabilizing of the science of psychology and the vogue among economists of the scientific method will not allow these psychological findings to be shouldered out by the careless a priori deductions touching human nature which still dominate our orthodox texts" (215). Parker suggested that a bridge between economics and psychology might be constructed as a result of their common attention to urgent public policy problems.

> The confusion and metaphysical propensities of our economic theory, our neglect of the consequences of child labor, our lax interest in national vitality and health, the unusableness of our theories of labor unrest and of labor efficiency, our careless reception of problems of population, eugenics, sex, and birth control; our ignorance of the relation of industry to crime, industry to feeble-mindedness, industry to functional insanity, industry to education; and our astounding indifference to the field of economic consumption—all this delinquency can be traced back to our refusal to see economics as social economics, and that a full knowledge of man, his instincts, his power of habit acquisition, his psychological demands were an absolute prerequisite to clear and purposeful thinking in our industrial civilization. (215)

He quoted McDougall to the effect that "classical political economy was a tissue of false conclusions drawn from false psychological assumptions" (215).

Parker found in McDougall and Veblen "a galaxy of instincts" that he hoped would explain those "impulses" that are "the mental forces which maintain and shape all the life of individuals and societies, and in them we are confronted with the central mystery of life and mind and will" (216). He looked for a better understanding of what "Thorndike, the Columbia psychologist, in his analysis of human motives, has written." Thorndike hoped to explain "the behavior of man in the family, in business, in the state, in religion, and in every other affair of life [that is] rooted in his unlearned original equipment of instincts and capacities" (216). It was clear that Veblen was Parker's main inspiration, with lesser influence from John Dewey, William McDougall, and Walter Cannon, the Harvard physiologist working on the biology of instincts and emotions. Parker drew on all of these to prepare his own extensive taxonomy of the innate tendencies or instincts, according to their persistence, repression in certain environments, and their normality in others. He reported uneasily that most of the authorities he consulted had different lists of instincts, and it was necessary, therefore, for any analyst to settle on his own list of "those motives to conduct which, under observation, are found to be unlearned, are universal in the species, and which must be used to explain the innumerable similarities in behavior, detached in space and time from each other" (220). Some of the instincts on Parker's list of sixteen came straight from Veblen; others were his own, like the first, "the instinct of gregariousness," and the fifteenth, "the instinct of display: vanity" (220–25). Still others were taken from Veblen but modified, such as "3. Instinct of curiosity: manipulation: workmanship" and "4. Instinct of acquisition: collecting: ownership." He thought that some instincts, such as this last one, if too intense, could lead to mania. "Asylums are full of pitiful, economic persons who, lost to the laws of social life, continue as automatons to follow an unmodified instinct in picking up and hoarding pins, leaves, scraps of food, paper. The savings banks in large part depend on this inborn tendency for their right to exist" (221–22). Some of the new instincts that Parker proposed were hopelessly vague, such as "9. The instinct of hunting," where he found an explanation for many of the things he disliked. "Historic revivals of the hunting urge make an interesting recital of religious inquisitions, witch burnings, college hazings, persecution of suffragettes, of the I.W.W., of the Japanese, of pacifists. All this goes on often under naïve rationalization about justice and patriotism, but it is pure and innate lust to run something down and hurt it" (223). Through "10. Instinct of anger: pugnacity," Parker sought to explain some of the horrors of the Great War. "In fighting, there is a subtle reversion to the primitive standards, and early atrocities become the trench vogue of later months. Patriotism without fighting seems, to western nations, a pallid thing. Most of the vigorous phases of modern civilization remain highly competitive and warlike. Ethics has a long psychological way to go in its vitally necessary task of sublimating the pugnacious bent in man" (224).

In one respect Parker's catalog of instincts seemed helpful, but at the same time disturbing, by revealing the complexity of human behavior. It pointed up how difficult it was to explain complex phenomena using sixteen variables, most of them unquantifiable. He complicated the picture by suggesting that perverted instincts too often entered the picture in place of normal ones. "Instinct perversion rather than freely selected habits of instinct expression seems broadly a just characterization of modern labor-class life. Modern labor unrest has a basis more psychopathological than psychological, and it seems accurate to describe modern industrialism as mentally insanitary" (227). Business people as well as workers suffered from economic pathology. "Even the conventional competitive efficiency of American business is in grave question. I suggest that this unrest is a true revolt psychosis, a definite mental imbalance, an efficiency psychosis, as it were, and has its definite psychic antecedents; and that our present moralizing and guess-solutions are both hopeless and ludicrous" (230–31). Parker ended his long paper with a modulated attack on the capitalist system in terms taken from social psychology and a challenge to other economists to broaden their perspectives.

> We must know more of the meaning of progress. The domination of society by one economic class has for its chief evil the thwarting of the instinct life of the subordinate class and the perversion of the upper class. The extent and characteristics of this evil are only to be estimated when we know the innate potentialities and inherited propensities of man, and the ordering of this knowledge and its application to the changeable economic structure is the task before the trained economists today. (231)

Parker's American Economic Association paper in 1918 was a high-water mark in the application of instinct psychology to economics. It was the paper to which reference was made most often in later years when the uses of psychology were discussed by economists. But what readers must have taken from this presentation was less excitement about a new analytical tool than the sense that the application of psychology would lead to sharp criticism of the market economy on the ground that dynamic and evolving instincts and habits were in constant tension with the static institutions of society, leading to repression of emotions and ultimately frustration and violence such as that manifested by the Wobblies (International Workers of the World). Parker died in the flu epidemic of 1918, and his wife, Cornelia, wrote a moving and best-selling account of their life together titled *American Idyll*. She attempted also to spread his message through her own writings (e.g., Cornelia Parker 1919) and republication of his work (Carleton Parker 1920). But his influence soon waned (Richardson 1920; Bogardus 1921).

The third economist, after Tannenbaum and Parker, who speculated soon after World War I that the mounting conflicts in industrial relations might be understood best and resolved through the application of psychology rather than through economics on its own was Wolman, a young midwesterner whose career included appointments at the New School, the University of Wisconsin, and Columbia University. Like the other two, he spent a lifetime trying to reduce labor strife, and he found that the conditions on the ground could not be adequately explained by the economics in which he had been trained (Wolman 1916). Theories of production and distribution, he thought, were typically based on unrealistic assumptions and ignorance of the way the world really worked. At the American Economic Association annual meeting in 1920, he proposed the development of a new subdiscipline of economics, later known as "industrial relations," that would replace simplistic abstract models based on unreasonable assumptions with those grounded on facts: "So profoundly has the study of market phenomena and price determination directed scientific economic thinking, that technological and psychological phenomena, fundamental in more ways than one to a proper understanding of the machinery of production, have been almost wholly neglected" (Wolman 1921, 41). He noted sarcastically that Allyn Young in an article in the *Quarterly Journal of Economics* had praised a recent book because "free from irrelevant and insignificant detail, it represents a courageous and painstaking attempt to get at the larger facts in the situation" (41n). But what, Wolman asked, "are the 'larger facts' as separate and distinct from 'irrelevant and insignificant detail'?" Because of this kind of misguided thinking, he wrote, "technological and psychological phenomena have been subordinated to those of the market, and inadequate theories of production have gained currency. From the standpoint, therefore, of both economic theory and economic measurement, the dominance of a money attitude has had the effect of diverting investigations from fields in which the scientific yield should be very high indeed" (42). To give one example, he noted that, except "for the observations of Adam Smith and the criticisms of Jevons, economic treatises are surprisingly barren of any adequate treatment of the course of invention" (43).

Little had been done, Wolman complained, on this important question by economists other than Marshall and Frank Taussig (see below). "At any rate, the problem is one that can be investigated with a hope of creditable, if not revolutionary, results; and economic dicta with regard to the matter can be removed from the realm of pure speculation to one of experience" (45). Important questions to be asked about modern inventors were, "What factors determine the problems on which this army of scientists is put to work? What is the relation between the importance of their discoveries and the pecuniary reward they receive?" And closer to home he asked, what "are the differences and similarities between the discoveries of university investigators and those of public and private servants? Can it be that the great basic discoveries which make possible the later progress in the industrial arts originate within the walls of our universities? Or are they the product of the well-equipped and efficiently organized laboratories of private business?" (45–47). Like Irving Fisher and Eugen von Böhm-Bawerk, Wolman recognized the pioneering work on the progress of invention of the Scotch-Canadian economist John Rae.

For Wolman, questions surrounding the labor market were as important as those in the product markets, especially those regarding "the attitude of the worker toward his work." Here the discipline of psychology had much to contribute: "A science of economics, dealing as it does largely with the motives and acts of men, must build its principles upon a foundation of psychological observation. This necessity political economy has met in the past with a substratum of psychology characterized by extreme simplicity and uniformity. Human nature is regarded as simple, and everywhere and at every time the same. Differences between men are external and ephemeral, similarities, deep-rooted and dominant" (49–50). To replace this caricature, there needed to be study, above all, of how "technology and psychology—act and react upon one another. It is impossible to conceive scientific progress without a painstaking and detailed study of both" (51). Just as he argued for a new field in economics to be called "industrial relations," he argued also for another field that later would be called "industrial organization," both of which would depend heavily on psychology. Only with knowledge gained from a wider spectrum of research could progress be made in economics, not only in industrial conflict and the impact of technical change, but also on such pressing issues as population growth, resource depletion, and competition among communities for new business enterprise. "With a background of psychology and technology, the future economists will enter an unploughed field, full of promise and hope for economics as a science" (56).

5. Unstable Preferences
and Wartime Propaganda:
George Creel, Norman Angell,
and Leonard Doob

A second consequence of the interaction of psychology with economics in, and after, the Great War was some loss of confidence in stable preferences, the foundation on which both economics and political science depended for their defense of a free market economy and democracy. Economists argued that a triumph of the competitive market economy was that it responded to the wishes of demanders, who exhibited relatively stable preferences among goods available to them. Similarly, political scientists claimed that in a well-ordered democracy citizens expressed through the ballot box their preferences for public goods and public policies. The appropriate roles of the business people and the public servants were to respond to the instructions they received from sovereign consumers and voters. But what if consumers and voters could easily be manipulated to want things that others told them they wanted or should want, or to experience sudden shifts in their preferences overall? Where was the sovereignty then? This question was asked forcefully as the result of experience with propaganda during the war.

George Creel, chairman of the Committee on Public Information and known popularly as the federal propaganda czar, was portrayed increasingly as the evil genius who had learned how to manipulate "public opinion," that is, preferences of consumers and voters. He, of course, did not see it that way. His faith in stable preferences was unshaken. He saw his role being to tease out views of the people that they might not even know that they had. He said: "I do not believe that public opinion has its rise in the emotions, or that it is tipped from one extreme to the other by every passing rumor, by every gust of passion or by every storm of anger. I feel that public opinion has its source in the minds of people, that it has its base in reason, and that it expresses slow-formed convictions rather than any temporary excitement or any passing passion of the moment" (Creel 1918, 185). At times Creel spoke like an economist. He claimed that all his propaganda machine was doing was giving the "facts in the interest of full understanding," and for this purpose he had "called together three thousand historians of the country for pamphlet production, to set down causes in black and white, to put it so simply that a child could grasp just what we meant by democracy" (186). Creel reported that in addition he had engaged the advertising community, always in his eyes just to give the facts at home and abroad. "We mobilized the advertising experts of the nation, and today every great advertising man in the United States is working for the Committee on Public Information, preparing the matter that goes into periodicals and on the billboards, and contributing millions in free space to the national service" (188). Creel even admitted that his objective was propaganda, but it was good propaganda, that is, material designed to change people's perceptions and responses, not their preferences. "So we cover the whole world today with our American news. That is the best propaganda possible because it tells them what we are doing and what we are thinking" (190). Creel's firm conviction was that what he was doing was not propaganda of the usual sort but delivery of truth to a public that needed to know. "We do not want a public opinion that is based on the happenstance of the moment. We want a public opinion that springs from the heart and soul—that has its root in the rich soil of truth" (191).

But others were less certain than Creel about the consequences of providing "public information" to the people, if public opinion was indeed as malleable as it seemed to be in wartime. This also raised the larger question of whether economic and political preferences were as stable as social scientists had thought them to be overall. Norman Angell, the British political economist and journalist, took issue with the positive picture of the propagandist presented by Creel. In a pre-Orwellian manifesto prepared for the American Academy of Political and Social Science, Angell rejected the claim for the benign role played by propaganda in forming public policy, and he urged governments to stay away from controlling public discussion of policy issues. He rejected the charge that free discussion was inimical to national security even in wartime, or any other time (Angell 1918). The real problem was to get the public to focus on policy in the first place, even after a crisis as serious as the sinking of the *Lusitania*. "Now, how can you have an informed public opinion when you cannot get a degree of continued attention, even as relative as that? Our first problem is to see how we can direct the attention of our people, how we can get the great mass to discuss, to realize the importance of foreign policies as affecting their domestic concerns" (Angell 1916, 138). Government should neither muzzle criticism in a free society nor attempt to direct discussion of it.

It was only a short step from Angell's view of the iniquity of propaganda to the position that public attitudes on any subject should be allowed to evolve without interference from government. Alvin Hansen, soon to become a convinced Keynesian, worried in 1920 that there might be efforts afoot to deal with macroeconomic problems by manipulating consumer preferences and to increase spending at the expense of thrift. Human preferences, he was convinced, should be accepted as given and not as macroeconomic policy variables: "Neither under-consumption nor over-production produce the business cycle. In brief the solution of the problem of the business cycle must be found in the movements of money, credit, prices and profits. . . . Enlarged spending is not the solution for this modern evil which so vitally affects labor" (47). Thomas Nixon Carver also objected to manipulating human preferences to increase aggregate demand. For these critics, it was dangerous to contemplate meddling with any aspect of the human psyche that economists thought of as exogenous. They mistrusted anyone, economist or psychologist, who wanted to play sorcerer's apprentice. "To misdirect our productive power, causing it to produce things of little importance, is quite as great a loss, and quite as great a hindrance to our prosperity, as to allow it to do things in a wasteful and slipshod manner" (Carver 1920, 4). Two books by the young journalist Walter Lippmann published soon after the war, *Public Opinion* (1922) and *The Phantom Public* (1927), drew attention and praise from both psychologists and economists for suggesting that unstable preferences might be corrected not by propaganda or by psychological manipulation but by improved public education in the social sciences for consumers, voters, businesspersons, politicians, and public servants (Wright 1922; Smith 1933; and Goodwin 2014).

Edward Bernays, a psychologist active in government propaganda during the war and thereafter, had a different view and proposed that public opinion be consciously molded by political leaders to achieve positive benefit. For example, they might encourage cooperative rather than competitive behavior. Like others, he had concluded that preferences for competition might lie behind warlike behavior. The leaders should understand the circumstances that conditioned human responses and manipulate opinion rather than search for existing preferences when they constructed public policy: "What are the great basic motivations of people, wherever they are and to whatever groups they belong? Self-preservation, ambition, pride, hunger, love of family and children, patriotism, imitativeness, the desire to be a leader, love of play—these and others are the psychological raw materials of which every leader must be aware in his endeavor to win the public to his point of view" (Bernays 1935, 83). This sounded like dangerous advice to a free market economist.

Leonard Doob, a Yale psychologist, saw the movement for consumer cooperation in the 1930s as potentially a metaphor for constructive change within society and the economy. Cooperating consumers were willing to accept higher costs, he observed, so as to avoid the cutthroat world of large grocery chains and take part instead in the friendly, small-scale interactions of consumer cooperation. Could this regard for cooperation be extended around the world? He identified four conditions that would cause an economic actor to leave a competitive environment and embrace cooperation, in effect to change his preferences for the kind of economic and political system in which to engage.

> (1) There is a discrepancy between his level of achievement and his *level of aspiration*; i.e. he is motivated to attain a goal; (2) his *knowledge* of the goal which he seeks indicates that it can be reached by striving with others; i.e., his ideas, stereotypes, philosophy of life, and so forth, bias him in favor of cooperation; (3) his *attitudes* toward cooperating with others are stronger than any other possibly conflicting ones; i.e. he is emotionally disposed to cooperate; (4) his *skill* is of such a nature that under the rules of the situation he has a reasonable chance of success by cooperating; i.e. he is able to participate. (Doob 1937, 47)

Doob's faith in the possibility that the spirit of cooperation would somehow contribute to the maintenance of world peace was reflected in a large study by the Cambridge economic historian C. R. Fay titled *Co-operation at Home and Abroad* (1925).

As war again drew close in 1935, Doob and a colleague, Edward S. Robinson, discussed how propaganda for cooperation might be used to stave off war. The issue for them was not whether information disseminated was "correct" but whether it would be effective in manipulating minds. Such manipulation, they reminded their readers, was widespread in society any way, and one should not be squeamish about employing it if for the public good. "Pedagogues, for example, may honestly believe that they are elucidating a portion of the 'truth' when they condemn the idea of sudden social change; and yet the fact remains that they are influencing their students by the same means employed by the public utility companies in their campaign to gain support for private ownership in the raw" (89). The important point to note here is that preferences that were traditionally viewed as given by economists were now being treated openly as variables to be adjusted by psychologists. "The psychologist is interested in the fact that attitudes may be altered or constructed either through the arousal of reflective thought or through the devices of propaganda, but he does not assume that either of these procedures is a guarantee of the social value of its own results" (89). To those who complained that propaganda was simply one form of infringement of free speech, these psychologists replied that free speech was substantially a myth, and manipulation of speech that was undesirable had to be countered by manipulation that was desirable. "In the face of economic, political, social, and spiritual cartels, the literal doctrine of noninterference with speech has plainly broken down. . . . In the psychological as well as in the economic realm, it is seen that freedom is tolerable only within limits" (94).

Harwood Childs, a professor of political science at Princeton and editor of *Public Opinion Quarterly*, went so far as to suggest that the roots of the next war would be as much psychological as economic or political, and psychologists were needed immediately to intervene. "Struggles for control over the minds of men have a tendency to pass over into physical warfare when the will to resolve these conflicts peacefully, or the mechanism for doing so, does not exist" (Childs 1937, 31). In wartime, for sure, the presumption of rationality would have to go by the board. He said in 1937, "As far as I can now see, there is no evidence that we are likely to pursue a more rational course in case another European war breaks out than we did in 1917" (37). In 1938, with the European war a year away, he urged close attention to the psychological roots of the upcoming conflict. The psyche had, in his mind, replaced the economy as the likely source of trouble.

> International tensions are psychological phenomena. They are the product of acts as well as words. They reflect states of mind characterized by uneasiness, dissatisfaction, insecurity, fear. It is very unlikely that such tensions can ever be resolved permanently. Hunger and poverty create such tensions. But food and riches do not guarantee peace of mind. To allay and resolve international tensions completely it would be necessary to do away with all those factors that produce dissatisfaction,

whether real or imaginary. And very often it is the imaginary rather than the real that disturbs our peace of mind. The assumption that mere changes in material conditions will free the world from psychological tenseness is an illusion. (Childs 1938, 113–14)

Peace-loving nations should quickly disseminate propaganda that would contribute more to prevent war than any preemptory acts.

6. Macro-irrationality:
Financial Panic and Warfare;
John Bates Clark and Elton Mayo

The third way in which the Great War affected the image of psychology in the social sciences, and particularly in economics, was to confirm that there might be a difference between the way humans behaved as isolated individuals and as part of a "crowd" or "herd." While the rational actor might be kept as the model for buyer or seller in a competitive market, another set of assumptions and another model might be required for the macroeconomy. The financial crisis of 1907 was the first big test of this proposition, and a few economists admitted at that time that "irrational behavior" seemed to be a cause of the crisis. Speaking before the American Academy, Frank A. Vanderlip, vice president of the National City Bank, denied that the cause of the crisis lay in the financial system, as often alleged. The crisis called instead for a psychological explanation. "It has, in large measure, been a matter of what was in men's minds" (Vanderlip 1908, 3; see also Johnson 1908 and Marburg 1908). He blamed the media, and especially the "muckrakers" like Lincoln Steffens and Ida Tarbell, for stirring up hysteria among the people.

> Perhaps the most significant of all the lessons of the crisis, one that will, in the end, sink more deeply into our understanding than any of the others, will come to us when we comprehend the full weight of what it means to destroy confidence; what it means to destroy the confidence of the people in the financial leaders, to destroy the confidence of capitalists in the fairness of the people as reflected in legislation and in the decisions of the courts. (7)

The only way to restore confidence, he concluded, as had Walter Lippmann, was to educate the people. "I am afraid that the bankers would show, in some cases, as great ignorance of what is needed, and as little comprehension of the principles underlying any really intelligent reform, as our senators and congressmen. That leads me to believe that there never was a time when education of the people in the principles of banking and currency was more seriously needed" (5–6). This assumed, of course, that better educated people would act more rationally than uneducated ones. The possibility of economic agents acting irrationally and changing their patterns of spending and investing because of fear and panic returned for discussion during the late 1920s and 1930s (Stamp 1927). It seemed apparent that in cases where economic rationality was in question in a financial crisis, the economist had need of a psychologist.

The possibility that irrational behavior lay behind warfare came up early in the twentieth century. After decades of peace the new century began with the Russo-Japanese War, the South African War, and the Spanish-American War. An arms race that ensued among the great powers suggested that something even bigger might follow. Economics by this time had had a long engagement with questions of national security. Adam Smith and those who followed him addressed the costs and benefits of war, how best to deter an aggressor, how to mount an armed force and other issues of the kind, all for the most part modeled with rational actors optimizing economic variables (Goodwin 1991). An unplanned test of the contributions that orthodox economics might make to the prevention of war began in 1911 when the recently created Carnegie Endowment for International Peace, established by Andrew Carnegie in New York, began a program to explore "the causes of war and the practical methods to prevent and avoid it," with the Columbia economic theorist John Bates Clark as director of a division of economics and history. Clark gathered together economists from around the world to plot strategy. His program was rooted in a presumption that no rational country would go to war when the perceived costs exceeded the benefits. A sensible economist's strategy, therefore, was to discover ways to increase those potential costs and benefits through international economic integration. Ironically, the Carnegie economists were scheduled to reconvene to discuss their research in August 1914, the month when the Great War began, and rational actors became hard to find or even to imagine. Faced with these new facts on the ground, Clark turned to other disciplines than economics and began an economic history of the war that concluded with 133 volumes.

After Clark's apparent failure to discover ways to explain or prevent war using economics alone, some economists turned to smaller questions about war such as how to increase munitions production, stabilize labor markets, and accomplish war finance. They were joined by psychologists in fields like public relations, personnel management, and advertising. But some psychologists also took up the deeper questions abandoned by the economists of what caused wars and what could be done about them. For example, Elton Mayo (1923, 117), a young Australian social psychologist at the Harvard Business School who worked on problems of industrial relations, suggested that war was not an economic but a psychological phenomenon: "The human mind and the social organism are still very largely uncivilized." Emotions, the purview of the psychologist, rather than the rational acts of the economists, had increased the amount of irrational behavior. "Social development has intensified emotions and multiplied the occasions of emotion; the right ordering of emotion is a task but little advanced. . . . We have long since ceased to smash inanimate things when they happen to displease us. But we still apply the primitive method to our brother man" (117). Stress often led to conspiracy theories and violent actions such as strikes and lockouts, even breakdowns at international conferences. "'Capitalist' and 'Bolshevist' conspiracies exist mainly in the minds of those who bring fear and anger to bear upon the problem, rather than dispassioned thought. Diabolism is chiefly a bogey created by the terrors which still lie near the surface in civilized thinking" (118).

Mayo suggested that simple misery affected the equilibrium of people and reduced their capacity to think rationally. Laboratory study by psychologists of assembly-line workers demonstrated this effect.

Modern methods of machine production are monotonous; long periods of revery-thinking are made inevitable. Life in a city slum and long hours in the factory combine to make such reveries pessimistic or melancholic. Socialism, Syndicalism, Bolshevism—irrational dreams of anger and destruction—are the inevitable outcome. As theories of society or social science these movements are of small importance. As symptoms of a human need, as evidence of the failure of civilization to study human problems, these expressions of working class feeling are of the first order of value. (122–23)

Mayo wrote of the "night-mind" of the common people that could not be confronted successfully with rational thinking. "A belief in the efficacy of magic and sorcery is not the only character [istic?] of the night-mind; it is also curiously animistic. Being the product of unacknowledged reveries and therefore irrational, it makes no use of scientific notions of causation" (124). Mayo called for psychology to work with the other social sciences so that conditions for rational thought might be reestablished. "If psychology were to confine itself to investigation of the human situation in industry, to elimination of superstition, delusions of conspiracy and unnecessary hatred—if psychology were to do no more than this for the next twenty years, it would still be possible for it to make the greatest contribution to civilized progress that any science has made" (124).

Leon Marshall at Johns Hopkins, another pioneer in industrial relations, argued that a successful economy and polity could be achieved only with attention to the social context in which attitudes and behavioral assumptions were important.

> We have become quite well convinced that the first fundamental assumption of the *laissez faire* regime is false. This first assumption, you will remember, was that every individual of sound mind and mature age knows reasonably well his own self-interest. While this may be said to have been substantially true of the simpler society of the past, the kaleidoscopic changes of the last generation have made it highly improbable that every individual can know his own self-interest even reasonably well. The second assumption of the *laissez faire* regime was that the individual will follow his self-interest and in so doing will be led 'as by an invisible hand' to promote the public welfare. This second assumption we can no longer grant; the last hundred years of history have furnished abundant evidence to the contrary. (Marshall 1930, 7)

Using the language of contemporary institutionalism, Marshall argued that satisfactory psychic conditions, not just competitive markets, were essential for peace and prosperity. "The relationships of labor, capital and management; the need of a social minimum as a basis of sturdy individualism; the opportunity for a more effective utilization of our various forms of social control—these are but three illustrations out of many of the new institutional situations which are emerging from the vast cultural changes of our generation" (Marshall 1930, 8; Rutherford 2011, 144).

The most provocative charges made by psychologists against economists after World War I in the multidisciplinary journals in which they both wrote was that the selfish competitive behavior glorified by economists had led perhaps to intolerant and mutually destructive attitudes when carried over to relations among nations. These attitudes became reflected especially in exaggerated nationalism that led to conflict. Norman Hapgood, a prominent journalist and peace activist writing in the *Annals of the American Academy of Political and Social Science*, suggested that all of American culture had been permeated with the notion that international relations required a hostile and suspicious attitude to others, as in a market. For peace to be secured, this attitude must be changed to emphasize cooperation rather than conflict: "Where the word 'patriotism' tends to make us think of our country in opposition to other countries, tends to give us the kind of school-books that I was given when I was a child, I say that that creates a poisonous atmosphere for the young to grow up in" (Hapgood 1925, 158). In a similar vein, Thorstein Veblen (1917, 1998) wrote a steady stream of articles on the Great War and its aftermath from an institutionalist perspective.

7. Institutionalists Weigh In:
Wesley Clair Mitchell, Frank Taussig,
John Maurice Clark, and Paul Douglas

Young institutionalist leaders in economics in the early twentieth century greeted the attacks on marginal economics from the social psychologists and their sympathizers in economics with cautious enthusiasm (for discussion of the institutionalist literature on psychology, see Rutherford 2011, 45–47). Perhaps, they thought, these attackers could become allies in the struggle against the traditionalists. The institutionalists were interested, especially, to see if the integration of social psychology with economics might make microeconomics more dynamic and evolutionary. They explored both the new behaviorism and the older instinct and habit theories. At the same time, institutionalists were all trained in marginal economics, and, to some degree, the rational actor was an old friend whom they were reluctant to abandon before they were persuaded there was a plausible replacement in the wings. Wesley Clair Mitchell was the first leader of the burgeoning institutionalist movement to dip his toe in the psychological waters.

Mitchell (1910, 197) accepted that McDougall's claim had to be faced that "mankind is only a little bit reasonable and to a great extent very unintelligently moved in quite unreasonable ways." Mitchell began by offering a list of the assumptions employed by price theorists to see if they were contradicted by McDougall's claims.

> For most purposes the list would be limited to the irksomeness of labor, the satisfaction derived from the consumption of goods, the increasing intensity of the first and decreasing intensity of the second as labor and

consumption proceed, the emergence of new wants as the old become partially satisfied, the preference for present over future satisfactions, and sufficient intelligence to recognize and to act in accordance with these simple conditions so as to attain ends in the easiest known way. These assumptions, it is commonly believed, are not artificial; on the contrary they are held to be substantially verified by observation. And they contain the measure of 'rationality' really imputed to men by economic theory. (198)

Mitchell was convinced that most market participants were, in fact, quite rational and took only those actions that would achieve their desired ends. However, he conceded that in this process demanders and suppliers often settled on routines (habits?) that fulfilled their goals; this too was perfectly rational. Especially on the supply side, the large corporations were exceptionally rational. "The very perfection of rationality is exhibited by the industrial organization and management of the great industrial plants already typical of economic life—and clearly increasing their sway" (199).

But for the rest of the economy Mitchell was not so sure of the rationality, and here, he thought, McDougall might be helpful. "The conspicuous psychological facts here are facts of habit, amenability to suggestion, tendency toward imitation, and the instinct of construction. In other words, the economist who makes a faithful effort to represent human activity as it is, must have recourse to such analysis as McDougall recommends and practices" (200). In consumption, less rationality was exhibited than in production. "Passing whims, carelessness about prices, ignorance of qualities, obstinate preference for old ways are left wide scope. In McDougall's terms, habit suggestibility, and the instincts of emulation and imitation are brought in, if we are to account for our own subservience to fashion, our conspicuous waste, and our slovenly dependence on the advertiser. The assumption of rationality is inadequate to explain the facts" (200).

Mitchell defended the deductive method and the need to make assumptions about the behavior of producers and consumers in economic models. But the need for assumptions was no excuse for failing to examine the appropriateness of assumptions. The appeal of any hypothesis should never be an excuse for ignoring legitimate questions about the assumptions. Exclusion of the discipline of psychology from the construction of economic theory had led to impoverishment of the economics discipline. "So far, psychological criticism indicates that the assumption of economic rationality is not so much mistaken as inadequate. It applies to the work of the captains but not to the work of the rank and file in industry and business; it does not explain the activities of consumption; and it betrays the economist into neglect of his chief problem" (201). As he warmed to his subject, Mitchell charged the community of economic theorists with avoiding hard work by suggesting that others would deal with psychological issues.

> The tasks of accounting for the present economic institutions and the leading traits of human nature it hands over to economic history, ethnology, and psychology. For itself it reserves the field within which intelligent choice prevails, under the conditions established by an organized set of institutions and a well-developed human nature. And this field it holds wide enough to require all the energy of one company of scientific workers. . . . This division of labor betrays the economic theorist into tacitly misconceiving the mental processes involved in economic activity. The most serious of his misconceptions concerns the role played by concepts having a social origin. (202)

A systematic and fundamental misdirection occurred in economics, Mitchell thought, when the psychological perspective was excluded. Then the institutions through which the economy operated were misconceived. "Social concepts are the core of social institutions. The latter are but prevalent habits of thought which have gained general acceptance as norms for guiding conduct. In this form the social concepts attain a certain prescriptive authority over the individual" (203). Those economists who simply dismissed psychology were the poorer for it. "Economists who have 'some understanding of the human mind and its modes of operation' regard the study of these concepts as an integral part of their own task. Economists who would delegate this task to others, on the contrary, seldom have such understanding of the human mind" (204). Mitchell specifically criticized John Bates Clark and Irving Fisher for neglecting psychology. "Nothing shows more clearly how unfit hedonistic psychology is for the uses of a modern science than this fact that the more perfectly the old hedonistic preconceptions are worked out in economics the less does the theory have to do with the facts" (207). Mitchell found modern theorists to be misguided in paying so little attention to habitual "pecuniary concepts" that often overrode calculations of greatest utility. These concepts establish "norms of conduct which exercise a prescriptive authority over recalcitrant individuals" (208). The picture of individuals making careful marginal calculations as a preface to action was just a crutch to avoid hard thought. "When economists ignore the use of pecuniary concepts by mod-ern men, they must find other concepts to play the vacant role. Their usual device is to picture their own contemporaries as thinking in terms of mar-ginal utility and disutility" (209).

The economic man as conceived by the modern economic theorist was, in Mitchell's view, far from a realistic conception. "The man created by the imagination of economists is indeed a thin and formal character in comparison with the heir of all the ages, with his rich inheritance of instincts, his dower of social concepts, and his wealth of habits" (210). The consequences of this misperception were visible in thinking about policy as well as theory.

> That the making of goods is subordinated to the making of money; that industrial experts are similarly subordinated to business experts; that the orderly working of industrial processes is strictly dependent upon the maintenance of the precarious adjustments between various sec-tions of the system of prices; that the rate at which gold is produced and the way in which banking is practiced affect the material welfare of millions of men; that different economic classes feel the disciplining hand of the money economy in such unlike measure as to find difficulty in understanding each other's preconceptions—these are a few among the pregnant consequences resulting from the use of pecuniary con-cepts which our marginal-utility theorists are prone to overlook. . . . At present we remain ignorant, because we have leaped past pecuniary concepts in our haste to reach the marginal utilities assumed to be behind them. (210–11)

Like other critics of marginal utility theory at the time, Mitchell blamed Jeremy Bentham for establishing the simplistic frame that dominated eco-nomics. As rational actors businesspeople and consumers had become two sides of the same coin.

> The formulation of the mental operations of an ideally perfect money-maker can be converted into a passable formulation of Bentham's hedo-nism by merely turning pecuniary into psychological terms. Substitute pleasure for profit and pain for loss, let the unit of sensation stand for the dollar, replace accounting by the hedonic calculus, interpret self-interest as the maximizing of net pleasures instead of net profits, and the trans-formation is complete. The creature of hedonic psychology, like the creature of the money economy, has substantially no instincts, emotions,

or habits, which are not embodied in the pursuit of pleasure along the road of calculation. . . . Complete reliance may be placed upon the rationality of both the pecuniary and the hedonic subject. (213)

McDougall had suggested that all economists be required to have training in psychology. In 1910 Mitchell agreed with him: "The counsel and example of a trained psychologist must seem most welcome" (216).

In 1914 Mitchell produced for the *Quarterly Journal of Economics* an important survey of the recent literature on human behavior. His impression was that up until early in the twentieth century, economists preferred mainly to ignore psychology, but then focused attacks on marginal utility by psychologists and some economists had forced economic theorists to make a choice: either they could claim that the facts of behavior being brought forward were of no interest to them on the ground that economics was the science of choice, and what was chosen, and how, was none of their business; or they could agree that the facts behind their assumptions should as much as possible approximate reality. On the whole Mitchell was encouraged by the progress that had been made over the four years since his first article in moving to the second approach. Now the explanation of human behavior was seen as a challenge in many disciplines. "Physiologists, neurologists, psychologists, ethnologists, sociologists, political scientists, economic historians, even a few economic theorists, are not only working at the problem from their several viewpoints, but also endeavoring to pool their contributions" (Mitchell 1914, 3). For illustration, he examined in some detail the work of Maurice Parmelee, a biologist and physiologist. He found Parmelee's work highly suggestive, and he regretted that economists paid so little attention to it. Naturally, "Mr. Parmelee's discussion of human behavior is biological rather than psychological in character. He finds the criteria by which to discriminate between the different types of activity, not in what the organism does, but in the anatomical structure of the nervous tissues involved. Interesting as this viewpoint undoubtedly is, important as are certain conclusions which it suggests, it still remains a matter of secondary interest to students of the social sciences" (5–6). As Mitchell had observed in 1910, the main issues for the social sciences should be whether human behavior could be improved and reformed, and if so how: "Since we have come to discredit the inheritance of acquired characteristics, the possibility of reforming human nature turns largely on what part of that nature is inherited and hence presumably unchangeable, and what part is formed by experience and hence presumably capable of modification. Keen and widespread interest will be felt, therefore, in the effort of a distinguished psychologist [his Columbia colleague Edward Thorndike] to determine what is The Original Nature of Man" (6).

Mitchell was optimistic by 1914, on the basis of evidence provided by Thorndike, that human nature could actually be changed for the better through training and experience, and that this might reduce the need for policy intervention in the economy. He remained unsure, however, just how much this "nurture" could do to affect characteristics that were deeply embedded in "nature."

> Nurture cannot indeed eradicate unlearned capacities, it cannot supply them; but it can select certain among them for development and others for repression; it can make the most various combinations among them as well as modify their forms. . . . Most important of all, the influence of nurture may be cumulative. Every increase of social wisdom may be applied in bettering the nurture given to the generation that follows, so that this generation in turn may give its successor training better than it received. (11)

As Graham Wallas (1914) put it, "complex dispositions" could control and modify those "propensities" that we acquire by inheritance and from experience.

Wallas was, in fact, after Parmelee and Thorndike, the third writer Mitchell reviewed in detail. He found that Wallas shared his wish to bring "the knowledge which has been accumulated by psychologists into touch with the actual problems of present civilized life," and Mitchell was pleased especially that Wallas's two books, *Human Nature in Politics* (1908) and *The Great Society* (1914), were written with "a charm nourished by the classics, and both sparkle with vitality" (Mitchell 1914, 12). Mitchell was glad that Wallas had made the case, and contradicted McDougall, that instinct and the independent use of human intelligence were perfectly consistent. "McDougall in his *Social Psychology* (p.44) advanced the view that intelligence is but a complex apparatus for finding ways and means toward the ends which are set by instinct. Mr. Wallas, on the contrary, holds 'that we are born with a tendency, under appropriate conditions, to think, which is as original and independent as our tendency, under appropriate conditions, to run away'" (16). By this interpretation, man was not seen as an automaton, as economists typically pictured him, but as an economic actor making choices influenced now by a multitude of psychological forces. Wallas provided an inventory of traditions in social psychology that should be useful to economists. "The leading doctrines treated are the habit philosophy of Sir Henry Maine and others, the fear philosophy of Hobbes, the pleasure-pain philosophy of Bentham, the psychology of the crowd based upon imitation, sympathy and suggestion by Bagehot, Tarde and their disciples, the social psychology of love offered by Comte and less definitely by later writers, and finally, the doctrine of ineradicable national hatred proclaimed by contemporary militarists" (16–17). Wallas, Mitchell concluded, had demonstrated that psychology should not be seen as in tension with modern economics but as a subject capable of enriching other disciplines. "Mr. Wallas accepts the evidence of psychologists that we cannot control the movement of thought; but he contends that we can control the material circumstances necessary for thought, the mental attitudes which are favorable to thought, and our relations to the subject matter of thought" (17). In a word, Wallas had argued persuasively that psychology could assist economists in finding solutions to the many issues facing them. "Any one who doubts the helpfulness of looking at such issues from the psychological viewpoint will be rapidly converted to faith if he will entrust himself for a few hours to Mr. Wallas' wise leading" (18).

Mitchell found Veblen's recent book *The Instinct of Workmanship and the State of the Industrial Arts* (1914) to be stimulating but less disciplined than the work of Thorndike, Parmelee, and Wallas. He thought that Veblen's main contribution was in ascribing to the instinct of workmanship "the highest survival value" in human evolution, "its primacy is disputed only by the closely-related 'parental bent'" (24). Mitchell concluded his review of social psychology by suggesting how this was relevant to his larger concern with human institutions in the economy and their relevance to policy. "As the instincts constitute the first great factor in culture, so modifications of instinctive behavior through intelligence and habits constitute the second" (24). Veblen had demonstrated that institutions could shape habits so that instincts would lead humans into constructive rather than destructive directions. While "'the typical human endowment of instincts' changes but little, 'the habitual elements of human life change unremittingly and cumulatively'" (25). Some races, such as the "Dolicho-blond," were endowed with strong instincts of workmanship, parental bent, and a "spirit of enterprise," and they had advanced rapidly. But progress was not inevitable. The recent outbreak of war had demonstrated how predatory institutions could lead to destructive tendencies. "Interest is shifted from the fullness of life of the community and centers in the war-like glory of the tribe, its leaders, and its god" (27). Persuaded, apparently, by the first book of the young Walter Lippmann (*A Preface to Politics* [1913]) that something might be learned from Freud, Mitchell conceded that "only by supplying our passions with civilized interests can we escape their destructive force" (39).

Mitchell concluded his 1914 survey with a rather gloomy observation, quoting from "a distinguished psychologist [McDougall]," that the failure of psychology to penetrate economics as it should was its own fault: "The lack of practical recognition of psychology by the workers in the social sciences has been in the main due to its deficiencies. . . . The department of psychology that is of primary importance for the social sciences is that which deals with the springs of human action, the impulses and motives that sustain mental and bodily activity and regulate conduct; and this, of all the departments of psychology, is the one that has remained in the most backward state, in which the greatest obscurity, vagueness, and confusion still reign" (46–47). So, at least, economics might not be entirely to blame for its own weakness.

Of all the economists who discussed the enrichment of economics through psychology, Mitchell was the most thoughtful and most engaged. He concluded that improved understanding of human motives and human behavior must be gained from incorporating the insights of psychology with the rigor of economics. It is surprising, therefore, that over his long career he did not enter into collaboration with psychologists or attempt to make progress on his own. Some of his initiatives showed promise. For example, he published an essay titled "The Backward Art of Spending Money" in 1912 in the *American Economic Review* that sounded as if it might be an exploration into human consumption, a subject on which he called for more work. But it was mainly a discussion of family budgeting and the amateurish way in which consumer expenditures were determined. He claimed, "We may rely upon progress in physiology and psychology to make wider and more secure the scientific foundations of housekeeping" (Mitchell 1937, 18; Rutherford 2011, 143), but he did not say why. Others did follow up this initiative to some extent in later years (e.g., Andrews 1929). He continued to lament the failure of economists to take advantage of psychology and to predict that soon the tide would turn. He wrote in Tugwell's collection of essays, *The Trend of Economics*, in 1924 that he was optimistic "partly because the younger men are reading psychological literature, but mainly because certain among the older men have been cultivating an unorthodox type of economic theory—a type of theory that deals with a range of problems undreamt of in the philosophy of value and distribution. This type is perhaps best called institutional economics" (Mitchell 1924, 17). In this and later work Mitchell renewed his call for a real engagement of economics with psychology, not just a rhetorical one, and he rejected as unsatisfactory the simple repudiation of Benthamite hedonism by the "American Psychological School" of Fetter, Davenport, and Fisher (Mitchell 1969, 251–344). A redefinition of price theory as simply a theory of choice begged the question of what determined the choice.

Mitchell struggled hard to understand Bentham's construction of the felicific calculus and indicted him for the misconception of human nature that had misled economists (Mitchell 1918). But he concluded that the guilt rested as much with Bentham's followers as with himself, for they had declined to move on. Bentham had anticipated many of the problems with an unsophisticated use of utility, but his disciples had kept them quiet. It was the responsibility of modern social scientists to abandon Bentham's utility and to adopt modern psychology. "The real reason why we find the conception artificial is that we have another stock of ideas about behavior with which Bentham's ideas are incompatible. Our business is to be consistent as he was, and to use the set of ideas in which we believe as fully as he used the set in which he believed. Then if our ideas prove wrong, as is not unlikely, we may at least give late comers the same kind of help that Bentham now gives us" (Mitchell 1937, 202). Yet here as elsewhere Mitchell does not give precise guidance as to how this new "set of ideas" should be used. Once more Mitchell followed Wallas (1923), who also had sought to solve the riddle of utility by going back to Bentham.

Perhaps because of the recent visiting professorship of Graham Wallas at Harvard, or the review of the literature in psychology relevant to economics by Wesley Mitchell, or even the enthusiasm of his prize student Walter Lippmann, Frank Taussig, the highly respected senior Harvard economist with institutionalist leanings, delivered a series of lectures at Brown University in 1915 on "some relations between economics and psychology." He took as his focus several instincts that had been proposed by William James, William McDougall, and Thorstein Veblen as alternative explanations to hedonism for the behavior of inventors, entrepreneurs, and philanthropists. He began the lectures by observing that Adam Smith had deliberately pointed to psychology with his discussion of the instinct to "truck, barter and exchange" in chapter 1 of the *Wealth of Nations*. The utilitarians who followed, however, had rejected this insight and directed attention instead to simple conscious optimizing behavior, and this had been little challenged since. Only recently the balance had been shifted back by Werner Sombart, McDougall, Wallas, and Veblen. Taussig preferred McDougall's term "instinct of contrivance" to Veblen's "instinct of workmanship," but he found that they both referred roughly to the same phenomena. To illustrate this instinct, he examined the careers of several prominent inventors: John Ericsson, Thomas Edison, Edmund Cartwright, James Watt, Robert Fulton, and Samuel Morse. He found that, as the instinct predicted, they all responded more to "an inborn and irresistible impulse" than to any calculation of future profit (Taussig 1915, 21). Profit typically affected the "*direction* in which the contriver turns his bent" (50), but the force comes from the instinct rather than any calculation of net profit. The same was true of the ordinary businessperson who did not find most work "irksome," as claimed in orthodox economics. There too the force of the instinct of contrivance was directed but not driven by profit and was reflected in a "passion for building" (59). Taussig was writing in the early days of the "scientific management" movement, and he was concerned that this doctrine might neglect the human dimension of production as manifest in the instincts that motivated a workforce: "The management must be not only scientific, but human. The familiar schemes have too much of the mechanical and non-human element" (71).

To understand the behavior of the typical businessperson, Taussig reviewed the various instincts that might be relevant. In addition to the instinct of contrivance, he mentioned the instinct of acquisition and ownership, and the instinct of domination (encompassing the instincts of pugnacity and predation). "Domination, power, conquest,—this plays a great part in the industrial world as well as in the political. It goes with the love of adventure, to which we give in business life the more euphemistic term 'enterprise'" (87). The disposition or tendency to emulation and its concomitant "imitation" "combines spontaneously with the instincts of play, of the chase, of construction, of domination" (96). Although Taussig did not admit it, his explanation of business behavior was becoming bewilderingly complex.

Taussig concluded with reflections on some instincts usually thought to be noneconomic and "variously described by the terms pity, sympathy, love, altruism, the moral sentiment, devotion" (102). He paid attention especially to the last of these and to what he called "the moral sense," referring perhaps to Francis Hutcheson but more likely to Adam Smith's moral sentiments. He thought that the neglect of the phenomenon of devotion was the result in part of the kind of person who became an economist. Such a person "likes results that are clean-cut. He is apt to disregard the admitted qualifying factors, and to treat the qualifications as aberrations from the truth, not modifications of his conclusions. And among the things which he is thus tempted to push aside as aberrations, negligible in the formulation of accurate results, is the influence of sympathy, or altruism, or devotion" (111–12). It was a mistake, Taussig said, to think of devotion as characteristic only of public affairs and selfishness of private affairs. On the question of what public policy prescriptions emerged from his study of instincts and invention, Taussig was rather vague. He thought, "It would be presumptuous to pretend to offer anything more than hints" (122). At least, he was prepared to argue, some instincts deserved to be encouraged and others restrained. "Some of the constituent instincts, it would seem, can be enlisted and encouraged almost without reserve. Others, though they are too strong to be entirely suppressed, must in some way be held in check" (123). Taussig concluded on a cautiously optimistic note that his preliminary exploration into the usefulness of psychology to economics would be followed by others. "We must be content to face and accept the complexity of human motivation, the interplay of conflicting instincts, a tantalizing uncertainty concerning the possibilities of modifying their relative strength. And yet we may cherish none the less a hope that in the future they may be made to work for human happiness more effectively than has been the case in the past" (135).

Another young leader of the institutionalist movement, John Maurice Clark, son of the theorist John Bates Clark, took up at the end of the Great War the questions that Mitchell had addressed at the beginning. In a two-part article in the *Journal of Political Economy*, he asked whether economics and psychology should forge a new set of bonds. At a minimum, he insisted, economists should explore the possibility that psychology might give to economics the dynamism it lacked.

The economist may attempt to ignore psychology, but it is a sheer impossibility for him to ignore human nature, for his science is a science of human behavior. Any conception of human nature that he may adopt is a matter of psychology, and any conception of human behavior that he may adopt involves psychological assumptions, whether these be explicit or no. If the economist borrows his conception of man from the psychologist, his constructive work may have some chance of remaining purely economic in character. But if he does not he will not thereby avoid psychology. Rather he will force himself to make his own, and it will be bad psychology. (Clark 1918, 4)

But at the same time, Clark was more restrained than Mitchell in his advice to economists, and he suggested that they avoid those parts of psychology that were especially controversial and threatening to the core of price theory. Their objective should be to enrich price theory and not to replace it. They should avoid such contentious notions as instincts and habits and should keep away from anthropology. The specter of Freud undoubtedly lay behind such advice. Clark was like an arbiter seeking common ground between two contending parties.

> Some phases of the study of human nature there may be which are of no direct use to the economist. For our present purpose we need not take up the detailed study of particular instincts and dispositions, nor the greater part of social psychology, being concerned first and foremost with the general theory of individual desires, Even the study of the social origin of wants does not seem to be universally recognized as belonging to the economists' study of value. "Quite true but what of it?" may be the reaction. "We begin by taking wants as we find them, and our doctrines are drawn up on that basis: hence one want is as good as another in our eyes. Indeed it is only this impartial attitude that makes economics possible as distinct from ethics. Our doctrines trace prices back to their basis in finished wants, so to speak, but no farther, and hence they cannot be disturbed by new studies of the origins of desire, interesting as these may be." This attitude is quite natural but quite misleading. (5)

Clark was most attracted to psychology as a way to make price theory dynamic. Marginal utility could remain intact but would be invigorated by challenges to its static procedures. "In psychology proper the first importance of the newer knowledge seems to lie not so much in new ideas of welfare as in changed conceptions of the way wants are aroused, their relations to human action, and the way they behave from moment to moment and from day to day. In these respects psychology does seem to call for some real changes of doctrine in economics, both as to marginal utility and as to the nature of production. In a word, it offers a dynamic interpretation of consciousness in place of the static conception which plays so large a part in theoretical economics" (7). Although expressing caution, Clark did drift a little toward the McDougall-Veblen emphasis on instincts and habits. For example, he wrote, "The problem of welfare now-adays appears largely as the problem of what to do with misplaced instincts. Natural selection is an extremely wasteful process. A trait survives because it fitted a past environment, and persists in inappropriate situations in which it is useless or worse" (9).

Clark observed that one consequence of adopting either of the psychological approaches to human behavior, instinct theory or behaviorism, was to diminish the image of the heroic economic agent optimizing his situation internally and responding to the internal but not the external environment that contained forces over which he had little control. This was likely to be a profoundly displeasing image of economic man to those who studied him. "Of the many cruel shocks which the study of psychology has in store for the self-satisfaction of the naïve and innocent beginner, perhaps the most disconcerting comes when he is forced to conceive of his sovereign personality as reacting to the stimuli furnished by the outside universe rather than as generating its own stimuli and acting independently upon the universe from an inner self, possessed to some extent of a quality called 'originality'" (11). But, like it or not, "the stream of consciousness is guided by outside forces" (13). Clark regretted that the typical economist was so ignorant of psychological forces that he even denied the possibility of manipulation through advertising: "One can read orthodox texts in economics and find utility and production treated in a way which either ignores entirely the implications of the psychology of advertising or is absolutely inconsistent with it" (14). Inattention to advertising reflected the static character of contemporary market theory that he so much deplored. "This virtually says that the demand schedule is an ultimate fact for the seller, as the supply schedule is for the purchaser; or that the buyer has one and the same demand schedule throughout his relations with the seller" (15). Marginal utility when seen as a static concept had misled economists: "What economists have gained in 'marginal utility' is in appearance a theory of equilibrium and something to gratify the treacherous yearning for a psychic entity which price can be said to measure" (21–22). Psychology offered one way out of this trap.

Clark regretted the disappearance of ethics from much of economics, and he saw in psychology one way to reconcile the two: "Since desires are roused and directed, as we have seen, in ways that are matters of business, it would seem that ethics cannot take command of this compartment of life to the exclusion of economics any more than an economic study precludes

an ethical one" (23). He found the psychological attention to habit formation likely to be useful in economics, and also Fetter's notion of "impulsive
action." At the same time, Clark was unclear, as were other economists
who found promise in psychology, about precisely what the next steps
should be to improve the relationship between the two disciplines.

A chapter in Tugwell's collection of essays *The Trend of Economics*
(1924), "The Reality of Non-Commercial Incentives in Economic Life,"
by the young, and later to be senator, Paul Douglas was a follow-up to
Taussig's little book a decade earlier. Like Taussig, Douglas examined the
careers of a group of scientists, inventors, and "captains of industry," different from those of Taussig, to see what made them tick. He too found
that the "economic motive" was only one among many. Others were "1.
The desire to benefit humanity. 2. The fascination, or joy, of the work
itself. 3. The desire to project one's own personality in the work at hand. 4.
The desire to be esteemed by one's fellows in the same field of activity. 5.
The desire for the esteem and approval of the general public. 6. The craving for notoriety (This may be quite distinct from the two previous incentives). 7. The desire for power over men and over things" (Douglas 1924,
188). Douglas drew at least one policy conclusion from his findings: "If
we know that there are these other sources of energy in men, we can then
more confidently apply ourselves to the creation of devices and attitudes
which will call them forth" (188).

An attempt was made in 1931 to synthesize the institutionalist position
on human behavior in a large, two-volume textbook titled, appropriately,
Economic Behavior: An Institutional Approach (Atkins et al. 1931; Rutherford 2011, 29, 44). Malcolm Rutherford (2011, 346, 352) argues persuasively that the failure of institutionalism to prosper in the second half of
the twentieth century may be explained partly by the failure to fulfill the
promise to rebuild economics on the basis of modern psychology. The
institutionalists discovered that psychology was a difficult partner with
whom to arrange a marriage because it never achieved a single paradigm
and seemed always to be a moving target: from instinct to habit, and then
to an open-ended behaviorism. By the end of the 1920s economists and
psychologists both had moved away from attempts to substitute instinct
theory for marginal utility because no agreed set of instincts had emerged,
and the whole approach had an increasingly unpleasant metaphysical
odor. Rutherford (2011, 97) reports that in the 1920s the psychologist
J. R. Kantor organized an "anti-instinct cult" at the University of Chicago
that attracted Clarence Ayres and perhaps Morris Copeland. Those who

abandoned instinct theory tended to move toward behaviorism, but they soon found that they had not left criticism behind. They also found that the loss of the rational actor was a threat not only to conventional market theory. Many of the institutions embodied in President Roosevelt's New Deal depended as much on predictable responses from self-interested actors as did competitive markets (Eaton 1934).

8. The Establishment Strikes Back:
Herbert Davenport, Frank Fetter,
A. C. Whitaker, Thomas Nixon Carver,
Jacob Viner, and Frank Knight

Within the economics profession it was one thing for a gadfly like Simon Nelson Patten or young whippersnappers like Parker, Tannenbaum, and Wolman to argue for a merger of economics with psychology. It was even understandable for a few slightly older but eccentric members like Johnson and Tugwell to take up the cry; but it was quite another thing for leaders of the profession like Mitchell, Taussig, and Clark to become advocates for psychology. It was necessary then for the establishment in the profession to take a stand. The responses began toward the end of the Great War. In some, critiques of psychology, and particularly of behaviorism, were concealed behind a spirited defense of marginal utility. It was conceded that some of the findings from psychology were mildly interesting, but they were found to be trivial in the scheme of things. Respected senior figures like Frank Fetter, who flirted with psychology as an American Austrian and waffled over what to do about it, were severely criticized for taking that subject too seriously. The critics claimed repeatedly that all that was needed from psychology could be found already in the theory of choice. Herbert L. Davenport, from the University of Missouri, was distressed to find traces of "modern theory," meaning rejection of marginal utility, in Fetter's textbook of 1915. Davenport conceded that utility had occasionally been misused by economists, but any faults in orthodox economic theory could be corrected without joining up with psychology.

It is not to be questioned that the earlier economists, with most of the later, have been grossly addicted to hedonism. But the harm of it all is not so clear. There need be none for those economists who, in the main—as does Fetter—find no occasion to go back of the facts of desire and of choices among the things desired. No psychological economist, or any other, is concerned to commit himself to any view more controversial than merely that men have actually wants and needs—desires—and do somehow come to make choices among the things desired as ends and among the things employed as means. No theory of desire nor any genetic account of its derivation is essential to the case. Habit, imitation, instinct—there is room for all within the simple assertions *one wants* and *one chooses*. (Davenport 1916, 319–20)

Davenport thought it not worth the trouble to abandon the terms *hedonism* and *marginal utility* that had served well for so long. In making his point, he trivialized the case for paying more attention to psychology:

The advantage must be small in abandoning a term of long and thoroughly established usage. And even were it worth the trouble to convert from their error that majority of economists who still benightedly, obstinately, and, in the main, unconsciously, cling to their hedonism, what shall be done if they will not be converted? Shall there be a different terminology for each of the disciples of the various warring psychological and ethical schools? Or shall those folk who mistakenly disagree with Fetter and Davenport give up their foolishness, and, blinded by the new light, accept that which they have not yet received? Or shall the first volume of the coming final work in economics devote itself to the establishment of certain doctrines in the field of philosophy and psychology, by the compulsion of which there shall no more anywhere be division or change in the ultimates of psychological theory? Utility has come to connote neither beatitude nor wisdom, but mere desire—the fact of *wantedness*. Why not be content with it so? (320)

Davenport thought that the proposals to abandon the notion of marginal utility were a storm in a teacup and that Fetter, despite his talk of impulses and volition, like other reformers, had succeeded "in finding nothing in its stead" (325).

A. C. Whitaker of Stanford University, in the same year (1916) as Davenport, offered a similar critique "of that group of gentlemen engaged in demolishing everything tinged with hedonism in our fair science." He suggested that removal of hedonism from economics, as proposed by "the new psychologists," would eviscerate economics. "It seems according to their way of thinking, that the banishment of hedonism will leave nothing much in economics but the 'genetical' account" (Whitaker 1916, 430). Like Davenport, he found that the "impulse theory" proposed to replace hedonism was unsatisfactory on all counts, and he admonished Fetter for toying with the idea. He blamed McDougall for getting both Fetter and Mitchell on the wrong track. The marginal revolution remained intact: "It can be shown that neither Jevons's theory of final utility nor the similar Austrian theory of marginal utility rests on the technical hedonistic prem- ises that pleasure is the end of life, or the object of desire, or that pleasures differ only in intensity, or what not. The utility theory remains unscathed by the new psychology" (436). Whitaker found that the so-called new theory of psychology that supposedly contradicted marginal utility theory was like the clothing of the *bourgeois gentilhomme*: it did not exist. "It all comes to this, that the instinctive elements of choice are very potent. And this is all it comes to. What there is in this to contradict the utility theory the reviewer does not know" (438). The concept of the rational actor had been misunderstood: "The utility theory makes no assumption that men are rational in the sense that their desires are wise or well-considered according to standards of some person or other" (439). Whitaker was relieved that, given the weakness of the case, few psychologists were actu- ally involved in the attack on economics: "No large number of profes- sional psychologists have been showing an interest in the reform of eco- nomics in the name of their science" (441).

Thomas Nixon Carver, the conservative Harvard economist, was more magnanimous than Whitaker. He welcomed more study of instincts and habits, but he thought that the new psychologists, and especially the behaviorists, were thinking mainly about the losers in the economy and too little about the winners.

> It may be that successful men are influenced somewhat more by the rational factors than are unsuccessful men. At any rate, the classical school with its so-called economic man was as truly a behaviorist school as any group of recent students. They were studying a different class of men in the industrial system. Perhaps both schools develop a one-sided theory of human nature because of the fact that each is study- ing a different class—one the successful, the other the unsuccessful class. (Carver 1918, 198)

The implication of this conclusion for Carver was that the rational actors should be encouraged and the irrational ones discouraged. "A nation which encourages this kind of calculation on the part of its citizens is more likely in the long run to prosper than the nation which does not" (199). From across the water D. H. Robertson (1923, 179–80) commented that after watching this debate in America, he was relieved to find that "the gap between the old hedonist doctrines and those of modern Behaviourism is much narrower than is often suggested, and that for the practical purposes of the economist the former remain substantially valid."

In the 1920s, after watching the debate with the psychologists and their admirers in economics evolve, the heavy hitters in economic theory became involved. In 1925 Jacob Viner in two articles in the *Journal of Political Economy* reviewed the long history of utility theory, from the eighteenth century to date, and found that improvements had repeatedly been made in response to criticisms, but by the end of the nineteenth century stabilization had occurred. "In its developed form it is to be found sympathetically treated and playing a prominent role in the exposition of value theory in most of the current authoritative treatises on economic theory by American, English, Austrian, and Italian writers" (Viner 1925, 371). Yet for some reason, in recent years critics of the concept had turned nasty and advocates were treated with disrespect.

> In the scientific periodicals, however, in contrast with the standard treatises, sympathetic expositions of the utility theory of value have become somewhat rare. In their stead are found an unintermittent series of slashing criticisms of the utility economics. Its psychology, it is alleged, is obsolete; its logic faulty; its analysis and conclusions tainted with class bias; its service to economic enlightenment nil. The critics vie with one another in finding terms sufficiently vigorous to express to the full their dissatisfaction with it. (371)

He gave Rexford Tugwell as an example of an especially intolerant critic. Viner's response was vigorous.

> The utility economics, as ordinarily formulated, is bad psychology. But what of it? How vital is its dependence upon its erroneous psychology? How extensive would be the changes required in its mode of analysis and its conclusions if all of its psychological elements which were in conflict with the current fashions in psychological doctrine were either brought into accordance with it or ruthlessly excised? The critics, of course, have said that the utility economics stands or falls with its psychology, but have they made their case? (374)

To clarify some points at issue, Viner reported that from a study of the literature he was persuaded that, contrary to what some critics claimed, economists had not simply taken up early notions in psychology and then failed to note when they became obsolete and discredited. The two disciplines had moved forward, each on its own path. "The law of diminishing utility, whether sound or not, has been developed by the economists as a product of their own observation and has not been borrowed from psychology" (376). The downward-sloping demand curve, which was the real matter at issue, did not depend on the concept of marginal utility for its legitimacy: "The negative slope of the demand curve is a direct inference from experience, and the law of diminishing desire is a working hypothesis serving to explain the general recurrence of that phenomenon. Until it is demonstrated to be contrary to established fact, or until a better hypothesis is available, the law of diminishing desire can stand on this fact alone" (381). Viner was not sure that the critics appreciated that marginal utility was a tool intended to help understand individual human behavior. It could not reveal anything about aggregate social welfare. In an unexpected anticipation of Galbraithian ideas some decades down the road, he wrote: "Is it not possible that there is a common underestimate of the contribution which government services make to individual welfare, resulting from the favorable advertising which private enterprise provides for its own products—and to the unfavorable advertising which it often spreads with respect to the products of government activity?" (Viner 1925, 650). Humans acted in groups as much as alone, and this led to externalities that had to be taken into account in calculating social welfare. "A group concept of welfare, on the other hand, would endeavor to take into account the totality of influences, favorable or unfavorable, of such institution or activity on all who are affected thereby, directly or indirectly. It would thus take into account in connection with any particular price-transaction not merely those utilities which influence the determination of that price, but also those utilities, which accrue therefrom to persons who played no direct part in the transaction" (633).

Just as Wesley Mitchell's rather positive review of the possible contributions that might come to economics from psychology was the most important assessment on the positive side of the debate, the response from Knight was the most influential on the negative side. Viner provided a full bibliography of Knight's publications on the subject in Viner 1925. While still at the University of Iowa before coming to the University of Chicago, Knight published three articles, one in the *Quarterly Journal of Economics* (1925a), another in the *American Economic Review* (1925b), and the third in Tugwell's *Trend* volume (1924) that made his case. The key issue, he made clear, was whether humans acted only after conscious deliberation. Behavioral psychologists seemed increasingly to argue that they did not; humans, they said, were creatures dependent wholly on their unconscious condition. Stimulus and response from that perspective was the essence of human behavior.

> This central issue is nothing less than the question whether conscious desires or conscious states of any sort can be regarded as "causing" or "explaining" conduct. The scientific study of behavior is notoriously unable to find a place for conscious states as causes, and the weight of psychological opinion is increasingly against treating them as such. . . . Still more recently the tendency is simply to leave desire and satisfaction and all feelings out of the scientific discussion of behavior and treat every action as a response of the organism to a situation of stimulus. (Knight 1925a, 375)

"Feelings" of any sort were not legitimate scientific facts, and any theory based on them was baseless. "It is useless to know that a human being who feels in a certain way will act in a certain way, unless we have some perceptible indicator of the feeling, which indicator can be only a behavior fact. Equally useless is it from the standpoint of control unless we know how to produce and manipulate feelings, and this can be done only by means of established behavior sequences" (376). If behaviorism were accepted, economics would be eviscerated: "It is surely clear that if consciousness is denied and a behavioristic position assumed, an end is put at once to the possibility of discussing values or motives" (Knight 1924, 243).

Knight responded to the position of the psychologists with the observation that desires had long been used to explain behavior, and common sense required that they continue to be.

> From a scientific point of view the problem of economic behavior is parallel to that of the celestial motions. The 'desire' which we say 'makes' men buy goods is analogous to the 'attractive force' which makes objects fall to the surface of the earth and planets fall from the sun. What we really observe in the economic situation is the fact that a good is purchased, just as what we observe in the other case is the fact of movement. The notion of desire serves to simplify the statement in accordance with our mental prejudices, in the one case, as the notion of attractive force does in the other. (Knight 1925a, 380–81)

Knight saw in the new laboratory-based psychology the scientism that he thought was a curse on those attempting to understand the world around them. In this kind of science, agency, ethics, and the study of ends were all excluded from consideration.

> The corner-stone of the scientific attitude is skepticism; it must insist on nothing so much as the repudiation of all "emotion" as a source of knowledge; to science, faith and will-to-believe are synonyms for sin. . . . Morality, as the term is used, is therefore as antithetical to science as faith itself. The effect of the skeptical attitude is sharply to accentuate the naïve dualism of the plain man, the distinction between the real and the imaginary, the objective and the subjective, or, as Walter Lippmann most naively puts it, between the world outside and the pictures in our minds. (392)

In Knight's telling, psychology in its new behavioral rendition was not just irrelevant to economics, or a mild irritant, as some earlier critics had suggested: it was the pied piper leading gullible economists down a road they should not take, away from the issues that really mattered. While the kind of science represented by behavioral psychology purported to bring studies of the mind and economics into closer relation to reality, it did just the opposite. "It is always possible to assert that there is a mechanical law covering every detail of conduct if we could discover it, but the assertion is mere dogma, and practical procedure calls for the opposite assumption" (401). Reliable generalizations about human behavior in the aggregate could never be developed: "Human phenomena are not amenable to treatment in accordance with the strict canons of science. They will not yield generalizations which can be used as the basis of prediction and the guidance of policy, because there are no generalizations about them which are true; that is, no generalizations about our observations of them" (Knight 1924, 251). Economists in Knight's time may have been surprised to learn that the correct province for economics was with ethics and aesthetics rather than with the natural sciences, and that danger lay in the mechanistic approach of behavioral psychology. But the implication was clear; in Knight's view, with the latter lay the possibility of apostasy and even heresy. In his *American Economic Review* article, Knight confirmed what he had said in the earlier *Quarterly Journal of Economics* piece.

> The essence of behaviorism is the insistence that we ignore in the study and description of behavior everything but the observed physical facts of the behavior itself, which of course means practically denying the existence of consciousness. This, again, is what we have done in the

study of other natural phenomena. . . . We are thus *compelled*, as well as impelled, to recognize that man is *more* than an observed object. In fact he is more in two senses. He is, and has to be recognized as being, first an *observer* as well as an observed object, an observer in a sense which cannot ultimately be identified with object observed. And second, he is an *agent* in a sense ultimately distinct from that in which natural objects are treated as agents in scientific discussion. No discussion of man and conduct which ignores these "facts" can, I shall contend, be genuinely useful or intelligent. (Knight 1925b, 248–49)

This was strong language for those already engaged in such "discussion."

Undoubtedly with an eye on the growing institutionalist movement that promised improvements in human welfare through "social control," Knight warned that the prediction required for such public intervention would never come to pass. "We *like* to predict, entirely aside from the utilitarian motive of prediction for the sake of control. It is the control motive which is overdone in contemporary discussion, in spite of the flagrant contradiction already pointed out between an instrumental view of science (which is to say a teleological view) and the insistence upon confining it exclusively to verifiable fact" (256). Laboratory data compiled by behavioral psychologists could never yield the kind of understanding dreamed of by the institutionalists as the basis of social control. "The striving after natural science ideals in the social sciences is a false steer. For practical purposes of prediction and control of human behavior, and finally for the theoretical purpose of understanding it, we can learn more by studying the ways in which *minds* know and influence each other than we ever can by attempting to analyze mechanically the process of interaction between bodies" (265). Behaviorism was based simply on false promise. "We seem to be forced to the conclusion, not that prediction and control are impossible in the field of human phenomena, but that the formal methods of science are of very limited application" (Knight 1924, 254). Knight's advice to economists about how to conduct their inquiry was somewhat vague, but he clearly recommended avoiding psychology as it had evolved: "We can learn about human phenomena, in the significant sense of knowledge, chiefly by studying, *and practicing*, communication with other minds, the process of which activity is art in its various forms, in contrast with science" (265).

Knight's hard-hitting methodological position against the "new" behavioral psychology ignited a lively controversy that lasted through the 1920s.

He was confronted directly by Morris Copeland, who claimed that Knight's position on psychology was an attack on heterodoxy in economics more generally. "The behaviorist does not deny mind, interest, value, etc., 'making all control an illusion' (which is what Professor Knight appears to think), and then proceed to act as if he believed in these things, science itself being avowedly instrumental and purposive. The behaviorist does reserve the right which Professor Knight assumes for himself—the right to conceive mind and value in his own way" (Copeland 1925, 143). Copeland said that behavioral psychologists and the institutional economists were most like biologists, working within a dynamic evolutionary system. They were not the mechanical physicists that Knight claimed them to be. Their methods were like those of all modern scientists. "The behaviorist and the institutionalist believe their subjects to be biological sciences, and they employ concepts and (statistical) methods appropriate to classes of which the individual members differ from one another, to species that originate and evolve. As biologists, their observational technique includes collecting specimens ('case work') and unearthing the remains of the past, as well as laboratory experiment" (147). Copeland had faith that in due course the behaviorists and institutionalists would be able to provide the deep understanding of human interactions that thus far had eluded conventional economists: "We may still proceed on the assumption that psychology and social *science* will be able, by improvement of statistical and laboratory technique, by a more exhaustive collection of data, by better definition of terms and formulation of problems, and by accurate reasoning, to render a scientific account of human purposes and values" (151).

Perhaps because of this tense confrontation between these major figures in the profession, when controversy flared up again from time to time, it tended to be more modulated. Allyn Young thought the controversy overblown and that conventional economics had emerged from it unscathed. "Most of its critics and some of its defenders appear to be agreed that it was and has remained essentially deductive, proceeding from a few questionable assumptions about human nature, and that it has assigned an especially important role to a lay figure, the economic man. Now the truth is that English political economy has never been, in any real sense, deductive or *a priori*, and that it has never put a very heavy burden upon the economic man" (Young 1928, 5). Similar positions were taken by P. Sargent Florence (1927) and Umberto Ricci (1932). Z. Clark Dickinson, who completed a dissertation at Harvard under Frank Taussig, published a book titled *Economic Motives* (1924a), attempted to be a peace-maker, and continued to claim that the wider use of psychology would only strengthen orthodox economics and did not threaten it (e.g., Dickinson 1919, 1924b, 1927). Dickinson was severely criticized for his peace-making by one psychologist, A. J. Snow (1924).

9. Cultural Context:
Henry Adams and Thorstein Veblen

It is not hard to appreciate the negative response from much of the economics profession to the greater use of psychology during the early years of the twentieth century. Concepts like instinct, habit, and emotion were not easily modeled or expressed quantitatively, and to compound the problem the descriptions of the psychological variables kept changing with the arrival of new authors. Moreover, claims for the potential achievements of behavioral psychology did appear to threaten the notion of free choice on which market economics rested. If it turned out that laboratory based studies could indeed predict human behavior from a study of the human brain, it would appear that economics must be replaced by biology and biochemistry. But the evident distaste for the potential contribution of behavioral psychology may have deep roots also in culture, especially American culture, beyond economics and even beyond the scholarly world. This is a slippery subject, but immersion in the American literature of the time must leave one with the sense that there is something in the distaste for psychology beyond the familiar disciplinary tension. It is possible only to offer some speculations on this subject with, admittedly, flimsy evidence.

The suggested hypothesis is that the identity story of the American people, with origins even before the American Revolution, is relevant to an understanding of attitudes toward psychology. Roughly, the story is that the United States is a nation of immigrants who fled the corrupt old world and came to the new to escape political, religious, and social tyranny. They left behind persecution, prejudice, and sometimes destitution. In America they found ample resources, personal freedom, and the possibility of achievement dependent only on their own energy and initiative. Infinite opportunity was open to them. The frontier awaited. Any man could become president, but never king. The brave and imaginative entrepreneur was seen as the one who triumphed in this new environment and by doing so made the country great. Thus he could, and should, be left free to achieve prosperity and liberty for himself, his family, and his neighbors, no matter whether on a frontier farm or in a new city in the burgeoning West. When some immigrants failed, it was because they did not have the necessary skills, or more likely the required ambition and drive. These failures should certainly not be supported at the expense of those who succeeded. Competition accomplished a filtering process wherein the best prospered and others were relegated to subsidiary roles. Social Darwinism and eugenics played a part in this telling, but the story was bigger than that. It was the heroic account of the growth of the greatest nation on earth, based on private initiative, the city on a hill inhabited by a population like no other of strong, healthy, independent citizens. The Horatio Alger stories of Ragged Dick and other young heroes who rise from poverty, of course, reflect this myth, as do the novels of James Fenimore Cooper, Mark Twain, and others. In Muncie, Indiana, the "Middletown" of the pioneering study by the sociologists Robert Lynd and Helen Lynd, a recent report on borrowings from the public library shows that between 1891 and 1902 one out of every twelve books checked out was by Horatio Alger, and Mark Twain was close behind (www.bsu.edu/libraries/wmr/).

The idea that each nation had its own distinct "life and character" was made popular in the 1890s by the British historian Charles H. Pearson and resonated well in America (see reviews of Pearson by C. H. Lincoln [1895] and Franklin Giddings [1895b]). The notion of special economic virtues indigenous to the American scene was not limited to the nineteenth century. For example, William L. Nunn, professor of economics at the University of Newark, observed as late as 1938 that the "concept of thrift" was grounded in the Puritan sense of duty where "individual thrift" became a primary virtue. "This conception of thrift as a moral virtue and as a utilitarian practice was a cornerstone in the development of capitalism as an economic system and individualism as its philosophy of control" (Nunn 1938, 52). Unhappily, wrote Nunn, this virtue was under threat. "In the urbanization of America, the successful application of the simple Puritan virtues of individual frugality and thrift has been lost or sidetracked, to a certain extent, in the bewildering maze of urban streets and city blocks" (54).

The heroes that loom large in American culture reflect this story. Neither Ragged Dick nor Tom Sawyer can be imagined in the culture of the old world. Instead of monarchs, soldiers, and great aristocrats, American literature celebrates entrepreneurs like Henry Ford, Thomas Edison, and Andrew Carnegie who, it was suggested, helped bring the millennium in sight, even if not yet to hand. There was a warm fuzzy feeling about these early entrepreneurs, similar to that felt today for Bill Gates and Warren Buffet, and their writings were welcomed even in scholarly publications (e.g., Carnegie 1909). A reviewer of Andrew Carnegie's *Gospel of Wealth* had this to say:

> It is a commentary on European conditions to read of Czar and Emperor trembling for personal safety, looking upon the common man as a menace to society. Under the freer conditions of America, Australia or Canada this same class, many of them the very ones whose attitude toward society has been considered most dangerous, revolutionists, even criminals, coming to lands where the hold of government is most lax, become strong, useful, patriotic citizens—liberty-loving, but strong in their attachment to law and order. It is quite as significant to find those who have labored in poverty, whose only shelter has been a shed, and whose reasonable hopes, under European conditions, could never rise above the associations of a thatched roof, becoming the sturdy, substantial men of affairs, or, possessed of uncommon ability, with broader opportunity given, coming to the forefront in the management of industry, commerce, in politics and in learning. (Cleveland 1901, 78)

How is this creation myth relevant to attitudes toward the application of psychology to economics and, by reference, to the American economy? In at least three ways, it would seem. First, psychology was widely perceived in the United States as a European import. Therefore it was the product of study in very different circumstances, and although it might be reasonable as the basis for treating those benighted and neurotic Europeans who had not escaped the oppression under which the American ancestors had suffered, it was not needed in the United States. It was treatment for a variety of malignant conditions that, thankfully, had not crossed the Atlantic Ocean. Second, study of psychology to most people in America, at least, implied the expectation that this new science could be used to manipulate the population in efforts to achieve social improvement. But if the American psyche was indeed of a special kind, the result of self-selection among immigrants coming to America and then natural selection in the new environment, the distinctive American psyche was something precious, even sacred, and certainly not to be manipulated by social scientists, like McDougall, with intellectual origins themselves overseas. Change in the fundamental behavior of the citizens was not an appropriate objective for scholars or politicians, and therefore why study it? Third, by the 1930s at least, some observers of the American economy thought that they saw a serious weakening of the self-confidence that had characterized the American psyche and the belief in exceptionalism. The closing of the frontier and failure to find ways to deal with the Great Depression had led to an "inferiority complex" in place of the creation myth and to the chimerical notion that "some superhuman psychoanalyst could take hold of us as a nation and cure us of our 'inferiority complex'" (Bullard 1929). No such cure was necessary, implied this observer. America should just buck up and recognize again its own good fortune and achievement of success through self-reliance.

How can we gain a sense of whether there is something to this hypothesis that a set of cultural beliefs helps explain the continuing great divide between economics and psychology? One way would be to put together, and attempt to make a synthesis of, the relevant commentary in American literature. But that is beyond the scope of this article. Instead, to get a sense of the times, we look briefly at the lives of just two American intellectuals, one of whom has been discussed already, Thorstein Veblen. His educational experience is examined briefly using the biography by Joseph Dorfman, a work that has been criticized by revisionist historians but remains a great achievement all the same. The other intellectual, a scholar-diplomat, grandson of one president of the United States and great-grandson of another, stands on the edge of this study, but over his lifetime he touched and reflected on many of the issues discussed here in his celebrated autobiography *The Education of Henry Adams*. These glimpses can provide only hints about the attitudes that we are trying to understand, but they are certainly suggestive.

The purpose of his autobiography, Adams ([1918] 1973, 12) explained, was to provide a "guide" to a good education for young American men like himself, the main objective of which should be to discover how to achieve "order through chaos." In his primary school Adams received a simple message that "human nature worked for Good, and three instruments were all she asked—Suffrage, Common Schools, and the Press. On these points doubt was forbidden. Education was divine, and man needed only a correct knowledge of facts to reach perfection" (33). Adams took from his father deep suspicion of the old world. He "felt no love for Europe, which, as he and all the world agreed, unfitted Americans for America" (70). When he did go to Europe seeking education beyond what he had obtained at Harvard College, Adams was revolted by the squalor resulting from industrialization, especially in Britain (72), and by the emptiness of the German universities, where "no other faculty than the memory seemed to be recognized. Least of all was any use made of reason, either analytic, synthetic, or dogmatic. The German government did not encourage reasoning" (78). When he became a member of the American legation in London during the American Civil War, his regard for Britain fell even more, mainly because of its bloodthirsty attitude toward the conflict: "He wanted nothing so much as to wipe England off the earth. Never could any good come from that besotted race!" (128). By contrast, he heaped praise on other members of the American legation. One was "a complete American education in himself. His mind was naturally strong and beautifully balanced; his temper never seemed ruffled; his manners were carefully perfect in the style of benevolent simplicity, the tradition of Benjamin Franklin" (146). Adams studied the British character quite seriously. "Psychological study was still simple, and at worst—or at best—English character was never subtle [*sic*]" (163), and the more he examined it the less he liked it. "The English mind was one-sided, eccentric, systematically unsystematic, and logically illogical. The less one knew of it, the better" (180) He extended his indictment to Europe as a whole. "From an old world point of view, the American had no mind; he had an economic thinking-machine which could work only on a fixed line. The American mind exasperated the European as a buzz-saw might exasperate a pine forest" (180). The British in particular were wasteful and eccentric, two vices that Americans had been required to cure in their challenging environment. "Americans needed and used their whole energy, and applied it with close economy; but English society was eccentric by law and for sake of the eccentricity itself" (181). American "national character" rested on "native vigor—robustness—honesty—courage" (181).

While living in Britain, Adams found himself, with regret, being drawn into some of the British national characteristics, "catching an English tone of mind and processes of thought, though at heart more hostile to them than ever" (211–12). One of the most dangerous aspects of British character for an American was that it might become addictive. "Once drawn into it, one had small chance of escape" (213). It was best avoided whenever possible. Adams looked to psychology for guidance in maintaining his American cultural integrity, but without much luck. "Psychology was to him a new study, and a dark corner of education" (231). His father was not much help. "He put psychology under lock and key; he insisted on maintaining his absolute standards; on aiming at ultimate Unity" (232). To maintain his balance among the cultural attractions of London society, he kept before him the models of men like Commodore Vanderbilt and Jay Gould, who "naturally and intensely disliked to be told what to do, and how to do it, by men who took their ideas and methods from the abstract theories of history, philosophy, or theology. They knew enough to know that their world was one of energies quite new" (239). Adams sometimes seemed almost obsessed with explaining and defining what was distinct in the American character. After the Civil War, he reflected that an American came to see himself as "a restless, pushing, energetic, ingenious person, always awake and trying to get ahead of his neighbors. . . . That the American, by temperament, worked to excess, was true; work and whiskey were his stimulants; work was a form of vice; but he never cared much for money or power after he earned them" (297).

Whether Henry Adams was right in his depiction of the American character is not the issue here. What is significant is that he sought to understand this character and that he found it to be superior in most ways to the European character to which he was exposed as a diplomat. It is significant also that by the 1890s he found that "the new psychology" was not of help to him in his search for understanding (433).

In the case of Thorstein Veblen, we shall look only at his formal education to gain some sense of the cultural environment in which he developed his cynical picture of the treatment then in vogue of the human psyche. Veblen attended Carleton College in Minnesota, an evangelical Christian institution not unlike many others in America at that time. There he learned through courses in philosophy, religion, and political economy that the "self-regarding passions" were the motive power to action. This power was nourished by the right to property. The health of the economy became a desideratum in just about every course. Even his textbook in moral philosophy stated, "'We . . . get knowledge' in order to 'get wealth'" (Dorfman 1934, 21). His textbook in political economy by Rev. A. L. Chapin taught that "competition is 'a beneficent, permanent law of nature', and self-interest is 'the mainspring of human exertion'" (23). Moreover, competition was the best arbiter of economic justice. "By the competitive process of acquisition every man finds the place and reward to which his abilities and talents entitle him" (24). Economic failure was likely "due to the lack of moral character and intelligence, that is a self-regarding interest among the 'weaker and lower'. They are still 'barbarians,' men of 'feeble races' and 'savage society,' since they do not feel the force of the pursuit of gain" (26). John Bates Clark taught economics at Carleton while

Veblen was there, and he agreed with the orthodox view that the desire for acquisition was the "constant motive power in industrial progress" (28).

In graduate school Veblen continued to hear that vigorous self-interest was essential for the smooth running of the economy. At Yale he learned from reading Herbert Spencer that strong self-interest guaranteed both efficiency and fairness. "From the psychological point of view 'the normal working of the pleasures and pains become incentives and deterrents so adjusted in their strength to their needs that the moral conduct will be the natural conduct'" (47). In his graduate training Veblen encountered several of the pioneering American psychologists who were attempting to make their subject a laboratory science. They included Gorge Trumbell Ladd and Lester Frank Ward at Yale and G. Stanley Hall at Johns Hopkins. Most of them had received divinity degrees and continued to align their subject with Christian doctrine; they emphasized that self-interest was a force for good and the means to advance civilization (53–55). At the University of Chicago Veblen received more "common sense economics" through J. Laurence Laughlin and only a mild critique of "the greed philosophy" from Charles S. Peirce (94).

It seems clear that for these two intellectuals in the nineteenth century, the picture of the economic man they encountered in their education was much more than an abstraction employed for convenience in modeling the economy. This man was first and foremost a normative concept, the picture of an economic actor who had made the country great and would continue to do so if not impeded by do-gooder reformers. His psyche had been forged on the anvil of struggle, first to escape a corrupt old world and then to create a new one in the wilderness. To meddle with the psyche of this actor could be a dangerous and potentially destructive undertaking.

10. Truce: Psychology Moves to the Subdisciplines

In the late 1920s and 1930s an uneasy disengagement took hold between the advocates and critics of greater contact between economics and psychology. Several explanations may be suggested for this development. One is that the leaders of the economics discipline needed time to recover from the ill-tempered exchanges early in the 1920s between the marginalists and the institutionalists. The language used on both sides in these exchanges had implied disrespect and even contempt for the other. Leaders of these comparatively new fields may have come to appreciate that unity in public might be an important determinant of professional success. Undoubtedly another factor was the rise of other issues for attention, notably the onset of the Great Depression and means to combat it. Here the main combatants in the earlier conflicts were much involved. Rexford Tugwell soon became a key member of President Roosevelt's brains trust, using his institutional skills to propose and develop interventionist schemes to stimulate the economy like the National Recovery Administration and the Agricultural Adjustment Administration. Frank Knight and his Chicago brethren hunkered down to defend the free market that they thought was in peril from such policies. Proposals to import more psychology into economics loomed small against the backdrop of these greater themes.

Yet a third factor was also important in strengthening the truce. The economics discipline during this time went through a period of decomposition into semiautonomous subfields, and psychology, it was discovered, could be off-loaded into several of these where it would hardly be noticed and would not seriously threaten core price theory. Out of sight, out of mind. Whereas psychology came to be seen as banned from price theory, it was accepted into business cycle theory and industrial relations (Lewisohn 1938). The most important subfields of economics where psychologists settled were associated with the rise of business education, both in management programs in economics departments and in separate professional schools of business: most prominently, industrial (labor) relations, industrial organization, marketing, public and personnel relations, and advertising. The potential contributions of psychology to business had been noted before World War I, especially by the French psychologist Gabriel Tarde (1902), and as applied to advertising by Walter Dill Scott and Henry Foster Adams (Scott 1903, 1908; Adams 1916). Industrial efficiency using psychological tools was addressed by Hugo Munsterberg (1913, 1915). The subject was revived in the 1920s by Z. Clark Dickinson and others who argued that since most of the inputs and outputs of business involved human beings, businesspeople should understand human nature and engage in "human engineering." In an article in the *Journal of Political Economy*, Dickinson (1922, 88–89) drew attention particularly to the supposed success of US Army mental tests during World War I to find "the right man for the place," and he suggested a requirement that "all students taking the business degree shall have passed an introductory psychology course" (see also Kornhauser 1923, 1925; Kingsbury

1923; Crennan 1923; Miller 1923; and Link 1919, 1923). The application of psychology to business was presented as an important part of "scientific management" advocated by the Taylor Society, where it could facilitate the optimum use of inputs in the productive process (Link 1919; Brown 1925). Soon there was a spate of articles and texts from both economists and psychologists that responded to this perceived opportunity (Twitmyer 1924; Snow 1925; Florence 1925; Poffenberger 1925; Stone 1930; Burtt 1930; Viteles 1932; Lucas and Benson 1930; Ball 1934; Edwards 1934; Baster 1934; Strong 1938; Moore 1939). Psychology found an especially happy home in the subdiscipline of "marketing," where analysis of consumer demand became a growth industry (Stevenson 1923; Hess 1924; Nystrom 1940). That is not to say there was no criticism of these intrusions. In the *Journal of Political Economy* Frank Knight (1929) and Harry Dexter Kitson (1920) complained that the new literature depended too much on contentious figures in psychology, especially McDougall and Freud.

One of the most prominent and prolific commentators on the place of psychology in business studies, and especially personnel management, during this period was Ordway Tead, publisher and public servant. He deserves special mention. He wrote, "Today there is hardly a major management problem recognized but that thinking on it discovers it to be in part psychological" (Tead 1930, 110). He looked at industrial relations and prepared an extensive catalog of worker responses to the industrial world that went far beyond wage rates. To understand worker behavior, he suggested some of the instincts proposed by McDougall and Veblen, suitably modified for his purposes. "The impulses to create and construct, to satisfy one's curiosity, to satisfy one's desire for the approval of others and one's sense of significance in work, are all legitimate parts of the human equipment and they demand satisfaction" (Tead 1920, 178). To understand how firms behaved and, anticipating John Kenneth Galbraith's *New Industrial State* three decades ahead, Tead pointed out that the objectives of the firm are never as simple as profit maximization, and to understand industrial behavior, these must be taken into account. "Corporate objectives are never single, if analysis is profoundly pressed. They are plural in fact, if not in law. Once you start talking about considerations of 'service,' quality, low price, good name, good will, community standing, employee loyalty, or any other related and secondary aim, the singleness of all operating aims goes by the board" (Tead 1930, 111). Tead suggested that psychologists might help economists understand priorities in consumption, a topic they had been reluctant to explore: "The service of a still infant science of psychology is already beneficent because it calls us all back to preoccupation with those problems in economic living, in the solving of which lies one of the abiding sources both of personal satisfaction and of a deep conviction as to the worth of life itself as a creative reality" (119).

Business studies was not the only remote segment of applied economics to which psychology migrated in the 1920s and 1930s. There were contributions to educational policy (Sherman 1930), maintenance of law and order (Larson 1929), and economic ethics (Hadfield 1923). But it would be some years before psychologists would again challenge the innermost citadels of high economic theory.

11. A Freudian Beachhead:
Walter Lippmann and John Maynard Keynes

Psychoanalysis found few admirers among economists when it appeared on the scene early in the twentieth century. There were many reasons why. It was based mainly outside academe and the accepted seats of science, and on case studies by clinicians operating as scientists without the usual devices for quality control. Few reliable data sets emerged from their work that could lead to confident generalizations. The approach made use of strange metaphysical notions like the unconscious and dreams, not susceptible to measurement or even clear definition. It was conducted with terms like *the ego* and *the id* that could not easily be understood by newcomers, such as economists, without more close attention than they were prepared to give. The foundational literature was primarily in German, with few reliable translations into English until well into the twentieth century. For the most part, the subject was viewed with suspicion and distaste by respectable academics, even by many psychologists. The emphasis on sexuality and concepts like the libido must have seemed borderline pornographic to those scholars who were known especially for their piety and, in the case of the economists, for their "social gospel." G. Stanley Hall, one of the founders of modern psychology in America, wrote in 1924: "Many have testified to a new freedom in recent years in speaking frankly on subjects formerly tabooed, but I am old-fashioned enough to have felt slightly shocked at a few of the more frank discussions in which both sexes have participated, even in my seminary, and still franker discussions of which I have learned outside it." At the same time, he conceded, "I certainly have yet to learn of any immorality that can be ascribed to our cult of psychoanalysis here" (413). Frank Knight (1924, 247) in the same year gave his views of the "psycho-analytic method in psychology": "While its postulates may be useful as the basis of a technique of control in certain special cases, they introduce enormous new difficulties and uncertainties in the way of reducing behavior at large to general laws. . . . The procedure would be much more accurately called psycho-interpretation."

But there were exceptions to this negative view. For example, Carleton Parker included a book by Freud in the readings for a course at Berkeley in 1915 (Rutherford 2011, 22, 139). Most significant were two readers of psychoanalysis who stood at the center of the macroeconomic revolution of the 1930s: the journalist Walter Lippmann and John Maynard Keynes (Goodwin 2014). Although unknown to each other before they met at the Paris Peace Conference in 1919, their early engagements with psychoanalysis, and especially with Sigmund Freud, were remarkably parallel, and they maintained a close friendship in which these were undoubtedly discussed.

Early in their careers Lippmann and Keynes became deeply interested in human behavior, not only in the economy but elsewhere. Yet they were both repelled by the three accepted interpretive frameworks used to explain this behavior: the simple hedonistic brand of utilitarianism that gave birth to *homo economicus*, the instinct theory of William McDougall that seemed to suggest a kind of biological determinism for human action, and the new behaviorism that rejected all reference to consciousness and depended exclusively on external observation. Both men were embedded during their student days and soon thereafter in groups of friends who became fascinated by psychoanalysis for a variety of reasons, one of which was that it seemed to provide a fourth explanatory approach to understanding human activity. They both conceded that the three conventional explanations might do for an understanding of the mass of the people, but for the subsets that interested them it would not do: people engaged in public affairs in the case of Lippmann and artists and scientists for Keynes and his friends. For both men, the exciting early appeal of Freud did not last into middle age, but it did seem to relieve them of any commitment to psychological orthodoxy, and it opened their minds to revolutionary conclusions, for example, Lippmann's discovery that human preferences expressed as public opinion were easily malleable, and Keynes's psychological differentiation of the behaviors of consumers, savers, investors, and those in search of liquidity.

Lippmann left Harvard in 1910 fond of his economics teacher Frank Taussig and his mentor in psychology William James, but deeply disillusioned with the economics and psychology he found to be in fashion. His heart lay with philosophy, in which he majored, but his interest moved more and more toward politics and public affairs where he looked to the social and behavioral sciences increasingly for illumination. He complained in his first book, A *Preface to Politics*, of the mechanical view of the economy that he had been exposed to in his classes, with its roots still in the eighteenth century and seemingly unaffected by the Darwinian revolution (Lippmann 1913, 16). Economists, he concluded, spent too much time building protective walls around their behavioral assumptions and not enough time challenging them: "We decide beforehand that things must fit a few preconceived ideas. And when they don't, which is most of the time, we deny truth, falsify facts, and prefer the coddling of our theory to any deeper understanding of the real problem before us" (124). He objected especially to what he saw as the glorification of selfish practices in the marketplace. "That was the nauseating method of nineteenth century economists when they tried to identify the brutal practices of capitalism with the beneficence of nature and the Will of God" (160). The modern economist was little better. "The orthodox economists are in the unenviable position of having taken their morals from the exploiter and having translated them into the grandiloquent language of high public policy. They gave capitalism the sanction of the intellect" (70). The mechanical view of the economy treated issues such as the tendency toward monopoly as problems to be solved once and for all through gimmicks like the Sherman Act into which potential malefactors "can bump" instead of through imaginative policies that require government to "take the wheel and to steer" (22). "Routineers" and "stand-patters" opposed all significant social and economic reforms on the ground that they would be "against human nature" when in fact they were mainly ignorant of human nature. Moreover, they were not even trying to learn. The evolutionary approach to economic policy, with which Lippmann associated Freud, offered some hope for progress. "The lasting value of Darwin, for example, is not in any concrete conclusion he reached. His importance to the world lies in the new twist he gave to science. He lent it fruitful direction, a different impetus, and the results are beyond his imagining" (57). Contemporary economics was firmly on the rocks because it stayed with stereotypes. "The Economic Man—that lazy abstraction—is still paraded in the lecture room; the study of human nature has not advanced beyond the gossip of old wives" (61–62). Lippmann's contempt for the economics that he had been taught was so great that he accused the discipline of professional malfeasance. "We have had economists who set out with the preconceived idea of justifying the factory system. The world has recently begun to see through this kind of intellectual fraud" (123). In government now, "the bogs of technical stupidity and empty formalism are always near and always dangerous" (78).

The current state of psychology, Lippmann found, was no better than that of economics. He found some glimmers of enlightenment in the French psychologists Gabriel Tarde and Gustave Le Bon, but in the English-speaking world the prospects were universally discouraging. "There are, too, any number of 'social psychologies,' such as those of Ross and McDougall. But the trouble with them is that the 'psychology' is weak and uninformed, distorted by moral enthusiasms, and put out without any particular reference to the task of statesmanship" (63). Lippmann was concerned especially to understand political and economic behavior, and he wondered whether failure to include these realms in the larger culture was one cause of their poverty. "It is enough that we remember the close alliance of art, science and politics in Athens, in Florence and Venice at their Zenith. We in America have divorced them completely: both art and politics exist in a condition of unnatural celibacy. Is this not a contributing factor to the futility and opacity of our political thinking?" (88). To understand and improve political and economic behavior, Lippmann thought it necessary to create a "willful humanistic culture." "Without a literature the people is dumb, without novels and poems, plays and criticism, without books of philosophy, there is neither the intelligence to plan, the imagination to conceive, nor the understanding of a common purpose. Without culture you can knock down governments, overturn property relations, you can create excitement, but you cannot create a genuine revolution in the lives of men" (227–28). This perspective of seeing psychology as a way not only to understand the psyche but also to change it left Lippmann open and receptive to Freud.

Lippmann seems to have become aware of Freud as an undergraduate through his college friend Alfred Booth Kuttner, an early patient of A. A. Brill, one of the first Freudian practitioners in America. Indeed, Lippmann wrote *A Preface to Politics* in part in a cabin in the Adirondacks while Kuttner was with him translating Freud's *Interpretation of Dreams* in collaboration with Brill. Lippmann reports: "I read the translation as he worked on it and discussed it with him and began to see how much Freud

had to contribute to the psychology which I had learned at college"
(Lippmann 1942). Lippmann attempted immediately to explore how
Freud might help solve current policy problems. Perhaps, he suggested,
the "lusts of the city" that drove street gangs could be redirected into art.

> The Freudian school of psychologists calls this "sublimation." They
> have brought forward a wealth of material which gives us every reason
> to believe that the theory of "moral equivalents" is soundly based, that
> much the same energies produce crime and civilization, art, vice,
> insanity, love, lust, and religion. In each individual the original differ-
> ences are small. Training and opportunity decide in the main how
> men's lust shall emerge. Left to themselves, or ignorantly tabooed, they
> break forth in some barbaric or morbid form. Only by supplying our
> passions with civilized interests can we escape their destructive force.
> (Lippmann 1913, 43–44)

Lippmann had high hopes that the study of dreams and myths could contribute to the construction of sound public policy. "No one can any longer
dismiss the fantasy because it is logically inconsistent, superficially
absurd, or objectively untrue" (175, also 129). Soon after his summer in
the woods with Kuttner, together with A. A. Brill Lippmann introduced
Freudian psychology to the avant-garde salon held by patron of the arts
Mabel Dodge in Greenwich Village. Indeed, in 1932 Brill invited
Lippmann as a pioneer of Freudian thinking to speak at an anniversary of
the founding of the New York Psychoanalytic Society (Brill 1932).
Lippmann replied modestly, "I have, of course, been a pretty consistent
reader of Freud in a poor amateur sort of way. But I am hardly a man for
such a formidable occasion. I wish I could come to the dinner nevertheless, and if I could I might be tempted to get up and say a few words
expressing my personal gratitude to him" (Lippmann 1932).

After his initial engagement with Freud through Kuttner, Lippmann's
enthusiasm continued but with less intensity and in balance with the rest
of psychology. He cites Freud in his most scholarly work *Public Opinion*
(1922), but on a par with Trotter, McDougall, Jung, Titchener, and Edward
Ross, and much less than with William James. In later life he portrayed
his engagement with Freud as a feature of his youth. He wrote in 1942, "I
can say that serious young men took Freud quite seriously, as indeed he
deserved to be taken. Exploitation of Freud into a tiresome fad came later
and generally from people who had not studied him and had only heard
about him" (Lippmann 1942). In 1922 Lippmann was part of a discussion

group organized by Dorothy Straight, the patron of the *New Republic* magazine, "to discuss together certain psychological questions" in which the work of Freud did not appear to loom especially large (Straight 1922). Lippmann's one attempt to introduce Freud to economics does not appear to have been successful. In 1915 he tried to persuade Wesley Mitchell to take Freud seriously, and Mitchell replied, "Of course I realize that you have gotten good service out of the Freudian view-point in discussing certain of your topics, but I still feel much as I did after reading 'A Preface to Politics,' viz., that the service rendered by Freud's ideas is quite capable of being gotten from the psychological analysis of people like Thorndike, for example. So I need the help which you kindly offered to give me as much as ever. Won't you set a date in the near future when you can dine with us quite alone and talk the matter out?" (Mitchell 1915). Lippmann was pleased that Freud arranged for *Preface* to be reviewed (favorably) in his magazine *Imago,* and he was glad to meet Freud in person in Vienna some time later. But by then the love affair had cooled.

There are striking parallels between the ways in which Keynes and Lippmann came to know about Freud and his works. They did not go in search of or react to Freud. He was made known to them, almost by accident, by friends with little interest in economic or social policy. Like Lippmann, Keynes as an undergraduate developed a deep interest in philosophy, literature, and the arts. Economics came later. Vincent Barnett reports that Keynes read some of the late nineteenth-century texts in psychology while preparing for the civil service in 1905–6, and some of the ideas contained therein may be seen in his later economics (Barnett 2015). But his exposure to psychoanalysis came not much later. He, too, like Lippmann, developed friendships in the arts and humanities that exposed him to this branch of psychology and to Freud. For Keynes, these contacts were first at Cambridge with the so-called Apostles, members of a secret society for exalted conversation on many subjects. Later it was the Bloomsbury Group, a loose association of artists, writers, and others that met informally but often in central London. The Bloomsburys became one of the most important communities for spreading Freudian ideas in the English-speaking world. Most members were influenced one way or another by Freud. The two pioneers were James Strachey, younger brother of Lytton Strachey, and Alix Sargent Florence, who later married James. Alix and her brother Philip were together at Cambridge in the years just before World War I, and she experienced some sort of nervous collapse while a student at Newnham, somewhat like that of Lippmann's friend

Alfred Kuttner; she too looked to psychology for answers. After Cambridge Alix moved with Philip to a flat in Bloomsbury and came to know the other members of the Group, including Keynes. By this time James Strachey was becoming increasingly interested in psychology, and especially psychoanalysis, with which he had become acquainted through his engagement with the Society for Psychical Research begun by Henry Sidgwick and others in 1887. Freud contributed a paper to the society's proceedings in 1912 with which James must have been familiar. His interest dates from that time, and when Keynes invited him to a party in that year he replied jokingly, "D'you really think I had better come, though? It might make your party psychological—which is always a thing to be avoided" (quoted in Meisel and Kendrick 1985, 27). James enrolled briefly in medical school, aiming to become a psychiatrist, but abandoned this path. He lent a copy of Freud's *Interpretation of Dreams* to Alix in 1915 (Meisel and Kendrick 1985, 27), the work translated by Brill in collaboration with Kuttner in part in Lippmann's cabin in the woods three years before, and this seems to have sparked her lifelong interest in Freud.

Over the next years Freud made his mark on Bloomsbury in many ways, some direct and some indirect. He was clearly an influence on Lytton Strachey and his *Eminent Victorians* (published 1918), and on one of Keynes's lovers, Sebastian Sprott, a Cambridge Apostle and demonstrator at the Cambridge Psychological Laboratory who translated a work by Freud. It is not hard to see the influence of Freud on the novelists in the Group, Virginia Woolf and E. Morgan Forster. Ultimately members of the Group became practicing psychoanalysts, including Virginia Woolf's younger brother Adrian Stephen and his wife, Karen. In 1914 Virginia's husband, Leonard, contributed to the *New English Weekly* one of the first reviews in English of a work by Freud (Meisel and Kendrick 1985, 40). In 1920 Alix and James were married and set off for Vienna to be analyzed. In 1924 James persuaded Leonard and Virginia Woolf to publish all of Freud's work in definitive English translations from their Hogarth Press, and the first two volumes appeared in that year. The Standard Edition of Freud began from Hogarth in 1953.

Because from 1915 Freudian ideas were so pervasive in Bloomsbury, it is seldom possible to pinpoint them precisely. But the most significant impact was to strengthen the anti-utilitarian message of the Cambridge philosopher G. E. Moore, with whom some of them had studied and by whom most of them had been influenced; Freud opened minds to the complexity of human behavior. The image of the rational actor seldom appears thereafter in Bloomsbury. The success of the many creative and imaginative biographies of major and minor public figures that came out of Bloomsbury was based on the premise that lives could not be understood by rational reconstructions of events. Humans were more interesting than that. In this Lytton Strachey was the pioneer, but Keynes was not far behind with *The Economic Consequences of the Peace* (1919) and *Essays in Biography* (1933).

Freud was exceptionally productive during the 1920s, with James Strachey rushing along behind with translations. One of the greatest accomplishments of James and Alix in that decade was the translation, and publication by Hogarth in 1925, of five selected case studies by Freud written between 1899 and 1919 (Meisel and Kendrick 1985, 47). They were widely read. James wrote to Alix, who was in Germany: "By the way, Maynard said he was engrossed in the Case Histories, & made complimentary remarks about the translation. According to him he's going through the whole of the Dr.'s works, so as to get a real grasp of the subject" (Meisel and Kendrick 1985, 289).

The initial application of Freudian psychology by the Bloomsburys to problems that interested them was to the behavior of iconic public figures in, for example, *Eminent Victorians* and *The Economic Consequences of the Peace*. But they moved on to the study of artists and scientists (including economists) whose special gifts intrigued them and whose survival in a market economy they wished to assure. Freudian ideas can be found as late as the 1930s and 1940s in Keynes's famous essay *Newton the Man* (1942) and Virginia Woolf's biography *Roger Fry* (1940). But at the same time, like Lippmann, they began to lose faith in the general applicability of the ideas.

Roger Fry, a good friend of Keynes and deeply concerned with questions of method in the social and behavioral sciences, in a sense acted for the Group in expressing doubts about the use of psychoanalysis. In a talk to the Psychoanalytic Society, published by the Hogarth Press in 1924, he made clear his misgivings about the Freudian approach. He complained that psychoanalysts, when thinking about artists, confused two groups of professionals whose "aims and activities" were very different under the single heading of "artist." One group that most of the world, as well as the psychoanalysts, thought of as artists was in fact "mainly preoccupied with creating a fantasy-world in which the fulfillment of wishes is realized" (Fry [1924] 1996, 352). Theirs was an "instinctual life" in which Freud's largely sexual explanations might be plausible. True artists, by contrast, were "concerned with the contemplation of formal relations," which was "the distinctive esthetic activity." These two types of behavior were "fundamentally different, if not in their origins, at least in their functions" (352). The same was true of pure as contrasted with "impure or useful" science. To understand "pure scientific activity you must note that its scientific essence is precisely the complete detachment from the instinctive life, its complete uselessness, its abiological nature, since it exists not to serve life but truth, and this is precisely why those who devote themselves to this activity are constantly in conflict with the mass of mankind which is deeply concerned with life and completely indifferent to truth" (353). Pure science, just as pure art, could not be explained by such devices as Freud's analysis of sex: "The fundamental truth-seeking passion of pure science is distinguished precisely by its independence of, and its indifference to, biological necessity" (353).

Fry, who was familiar with Veblen's contributions to psychology, noted that pure and impure art were often mixed together, making analysis difficult: "The esthetic appeal is mixed with all sorts of appeals to other feelings than the love of beauty—appeals to our sense of social prestige, to our avarice, to our desire for personal display, and so forth" (354). Pure and impure art were reflected in different kinds of emotions. "Now these emotions about forms may be accompanied by other emotions which have to do more or less with what I call the instinctive life" (354). The problem of disentangling pure from impure art was as great for the audience as for the analyst. "Now since very few people are so constituted by nature or training as to have developed the special feeling about formal design, and since everyone has in the course of his life accumulated a vast mass of feeling about all sorts of objects, persons, and ideas, for the greater part of mankind the associated emotions of a work of art are far stronger than the purely esthetic ones" (355). Psychoanalysts had failed to understand the arts because they did not understand this complexity. Freud had attempted to understand the artist by examining his "instinctive needs," and this was a misguided approach: "The portrait of the artist here given is drawn on the lines of a widespread popular fallacy about the 'artistic temperament'" (358). Freudian tools of analysis did not help clarify the process of artistic creation. For example, "the novels that have endured do not represent wish-fulfilment to any considerable extent" (359). It was the case that "qua artist, the creator has other aims than that of wish-fulfillment and that the pleasure which he feels is not thus directly connected with the libido" (360). Some of the factors identified by Freud in the creative process were in fact irrelevant. For example, "nothing is more contrary to the essential esthetic faculty than the dream. The poet Mallarme foresaw this long before Freud had revealed the psychological value of dreams" (361). Fry concluded that Freud had usefully drawn attention to the question of artistic creation, but it was left for other psychologists to provide a more satisfactory explanation.

> One thing I think we may clearly say, namely that there is a pleasure in the recognition of order, of inevitability in relations, and that the more complex the relations of which we are able to recognize the inevitable interdependence and correspondence, the greater is the pleasure; this of course will come very near to the pleasure derived from the contemplation of intellectual constructions united by logical inevitability. What the source of that satisfaction is would clearly be a problem for psychology. (365)

The significance of Fry's essay on psychoanalysis is that while he and the other Bloomsburys admired Freud and found his work stimulating, they were doubtful of its direct application to the issues that interested them the most. Freud opened their minds to the complexity and fascination of human behavior, but his works were far from providing a road map of how they should proceed to gain a better understanding.

12. Conclusion

What, then, can we take away from this examination of the engagement, or disengagement, of economics and psychology during the first half century of their existence as modern social sciences? What of the hypotheses with which this article began? The first of these, that methodological differences sustained the schism, was undoubtedly crucial. Economics from its origins in the eighteenth century, and strengthened by the marginal revolution of the 1870s, was a resolutely deductive science. It progressed by constructing simple models with relatively few variables and plausible behavioral assumptions that made possible predictions and advice on public and private policies. Psychology was, by contrast, an inductive science based first on introspection and personal experience, and then on insights from other disciplines like philosophy, sociology and anthropology, animal behavior, and laboratory experiments that all yielded exceptionally complex models, sometimes with dozens of variables, many unquantifiable but plausible on the surface. To reconcile these starkly different methodological approaches to explaining human action would have been a demanding task, and no superhuman stepped forward to try. The task was complicated even more by the lack of sympathy, and sometimes even derision and contempt, of one profession for the other.

The ideological hypothesis, although difficult to defend, was also sustained. The image of the economic man that emerged from Bentham and the marginal revolution in economics was not simply a methodological convenience. The man had normative content as well. William Stanley Jevons, Alfred Marshall, and others among the revolutionaries were Victorian prudes, and the rational actors from their imagination were to them role models as much as assumptions. Sober, clear-thinking participants in the markets who thought before they acted would, leaders in economics believed, sustain morally righteous policies free of the irresponsible and selfish behavior so deplored by all Victorian moralists. The picture of a society they saw in psychology, made up of poor tormented souls, driven by their unconscious, and by uncontrollable forces rooted in their past, was disturbing to economists. At the same time, psychologists like McDougall and Freud found the economists' vision as implausible as the economists found theirs distressing.

The hypothesis that cultural constraints played a role in this disciplinary estrangement seems also to be supported by the evidence, but rather tentatively. The belief in a distinctive American psyche shared by economists, of an American character, heroic and exceptional, the result of repeated challenges through the years, does seem to have been a barrier to the kind of open-ended inquiry conducted by psychologists.

Finally, the accidents of history unquestionably played a crucial part in this evolution. To have brought these two disciplines together constructively, in common cause, would have required scholars of uncommon breadth, tolerance, and imagination. Such persons did appear from time to time but none delivered on their promise. Simon Nelson Patten and Thorstein Veblen saw the problems and potential payoff in integrating the disciplines, but they were both too cynical and too much the gadflies to pull it off. The American institutionalists were the most promising movement to address the questions and to demonstrate what might be achieved from working together, but they did not follow up. There were numerous accidents along the way such as the untimely death of Carleton Parker and the leading part played by the contentious William McDougall that may explain stops and starts. Several of those who seemed to understand best the possibilities from cooperation, such as Wesley Mitchell, J. M. Clark, and Rexford Tugwell, were pulled away by other demands including government service and the creation of interdisciplinary academic institutions of various kinds. There is also the possibility that the vigor of the attacks on those who contemplated working across these disciplinary lines was enough to make younger scholars, looking forward to long careers ahead, find it more prudent to direct their efforts into less contentious endeavors.

References

Adams, Henry. (1918) 1973. *The Education of Henry Adams.* Boston: Houghton Mifflin.

Adams, Henry Foster. 1916. *Advertising and Its Mental Laws.* New York: Macmillan.

Anderson, B. M., Jr. 1913. "Patten's Reconstruction of Economic Theory." *Political Science Quarterly* 28: 123–29.

Andrews, Benjamin R. 1903. "Habit." *American Journal of Psychology* 14: 121–49.

———. 1929. "The Home Woman as Buyer and Controller of Consumption." *Annals of the American Academy of Political and Social Science* 143 (May): 41–48.

Angell, Norman. 1916. "Public Opinion in Foreign Policies." *Annals of the American Academy of Political and Social Science* 66 (July): 136–39.

———. 1918. "Freedom of Discussion in War Time." *Annals of the American Academy of Political and Social Science* 78 (July): 194–204.

Asso, P. F., and L. Fiorito. 2004. "Human Nature and Economic Institutions: Instinct Psychology, Behaviorism, and the Development of American Institutionalism." *Journal of the History of Economic Thought* 26 (4): 445–77.

Atkins, Willard E., et al. 1931. *Economic Behavior: An Institutional Approach.* 2 vols. Boston: Houghton Mifflin.

Ball, Robert J. 1934. "Clinical Psychology in the Diagnosis and Treatment of Delinquents." *Annals of the American Academy of Political and Social Science* 175 (September): 224–28.

Barnett, Vincent. 2015. "Keynes and the Psychology of Economic Behavior." *History of Political Economy* 47 (2): 307–33.

Baster, A. S. J. 1934. *Advertising Reconsidered.* London: P. S. King.

Bernays, Edward L. 1935. "Molding Public Opinion." *Annals of the American Academy of Political and Social Science* 179 (May): 82–87.

Bogardus, E. S. 1921. Review of *The Casual Laborer and Other Essays,* by Carleton H. Parker. *American Journal of Sociology* 26: 527–28.

Brill, A. A. 1932. Letter to Walter Lippmann, October 28, 1932. Walter Lippmann Papers, MS 326, Manuscripts and Archives, Yale University Library III F294.

Brown, Percy S. 1925. "The Work and Aims of the Taylor Society." *Annals of the American Academy of Political and Social Science* 119 (May): 134–39.

Bruni, L., and R. Sugden. 2007. "The Road Not Taken: How Psychology Was Removed from Economics, and How It Might Be Brought Back." *Economic Journal* 117: 146–73.

Bullard, Arthur. 1929. "The American Inferiority Complex." *Annals of the American Academy of Political and Social Science* 144 (July): 32–33.

Burtt, Harold E. 1930. *Psychology and Industrial Efficiency.* New York: Appleton.

Carnegie, Andrew. 1909. "The Future of Labor." *Annals of the American Academy of Political and Social Science* 33 (March): 15–21.

Carver, T. N. 1905. Review of *The Theory of Business Enterprise,* by Thorstein Veblen. *Political Science Quarterly* 20: 141–43.

———. 1918. "The Behavioristic Man." *Quarterly Journal of Economics* 33:195–201.

———. 1920. "The Relation of Thrift to Nation Building." *Annals of the American Academy of Political and Social Science* 87 (January): 4–8.

Chase, H. W. 1917. "Psychology and Social Science." *American Journal of Psychology* 28: 216–28.

Childs, Harwood L. 1937. "Public Opinion and Peace." *Annals of the American Academy of Political and Social Science* 192 (July): 31–37.

———. 1938. "Public Opinion—First Line of Defense." *Annals of the American Academy of Political and Social Science* 198 (July): 109–15.

Clark, J. M. 1918. "Economics and Modern Psychology." *Journal of Political Economy* 26:1–30, 136–66.

Cleveland, Frederick A. 1901. "Mr. Carnegie as Economist and Social Reformer." *Annals of the American Academy of Political and Social Science* 17 (May): 78–84.

———. 1907. "The Psychology of Chess and of Learning to Play It." *American Journal of Psychology* 18:269–308.

Coats, A. W. 1976. "Economics and Psychology: The Death and Resurrection of a Research Programme." In *Method and Appraisal in Economics,* edited by Spiro J. Latsis, 43–64. Cambridge: Cambridge University Press.

Copeland, Morris A. 1924. "Communities of Economic Interest and the Price System." In Tugwell 1924, 105–50.

———. 1925. "Professor Knight on Psychology." *Quarterly Journal of Economics* 40: 134–51.

Creel, George. 1918. "Public Opinion in War Time." *Annals of the American Academy of Political and Social Science* 78 (July): 185–94.

Crennan, C. H. 1923. "Human Nature in Business." *Annals of the American Academy of Political and Social Science* 110 (November): 1.

Dallenbach, Karl M. 1937. "The American Journal of Psychology: 1887–1937." *American Journal of Psychology* 50: 489–506.

Davenport, H. J. 1916. "Fetter's 'Economic Principles.'" *Journal of Political Economy* 24:313–62.

Day, A. M. 1901. "*The Theory of the Leisure Class* by Thorstein Veblen." *Political Science Quarterly* 16: 366–69.

Dewey, John N. 1887. "Professor Ladd's Elements of Physiological Psychology." *New Englander and Yale Review* 10: 207.

Dickinson, Z. Clark. 1919. "The Relations of Recent Psychological Developments to Economic Theory." *Quarterly Journal of Economics* 33: 377–421.

————. 1922. "The Psychology Course in Business Education." *Journal of Political Economy* 30:88–97.

————. 1924a. *Economic Motives.* Cambridge, Mass.: Harvard University Press.

————. 1924b. "Quantitative Methods in Psychological Economics." *American Economic Review* 14 (supplement): 117–26.

————. 1927. "Economics and Psychology." In *The Social Sciences and Their Interrelations*, edited by W. M. Ogburn and Alexander Goldenweiser. New York: Houghton Mifflin.

Donnelly, Margaret E., ed. 1992. *Reinterpreting the Legacy of William James.* Washington, D.C.: American Psychological Association.

Doob, Leonard. 1937. "Psychological Aspects of Consumers' Cooperation." *Annals of the American Academy of Political and Social Science* 191 (May): 46–54.

Doob, Leonard W., and Edward S. Robinson. 1935. "Psychology and Propaganda." *Annals of the American Academy of Political and Social Science* 179 (May): 88–95.

Dorfman, Joseph. 1934. *Thorstein Veblen and His America.* New York: Viking.

Douglas, Paul H. 1924. "The Reality of Non-Commercial Incentives in Economic Life." In Tugwell 1924, 153–88.

Downey, E. H. 1910. "The Futility of Marginal Utility." *Journal of Political Economy* 10: 253–68.

Dunlap, Knight. 1932. *Habits: Their Making and Unmaking.* New York: Liveright.

Eaton, Harry. 1934. "Human Elements in the Recovery Program." *Annals of the American Academy of Political and Social Science* 172 (March): 15–21.

Edie, Lionel D. 1925. *Review of Essays in Economic Theory*, by Simon N. Patten. *Political Science Quarterly* 40 (2): 302–4.

Edwards, Corwin D. 1934. "Marketing." *Annals of the American Academy of Political and Social Science* 173 (May): 86–92.

Ely, Richard T. 1900. "A Decade of Economic Theory." *Annals of the American Academy of Political and Social Science* 15 (March): 92–112.

Fay, C. R. 1925. *Co-operation at Home and Abroad.* London: P. S. King and Son.

Fay, Jay Wharton. 1939. *American Psychology before William James.* New Brunswick, N.J.: Rutgers University Press.

Fetter, Frank. 1919. "Discussion of Ogburn." *American Economic Review* 9: 306–8.

Florence, P. Sargent. 1925. *The Economics of Fatigue and Unrest.* London: George Allen and Unwin.

————. 1927. *Economics and Human Behavior: A Reply to Social Psychologists.* New York: Norton.

Frank, Lawrence K. 1924. "The Emancipation of Economics." *American Economic Review* 14: 17–38.

Fry, Roger. (1924) 1996. *The Artist and Psycho-analysis.* In *A Roger Fry Reader*, edited by Christopher Reed, 351–65. Chicago: University of Chicago Press.

Giddings, Franklin H. 1895a. "Sociology and the Abstract Sciences: The Origin of the Social Feelings." *Annals of the American Academy of Political and Social Science* 5 (March): 94–101.

————. 1895b. Review of *National Life and Character: A Forecast*, by Charles H. Pearson. *Political Science Quarterly* 10: 160–62.

Ginsberg, Morris. 1924. Review of *An Outline of Psychology*, by William McDougall. *Economica*, no. 11: 252.

————. 1925. Review of *Some Modern World Problems*, by William McDougall. *Economica*, no. 13: 98–100.

Giocoli, N. 2003. *Modeling Rational Agents: from Interwar Economics to Early Modern Game Theory*. Northampton, Mass.: Edward Elgar.

Goodwin, Craufurd D., ed. 1991. *Economics and National Security: A History of Their Interaction*. Durham, N.C.: Duke University Press.

————. 2014. *Walter Lippmann: Public Economist*. Cambridge, Mass.: Harvard University Press.

Guggenheim, Daniel. 1915. "Some Thoughts on Industrial Unrest." *Annals of the American Academy of Political and Social Science* 59 (May): 209–11.

Hadfield, J. A. 1923. *Psychology and Morals*. London: Methuen.

Hadley, Arthur T. 1889. Review of *The Consumption of Wealth*, by Simon N. Patten. *Political Science Quarterly* 4: 534–36.

————. 1892. Review of *The Theory of Dynamic Economics*, by Simon N. Patten. *Political Science Quarterly* 7: 562–63.

Hall, G. Stanley. 1924. *Life and Confessions of a Psychologist*. New York: D. Appleton.

Hall, G. Stanley, and E. B. Titchener. 1921. "The American Journal of Psychology." *American Journal of Psychology* 32: 1–4.

Hands, D. Wade. 2010. "Economics, Psychology, and the History of Consumer Choice Theory." *Cambridge Journal of Economics* 34: 633–48.

Hansen, Alvin H. 1920. "Thrift and Labor." *Annals of the American Academy of Political and Social Science* 87 (January): 44–49.

Hapgood, Norman. 1925. "Psychology of Education in Outlawing War." *Annals of the American Academy of Political and Social Science* 120 (July): 157–58.

Hess, Herbert W. 1924. "Selling Distribution and Its New Economics." *Annals of the American Academy of Political and Social Science* 115 (September): 1–7.

Hobson, J. A. 1937. "The Economics of Thorstein Veblen." *Political Science Quarterly* 52: 139–44.

Hopkins, Ernest Martin. 1916. "Democracy and Industry." *Annals of the American Academy of Political and Social Science* 65 (May): 56–67.

Hunter, Walter S. 1923. "Behaviorism and Psychology." *American Journal of Psychology* 34: 464–67.

Jastrow, Joseph, et al. 1890. "Psychology in American Colleges and Universities." *American Journal of Psychology* 3: 275–86.

Johnson, Alvin S. 1902. "Patten's Theory of Prosperity." *Political Science Quarterly* 17: 313–19.

Johnson, Joseph French. 1908. "The Crisis and Panic of 1907." *Political Science Quarterly* 23: 454–67.

Kingsbury, Forrest A. 1923. "Applying Psychology to Business." *Annals of the American Academy of Political and Social Science* 110 (November): 2–12.

Kitson, Harry Dexter. 1920. "Economic Implications in the Psychological Doctrine of Interest." *Journal of Political Economy* 28: 332–38.

Knight, Frank H. 1924. "The Limitations of Scientific Method in Economics." In Tugwell 1924, 229–67.

———. 1925a. "Economic Psychology and the Value Problem." *Quarterly Journal of Economics* 39: 372–409.

———. 1925b. "Fact and Metaphysics in Economic Psychology." *American Economic Review* 15: 247–66.

———. 1929. Review of *Economics and Human Behavior: A Reply to Social Psychologists*, by P. Sargent Florence. *Journal of Political Economy* 37: 363–64.

Kornhauser, Arthur W. 1923. "Scientific Method in Constructing Psychological Tests for Business." *Journal of Political Economy* 31: 401–32.

———. 1925. "Intelligence Test Ratings of Occupational Groups." *American Economic Review* 15 (supplement): 110–22.

Larson, John A. 1929. "Psychology in Criminal Investigation." *Annals of the American Academy of Political and Social Science* 146 (November): 258–68.

Le Bon, Gustave. 1913. *The Psychology of Revolution.* New York: Putnam.

Leuba, James H. 1909. Review of *An Introduction to Social Psychology*, by William McDougall. *American Journal of Psychology* 20: 285–89.

Lewin, Shira B. 1996. "Economics and Psychology: Lessons for Our Own Day from the Early Twentieth Century." *Journal of Economic Literature* 34 (3): 1293–323.

Lewisohn, Sam A. 1938. "Psychology in Economics." *Political Science Quarterly* 53: 233–38.

Lincoln, C. H. 1895. Review of *National Life and Character: A Forecast*, by Charles H. Pearson. *Annals of the American Academy of Political and Social Science* 5: 140–43.

Lindsay, Samuel McCune. 1900. Review of *The Theory of the Leisure Class*, by Thorstein Veblen. *Annals of the American Academy of Political and Social Science* 15: 138–42.

Link, Henry C. 1919. *Employment Psychology.* New York: Macmillan.

———. 1921. "Emotions and Instincts." *American Journal of Psychology* 32: 134–44.

———. 1922. "Instinct and Value." *American Journal of Psychology* 33: 1–18.

———. 1923. "Psychological Tests in Industry." *Annals of the American Academy of Political and Social Science* 110 (November): 32–44.

Lippmann, Walter. 1913. *A Preface to Politics.* New York: Mitchell Kennerley.

———. 1922. *Public Opinion.* New York: Harcourt Brace.

———. 1927. *The Phantom Public.* New York: Macmillan.

———. 1932. Letter to A. A. Brill, November 2, 1932, Walter Lippmann Papers, MS 326, Manuscripts and Archives, Yale University Library, III F294.

———. 1942. Letter to Frederick J. Hoffman, November 18, 1942, Walter Lippmann Papers, MS 326, Manuscripts and Archives, Yale University Library, III F1059.

Lucas, D. B., and C. E. Benson. 1930. *Psychology for Advertisers.* New York: Harper.

Luckey, G. W. A. 1895. "Review Essay on *Pleasure and Aesthetics* by Marshall et al." *American Journal of Psychology* 7: 108–23.

Marburg, Theodore. 1908. "The Panic and the Present Depression." *Annals of the American Academy of Political and Social Science* 32 (July): 55–62.

Marshall, Henry Rutgers. 1894. *Pain, Pleasure, and Aesthetics*. New York: Macmillan.

Marshall, Leon C. 1930. "The Changing Economic Order." *Annals of the American Academy of Political and Social Science* 147 (January): 1–11.

Mavor, J. 1894. "The Relation of Economic Study to Public and Private Charity." *Annals of the American Academy of Political and Social Science* 4 (July): 34–60.

Mayo, Elton. 1923. "The Irrational Factor in Human Behavior: The 'Night-Mind' in Industry." *Annals of the American Academy of Political and Social Science* 110 (November): 117–30.

McDougall, William. 1908. *An Introduction to Social Psychology*. London: Methuen.

———. 1923. *An Outline of Psychology*. London: Methuen.

———. 1924. *Ethics and Some Modern World Problems*. London: Putnam.

Meisel, Perry, and Walter Kendrick, eds. 1985. *Bloomsbury/Freud: The Letters of James and Alix Strachey, 1924–1925*. New York: Basic Books.

Miller, Karl G. 1923. "The Function of Psychology in the School of Business Administration." *Annals of the American Academy of Political and Social Science* 110 (November): 200–206.

Mitchell, Wesley C. 1910. "The Rationality of Economic Activity." *Journal of Political Economy* 18: 197–216.

———. 1914. "Human Behavior and Economics: A Survey of Recent Literature." *Quarterly Journal of Economics* 29: 1–47.

———. 1915. Letter to Walter Lippmann, February 16, 1915, Walter Lippmann Papers, MS 326, Manuscripts and Archives, Yale University Library, I F827.

———. 1918. "Bentham's Felicific Calculus." *Political Science Quarterly* 33: 161–83.

———. 1924. "The Prospects of Economics." In Tugwell 1924, 3–34.

———. 1937. *The Backward Art of Spending Money and Other Essays*. New York: McGraw-Hill.

———. 1969. *Types of Economic Theory*, edited by Joseph Dorfman. Vol. 2. New York: Augustus Kelley.

Moore, Herbert. 1939. *Psychology for Business and Industry*. New York: McGraw Hill.

Moore, V. F. 1899. "The Psychology of Hobbes and Its Sources." *American Journal of Psychology* 11: 49–66.

Munsterberg, Hugo. 1913. *Psychology and Industrial Efficiency*. London: Constable.

———. 1915. *Business Psychology*. Chicago: LaSalle Extension University.

Nunn, William N. 1938. "Revolution in the Idea of Thrift." *Annals of the American Academy of Political and Social Science* 196 (March): 52–56.

Nystrom, Paul H. 1940. "Education and Training for Marketing." *Annals of the American Academy of Political and Social Science* 209 (May): 158–64.

Ogburn, William F. 1919. "The Psychological Basis for the Economic Interpretation of History." *American Economic Review* 9 (supplement): 291–305.

———. 1920. "Psychological Bases for Increasing Production." *Annals of the American Academy of Political and Social Science* 90 (July): 83–87.

Ogden, R. M. 1933. "Gestalt Psychology and Behaviorism." *American Journal of Psychology* 45: 151–55.

Parker, Carleton H. 1918. "Motives in Economic Life." *American Economic Review* 8 (supplement): 212–31.

———. 1920. *The Casual Laborer and Other Essays*. New York: Harcourt, Brace and Howe.

Parker, Cornelia S. 1919. *An American Idyll*. Boston: Little Brown.

———. 1920. "The Human Element in the Machine Process." *Annals of the American Academy of Political and Social Science* 90 (July): 88–93.

Patten, Simon Nelson. 1888. Review of *The Present Condition of Economic Science*, by Edward Clark Lunt. *Political Science Quarterly* 3: 687–90.

———. 1892. "The Economic Causes of Moral Progress." *Annals of the American Academy of Political and Social Science* 3 (September): 129–49.

———. 1896. "The Relation of Sociology to Psychology." *Annals of the American Academy of Political and Social Science* 8 (November): 1–28.

———. 1924. *Essays in Economic Theory*, edited by Rexford G. Tugwell. New York: Knopf.

Pattie, Frank A. 1939. "William McDougall: 1871–1938." *American Journal of Psychology* 52: 303–7.

Pigou, A. C. 1903. "Some Remarks on Utility." *Economic Journal* 13: 58–68.

Poffenberger, Albert T. 1925. *Psychology in Advertising*. New York: A. W. Shaw.

Ricci, Umberto. 1932. "The Psychological Foundation of the Law of Demand." *Journal of Political Economy* 40: 145–85.

Richardson, Florence. 1920. Review of *The Casual Laborer and Other Essays*, by Carleton H. Parker. *Journal of Political Economy* 28: 622–24.

Roback, A. A. 1924. "A Supplement to 'Behaviorism and Psychology.'" *American Journal of Psychology* 35: 103–9.

Robertson, D. H. 1923. "Economic Psychology." *Economic Journal* 33: 178–84.

Rosenow, Curt. 1925. "The Problem of Meaning in Behaviorism." *American Journal of Psychology* 36: 233–48.

Rutherford, Malcolm. 2011. *The Institutionalist Movement in American Economics, 1918–1947*. Cambridge: Cambridge University Press.

Scott, Walter Dill. 1903. *The Theory of Advertising*. Boston: Small, Maynard.

———. 1908. *The Psychology of Advertising*. Boston: Small, Maynard.

Seager, Henry R. 1902. "Professor Patten's *Theory of Prosperity*." *Annals of the American Academy of Political and Social Science* 19 (March): 75–91.

Sherman, Mandel. 1930. "The Contribution of Psychiatry to Some Educational Problems." *Annals of the American Academy of Political and Social Science* 149 (May): 124–32.

Sherwood, Sidney. 1897. "The Philosophical Basis of Economics: A Word to the Sociologists." *Annals of the American Academy of Political and Social Science* 10 (September): 58–92.

Slichter, Sumner. 1924. "The Organization and Control of Economic Activity." In Tugwell 1924, 303–55.

Small, Albion W. 1895. "The Organic Concept of Society." *Annals of the American Academy of Political and Social Science* 5 (November): 88–94.

Smith, T. V. 1933. "The Voice of the People." *Annals of the American Academy of Political and Social Science* 169 (September): 101–9.

Snow, A. J. 1924. "Psychology in Economic Theory." *Journal of Political Economy* 32: 487–96.

———. 1925. *Psychology in Business Relations.* Chicago: A. W. Shaw.

Soule, George. 1924. "Economics—Science and Art." In Tugwell 1924, 359–67.

Speek, Peter Alexander. 1917. "The Psychology of Floating Workers." *Annals of the American Academy of Political and Social Science* 69 (January): 72–78.

Stamp, Josiah. 1927. *On Stimulus in the Economic Life.* Cambridge: Cambridge University Press.

Stevenson, John Alford. 1923. "Psychology in Salesmanship." *Annals of the American Academy of Political and Social Science* 110 (November): 144–55.

Stone, C. L. 1930. Review of *Psychology and Industrial Efficiency*, by Harold E. Burtt. *American Economic Review* 20: 506–7.

Straight, Dorothy. 1922. Letter to Walter Lippmann, November 21, 1922, Walter Lippmann Papers, MS 326, Manuscripts and Archives, Yale University, I F1166.

Strong, E. K. 1938. *Psychological Aspects of Business.* New York: McGraw-Hill.

Sutherland, Alexander. 1898. *The Origin and Growth of the Moral Instinct.* London: Longmans, Green.

Tannenbaum, Frank. 1920. "Labor Movement Psychology." *New Republic*, July 7, 169–72.

Tarde, G. 1902. *Psychologie economique.* Paris: Felix Alcan.

Taussig, Frank. 1915. *Inventors and Money-Makers.* New York: Macmillan.

Tead, Ordway. 1920. "The Problem of Incentives and Output." *Annals of the American Academy of Political and Social Science* 89 (May): 170–79.

———. 1930. "Trends in Industrial Psychology." *Annals of the American Academy of Political and Social Science* 149 (May): 110–19.

Tugwell, Rexford G. 1922. "Human Nature in Economic Theory." *Journal of Political Economy* 30: 317–45.

———. 1924. *The Trend of Economics.* New York: Knopf.

Twitmyer, Edwin B. 1924. "The Place of Human Sciences in Modern Organized Business." *Annals of the American Academy of Political and Social Science* 115 (September): 47–51.

Vanderlip, Frank A. 1908. "The Panic as a World Phenomenon." *Annals of the American Academy of Political and Social Science* 31 (March): 2–7.

Veblen, Thorstein. (1899) 1953. *The Theory of the Leisure Class.* New York: New American Library.

———. 1900. "The Preconceptions of Economic Science." *Quarterly Journal of Economics* 14: 240–69.

———. (1904) 1965. *The Theory of Business Enterprise.* New York: A. M. Kelley.

———. 1909. "The Limitations of Marginal Utility." *Journal of Political Economy* 17: 620–36.

————. 1914. *The Instinct of Workmanship and the State of the Industrial Arts*. New York: Macmillan.

————. 1917. *The Nature of Peace and the Terms of Its Perpetuation*. New York: Macmillan.

————. 1998. *Essays in Our Changing Order*. New Brunswick, N.J.: Transaction.

Viner, Jacob. 1925. "The Utility Concept in Value Theory and Its Critics." *Journal of Political Economy* 33: 369–87, 639–59.

Viteles, Morris. 1932. *Industrial Psychology*. New York: Norton.

Wallas, Graham. 1908. *Human Nature in Politics*. London: Constable.

————. 1914. *The Great Society: A Psychological Analysis*. London: Macmillan.

————. 1923. "Jeremy Bentham." *Political Science Quarterly* 38: 45–56.

Ward, Lester. 1893. "The Psychologic Basis of Social Economics." *Annals of the American Academy of Political and Social Science* 3 (January): 72–90.

Watson, J. B. 1913. "Psychology as the Behaviorist Views It." *Psychological Review* 20 (2): 158–77.

Whitaker, A. C. 1916. "Fetter's Principles of Economics." *Political Science Quarterly* 31: 430–44.

Williams, Katherine. 1931. "Five Behaviorisms." *American Journal of Psychology* 43: 337–60.

Williamson, Charles C. 1909. Review of *Human Nature in Politics*, by Graham Wallas. *Political Science Quarterly* 24: 696–701.

Wolfe, Albert B. 1924. "Functional Economics." In Tugwell 1924, 445–82.

Wolman, Leo. 1916. *The Boycott in American Trade Unions*. Baltimore: Johns Hopkins Press.

————. 1921. "The Theory of Production." *American Economic Review* 11: 37–56.

Wright, Helen R. 1922. Review of *Public Opinion*, by Walter Lippmann. *Journal of Political Economy* 30: 717–20.

Wright, H. W. 1937. "Social Significance." *American Journal of Psychology* 49: 49–57.

Young, Allyn, 1928. "English Political Economy." *Economica*, no. 22: 1–15.

Behaviorism and Control in the History of Economics and Psychology

José Edwards

There is a misunderstanding about the meaning of behaviorism in recent discussions on the history of economics and psychology. This essay explores that history by highlighting the role of "control" as understood by behaviorists and contrasting their views against those of economists. This exploration reveals that, rather than affecting consumer demand theory during the "ordinalist revolution" of the 1930s (i.e., what many economists think), behaviorism related to the early American institutionalism of Thorstein Veblen, Wesley Clair Mitchell, and John Maurice Clark, who strongly criticized the teleological aspect of that theory.

I make three claims about the history of economics and psychology. First, that behaviorism in psychology is mainly about "behavior control": that is, the idea that because behavior results from the interaction of an organism with its environment, it can be experimentally controlled so as to produce causal (i.e., "scientific") accounts of behavior. Second, that consumer demand theory has never been about "control," especially not in

Correspondence may be addressed to José Edwards, Escuela de Gobierno, Universidad Adolfo Ibáñez, at jose.edwards@uai.cl. This essay, having a long history, has benefited from comments by many people (the usual disclaimers apply): Neil De Marchi, Marina Bianchi, Ivan Moscati, Jeff Biddle, and Harro Maas (*HOPE* conference, 2015); Annie Cot (AEA-ASSA, 2015); Roy Weintraub, Erik Angner, and John Staddon (*HOPE* seminar, 2014); Philippe Fontaine, Ross Emmett, Tiago Mata, Marcel Boumans, Steven Medema, and Teresa Tomás Rangil (HIS-RECO, 2009); Wade Hands, Jérôme Lallement, and Richard Arena on different occasions; and two anonymous referees. Financial support for the last part of this project came from CONICYT (FONDECYT no. 11130072).

History of Political Economy 48 (annual suppl.) DOI 10.1215/00182702-3619262

Paul Samuelson's ordinalist approach, which economists (including some historians of economics) think was "behaviorist" (but was not). Third, that the concept of behavior control itself can be used as a viewpoint from which to analyze the history of economics and psychology.

By using behavior control as a viewpoint, my exploration offers a new way to look at the history of the two disciplines. Instead of studying whether psychology has remained "in" or "out" of economics—which is so far the standard approach—it interprets the two disciplines in terms of how each relates to the behaviorists' functionalist aim of controlling and predicting behavior at both the individual level (i.e., behavior control) and the social level (i.e., social control). In advancing this new approach this essay also contributes to the general theme of this volume, by briefly exploring early American institutionalism and recent behavioral economics as specific instances in which psychology and economics have met.

The following text is structured in four sections. Section 1 begins with a sample of economists' views on what behaviorism stands for. According to what appears in most standard narratives of the history of economics and psychology, consumer demand theory—especially that following Samuelson's revealed preference analysis—became "behaviorist" during the 1930s as it progressively rid itself of psychic elements such as preferences and marginal utilities. Scholars involved in advancing behavioral economics claim to be reacting to this so-called behaviorist turn by providing a theory of choice "with more psychologically plausible foundations" (Angner and Loewenstein 2012, 642).

Section 2 presents portions of the history of behaviorism as written by historians of psychology. These accounts present behaviorism as having emerged from American functional psychology and argue that its main aim was to control and predict behavior. This went beyond simply "observing behavior," which is what most economists think was the key notion in the so-called behaviorist turn of the 1930s. For behaviorists like John B. Watson and B. F. Skinner, behavior was always controlled, since it resulted from the interaction of an organism with its environment. Based on that premise, they developed behaviorism by claiming that manipulating environments could lead to shaping/controlling behavior of all sorts.

In section 3 I show that behaviorists experimented on behavior in ways that were fundamentally different from the economists' (ordinalist) project of deducing preferences and utility functions from observed choices. I use references to Percy Bridgman's operationalism by Samuelson, on the one hand, and Edward C. Tolman and B. F. Skinner, on the other, to illustrate that even methodologically speaking, Samuelson's ordinalist / revealed preferences program was far removed from behaviorism. In short, that Samuelson attempted to operationalize consumer demand theory does not imply that the theory became behaviorist. Despite attempts to operationalize/mathematize economics, neoclassical economists such as Samuelson continued to conceive of behavior as being essentially purposive (i.e., teleological) and based on "mentalist" concepts like utility and preferences. These economists fundamentally rejected epistemologies encompassing behavior control and, in so doing, rejected the core of behaviorism.

Section 4 uses behavior control as a viewpoint to analyze two episodes in the history of economics and psychology. It outlines how early American institutionalists, Veblen, Mitchell, and Clark in particular, related to both functionalism and behaviorism. I then briefly discuss the "nudge" thinking of Richard Thaler and Cass Sunstein, whose book with that title appeared in 2009. I argue that consumer demand theory (even by these self-designated "behavioral" economists) is still fundamentally at odds with the idea of explicitly conceiving of behavior as controlled. While options—for example, to participate or not in retirement savings schemes—may be presented in ways such that choice is made easier in one option (in this case, automatic enrollment) than its alternative (here actively opt out), there is still volition, and choices are made. The basic distinction between control (behaviorism) and choice (economics) is thus preserved.

1. A "Behaviorist Turn" in Economics?

A so-called behaviorist turn supposedly was taken in economics during the 1930s, according to economists interested in relating their field more closely to psychology. Prominent among this group are Richard Layard (2005), Luigino Bruni and Robert Sugden (2007), and Erik Angner and George Loewenstein (2012). These economists interpret that turn as a dark episode in the history of the two disciplines, for it discouraged the economic analysis of concepts like utility, happiness, and preferences. Behaviorism is also blamed for the fact that for decades "happiness" (self-reported by individuals) was not part of the agenda of mainstream economists.

In this section I explore the views of economists who wish for closer ties between economics and psychology, including those who welcome a resurgence of interest in happiness. I argue that these economists have mistaken notions about behaviorism and have created a sort of "behaviorist myth." I also stress connections between economics and psychology that are different from those acknowledged by recent advocates of behavioral economics. I introduce functionalism as an element with potential for generating more adequate histories of the interactions between the two disciplines—economics and psychology.

Psychology "in" and "out" of Economics

As hinted at already, there is a recent construction of the history of psychology and economics that pits adherents of standard consumer demand theory against behavioral economists who are critical of it. In that narrative (Hands 2010), the issue is whether psychology has remained "in" or "out" of economics. It begins by showing that psychology came into consumer demand theory during the so-called marginalist revolution of the 1870s, but was "driven out" during the subsequent ordinalist and revealed preferences developments (especially during the 1930s and 1940s). As noted above, behavioral economists now claim to be bringing psychology "back" into the analysis of consumer behavior.

According to a recent survey by Angner and Loewenstein (2012, 642), the readmitting of psychology began during the early 1980s, since behavioral economists increased the "explanatory and predictive power of economic theory" by giving it foundations "consistent with the best available psychology." That new literature, they claim, developed "in opposition to neoclassical economics, which was heavily influenced by behaviorism and associated doctrines, including verificationism and operationalism" (642).

A theme throughout my essay is that this partial interpretation is misleading. In telling their story about economics and psychology, Angner and Loewenstein argue that "before the emergence of behaviorism," psychologists such as William James were "comfortable with talking about mental states and other unobservables" as were "classical and early neoclassical economists," who "made frequent references to cognitive and affective states" (644). Angner and Loewenstein then show how this comfortable situation was upended by "the emergence of behaviorism marked by the appearance of Watson's article "Psychology as the Behaviorist Views It" (1913), which included an attack on relying too heavily on both introspection and mental states. Watson argued, first, that all scientific methods should be public (hence disallowing the use of, for example, introspection). Second, Watson asserted that a science of behavior should focus on behavior only, avoiding references to unobservables such as beliefs, desires, plans, and intentions (Gardner [1985] 1987, 11). Angner and Loewenstein (2012, 647) find these same ideas clearly present in the writings of post–World War I neoclassical economists as well.

There are also historical claims by economists to the effect that the rise of behaviorism was part of how neoclassical economics "escaped from" psychology (Giocoli 2003) or to how psychology was driven "out" (Hands 2010). It is not uncommon to find claims by economists that "postwar neoclassical economists wanted to gain distance from psychology of all kinds, objected to the tacit assumption that Economics should make reference to conscious states, and rejected the idea that introspection was a scientifically acceptable means to explore such states" (Angner and Loewenstein 2012, 647). Such narratives make no reference whatsoever to control, nor do they mention the connections between William James, functional psychology, and behaviorism.

"Behaviorism" as in the Standard (in/out) History of Economics and Psychology

This narrative about "behaviorism" has been written by economists who seldom look at the history of psychology. It appears chiefly (but not only) in surveys focused on behavioral economics, experimental economics, and related subfields. Representative references are Lewin 1996, Rabin 1998, Giocoli 2003, Asso and Fiorito 2004, Bruni 2004, Sent 2004, Layard 2005, Bruni and Sugden 2007, Caplin and Schotter 2010, and Angner and Loewenstein 2012. These authors tend to give quick reconstructions of the history of the two disciplines, economics and psychology. Particularly loose concerning psychology, their reconstructions give partial accounts of "introspection," "behaviorism," the "cognitive revolution," and other elements in that history while quite overlooking "functionalism," "control," and related topics. I partly restore the balance below.

Shira Lewin's (1996) survey exploring the "roots of today's disagreements" about economics and psychology contains a common version of the typical standard reference to "behaviorism" in the literature about the history of the two disciplines:

A behaviorist movement arose in economics, as theorists attempted to free economics of all psychological elements. This movement contributed to the replacement of the older theory of cardinal utility, with the new notion of ordinal preferences. Later, the theory of revealed preferences eliminated the need to interpret even ordinal preferences psychologically. Preferences were transformed from "metaphysical" entities into scientifically valid, truly empirical objects derived solely from behavior. (1295)

In this narrative, "the final step in the escape from psychology was completed by Samuelson's attempt to reconstruct consumer choice theory along completely behaviorist lines" (Hands 2010, 636).[1]

Behaviorism by Economists Using Subjective Outcomes

There is also a strand of the "escape from psychology" literature that characterizes as "behaviorism" the proposal that economists ought not use subjective outcomes from surveys.[2] This characterization, too, I suggest, is misleading, but it comes out in Angner and Lowenstein (2012, 649) as part of behavioristic "belief" that "the only valid method to collect information about preferences is to study market transactions or observable choices."

Economists using subjective outcomes also often invoke Amartya Sen, who noted at one point that "non-verbal behavior" may not be the only valid source of information about a person's preferences. Thus, in Sen (1973, 258), we read "that behavior is a major source of information on a person's preferences can hardly be doubted, but the belief that it is the only basis of surmising about people's preferences seems extremely questionable." Sen was criticizing the revealed preferences approach, but he also brought behaviorists into the debate about the use by some economists of surveys, as when he wrote:

> There is an old story about one behaviorist meeting another, and the first behaviorist asks the second: "I see you are very well. How am I?" The thrust of the revealed preference approach has been to undermine thinking as a method of self-knowledge and talking as a method of knowing about others. In this, I think, we have been prone, on the one hand, to overstate the difficulties of introspection and communication, and on the other, to underestimate the problems of studying preferences revealed by observed behavior. (258)

---

1. Another example is Asso and Fiorito's (2004, 465) view of the "Slutsky school" being a form of "behaviorist mainstream economics." For Frank Knight (1944, 289), they claim, the "diminishing 'coefficient of substitution' of one good for another" was a "purely behavioristic principle."

2. For an analysis of the history of the use of self-reports in economics, see Edwards 2012.

Applying the same kind of argument to the more general use of surveys, Richard Easterlin (2004, 21) identifies the "concept of behaviorism" as being the "typical" economist's attitude against the use of verbal statements: "The typical economist's view, encapsulated in the concept of 'behaviorism,' was put succinctly as follows by Victor Fuchs, president of the American Economic Association in 1995: 'Economists, as a rule, are not concerned with the internal thought processes of the decision maker or in the rationalizations that the decision maker offers to explain his or her behavior. Economists believe that what people *do* is more relevant than what they say.'" For Easterlin, the economists' predisposition against the use of subjective outcomes does not come from "uncertainty as to their robustness" but from the "disciplinary paradigm of behaviorism" (31).

Layard (2005) gives yet another warning about the difficulties faced by economists studying subjective outcomes. In *Happiness: Lessons from a New Science*,[3] he develops a peculiar account of the history of economics and psychology, mobilizing elements like "behaviorism," "William James," "J.B. Watson," "B.F. Skinner," and "happiness." Parts of Layard's story are reproduced below to give a final picture of what an economist's view of the history of the two disciplines may look like:

> The [GNP] concept was developed in the 1930s . . . . But very quickly it got hijacked to become a measure of national welfare, and nations now jostle for position in the national income stakes . . . . This hijacking was inevitable once economics had been captured by behaviorism in the 1930s. It is actually a rather sorry tale. In the late nineteenth century most English economists thought that economics was about happiness . . . . Their system was not fully operational, but it was a forward-looking agenda. It was also in tune with late nineteenth century psychology like that of William James, who was actively studying the strength of human feelings. Then psychology turned behaviorist. Along came John Watson and Ivan Pavlov (followed by Skinner), who argued that we can never know other people's feelings, and all we can do is to study their behavior. . . . So behaviorism became the intellectual climate, and in the 1930s it took over economics. This led to a much narrower concept of happiness. (133)

As pointed out earlier, this way of interpreting the history of interaction between economics and psychology is misleading. As in much of this lit-

---

3. For a historical/methodological analysis of the "economics of happiness," see Edwards 2010.

erature, Layard quickly connects "welfare," "behaviorism," "James," "Watson," and "Skinner," thereby giving a superficial account of how behaviorism affected economics (and psychology). The following text challenges that standard narrative by looking at the relationship between the two disciplines from a "behavior control" viewpoint. I show that behaviorism has been read by economists in ways that are inconsistent with what behaviorists themselves (and economists!) did, revealing so far overlooked aspects of the history of the two disciplines.

A "Behaviorist Myth"

Some of the authors involved in the above-mentioned discussion have identified (albeit not clarified) the peculiarity/complexity of the impact of behaviorism on economics. Sen, for instance, recognized that economics was never really influenced by behaviorism. He showed that the real interest of revealed preferences came from the "skillful use of the assumption that behavior reveals preference," which he identified as being different from what behaviorists did: explaining "behavior without reference to anything other than behavior" (Sen 1973, 258).

Along similar lines, Lewin (1996, 1307) pointed out that the relationship between economics and behaviorism was "far more complex" than usually understood. Noticing the "absurdity of behaviorist mainstream economics," Lewin showed how not even Samuelson (supposedly the most "behaviorist" among economists) followed what behaviorists were really doing:

> Behaviorist mainstream economics was doomed to fail, for the theoretical practice of "behaviorists" such as Samuelson contradicted their own professed methodological views. . . . if economists were to become behaviorists, they had to do so whole-heartedly and actually learn from the work of behaviorist psychologists. But even as they reformulated preference theory so as to make its behavioral implications more explicit, these mainstream economists nevertheless ignored the work of behaviorist psychologists. They continued to obtain their assumptions from introspection or a priori deduction, rather than looking to rigorous experimental results as their own behaviorist methodology indicated that they should. (1318)

More recently, authors such as D. Wade Hands (2010, 640) have written about how influential neoclassical economists like Lionel Robbins and Frank Knight realized that the "forward-looking notion of purposive

behavior" was "not susceptible of observation by purely behaviorist methods." These examples of deeper reading into the history of economics and
psychology suggest that there is an acknowledgment by those both knowl-
edgeable and sensitive to nuance that there is something not quite right
about what I called the myth among economists about the impact of behaviorism on their discipline.

From Functional Psychology to Early American
Institutionalism (and Behaviorism)

There is an interesting connection between economics and psychology in
the early institutionalism of Veblen, Mitchell, and Clark. As noted by
Angner and Loewenstein (2012, 652), these institutionalists were among
"the earliest and most vehement critics of ordinalist tendencies." While
ordinalists were attempting to rid economics of psychics, these institutionalists "believed that it would be a mistake for economists to ignore
psychology" (652). They criticized the teleological character of consumer
demand theory and claimed that economists should study "settled habits
of thought" (i.e., institutions) as they established in their "objective, imper-
sonal, materialistic character and force" (Veblen 1909, 625, 626).

Even though historical accounts like that of Angner and Loewenstein
acknowledge that there were connections between early American institutionalism and psychology, they tend to overlook the functionalist character of the psychology these institutionalists were looking at. Mitchell, for
instance, believed "that the incorporation of a more plausible psychology
would make for better economics" (Angner and Loewenstein 2012, 653).
As I show below, that more plausible psychology was functional psychology, which conceived of behavior as being controlled, rather than purely
resulting from self-interested purpose.

2. Importing Control to the History
of Economics and Psychology

Understanding the historical/academic context in which Watson wrote
"Psychology as the Behaviorist Views It" is essential to grasping the meaning of behavior control and its importance in behaviorism. Similarly, later
and more sophisticated versions, such as Tolman's "purposive" and Skinner's "radical" behaviorism, can be better understood if analyzed through
the problem of control in the history of psychology (and economics!).

This section then explores the connections between functionalism and behaviorism based on several writings by historians of psychology, including Edwin G. Boring (1950, 1961, 1964), Hamilton Cravens and John Burnham (1971), Kerry W. Buckley (1989), John A. Mills (1992, 1998), Christopher D. Green (1992, 2009), James H. Capshew (1993, 1999), Alexandra Rutherford (2003, 2006, 2009), and John Staddon (2014). Sections 3 and 4 relate this history to that of economics and psychology, to give support to the three main claims of the essay.[4]

Watson's Functionalism: From Animal
Psychology to Behaviorism

There is a consensus among historians of psychology that despite German influences, functionalism—the main force shaping American psychology—arose "not within psychology itself but within American society from about the 1880s onward" (Mills 1998, 2; Green 2009). Boring (1950, 551), one of the first and most prominent historians of psychology, explains how American functional psychology opposed the descriptive/structuralist aspect of German experimental psychology by the late nineteenth century:

> If influenced by your culture, you conclude that you should devote yourself to the description of nature, content to say *what* happens and *how* it happens, without asking the question why, then you are concerned with structure, are working in the descriptive tradition. . . . But if you ask *why*, if you try to understand causes, then you are interesting yourself in capabilities, in capacities, and are being a functionalist. It is as natural to be a functionalist as it is to want to predict, to be more interested in the future than in the past, to prefer to ride facing forward on the train. The future concerns you because you think you might change it if you have the ability. The past has gone by, lies there open to description but unalterable.

Trying to understand causes as well as wanting to predict and change the future were elements common to functionalist schools within American psychology. The first school was established at the University of Chicago

4. My grasp of the history of psychology is also based on writings by Edward Madden (1965), Lorraine Daston (1978), Mitchell Ash (1980), Ellen Herman (1995), David Hothersall (1995), Tim Rogers (1989), Uljana Feest (2005), George Mandler (2007), and Sarah Igo (2007), works that I consulted to avoid endorsing any specific view within that subfield. All these references to historians of psychology were also used to give balance to my history of the interactions between economics and psychology, a balance I find sadly lacking in the writings regarded as the standard narrative.

and had direct connections with English evolutionary theory (Green 2009). Functionalism was defined as the study of the adaptive role of mental animal life and behavior, and was also an "attempt to make psychology more appealing within the highly pragmatic American context" (Green 2009, 75).[5] The Chicago school included John Dewey (1859–1952), George Herbert Mead (1863–1931), Addison Webster Moore (1866–1930), and James Rowland Angell (1869–1949). Considering their connections with American pragmatism, it is not surprising that William James (1904, 1, 5) quite immediately acclaimed that new school: "Chicago has a School of Thought! . . . It coincides remarkably with the simultaneous movement in favor of 'pragmatism' or 'humanism.' . . . It probably has a great future, and is certainly something of which Americans may be proud."

The way in which historians of psychology consider behaviorism takes into account connections (via functionalism) between James, Dewey, Angell, and Watson (e.g., Boring 1950; Cravens and Burnham 1971; Mills 1998; and Green 2009) rather than just differences between James and Watson, which is what the economists' "in/out" narratives highlight (sec. 1). The Chicago school was key in the process leading to behaviorism, which was also a clear product of functionalism within psychology. Notably, Watson studied philosophy under Dewey and had Angell as a supervisor.[6]

According to Watson's 1913 article, "Psychology as the Behaviorist Views It," psychology should be based on the method of comparative (i.e., animal) functional psychologists, by performing experiments in which the "entire life history of [the] subjects [was] under careful control" (Cravens and Burnham 1971, 647). Watson "assumed that young animals had at their disposal a vast array of random movements and that habits emerged from that pool via a process of selection" (quoted in Mills 1998, 57). From there, he aimed at developing psychology into an "experimental branch of natural science," the main goal of which was precisely defined as "the prediction and control of behavior" (Watson 1913, 158).

The essence of Watson's approach was by no means equivalent to just focusing on (or passively observing) behavior, as told in the standard story of economics and psychology. Watson aimed at producing "the only consistent and logical functionalism" (167), which drew from the "observable fact that organisms, man and animal alike, do adjust themselves to their

5. Another department of functional psychology was settled at Columbia by James McKeen Cattel (1860–1944), Edward Lee Thorndike (1874–1949), and Robert Sessions Woodworth (1869–1962) (Boring 1950).

6. For an account of Watson's life, education, and career, see Buckley 1989.

environment by means of hereditary and habit equipments" (167). From there, he developed notions as to how psychologists should experiment on behavior:

> Some time ago I was called upon to make a study of certain species of birds. . . . to understand more thoroughly the relation between what was habit and what was heredity in [their behavior], I took the young birds and reared them. In this way I was able to study the order of appearance of hereditary adjustments and their complexity, and later the beginnings of habit formation. . . . if I had been called upon to work out the psychology of the educated European, my problem would have required several lifetimes. But in the one I have at my disposal I should have followed the same line of attack. . . . My final reason for this is to learn general and particular methods by which I may control behavior. (167)

More than just criticizing the use of introspection or the study of mental states (i.e., what economists think), Watson considered behaviorism important as a way to develop a useful/applicable form of psychology. By following Watson's behaviorist plan, "the educator, the physician, the jurist and the businessman could utilize" psychology in a "practical way," finding no more "need to complain" as they did at that time (168).

It is also interesting to realize that despite the title of Watson's 1913 paper, historians of psychology consider Watson's "published animal work" as showing "no trace of a behaviorist position" before 1917 (Mills 1998, 57). Cravens and Burnham (1971), for instance, draw a useful distinction between comparative psychology and behaviorism based on whether Watson's experimental findings (i.e., results from behavior control) were socially applied (i.e., social control exercised) or not.

Watson's "socially oriented and crudely speculative" behaviorism fully emerged only after his work on "the problem of human instincts in human infants" (Cravens and Burnham 1971, 646). Watson and John J. B. Morgan's (1917) "Emotional Reactions and Psychological Experimentation" is a clear example of that work. That study drew from the active "observation" of human infants (i.e., control) and aimed at investigating the emergence of emotional reactions like fear, rage, and love. It stated the whole experimental process in terms of "situation and response," thus giving it an impersonal/objective character:

> After observing a large number of infants, especially during the first months of life, we suggest the following group of emotional reactions as belonging to the original and fundamental nature of man: *fear, rage,*

and *love*. . . . We use these terms which are current in psychology with a good deal of hesitation. The reader is asked to find nothing in them which is not fully statable in terms of situation and response. Indeed we should be willing to call them original reaction states, X, Y, and Z. They are far more easily observed in animals than in infants. [. . .] our own observation of the first few months of infancy has not yielded any larger number. (Watson and Morgan 1917, 165)

It is of great importance to realize that the process by which Watson "observed" emotions was active experimentation on behavior rather than just "passive" observation. By behavior control, I mean that active way of "observing" behavior, as opposed to just passively describing things happening. It was through this process that Watson was able to study/control the emergence of emotional reactions such as rage: "An individual hampers my use of my arms and legs, constrains me, holds me badly when dressing me, etc. (original conditions for arousing rage)—shortly the mere sight of that individual arouses the rage components. Finally an entire stranger whose behavior is even slightly similar to that of the first individual may set off the responses" (169).

Watson and Morgan also developed behavior technologies by which emotions could be attached to "useful" behavior, thus allowing the transformation of psychology into a socially useful discipline (i.e., a means for social control).[7] Because emotions furnished the "drive" for activities, it would be helpful, they claimed, if behaviorists could find out how to "attach" them so as to serve useful ends like that of "helping individuals to form necessary but prosaic habits" (172). That early form of behaviorism declined abruptly, however, alongside Watson's academic career during the early 1920s. It remained just a distant precursor of the much more sophisticated and technical work of later behaviorists like Tolman and Skinner.[8]

Skinnerian Behaviorism

From the 1930s to the 1970s new behaviorists produced "highly sophisticated and, in some cases, comprehensive psychological theories" (Mills

7. Watson and Morgan (1917, 174) identified social control as already employed in practices like business, showing that "many drives have been hit upon in a practical way already," mainly by business houses, precisely through "threatening discharge (fear)," "ridicule (rage)," and "loyalty (love)."

8. In *The New Behaviorism* (2014), John Staddon gives a historical account of behaviorism, with an interesting focus on Watson's proposed aim of controlling and predicting behavior.

1998, 4). Of these, Skinner's were the most visible, as he vulgarized and applied his science to controversial subjects like baby care, infant teaching, and social philosophy.[9] As for the earlier behaviorists, for Skinner, behavior was strictly connected to the growth of habit structures that he conceived of as resulting from repeated stimulus-response-reinforcement chains.

In Skinner's terms, behavior was controlled/shaped by the "history of past reinforcements" encountered by an organism, and he thus claimed that desired forms of behavior could be produced through appropriate experiments.[10] Skinner's machine—the Skinner box—provided controlled environments in which the initially random behavior of animals under experiment (i.e., mainly hungry rats and pigeons) could be positively reinforced by giving them food through a mechanism (i.e., behavior control). Desired behavior could be obtained by applying positive reinforcements to originally random animal movements. That "operant conditioning" was documented in "behavior records," which were also provided by the Skinner boxes.

Skinner's (1938) system of behavior was thoroughly presented in *The Behavior of Organisms*,[11] and it was just shortly after (during and after World War II) that he became popular for applying his science to social subjects (i.e., applying behavior technologies to "social control"). However, the behavior technologies by which Skinner's science should serve society were widely debated and strongly criticized (A. Rutherford, 2000, 2003, 2009).[12] For Skinner, the negative reaction to his ideas proved the uneasiness with which government was viewed when attempting to control behavior by using positive reinforcements instead of punishments (quoted in Rogers and Skinner [1956] 1962, 17). Hostility against behaviorism, he claimed, revealed a generalized misunderstanding of concepts like volition and freedom. Because all "men control and are controlled,"

9. For an account of Skinner's life and work, see Rutherford 2009.

10. The history of past reinforcements was one of the main concepts advanced by Skinner. Because that history shaped behavior, Skinner proceeded by showing how seemingly cognitive behavior could be obtained after patient behavior control in a Skinner box. For Skinner, behavior was not free but guided/controlled by "one's history of past reinforcements" (see Mills 1998, 139).

11. For a description of Skinner's experimental method based on "operant behavior" and the use of "reinforcement schedules," see Staddon 2014, 38–43.

12. In 1945 Skinner produced an "Air-Crib" or "mechanical baby tender": a "labor-saving invention" designed for "the problem of the nursery" (Skinner [1945] 1999, 29), and in 1948 he spread his ideas to the general public in *Walden Two*, the first edition of his utopian novel about an experimental community. According to Capshew (1993, 836), that book represents the "first step in Skinner's public transformation from experimental psychologist to social philosopher."

for Skinner the question to ask was not how freedom should be preserved but "what kinds of control [were] to be used and to what ends" (17).

Freedom, or in Skinner's (1964, 483) terms behavior that "feels free," was *always* "the product of a history of conditioning." In *Beyond Freedom and Dignity* (a best seller) Skinner (1971, 42) showed that the main problem was "to free men, not from control, but from certain kinds of control."[13] He complained about the lack of progress of the science and technology of behavior compared with that of the natural sciences. A few years after, *Walden Two* (also a best seller, in 1976) showed how human behavior could be changed by changing its consequences through operant conditioning (i.e., by using positive reinforcements). For Skinner (1976, xvi, vii), "knowledge about human behavior and new ways of applying that knowledge to the design of cultural practices" was necessary to face social problems that had reached an "entirely new order of magnitude." Behavior technologies were thus proposed as efficient means to deal with, namely, "the exhaustion of resources, the pollution of the environment, overpopulation, and the possibility of a nuclear holocaust" (vii).

Sections 3 and 4 relate behaviorism, as described in this section, to the more general history of economics and psychology.

3. Were the Ordinalists Behaviorists?

No. This section shows that even by methodological standards, what economists proposed during the 1930s and 1940s was far removed from behaviorism. Many economists seem to think that the "ordinalist turn" was behaviorist mainly because of the economic (i.e., especially Samuelson's) references to Bridgman's operationalism (e.g., Hausman 1989; Lewin 1996; Hands 2001, 2004; Giocoli 2003; and Angner and Loewenstein 2012).[14] However, behaviorists like Tolman and Skinner applied Bridgman's methodology within programs that were fundamentally dif-

---

13. *Beyond Freedom and Dignity*, Skinner's "most widely debated" best seller (Rutherford 2006, 204), was "socially" rather than "scientifically" contested. His detractors did not argue against its "scientific validity" but against its "serious affront to traditional value systems" (A. Rutherford 2000, 385). According to Rutherford (2006, 218), that episode represents a "distinctly illustrative" example "of the processes through which psychological science and its products" are "shaped, regulated, and modified by the society in which they are embedded."

14. For accounts of the ordinalist turn taken by Irving Fisher, Vilfredo Pareto, Eugen E. Slutsky, John Hicks and Roy Allen, and Samuelson, see Lewin 1996, Giocoli 2003, Hands 2010, and their references. For an analysis of the influence of operationalism in economics, see Gordon 1955a, 1955b; Samuelson 1955; Machlup 1960; Seligman 1967; McCloskey 1983; Hausman 1989; and Cohen 1995.

ferent from that of Samuelson and his alleged "behaviorist mainstream economist" followers (those of the standard story—of, e.g., Lewin 1996—who do not really exist).

Samuelson's Operationalism, the Human Guinea Pig, and Gestalt Psychology

Bridgman's methodology was a reference for Samuelson as it was for behaviorists like Tolman and Skinner (Boring 1950; Green 1992; Mills 1992, 1998; Hands 2001, 2004). For Samuelson (1947), as for Bridgman, scientific propositions were operationally meaningful only if they could be tested through defined sets of operations. Similarly, economic concepts, like "preferences," could be defined by specific operations, thus rendering them operationally meaningful (Gordon 1955a, 1955b; Seligman 1967; Hands 2001).

In "Consumption Theory in Terms of Revealed Preferences" Samuelson (1948, 243) introduced a "human guinea-pig," which was intended to "reveal his preference pattern" by picking "different combinations of goods at different relative price situations." From there, Samuelson described a set of mathematical operations that defined an indifference curve, thus concluding that "the whole theory of a consumer's behavior" could be "based upon operationally meaningful foundations in terms of revealed preferences" (251).

Samuelson's operationalist-inspired project aimed at revealing a consumer's preference pattern through "theoretically observed" market behavior. However, Samuelson's experimental "animal" (i.e., the human guinea pig) was not trained, positively reinforced, or under any form of behavior control schedule (Samuelson never ran behaviorist experiments). Unlike Skinner's pigeons, the human guinea pig was just a concept (which was meaningless, operationally speaking) used by Samuelson (1948) as he, ironically, drew from Gestalt psychology (an approach very much opposed to behaviorism) to turn the "numerous little arrows" given by the guinea pig into indifference curves (figure 1).

In Samuelson's (1948, 245) terms:

> It is a well known observation of *Gestalt* psychology that the eye tends to discern smooth contour lines from such a representation, although strictly speaking, only a finite number of little line segments are depicted, and they do not for the most part run into each other. . . . There is an exact mathematical counterpart of this phenomenon in *Gestalt* psychology. . . . Later we shall verify that these solution curves are the conventional "indifference curves" of modern economic theory.

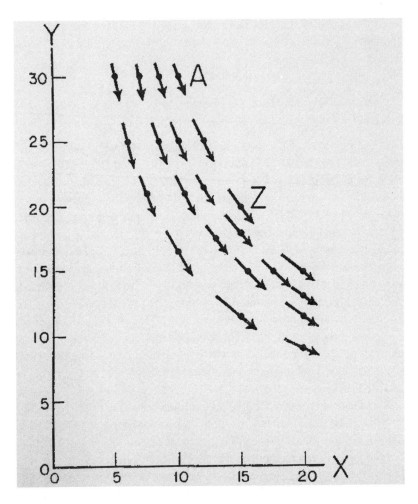

Figure 1. Revealed indifference curves. Source: Samuelson 1948, 244

Not only did that ordinalist / revealed preferences project fail to drop off "the last vestiges of the utility analysis" from consumer demand theory (Samuelson 1938, 62), but expected utility theory rehabilitated cardinal utility just shortly after Samuelson's (1948) revealed preferences paper (i.e., during the 1950s, as noted by Moscati, this volume). That rehabilitation happened within research programs, which were all as far removed from behaviorism as was Samuelson's, whose theory should have rather been labeled "*Gestalt* mainstream economics."

On Bridgman, the Pragmatic Tradition, and Functionalism

Bridgman-inspired approaches spread vigorously throughout the social sciences (i.e., beyond just economics and behaviorism). Among that diversity, Dewey's version is interesting, as his operationalism was "precisely the opposite of the message promoted by Samuelson in economics" (Hands 2004, 954).

Seeing the connection between Bridgman's approach and the pragmatic tradition, Hands (2004, 961) shows that, for Dewey, scientific operations were "directed and purposeful" and also "intelligent precisely because they serve[d] human designs": "The task of pragmatic reason is not to discover the essence or true nature of the objects of inquiry but rather to be successful in the active interaction with nature, and that success requires anticipation, deliberation, and intentional operations . . . . For Dewey 'the evidence' is not simply 'given' by nature; it is always interest laden and a product of active human operations" (960). By emphasizing "how diametrically opposed Dewey's version of operationalism" was to Samuelson's, Hands shows that "Dewey employed the concept of operations to give purpose and intentionality a legitimate role in scientific inquiry" (961).

As pointed out earlier in this essay (sec. 2), there are straightforward connections between Dewey's functionalism and Watson's behaviorism regarding their common pragmatic aim at controlling/predicting. It is thus surprising that authors like Hands group Samuelson together with behaviorists, since they were opposed to each other in such an essential aspect. By thinking that "precisely the same movement seemed to take place with respect to operational concepts" in both psychology and economics (Hands 2001, 68), one ends up seeing economics and behaviorism coming together during some sort of "operationalist turn" around the 1930s–1940s. For Hands, both Samuelson and the behaviorists produced just "theoretical redescription[s] of given empirical observations" so as to rid their science of "purpose and intention," which were not observable (Hands 2004, 961).[15]

15. Hands (2001, 2004) claims that "operational concepts ended up being used to defend and put a new scientific sheen on the traditional concepts" in both economics and psychology (see, e.g., Hands 2004, 958). That claim is based on the distinction of just two different uses of Bridgman's methodology: that of Dewey, who saw science "as something uniquely and enthusiastically human" (Hands 2004, 962), and the "project envisioned by Samuelson and various behaviorists within psychology" (961). This essay briefly presents two more uses of Bridgman's methodology, namely, Tolman's and Skinner's.

In the next subsection I show how, rather than working on "given empirical observations," behaviorists worked à la Dewey by actively producing behavior through different control methods.

From Purposive to Radical Behaviorism:
The Operationisms of Tolman and Skinner

Operationism (as opposed to operationalism) is the term used by historians of psychology to refer to Bridgman's approach transposed to psychology (e.g., Rogers 1989; Green 1992; Mills 1998; and Feest 2005). According to them, operationism began with Boring (the psychologist-historian who was not a behaviorist), S. S. Stevens, and also the behaviorists Tolman and Skinner (Green 1992). For behaviorists, operationism involved producing (i.e., not just observing!) causal accounts of behavior. To produce such accounts, they carefully controlled animal behavior under experimental settings. To understand behavior meant to give causal accounts leaving "no room for the action of forces lying outside the physical realm" (Mills 1998, 86). These behaviorists produced behavior in specific operational conditions by controlling all causal situations. Once "hidden" factors were controlled for, they studied the effects of manipulated (i.e., independent) variables on behavior (see Green 1992, 297–306). Controlling for (rather than neglecting) "hidden factors" was essential for matching predicted outcomes, which was what operationist-behaviorists aimed at. In line with Dewey's ideal, these behaviorists worked always with evidence that was the product of active human operations.

Tolman, arguably the least behaviorist among behaviorists, is nowadays considered a pioneer of cognitive psychology. His approach has been labeled "purposive behaviorism" or "cognitive behaviorism" (Kimble, Wertheimer, and White 1991), for his theory treated of purpose, also relating it to Gestalt psychology.[16] Methodologically speaking, Tolman's views drew from the New Realism studied at Harvard by E. B. Holt and R. B. Perry. Because one could not observe "raw purpose" but only "raw action" (Mills 1998, 95), Tolman's purposive behavior was produced and emerged only after animal training under control by the experimenter (i.e., behavior control). Tolman's instrument was the rat maze, and his observations were produced by running such animals through different kinds of mazes. He aimed at understanding "why rats turn the way they do, at a given

16. Tolman (1886–1959) received his PhD in psychology from Harvard University in 1915 and was introduced to Gestalt psychology while in Germany during his graduate training. After that, he spent most of his career at the University of California, Berkeley.

choice-point in a given maze at a given stage of learning" (Tolman 1938, 1), and in that process he developed the "cognitive map" concept. Finding that rats produced cognitive maps of mazes implied that the animals were able to learn maze configurations even in the absence of rewards (i.e., Tolman's "latent learning").[17]

In yet another Bridgman-inspired tradition, Skinner was operationist in the most radical way, as he used operations to eliminate "motivational states" (i.e., radical behaviorism). Skinner redefined "hidden factors" by introducing the concept of "drive," which was operationally defined. The drive "hunger," for example, was defined as the "reduction of an animal's body weight to 80% of the free-feeding level or placing the animal on a 231/2-hour feeding schedule" (Mills 1992, 76). Motivational states (like hunger) were thus replaced with operations that could be correlated with behavior, which Skinner produced as rates of bar-pressing or key-pecking in Skinner boxes.[18] Because they had precise control not only over the tasks performed by the animals but over all other relevant aspects of the history of their lives, radical behaviorists were well equipped so as to accurately predict the outcomes of their experiments (i.e., desired behavior).

Mills's (1998, 101–2) history of behaviorism gives an overall view of these operationist-inspired behaviorists who shared the common commitment of applying behavior technologies to social control: "Once operationism had reached its full development in psychology, a two-tiered differentiation of researchers was possible. On the one hand, there was a role for the Tolmans, whose primary interest was theoretical (but who were always aware of the possible practical applications of their work). On the other, we had those (especially Skinner and his followers) whose primary interest was in developing behaviorist-based social technologies. A commitment to social control linked the two tiers of behavioral science." The next section concludes by briefly using behavior control as a viewpoint from which to analyze parts of the history of economics and psychology.

4. Behavior Control as a New Viewpoint

It has been claimed throughout this essay that consumer demand theory has always been far removed from behaviorism. The main reason for that

17. Conceiving of cognitive maps reveals the influence from Gestalt psychology (Hothersall 1995) that made Tolman's approach distinct from that of radical behaviorists like Skinner.

18. For an exciting explanation of how Skinner developed the "Skinner box" after running rat maze experiments himself, see Staddon 2014.

is that economists conceive of behavior as being essentially purposive (i.e., teleological) rather than controlled (i.e., causally explainable). However, behavior control elements can be found both in the institutionalisms of Veblen, Mitchell, Clark, Lawrence Kelso Frank, and Morris A. Copeland, and in a few forms of behavioral economics—namely, that following Thaler and Sunstein's *Nudge* (2009). This last section briefly discusses these "unorthodox" economic views of behavior to show how different the history of economics and psychology looks when analyzed from this new viewpoint.

Institutionalism and the Backward Art of Spending

Accounting for "extravagant" (i.e., not rational/efficient) household behavior was one of the main features of the early institutionalism of Veblen (1898, 1899), Mitchell (1910, 1912, 1914), and Clark (1918). Although distinct, their views drew from the naturalist idea that the individual is an agent who acts "in response to stimuli afforded by the environment in which he lives" (Veblen 1898, 188). They conceived of man, as they did of other animal species, as a "creature of habit and propensity" (188) in line with what functional psychologists investigated at that time. These early institutionalists were critical toward the teleological aspect of what they labeled "neoclassical economics" or "mechanics of self-interest" (for an analysis of Veblen and Marshall, see Cook and Foresti, this volume). While Veblen analyzed human instincts, Mitchell (1910, 99) urged economists to stop their activity of "amateur psychologizing" and develop instead a "positive science of conduct" by relying "largely upon objective observation." Clark (1918, 4) called on economists to learn psychology from those who had "specialized in that field," who had already stopped thinking that "we sought things because they g[i]ve us pleasure" (8). Modern psychology, he claimed, considered wants as "molded by our environment" and referred to natural selection to explain how "the means of fulfilment existing had molded the desires of the race by determining which desires equip men for survival" (8). Based on this sort of literature, one can safely claim that (at least) these three economists were willing to bring their discipline closer to the "evolutionary natural history of mind," which was functionalism (Mitchell 1910, 100).

For Mitchell, in particular, neoclassical economics had strictly nothing to say about the "art of spending money" (i.e., consumer demand theory). Just like Veblen (also in Cook and Foresti, this volume), Mitchell (1910,

200) identified William McDougall's *Social Psychology* (1908) as the best available approach to explore household behavior:[19]

> The assumption of rationality fits the activities of consumption nowhere outside of economic treatises. Men, and more especially women, plan the spending of money upon personal satisfactions with far less attention that they give to their plans for the spending of money upon business ends. Passing whims, carelessness about prices, ignorance of qualities, obstinate preference for old ways are left wide scope. In McDougall's terms, habit, suggestibility, and the instincts of emulation and imitation must be brought in, if we are to account for our own subservience to fashion, our conspicuous waste, and our slovenly dependence on the advertiser. The assumption of rationality is inadequate to explain the facts.

Given his inclination for functionalism, it is not surprising that Mitchell followed instinct psychology in its transition into behaviorism (i.e., alongside Watson's transition, described earlier in this essay). A few years after proposing that economists study human behavior "by tracing the processes by which habits and institutions have grown out of instincts" (216), Mitchell (1925, 6) turned to promoting quantitative approaches that replicated the work of psychologists (i.e., behaviorists), who were "moving rapidly toward an objective conception and a quantitative treatment" of human behavior: "Their emphasis upon stimulus and response sequences, upon conditioned reflexes; their eager efforts to develop performance tests, their attempts to build up a technique of experiment, favor the spread of the conception that all of the social sciences have a common aim—the understanding of human behavior; a common method—the quantitative analysis of behavior records; and a common aspiration—to devise ways of experimenting upon behavior."

Mitchell was followed on this during the interwar period, especially by Frank (1923, 1924a, 1924b, 1925) and Copeland (1925, 1926, 1951), which gave rise to the short-lived form of "behaviorist institutionalism" (see Asso and Fiorito 2004; M. Rutherford 2000, 2002; and Edwards 2010). That institutionalism (which was never dominant) decayed by the end of the interwar period as it generated negative reactions within the broader institutionalist movement. Malcolm Rutherford (2000, 301) shows how differences within institutionalism were magnified by external circumstances

---

19. For an interesting debate between McDougall and Watson over functional psychology and behaviorism, see "The Battle of Behaviorism" (Watson and McDougall 1928).

like the Depression, the New Deal, and Keynesianism, knocking down what "had been at the very heart of interwar institutionalism."

This way of looking at the history of economics and psychology yields more than just pointing out that "institutionalists like Mitchell believed that the incorporation of a more plausible psychology would make for better economics" (Angner and Loewenstein 2012, 653). It reveals a long-lasting tension between teleological/free versus causal/controlled ideas about behavior in economics (see Hands 2010).

About Behavioral Economics and "Nudging"

Moving back toward the beginning of this essay (and at the same time forward to nowadays), I note that behavioral economists are not only motivated by bringing psychology "back" into economics but also interested in "how people's decision making can be improved" (Angner and Loewenstein 2012, 677). Behavioral economists have been showing for more than four decades how people fail to behave as predicted by standard demand theory. However, they now seem to take new directions by proposing "libertarian paternalism" as a way to "nudge" consumers toward desired behavior.

Unlike most other developments in behavioral economics (which more or less clearly relate to cognitive psychology), the approach initiated by Thaler and Sunstein's *Nudge* (2009) seems to renew behavior-control topics. As usually done by behavioral economists, *Nudge* uses elements "borrowed from psychology" to produce a theory, which in this case involves the concept of "choice architect": "If you indirectly influence the choices other people make, you are a choice architect" (Thaler and Sunstein 2009, 93). Choice architects are defined as those who nudge people into better or worse decision making (for Skinner, everyone did so). By assuming that there is no such thing as a "neutral" architecture for any context "in which people make decisions" (3), *nudgers* conceive of decision making as affected (controlled?) by rules and thus capable of being approached as early institutionalists believed. Translated into *Nudge* vocabulary, what these institutionalists sought was a scientific (i.e., cause and effect) analysis of how "choice architectures" emerge and evolve in time.

Like Skinner (but without mentioning him), *Nudge* also claims that "better governance requires less in the way of government coercion and constraint" and more of "incentives and nudges" (15). *Nudge* followers have perhaps found a way to reframe operant conditioning (i.e., the use of incentives as positive reinforcements) to make room for (veiled) control within the mainstream economist's toolbox.

This contribution to the history of economics and psychology has proposed alternatives to the standard narrative. Instead of considering psychology as being "in" or "out" of economics, it has focused on the relationship between the two disciplines from a behavior control viewpoint. It has claimed that there is a "behaviorist myth" among economists and revealed direct connections between American functionalism, behaviorism, and institutionalism, especially during the first half of the twentieth century.

References

Angner, E., and G. Loewenstein. 2012. "Behavioral Economics." In *Philosophy of Economics*, edited by U. Mäki, 641–89. Amsterdam: North Holland.

Ash, M. G. 1980. "Academic Politics in the History of Science: Experimental Psychology in Germany, 1879–1941." *Central European History* 13 (3): 255–86.

Asso, P. F., and L. Fiorito. 2004. "Human Nature and Economic Institutions: Instinct Psychology, Behaviorism, and the Development of American Institutionalism." *Journal of the History of Economic Thought* 26 (4): 445–77.

Boring, E. G. 1950. *A History of Experimental Psychology*. 2nd ed. New York: Appleton-Century-Crofts.

———. 1961. "The Beginning and Growth of Measurement in Psychology." *Isis* 52 (2): 238–57.

———. 1964. "The Trend toward Mechanism." *Proceedings of the American Philosophical Society* 108 (6): 451–54.

Bruni, L. 2004. "The 'Happiness Transformation Problem' in the Cambridge Tradition." *European Journal of the History of Economic Thought* 11 (3): 433–51.

Bruni, L., and R. Sugden. 2007. "The Road Not Taken: How Psychology Was Removed from Economics, and How It Might Be Brought Back." *Economic Journal* 117: 146–73.

Buckley, K. 1989. *Mechanical Man: John Broadus Watson and the Beginnings of Behaviorism*. New York: Guilford.

Caplin, A., and A. Schotter, eds. 2010. *The Foundations of Positive and Normative Economics: A Handbook*. Oxford: Oxford University Press.

Capshew, J. H. 1993. "Engineering Behavior: Project Pigeon, World War II, and the Conditioning of B. F. Skinner." *Technology and Culture* 34 (4): 835–57.

———. 1999. *Psychologists on the March: Science, Practice, and Professional Identity in America, 1929–1969*. Cambridge: Cambridge University Press.

Clark, J. M. 1918. "Economics and Modern Psychology: I." *Journal of Political Economy* 26 (1): 1–30.

Cohen, J. 1995. "Samuelson's Operationalist-Descriptivist Thesis." *Journal of Economic Methodology* 2 (1): 53–78.

Copeland, M. A. 1925. "Professor Knight on Psychology." *Quarterly Journal of Economics* 40 (1): 134–51.

———. 1926. "Desire, Choice, and Purpose from a Natural-Evolutionary Standpoint." *Psychological Review* 33 (4): 245–67.

———. 1951. "Institutional Economics and Model Analysis." *American Economic Review* 41 (2): 56–65.

Cravens, Hamilton, and John C. Burnham. 1971. "Psychology and Evolutionary Naturalism in American Thought, 1890–1940." *American Quarterly* 23 (5): 635–57.

Daston, L. J. 1978. "British Responses to Psycho-Physiology: 1860–1900." *Isis* 69: 192–208.

Easterlin, R. A. 2004. *The Reluctant Economist: Perspectives on Economics, Economic History, and Demography.* Cambridge: Cambridge University Press.

Edwards, J. M. 2010. "Joyful Economists: Remarks on the History of Economics and Psychology from the Happiness Studies Perspective." *Journal of the History of Economic Thought* 32 (4): 611–13.

———. 2012. "The History of the Use of Self-Reports and the Methodology of Economics." *Journal of Economic Methodology* 19 (4): 357–74.

Feest, U. 2005. "Operationism in Psychology: What the Debate Is About, What the Debate Should Be About." *Journal of the History of the Behavioral Sciences* 41 (2): 131–49.

Frank, L. K. 1923. "A Theory of Business Cycles." *Quarterly Journal of Economics* 37 (4): 625–42.

———. 1924a. "The Development of Science." *Journal of Philosophy* 21 (1): 5–25.

———. 1924b. "The Emancipation of Economics." *American Economic Review* 14 (1): 17–38.

———. 1925. "Social Problems." *American Journal of Sociology* 30 (4): 462–73.

Gardner, H. (1985) 1987. *The Mind's New Science: A History of the Cognitive Revolution.* New York: Basic Books.

Giocoli, N. 2003. "Modeling Rational Agents: From Interwar Economics to Early Modern Game Theory." Northampton, Mass.: Edward Elgar.

Gordon, D. F. 1955a. "Operational Propositions in Economic Theory." *Journal of Political Economy* 63 (2): 150–61.

———. 1955b. "Professor Samuelson on Operationalism in Economic Theory." *Quarterly Journal of Economics* 69 (2): 305–10.

Green, C. D. 1992. "Of Immortal Mythological Beasts Operationism in Psychology." *Theory and Psychology* 2 (3): 291–320.

———. 2009. "Darwinian Theory, Functionalism, and the First American Psychological Revolution." *American Psychologist* 64 (2): 75–83.

Hands, D. W. 2001. "Reflection without Rules: Economic Methodology and Contemporary Science Theory." Cambridge: Cambridge University Press.

———. 2004. "On Operationalisms and Economics." *Journal of Economic Issues* 38 (4): 953–68.

———. 2010. "Economics, Psychology, and the History of Consumer Choice Theory." *Cambridge Journal of Economics* 34 (4): 633–48.

Hausman, D. M. 1989. "Economic Methodology in a Nutshell." *Journal of Economic Perspectives* 3 (2): 115–27.

Herman, E. 1995. "The Romance of American Psychology: Political Culture in the Age of Experts, 1940–1970." Berkeley: University of California Press.

Hothersall, D. 1995. *History of Psychology*. 3rd ed. New York: McGraw-Hill.

Igo, S. E. 2007. *The Averaged American: Surveys, Citizens, and the Making of a Mass Public*. Cambridge, Mass.: Harvard University Press.

James, W. 1890. *The Principles of Psychology*. New York: H. Holt.

James, W. 1904. "Does 'Consciousness' Exist?" *Journal of Philosophy, Psychology, and Scientific Methods* 1 (18): 477–91.

Kimble, G. A., M. Wertheimer, and C. White. 1991. *Portraits of Pioneers in Psychology*. Edited by American Psychological Association, Washington, D.C.: American Psychological Association.

Knight, F. H. 1944. "Realism and Relevance in the Theory of Demand." *Journal of Political Economy* 52 (4): 289–318.

Layard, P. R. G. 2005. *Happiness: Lessons from a New Science*. New York: Penguin.

Lewin, S. B. 1996. "Economics and Psychology: Lessons for Our Own Day from the Early Twentieth Century." *Journal of Economic Literature* 34 (3): 1293–323.

Machlup, F. 1960. "Operational Concepts and Mental Constructs in Model and Theory Formation." *Giornale Degli Economisti e Annali Di Economia* 19 (9–10): 553–82.

Madden, Edward H. 1965. "E. G. Boring's Philosophy of Science." *Philosophy of Science* 32 (2): 194–201.

Mäki, U., ed. 2012. *Philosophy of Economics*. Amsterdam: North Holland.

Mandler, G. 2007. *A History of Modern Experimental Psychology: From James and Wundt to Cognitive Science*. Cambridge, Mass.: MIT Press.

McCloskey, D. N. 1983. "The Rhetoric of Economics." *Journal of Economic Literature* 21 (2): 481–517.

McDougall, W. 1908. *An Introduction to Social Psychology*. London: Methuen.

Mills, J. A. 1992. "Operationism, Scientism, and the Rhetoric of Power." In *Positivism in Psychology*, edited by C. W. Tolman, 67–82. New York: Springer.

———. 1998. *Control: A History of Behavioral Psychology*. New York: New York University Press.

Mitchell, W. C. 1910. "The Rationality of Economic Activity." *Journal of Political Economy* 18 (3): 97–113.

———. 1912. "The Backward Art of Spending Money." *American Economic Review* 2 (2): 269–81.

———. 1914. "Human Behavior and Economics: A Survey of Recent Literature." *Quarterly Journal of Economics* 29 (1): 1–47.

———. 1925. "Quantitative Analysis in Economic Theory." *American Economic Review* 15 (1): 1–12.

Rabin, M. 1998. "Psychology and Economics." *Journal of Economic Literature* 36 (1): 11–46.

Rogers, C., and B. F. Skinner. (1956) 1962. "Some Issues concerning the Control of Human Behavior." *Pastoral Psychology* 13 (8): 12–40.

Rogers, T. B. 1989. "Operationism in Psychology: A Discussion of Contextual Antecedents and an Historical Interpretation of Its Longevity." *Journal of the History of the Behavioral Sciences* 25 (2): 139–53.

Rutherford, A. 2000. "Radical Behaviorism and Psychology's Public: B. F. Skinner in the Popular Press, 1934–1990." *History of Psychology* 3 (4): 371–95.

———. 2003. "B. F. Skinner's Technology of Behavior in American Life: From Consumer Culture to Counterculture." *Journal of the History of the Behavioral Sciences* 39 (1): 1–23.

———. 2006. "The Social Control of Behavior Control: Behavior Modification, Individual Rights, and Research Ethics in America, 1971–1979." *Journal of the History of the Behavioral Sciences* 42 (3): 203–20.

———. 2009. *Beyond the Box: B. F. Skinner's Technology of Behavior from Laboratory to Life, 1950s–1970s*. Toronto: University of Toronto Press.

Rutherford, M. 2000. "Institutionalism between the Wars." *Journal of Economic Issues* 34 (2): 291–303.

———. 2002. "Morris A. Copeland: A Case Study in the History of Institutional Economics." *Journal of the History of Economic Thought* 24 (3): 261–90.

Samuelson, P. 1938. "A Note on the Pure Theory of Consumer's Behaviour." *Economica* 5 (17): 61–71; 5 (19): 353–54.

———. 1947. *Foundations of Economic Analysis*. Cambridge, Mass.: Harvard University Press.

———. 1948. "Consumption Theory in Terms of Revealed Preference." *Economica* 15 (60): 243–53.

———. 1955. "Professor Samuelson on Operationalism in Economic Theory: Comment." *Quarterly Journal of Economics* 69 (2): 310–14.

Seligman, B. B. 1967. "On the Question of Operationalism." *American Economic Review* 57 (1): 146–61.

Sen, A. 1973. "Behaviour and the Concept of Preference." *Economica* 40 (159): 241–59.

Sent, E.-M. 2004. "Behavioral Economics: How Psychology Made Its (Limited) Way Back into Economics." *History of Political Economy* 36 (4): 735–60.

Skinner, B. F. 1938. "The Behavior of Organisms: An Experimental Analysis." New York: D. Appleton-Century.

———. (1945) 1999. "Baby in a Box." In *The Blackwell Reader in Developmental Psychology*, edited by Alan Slater and Darwin Muir, 27–34. Oxford: Blackwell.

———. 1964. "Man." *Proceedings of the American Philosophical Society* 108 (6): 482–85.

———. 1971. *Beyond Freedom and Dignity*. New York: Knopf.

———. 1976. *Walden Two*. New York: Macmillan.

Staddon, J. 2014. *The New Behaviorism*. New York: Psychology Press.

Thaler, R. H., and C. R. Sunstein. 2003. "Libertarian Paternalism." *American Economic Review* 93 (2): 175–79.

———. 2009. *Nudge: Improving Decisions about Health, Wealth, and Happiness*. Rev. ed. New York: Penguin Books.

Tolman, C. W. 1938. "The Determiners of Behavior at a Choice Point." *Psychological Review* 45 (1): 1–41.

Veblen, T. 1898. "The Instinct of Workmanship and the Irksomeness of Labor." *American Journal of Sociology* 4 (2): 187–201.

———. 1899. *The Theory of the Leisure Class: An Economic Study in the Evolution of Institutions.* New York: Macmillan.

———. 1909. "The Limitations of Marginal Utility." *Journal of Political Economy* 17 (9): 620–36.

Watson, J. B. 1913. "Psychology as the Behaviorist Views It." *Psychological Review* 20 (2): 158–77.

Watson, J. B., and J. J. B. Morgan. 1917. "Emotional Reactions and Psychological Experimentation." *American Journal of Psychology* 28 (2): 163–74.

Watson, J. B., and W. McDougall. 1928. "The Battle of Behaviorism, an Exposition and an Exposure." London: K. Paul, Trench, Trubner.

Implementation Rationality: The Nexus of Psychology and Economics at the RAND Logistics Systems Laboratory, 1956–1966

Judy L. Klein

How do you translate the broad findings of normative microeconomics into detailed, implementable procedures for operations in a system? How do you get individuals or smaller organizational units that have been maximizing their own self-interests to act together as a rational organism? How do you convince managers to forsake customary rules of thumb and implement optimal decision rules derived by economists? How do you get economists designing those optimal rules to economize on their time and thought and, if necessary, make do with less-than-perfect rules of action that are good enough? One way to approach these questions is to pair experimental psychologists with thinking-at-the-margin economists. You underwrite the costly pairing with a considerable US Air Force war chest. You give license to the blurring of observing, designing, and controlling a system. You cultivate adaptation in the modeler and the subjects of the model. For over a decade, the RAND Logis-

Correspondence may be addressed to Judy L. Klein, Department of Economics, Mary Baldwin College, Staunton, VA 24401; e-mail: jklein@marybaldwin.edu. I am grateful for research support from the Institute for New Economic Thinking (grant number IN011-00054) and for the permission from the Institute for Operations Research and the Management Sciences to reproduce the image in figure 1. An earlier version of this article was discussed at the April 2015 *History of Political Economy* conference, "Economizing Mind, 1870–2015: When Economics and Psychology Met . . . or Didn't." I appreciated comments from participants at that conference and an anonymous referee for the *History of Political Economy*.

History of Political Economy 48 (annual suppl.) DOI 10.1215/00182702-3619274

tics Systems Laboratory's gamelike simulations with Air Force personnel fostered these conditions.

In 1946 the US Air Force funded the Project for Research and Development (RAND) at Santa Monica, California. It did so in hopes of continuing the cooperation the US military had initiated with the civilian scientific community in World War II. In the early 1950s economists at the RAND logistics department were doing what they called "classical" analytical studies to improve efficiency and reduce costs of Air Force logistics system functions. Military logistics involves procuring, maintaining, and distributing people, parts, and mechanisms of warfare. Most of the early RAND studies drew on normative microeconomics, including working on probability distributions for demand for parts, quantifying marginal costs and marginal military worth, and deriving optimal decision rules. This was an exemplary demonstration of Thomas Schelling's (1960, 4) assertion that during the Cold War, military think tanks hired economists to "practice the science of economizing." RAND economists and Air Force staff were often dissatisfied, however, with resistance to implementing the fruits of logistics research in such areas as optimal inventory control.

Normative economics focuses on what ought to be. It is usually framed in an indicative mood—the analysis only *indicates* the best choice outcome. Rarely does prescriptive economics follow through in an imperative mood to articulate or control a process for achieving that outcome.[1] The resistance of Air Force personnel to implementation of optimal decision rules led RAND economists such as Murray Geisler to seek insight from RAND experimental psychologists. In October 1956, RAND established the Logistics Systems Laboratory (LSL) to use simulation to "bridge the gap between research and implementation" (Geisler 1959, 360). At the LSL, marginal analysis that focused on rational choice outcomes was interwoven with the psychologists' focus on process, adaptation, and group behavior. This nexus generated persuasive evidence of the superiority of economizing protocols as well as data-reporting and rule-based implementation systems necessary to implement these protocols. Simulation also took the economists to complex problem-solving realms

1. The contrast of moods is drawn from Norbert Wiener's use of the terms. In clarifying his concept of cybernetics in control engineering, Wiener (1953) argued that outgoing messages could be in the indicative mood, with the aim of exploring the universe, or in the imperative mood, with the intention of controlling the universe.

off-limits to their mathematical equations. That journey often led to what Herbert Simon would call satisficing: the adaptation, in the face of bounded rationality, of optimal to good-enough decision rules.[2]

Simon's military-funded work on bounded rationality had led him to distinguish between "substantive rationality" and "procedural rationality."[3] In Simon's framework, substantive rationality was the achievement of the best outcome given an optimizing goal. Examples include the rational consumer achieving maximum utility or the rational producer achieving maximum profits. Procedural rationality was the process of adapting the original optimizing ends and means to take into account information-gathering and processing costs, by, for example, changing the model in an effort to minimize the use of limited computational resources. Simon perceived consumers, producers, and economizing mathematical model builders as organisms with limited computational capacity. He asserted that economists should learn from psychologists as well as from their own discipline's experience with normative operations research and focus more on the process of how decisions are made.

This history of the Logistics Systems Laboratory introduces the concept of implementation rationality, characterized by the attempt to maximize the speed and scope of implementation of optimal decision rules. The rationalization of the implementation process includes observing inconsistencies in and resistances to the attempted application of optimal theory, feeding back critical observations to the individuals and system designers, training the users to be more system-rational, and tweaking the rules of behavior that could discipline the individuals to be more system-rational.

This case study of the attempted mapping from the optimal to the operational illustrates the advantages of economists focusing on iterative modeling that includes human interactions. This history is also a thorny take on the microfoundations of a macro approach. One concern in this his-

2. Simon (2000, 26), channeling Voltaire, described the dilemma with "the best is the enemy of the good" or "optimizing is the enemy of satisficing." Although Simon was the one to name and leverage the concepts of satisficing, bounded rationality, and procedural rationality, it was all around him in want-to-be-optimizing economists working for a military client who required rules of action amenable to computation and implementation.

3. See, e.g., Simon 1973, 1974, and 1976. In his 1964 essay "Rationality," Simon contrasted two types of rationality, the economist's "attribute of an action selected by a choice process" and the psychologist's "processes of choice that employ the intellectual faculty" (574). It was not until 1973, however, that Simon explicitly used the phrases "substantial rationality" and "procedural rationality." After that, he used the terms frequently in economic articles (see, e.g., Simon 1978a, 1978b, 1979).

torical case study is with how economics leveraged psychology to grow a regulatory system when individual units pursuing their own interests did not promote the interests of society. This dilemma was one of a few stimuli generating a new focal point for rationality, that of efficient implementation. As with procedural rationality, this new focus prompted modeled optimization at the level of outcomes to evolve through an adaptive process. This in turn can lead to optimization at the level of the individual being purposely bounded to give priority to a best or good-enough outcome for the system.

This history of the Logistics Systems Laboratory starts with Geisler's work on optimization with George Dantzig in the Air Force Project for the Scientific Computation of Optimum Programs (Project SCOOP) in the late 1940s. The narrative proceeds to his use of classical economics at the RAND Logistics Department in the early 1950s. As Geisler was applying cost-benefit analysis, the RAND experimental psychologists were starting to use what they called "man-machine" simulations at the Systems Research Laboratory (SRL). Beginning in 1956, psychologists from the SRL and economists from the logistics department joined forces to work on several major Air Force optimization problems at the LSL.

Project SCOOP

Geisler started off his career in military research by doing simulations with mathematical equation structures. Armed with a master's degree in economics and statistics from Columbia University, Geisler joined Project SCOOP at the US Pentagon in Washington, D.C., in February 1948. In his directive to all echelons of the Air Force, General Hoyt Vandenberg gave a general indication of the Project SCOOP method envisioned to design military programs. Programming in this context meant planning rules of contingent action and resource allocation to support that action: "The basic principle of SCOOP is the simulation of Air Force operations by large sets of simultaneous equations. These systems of equations are designated as 'mathematical models' of operations. To develop these models, it will be necessary to determine in advance the structure of the relationships between each activity and every other activity. It will also be necessary to specify quantitatively the coefficients which enter into all of these relationships" (Vandenberg 1948, 1).

Project SCOOP was engaged in mechanizing the planning of USAF operations using the latest computer technology. In the late 1940s and first few years of the 1950s, a triumvirate guided the project: Dantzig, chief mathematician; Marshall Wood, chief economist and head of the Planning Research Division; and Geisler, head of the division's Standard Evaluation Branch. Dantzig was instrumental in developing the linear programming framework consisting of an optimizing objective function maximizing gain or minimizing pain, a Leontief-inspired input-output model indicating technological relationships, resource constraints in the form of linear inequalities, and the simplex algorithm that leveraged the constraints to get convergence to an optimal solution. The Project SCOOP team and its allies in the Air Force had great hopes that with electronic digital computers a near full-mechanization of operational planning could be achieved through computing optimal decision rules derived from linear programming.

Project SCOOP's first major mathematical simulation of a military operation was that of Operation Vittles, the US contribution to the airlift to aid Allied occupying troops and German civilians in the western sectors of Berlin during the Soviet blockade from June 23, 1948, to May 12, 1949.[4] The planning team used a model that included an objective function maximizing the tonnage of coal and vittles delivered to Berlin, subject to the resource constraints related to aircraft, trained crews, airfield runways, and budgets. The hope was that linear programming could lead to decision rules that acknowledged trade-offs such as the fact that the opportunity cost of delivering more food today was forgoing the delivery of equipment to construct more runways that would have led to a higher food delivery rate three months in the future. The US Air Force's electromechanical punched-card calculators, however, could not solve the multiplications connected with the large input-output rectangular matrix of the linear programming model of Operation Vittles.

Digital computers to solve large USAF linear programs would not be available until the installation of a UNIVAC computer in 1952. Even a UNIVAC, however, could not do the matrix procedures on the scale that Project SCOOP had envisioned for the programming of Air Force mobilizations with a planned input-output matrix of the entire US wartime or peacetime economy. Given limited computational resources, the SCOOP team programmed Operation Vittles and other larger military operations using a suboptimal triangular model that encompassed smaller optimizing rectangular matrices that could be computed.

---

4. The history of Project SCOOP and details of programming Operation Vittles is documented in the chapter on the bounded rationality of Cold War operations research in Erickson et al. 2013, 51–80.

Although the triangular model turned out to be a satisfactory procedural solution to limited computational resources, Project SCOOP was unable to fully combat resistance to the implementation of integrated planning, centralized control of information flows, and decision rules as suggested by optimizing economists and mathematicians. Reflecting on Project SCOOP, Geisler (1986, 11) remarked that "we learned a lot about the difficulties of introducing a new system and learned how far people might go to avoid change. We also learned how close the researchers had to be to the implementation process to be sure the technical procedure was being followed." In his next career move to RAND, Geisler would confront the issue of resistance to implementation head-on.

The RAND Logistics Department

James Huston (1966) and other military historians have described logistics as "military economics" or "the economics of warfare." A key dilemma facing US military logistics during the Cold War was to be ready for a potentially catastrophic Soviet nuclear strike with little advance notice. Such a strike had to be prevented with a credible threat of a swift and bold contingent counterstrike. These needs for readiness and for prepared, overwhelming force were countered by the need to cut defense budgets to ameliorate pent-up postwar demand for a private, peacetime economy to flourish. In this context, logistics resource allocation became one of the three key branches of military-inspired mathematical decision theory along with strategy and tactics. In 1953 the RAND Corporation established a logistics research program at the request of the US Air Force. Appropriately, it was housed in the Economics Division and staffed mainly by economists.

Geisler left Project SCOOP and joined the newly formed RAND logistics department in February 1954. His traditional economic approach to research on cost-effectiveness is best illustrated by his work with other RAND economists on "flyaway kits" for the bombers in the Strategic Air Command (SAC). These were war-readiness kits of spare parts that in the event of expected combat would have to be flown to bases overseas. The mathematical decision problem was to design these kits to minimize stockouts (depleted inventory) of parts likely to ground the bomber, subject to a given kit weight. The team of economists working on this problem determined empirically that a Poisson probability distribution was a good fit for modeling demand for the high-priced spare parts (see, e.g., Brown and Geisler 1954). This enabled the research team to compute the

Table 1 Hypothetical example of a Marginal Protection flyaway kit

Rank	Marginal Protection	Part and Unit	Unit Weight	Total Weight
1	2.827	D-1	0.1	0.1
2	1.264	A-1	0.5	0.6
3	.528	A-2	0.5	1.1
4	.451	D-2	0.1	1.2
5	.160	A-3	0.5	1.7
6	.142	C-1	2.0	3.7
7	.126	B-1	5.0	8.7
8	.053	B-2	5.0	13.7
9	.050	D-3	0.1	13.8
10	.038	A-4	0.5	14.3
11	.023	C-2	2.0	16.3
12	.016	B-3	5.0	21.3
13	.008	Z-5	0.5	21.8
14	.004	B-4	5.0	26.8
15	.004	D-4	0.1	26.9
16	.003	C-3	2.0	28.9
17	.002	A-6	0.5	29.4
18	.001	B-5	5.0	34.4

Source: Karr, Geisler, and Brown 1955, 24.

"marginal protection" of each additional unit of a line item part per one-pound weight. They then sorted the calculated marginal protections from highest to lowest value. At each rank in the descending marginal protection list, the economists calculated the cumulative weight of that extra addition and all the higher-ranked items. The weight constraint then determined where the cutoff was for the selection of items in the flyaway kit. Table 1 shows a hypothetical example of the selection protocol for up to five units for each of four line item parts. If the total weight constraint on the kit was fifteen pounds, the preferred kit would comprise line item parts, with unit number, in ranks 1 through 10.

A major step to getting the Air Force to implement this protocol was to prove that the Marginal Protection flyaway kits were preferable to the contemporary standard recommendation for kits by the SAC.[5] The logistics

5. The type of proof the US military usually needed before implementing a new protocol was not that it was optimal but that it was preferable to the status quo, and the proof of preferable had to be rigorously persuasive. During World War II Abraham Wald and his colleagues at the Columbia Statistical Research group used a large team to prove sequential analysis was superior

department had data on the frequency of stockouts of B-47 spare parts from Operation High Gear in a North African desert. Those data also measured the performance of the then currently used SAC flyaway kit. Geisler, Herbert Karr, and Bernice Brown compared how their Marginal Protection kit would have fared with the SAC kit. Both kits faced a forty-thousand-pound limit in combining fifteen thousand spare parts for seventy-eight B-47 bombers. According to their calculations, the Marginal Protection kit would have reduced the number of unsatisfied demands from 42 percent to 27 percent (Karr, Geisler, and Brown 1955, iv). The logistics department generalized and codified its protocol for designing military supply tables for spare parts based on marginal analysis suggested by the economists (see, e.g., Geisler and Karr 1956).[6]

The Air Force formally adopted the protocol for designing Marginal Protection flyaway kits and incorporated it into its *Supply Manual*. In practice, however, there appeared to Geisler little operational use of the protocol.[7] In "Reflections on Some Experience with Implementing Logistics Research," Geisler (1965, 2) acknowledged that Project RAND's relationship with the US Air Force "places some responsibility on us to make it work, particularly from the Air Force point of view. We have to help the Air Force to make use of our results." In that essay, Geisler dwelled on the problem of "effecting implementation in the logistics system of the US Air Force," and he acknowledged that "the implementation decision itself has generated its own 'cost-effectiveness' analysis" (3, 5).

---

to the then currently used sampling plan for testing and inspecting ordnance. It was not until after the war in 1948 that Wald and Jacob Wolfowitz proved that compared with all tests of identical power for deciding between two alternative hypotheses, the sequential probability ratio test minimized sample size (see Klein 2000, n.d.).

6. Other economists practicing normative optimization have gone to similar lengths to translate results into implementable optimal actions. For example, during World War II, Milton Friedman, George Stigler, and Allen Wallis constructed nomograms so that Navy personnel could construct accessible graphs to implement Wald's sequential analysis (Klein 2000). In another case, to disseminate his findings from experiments with empirical production functions at the Iowa Agricultural Experiment Station, Earl Heady (1957) constructed a template for a "pork costulator" disc for farmers to determine the least-cost corn and soybean meal mix for different hog weights.

7. Geisler thought that one reason the Marginal Protection protocols were not widely implemented was that weight became less of a crucial issue soon after the protocols were published. One could speculate that another reason was that although marginal benefit/marginal cost comparisons were the kernel of their protocol, the team never explained the economists' use of the term *marginal* in their reports to the Air Force, leaving the noninitiated to think that the adjective was synonymous with "not important."

The logistics department also encountered resistance to implementation of economizing inventory control policies. The value of these optimal policies had been demonstrated in computer simulations comparing the costs of alternative air base stocking and requisitioning policies (Petersen and Geisler 1955). The computer simulation of supply operations at a typical Air Force base introduced a flexible restocking policy sensitive to demand and price and based on a classical microeconomic comparison of the stockage costs with the alternative of resupplying on demand. One of the several conclusions was that "it is more economical to have items costing under $10 requisitioned from the depot every three or six months, rather than every month, even if obsolescence charges on base stocks are as high as 50 per cent per year" (Petersen and Geisler 1955, 69). Implementation of the "economical" policies revealed by all-computer simulations, however, was slow in coming. As Geisler and his colleagues later reflected, "Our experience in trying to secure Air Force acceptance of policy findings resulting from all-computer simulations led almost naturally to the development of the game-simulation technique as a potential means of providing the additional support and detail needed by the Air Force for implementing such policy recommendations" (Geisler, Haythorn, and Steger 1962, 20).

The game-simulation technique referred to was that adapted from the successful, psychology-led training simulations at the Systems Research Laboratory. It therefore relied heavily on the human factor and was focused on information processing. In 1956 the RAND logistics department began using the expertise and simulation techniques of the RAND experimental psychologists. As Geisler (1960, 1) noted after several years of game simulations, "Putting people into the simulation helps to ensure the completeness, compatibility and workability of the model being constructed. People thus provide quality control, feedback, and learning qualities which are most helpful and economically desirable in dealing with very large and complex models."

Systems Research Laboratory, 1951–56

If the US military was engaging economists to practice the art of economizing through optimization leading to quantifiable rules of action, what was it employing the psychologists to do? Essays in *Psychology in the World Emergency* (Flanagan et al. 1952) indicate that psychologists were examining psychological warfare, testing and matching personnel through classification and selection, training individuals and teams, and studying human capabilities. A 1989 review essay on "psychology and the military" described the strong two-way relationship that had begun in World War I and continued through the Cold War: "Perhaps no other institution has been as inextricably linked with the growth and development of psychology as the military. This symbiotic relationship, born of the expediency of World War I, rests on two roles: (a) the military as a test-bed or applied laboratory for the examination of psychological processes, and (b) the military as an impetus to initiate and direct research and innovation in psychology" (Driskell and Olmstead 1989, 43).

In 1916 the percentage of American Psychological Association (APA) members in academe was 75 percent. By the 1980s, only 34 percent of psychologists with PhDs were in academic positions. James Driskell and Beckett Olmstead (1989, 53) attribute this to the growth in applied psychology stimulated by the success of psychological contributions in World War II. In 1946 the APA created a Division of Military Psychology to facilitate discussion among the hundreds of psychologists doing military research after the war. John L. Kennedy was one of those psychologists channeling his interests in human engineering into military research. At the end of World War II he worked for the Special Devices Center of the Office of Naval Research to construct a model of an alertness indicator that would sound an alarm if the frequency of a drowsy sailor's alpha brain rhythm slowed below ten cycles per second (Kennedy 1953). By 1950 Kennedy (1952) was a senior social scientist at the RAND Corporation evaluating, among other things, the research on extrasensory perception (ESP) including telepathy, clairvoyance, and precognition.

In August 1950 Kennedy proposed a study of how groups of Air Force personnel behave under the stress of a possible intrusion of Soviet bombers into US air space. Kennedy was also interested in how they learn to improve their performance in response to stress. RAND accepted the proposal, and Kennedy began planning a man-machine simulation of an Air Force system with two more experimental psychologists, William Biel and Robert Chapman, as well as a mathematician, Allen Newell.[8] In 1951

---

8. The early history of the Systems Research Laboratory is discussed in Chapman and Kennedy 1955, Chapman 1959, Baum 1981, and Ware 2008, 94–98. In *Von Neumann, Morgenstern, and the Creation of Game Theory*, Robert Leonard (2010) examines the relationship between the SRL and the rest of the RAND mathematics department and stresses Kennedy's point that the limits of game theory and mathematical modeling made empirical research through simulation a necessity.

the four researchers set up the Systems Research Laboratory in a room behind a Santa Monica billiard hall and brought in a few more psychologists and coders. In its first RAND research memorandum in January 1952, the design team explained, "The Systems Research Laboratory will be studying particular kinds of models—models made of metal, flesh and blood. Many of the messy and illusive [*sic*] variables of human and hardware interactions will be put into the laboratory" (Chapman et al. 1952, 1).

It was the presence of these regular interactions and the interdependence of the components of the model that made it imperative that the experimental psychologists study the whole system, or organism as they often called it, rather than seeing the whole as a mere aggregation of individuals.[9] It was the performance of the whole that would be monitored, and human learning capacity would not be "realized without explicit identification of their dominant motivation with system purpose and reinforcement of proper response with system success" (11). The research program consisted of "getting the model to the laboratory, training the organism, and experimentation" (11). The psychologists' organism/system approach eventually became a key input in the future collaboration with economists at the LSL.

What was measured in this modeling of and experimentation on a system was the speed and accuracy of information processing, which the SRL team asserted was a more general class of behavior than decision making. The information-processing center that they chose to model in the laboratory was an Air Defense Direction Center (ADDC, or ADC for Air Defense Center). After the first successful Soviet test of an atomic bomb on August 29, 1949, the USAF had installed over one hundred ADDCs around the country to identify and track foreign intrusion into US air space. Effective human interactions with machines at these sites, including radar monitors, computers, and red telephones, were crucial to the defense of the United States. For the experimenters, the centers had the advantage that the typical behavior of the group was observable because most of the ADC responses to stimuli were verbal. Also the achievements, such as the percentage of aircraft correctly identified and effectively tracked by the crew, were easily measured.

9. They explained their "organism concept" with this definition: "An organism is a highly complex structure with parts so integrated that their relation to one another is governed by their relation to the whole" (Chapman et al. 1952, 10). Ironically, the artificially constructed system was invested with the biological analogy of the organism. The system's communication channels served as the neurological analogy of nerve networks. The human elements were treated as abstract atoms: "The Information Processing center has a number of human operators. There is division of labor among these humans and a command structure or hierarchy as well" (3).

Table 2 The four man-machine simulations of the RAND Systems Research Laboratory

Name of Experiment	Dates	Temporal Structure
Casey	February-May 1952	54 4-hour sessions
Cowboy	January 1953	22 8-hour sessions
Cobra	February 1954	22 8-hour sessions
Cogwheel	June 1954	14 4-hour sessions

The physical life-size model installed in the lab was a replica of the Tacoma air defense radar station. Printouts of symbols every thirty seconds from an IBM electronic card-programmed calculator simulated the airplane tracks that would have appeared on a radar screen. Over two and a half years the SRL ran the four air-defense experiments, listed in table 2.

A key laboratory concept was that of "'growing' human organizations under a set of realistic but controlled or controllable conditions" (Simon 1952, preface). The research team's working hypothesis was that performance in information processing could be improved at a greater rate and to a higher standard if the learning was done at the group level rather than training individuals separately. The human subjects in the first Casey experiment were twenty-eight UCLA students who had never worked in an Air Defense Direction Center. In subsequent experiments the subjects were thirty-three to forty ADDC personnel who had not worked together before. The task load for the Casey students was comparable to peacetime air traffic, and the experimenters only gradually and slightly increased the task load in the course of the simulations. The team soon "learned its way right out of the experiment"; in that respect, the experiment was a failure (Chapman et al. 1959, 260). The college students were able to quickly reach the performance of professionals in the field and started to lose interest in the experiment.

The SRL had begun as a study of how groups behaved under the stress of a realistic emergency situation, but during that first experiment the striking result was how quickly a group could learn to act effectively if the team had a daily debriefing with a report on the discrepancy between actual and desired performance and a forum for airing problems. By harnessing the team's learning ability, the designers had enabled the group to adapt to the most efficient use of resources and to grow as an organization.

When the research team was digesting the results of the Casey experiment in the summer of 1952, they brought in Herbert Simon, a consultant

210 Judy L. Klein

with the RAND mathematics division, as an expert on organization theory. Simon's first encounter with Newell and with experimental psychologists using simulation to look at an adaptive problem-solving process would be a defining step in his research trajectory.[10] The SRL team also benefited from that encounter, and Simon returned to the laboratory in subsequent summers.[11] In his first report for the SRL, Simon (1952, 8) defined a program as "the rules that guide the behavior of the subjects in choice situations."[12] He suggested that the experimenters write out the programs in functional forms that would lead to new functional categories. Simon noted that as the task load was increased for the Casey group, the subjects realized the inadequacies of their program and adapted it. Simon honed in on a key way in which they learned and adapted by establishing priorities for reporting air tracks. Simon suggested that for data analysis purposes the experimenters should distinguish the success rate on the important radar tracks from the success rate on the unimportant tracks that did not match the planes reported to the group as civilian aircraft with clearance from the Civil Aeronautics Administration's traffic controllers. As can be seen in figure 1, in subsequent experiments the key characteristic of group learning as the task load increased was learning how to distinguish important radar tracks and unimportant tracks and give priority to the former. This narrower focus led to major increases in the success rate for "carrying" the important tracks.

Simon (1952, 31) also said that in the laboratory's data analysis, they should "maintain a distinction between propositions about optimal programs, propositions about the ways in which programs evolve, and propositions about the ways in which the experimenters can influence the evolution of programs and the program that is reached in equilibrium." In the

10. Hunter Crowther-Heyck (2005, 205) discusses three salient gains for Simon from his interaction with the RAND SRL: the initiation of his long-lasting friendship and professional collaboration with Newell, Simon's exposure to cutting-edge computers ("his 'secret weapon' in his psychological research"), and his insights on artificial intelligence from simulation experiments with humans and computer processing symbols. Willis Ware (2008, 138–40) documents Simon, Newell, and Clifford Shaw's artificial intelligence research at RAND.

11. From 1952 to 1954, the social psychologist Robert Freed Bales was also a consultant at the SRL. Bales's connection of his earlier work on abstracted "situations" to the simulated communication and control system as well as his perception of the ADDC as a symbol-aggregating and transforming process leading to a decision is discussed in Erickson et al. 2013, 125–29.

12. Simon's definition captures the military's use of the word *program* in the 1940s and early 1950s to mean program of action for military operations. If you substitute the word *computer* for *subject*, the definition also captures the current computer science usage of *programming*, what the military in the early 1950s would have called coding.

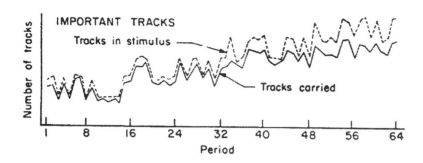

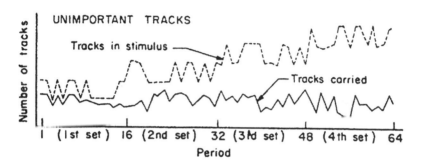

Figure 1. Two charts showing the nature of the learning process in the SRL simulations. As the task load increased with each set in the experiment, the crews learned to distinguish between important, unidentified tracks and the unimportant ones, which had been identified as domestic, civilian aircraft. Once the tracks were distinguished, the SRL crews gave priority to improving their carry rate in following the important tracks. Source: Chapman, et al. 1959, 265.

1970s, Simon came to perceive the first distinction about optimal outcomes as being associated with substantive rationality and the second with procedural rationality. The third is arguably associated with implementation rationality.

Kennedy's idea for a man-machine simulation laboratory had started as a study on stress and learning in groups. It culminated in a successful, fully incorporated training program for the Air Defense Command. In their 1959 reflective essay on the SRL, Chapman, Kennedy, Newell, and Biel (1959, 268) asserted that, at the very least, simulation was a technique "for building organization potential artificially when the price of failure in the real world while learning is prohibitive." The researchers did end up with a conclusion on stress: the stresses of failure and discomfort "guided the direction center's learning." They also drew several conclusions about learning. Most important was "to distinguish between information useful for task accomplishment and that which was not. Crews focused their attention on important classes of tracks at the expense of unimportant classes" (Chapman et al. 1959, 268). Why they learned that came down to "practice, under realistic conditions, and knowledge of results" (Chapman 1958, 72).

Over five years of laboratory simulations, the researchers had experienced their own group learning process. They developed into an effective organization that could manufacture and promote a lucrative "System Training Program." The SRL had channeled the capacity of man-machine simulation to grow groups that made system-rational choices. Their own organization grew rapidly after it codified the training program. In August 1954 the USAF and the SRL tried out the training program at the Boron California ADDC. Two months later, the Air Force asked the RAND group to install the System Training Program at all 150 radar sites. By 1957 the System Training Program employed five hundred people including two hundred psychologists. In October 1956 the newly named System Development Division joined forces with the MIT Lincoln laboratory to work on software for the SAGE (Semi-Automatic Ground Environment) systems of computers for Air Force defense. Within a month the Systems Development Corporation was an autonomous, fully incorporated enterprise that became one of the leading software contractors and employers of programmers and psychologists in the nation.[13] Biel became a corporate officer at the SDC, but Kennedy left for Princeton University to serve as chair of the psychology department. Newell went to the Carnegie Institute of Technology to collaborate and complete his PhD with Simon. Kennedy, Newell, and Simon continued to serve as occasional consultants to RAND. When the SDC abandoned its RAND simulation laboratory, the RAND Logistics System Laboratory moved in (see figure 2). In addition to the facilities, the LSL inherited several psychologists, including William Haythorn, laboratory staff, and the simulation conceptual framework from the SRL.

13. These landmarks are documented by Claude Baum in *The System Builders: The Story of SDC* and Martin Campbell-Kelly in *From Airline Reservations to Sonic the Hedgehog: A History of the Software Industry*. T. C. Rowan (1958) described the System Training program for both the manual air defense system and the planned SAGE system. A 1956 *Business Week* article, "At RAND: Massed Brains to Meet Air Threat," also gave insight into simulation details at the Systems Development Division and the burgeoning interactions between training and computer programmers on the SAGE system. In a "psychology in action" section of the *American Psychologist*, Goodwin (1957) discussed system training at the newly incorporated SDC.

Figure 2. Photograph of RAND Simulation Research Laboratory facilities that the RAND Logistics Systems Laboratory took over in October 1956. The undated photograph of the SRL shows the air surveillance crew of an ADC on the ground floor, the weapons direction personnel on the second floor. The psychologists and other SRL and USAF staff are monitoring the simulation on the third floor. Source: Baum 1981

Logistics Systems Laboratory

The researchers at the newly formed RAND Logistics Systems Laboratory classified their approach to simulation as a "game simulation" in contrast with the SRL's training simulations. Both were man-machine simulations that involved the processing of symbols rather than of physical goods, but the SDC training simulations had focused only on improving human performance while keeping the rest of the system elements fixed. For the logistics researchers, varying the other elements was the focus of the simulation. The human factor was added to the logistics simulations to augment the complexity that would facilitate detailed operational rules of action. The addition of Air Force personnel in a simulation experiment also ensured exposure to an economic way of thinking and enhanced postexperience persuasion and implementation.

Over a decade, the LSL conducted game simulations structured by the four separate laboratory problems (LPs) listed in table 3. Each iterative man-machine simulation experiment took two years and cost well over $1 million (over $8 million in 2016 dollars). Each LP employed over one hundred staff members, including twenty-five professional economists, psychologists, mathematicians, and logistics experts from the USAF.

There were four teams of twenty-five Air Force participants who were used for a month at a time in successive experiments of each laboratory problem. The primary machine in the first couple of simulations was an electronic IBM 702 to which punch cards had to be driven several blocks from the laboratory. The usual pattern for each laboratory problem was eight to nine months of designing, modeling, and creating the mock-up, followed by four months of actual simulation, and three to four months of analyzing and reporting on the results.

The evolution of economists' valuation of the function of simulation experiments is evident in the history of the four laboratory problems. Economists went from using the simulation to demonstrate the superiority of optimal policies derived from deductive economics to using the experiment as an inductive tool. As the experiments progressed, economists realized that simulation that incorporated information processing and problem solving revealed optimal or good-enough decision rules in a way that existing mathematical and computational tools could not. In a briefing to the Advanced Logistics Course of the Air Force Institute of Technology soon after LP-IV began, Geisler described the current perspective on the purpose of game simulations as "the study of decision rules in the context of a given organization and environment. . . . The definition of these tactical rules is usually only partly worked out in advance of a game-simulation. The function of the simulation itself is the further development of the rules by exposing them to a variety of situations, by determining the effects elsewhere in the organization, and by trying to discover better ways of making similar decisions" (Geisler, Haythorn, and Steger 1962, 21).

A key goal of each simulation was "to produce a reliable image of the real-world environment—so reliable, indeed, that the adaptation of proposed policies to such an environment would require the development of usable procedures, reports, and the like, in sufficient detail for ready transference to the real world" (Geisler 1959, 360). That transference, as well as the preliminary design of the first three LP simulations, was aided with the RAND logistics department's construction of three board games

Table 3 Comparison of Laboratory Problems.

Characteristic	LP-I	LP-II	LP-III	LP-IV
Primary Purpose	Pre-Service Test	Developmental	Pre-Service test	Developmental
Major policies	Supply and information system	Operations maintenance interactions	Degree of support centralization & integration	Maintenance management & maintenance information system
Simulated organizations	ADC bases & AMAs with data processing center	Titan-Atlas Missile Squadron and Wing	AMA, with missile bases sketched in	SAC multi-weapon base
Stresses	Operations	Operations, reliability, & resources	Program. Repair capacity & system responsiveness	Operations & responsiveness
Goal	Minimize budget, given operational program	Maximize alert, given resources	Minimize stockouts given program & budget	Maximize operations per support dollar, given operational program
Computer use	Great	Very little	Great	Medium to great
Participants' major role	Follow rules at base & manage an AMA	Develop management rules	Follow rules & evaluate feasibility	Develop management rules
Sources of participants	ADC, AMC & ATRC	SAC & ADC	AFLC	SAC, ADC, TAC, & AFLC
Number of participants	50	35	42	?
Number or runs	1	3	15	?
Lab Simulation Dates	Early 1957–end of 1957	Early 1958–late 1958	Mid 1959–mid 1960	On and off, late 1960–1965
Board game for designing LP and for post-simulation training	Monopologs	Baselogs	Misslogs	

Source: All of the rows but the last two are reproduced from Geisler, Haythorn, and Steger 1962, 5. ADC, Air Defense Command; AFLC, Air Force Logistics Command; AMA, Air Material Area; AMC, Air Material Command; SAC, Strategic Air Command; TAC, Tactical Air Command.

to train military personnel in an economic way of thinking in logistical decision making.[14]

The first of the four major experiments (LP-I) was on the optimal inventory control policies that the logistics department had explored two years earlier with the all-computer simulation. LP-I simulated and compared two different decision-making protocols for an Air Material Command depot supplying spare parts for fighter planes and bombers at ten bases: the current system and the one proposed by RAND economists. Each of the two logistics systems was given the same emergency stress tests as well as routine maintenance requirements. Participants followed the protocols of their respective system. The LSL compressed time with each day treated as a month, and the Air Force participants made decisions at the beginning and the end of each day (month). The RAND-proposed optimized system proved the most cost-effective over the "three-year" simulation, yielding half the procurement expenses on high-cost parts with no additional stockouts or planes out of commission. The economists' policies led to about the same expenditures on low-cost spare parts as the then current USAF policies did, but there were less than half the stockouts or planes out of commission. Participants, formal Air Force briefings, and the Monopologs board game spread news of the results, but RAND and the USAF also gained insight into the stumbling blocks to implementation. As Geisler (1962, 243) explained with optimal inventory control: "The implicit rationality of the policies does not always look right when they are put into use, and so amendments to them are made such that the resulting policy is something quite different." Indeed, the simulations at times resulted in recommending feasible solutions for good enough, rather than optimal, outcomes, what Simon would call "satisficing."

The LP-I game simulation ultimately led to a far greater degree of implementation than the all-computer simulation had. This was aided

14. In 1956 William Hamburger designed Monopologs, a board game to simulate an Air Force supply system consisting of a depot supplying widgets to five air bases and to train depot managers through feedback on player's total costs of thirty-one months of decision making. Jean Rehkop Renshaw and Annette Heuston made further revisions to Monopologs in 1957 and 1960. The logistics department also crafted two other games to help in the preliminary design of the next two man-machine simulation problems and ease the implementation of rules of action derived from optimization research: Baselogs, to study the interactions between logistics and operations on a fighter-interceptor Air Defense Command base (Gainen, Levine, and McGlothlin 1958); and Misslogs, developed to illustrate interactions among operations, supply, maintenance, and personnel in a ballistic-missile squadron. The latter was billed as an educational tool for USAF personnel "that gives the player, who must work within a limited budget, a clear-cut view of the tradeoffs he can make to achieve maximum readiness" (Voosen 1959, 1).

by the fact that personnel from the Air Material Command served as participants in the simulation, as well as part of the laboratory staff, and frequent observers during the floor run. When they returned to their base in Sacramento, the personnel who had served as the laboratory staff implemented many of the RAND logistics research policies that had fared well in the comparison with the status quo policies. These logistics department policies included the deferred procurement and the automatic supply of low-cost items (Geisler, Haythorn, and Steger 1962, 21).

With LP-II, the LSL researchers switched from demonstrating the effectiveness of predetermined optimal policies to investigating and exploring alternative policies. Observers to the LP-I run had included staffs from the Advanced Research and Logistics System who were working on inventory control systems for the new Thor, Atlas, and Titan missiles. They helped in providing data for LP-II, which simulated maintenance operations for a missile squadron. The USAF Air Material Command (AMC) and the RAND researchers were in uncharted territory for developing logistics policies for the first-generation missiles. For one thing, there were no existing bases to use in the modeling of a mock-up. The main purpose of LP-II was therefore developmental, with a goal to provide precise notions of significant decisions that would maximize the alert level of a missile squadron (minimize the time to launch) given resources.

The context for LP-III was the decision facing the AMC on whether to stick with a management structure based on inventory class lines of specialization in part type, no matter what the weapon, or to switch to an organizational structure based on each weapon system (Haythorn 1958, 77). As with LP-I, the researchers simulated the two organizational structures with a goal of minimizing stockouts given a fixed budget. The RAND logistics team also expected the simulations to lead to a determination of "the degree of responsiveness which seems both feasible and desirable from a cost-effectiveness standpoint" (Geisler, Haythorn, and Steger 1962, 53). Although the results indicated little difference in outcomes of the two management structures, the simulation generated new, detailed economizing procedures.

The LP-IV experiment was unique in that the simulation was used not to test previously determined policy rules or compare management structures but to fully solve for a rational choice framework for a complex base maintenance problem. The researchers resorted to simulation because such a solution had defied analysis with existing computational resources.

The specific LP-IV problem was how a primarily manual system at an air base could be designed to minimize maintenance turnaround time. Geisler (1962, 244) alluded to the significance of this nonstandard route to rational choice:

> The characteristics of analytic solutions are therefore optimality and calculability. Simulation, on the other hand, is a heuristic process in which the analyst attempts to obtain "optimal" solutions by iteration of the simulation model, but he must specify the conditions for each run by interpretation of the previous runs. . . . Thus the choice between analysis and simulation seems to be between optimal solutions of problems fitting certain calculable forms or smaller numbers of variables versus non-optimal, but more detailed and non-standard kinds of models.

With LP-IV, the simulations in the LSL facilities became more intermittent, popping up according to a need to examine a certain problem in base maintenance. For some parts of the problem, the logistics researchers relied on an all-computer simulator they had developed to be used in conjunction with the LP-IV man-machine simulation. The Base Operations Maintenance simulator was used to determine, for example, what shift-manning policies maximized sorties (Geisler and Ginsberg 1965, 21). Also, the LP-IV staff took the experiment to the real, real world, working at Air Force bases in Missouri and Thailand to run field tests. The field experiences in Thailand proved the most challenging because the base there was in combat mode with frequent sorties to support US engagements in Vietnam.[15] The LP-IV researchers were trying to develop base maintenance protocols to increase sorties subject to resource constraints. Even though the RAND staff had by then resorted to merely increasing, rather than maximizing, sorties, they still experienced in the urgency of a combat situation a far greater resistance to testing and implementation of new policies than they had at the Missouri base.

The logistics man-machine simulations ceased in 1966, by which time the attention of RAND and the Air Force was focused fully on the Vietnam War. Geisler concluded that the Logistics Systems Laboratory had "provided a good transition between the logistics researcher and the logistics operator." He was not able to claim the full implementation of optimal decision rules, but he asserted that the LSL had "helped to accelerate the transfer of sound feasible findings to the real world" (Geisler 1986, 33).

---

15. The US government dates its war in Vietnam from August 5, 1964, to May 7, 1975.

Conclusion

How do you translate the broad findings of normative microeconomics into detailed, implementable procedures for operations in a system? The RAND Logistics System Laboratory economists, with the help of psychologists, discovered that a big part of the answer was that you have to *grow* a system. This synthesis included building networks of information flows and feedback loops. Geisler and Ginsberg (1965, 4) summarized this research objective of game simulation designed for making decisions about resource allocation as achieving a "better definition of a system through suggesting new ideas, firming alternatives, integrating system functions, examining administrative feasibility and demonstrating effectiveness."

The chief contribution of economists to this enterprise was optimization, including a formal maximizing or minimizing criterion function for each of the laboratory problems (see goals on table 2). The economists also initiated optimal decision rules for most of the simulations and explicitly clarified trade-offs and opportunity costs. The contributions of the psychologists included experimentation through simulation, the analytical framework of a system or organism rather than the individual, a receptivity to adaptive processes, and a focus on interactions monitored and controlled within an information-processing structure.

One of the major obstacles the system definers/designers faced was the conflict between the goals of and incentives facing agents in different organizations that would make up a system. Haythorn (1958, 77), who had worked with the SRL before joining the LSL, described that dilemma: "Some components of the system emphasize operational support, some emphasize operational readiness, some emphasize economy. . . . That is, each component of the system may interact with other components so as to require coordination. Otherwise, the operational effectiveness of system components may be unrelated or negatively related to overall systems effectiveness."

Another lesson learned was that under the right conditions simulation is one way to grow an effective system by revealing the most effective reporting policies and communication channels. As the SRL psychologists found, "a system's environment can be inferred from, and its actions controlled by, information—a vital commodity to any organization" (Chapman et al. 1959, 251). Geisler (1959, 359–60) echoed this sentiment by declaring that "real-world needs generated a demand for specific detail which conventional research could not adequately provide; for example, the implementation of a policy based on mathematical formulae requires information-flow systems to provide the data needed for parameter review and estimation." For prescriptive economics, simulation proved an appropriate bridge between research and implementation when dealing with complex behavioral systems focusing on processing symbols, whether they were symbols of planes on a radar screen or reports on airplane parts needed.[16]

The economist's attention to implementation of rational choice protocols that maximized gains for an entire system has not been confined to military research and planning contracts. More recently, economists on the Basel Committee on Banking Supervision were engaging in implementation rationality through simulation in the form of the Regulatory Consistency Assessment Programme (RCAP). The Bank for International Settlements established the program to ensure consistent, effective implementation of Basel III banking regulations (see Basel Committee on Banking Supervision 2013). As with Geisler's work at the RAND Logistics Systems Laboratory, RCAP used simulation experiments to test for and further enhance consistent implementation. Over twenty trading days in the summer of 2012, the committee used a hypothetical test portfolio to conduct a simulation with sixteen international banks. Each day the banks calculated the weighting of the riskiness of their assets to determine the amount of capital they would set aside to meet the legal requirement of holding capital equivalent to 7 percent of the value of risk-weighted assets in their identical hypothetical portfolios of initial values and "common trading strategies implemented using primarily vanilla products" (see Basel Committee on Banking Supervision 2013, 67). The second stage of simulation introduced more exotic flavors of trading strategies. In response to the daily changes in the market-determined values of the portfolio assets over the twenty-day period for each simulation, banks calculated daily their ten-day 99 percent VaR (Value at Risk) and weekly their Stressed VaR and IRC (Incremental Risk Capital). The banks reported their risk metrics calculations on a common form.

The committee was surprised by the inconsistency in the investment banks' simulated calculations on risk-weighted assets. There were follow-up site visits to reveal the most likely sources of the inconsistency, and in particular to examine the relative importance of supervisory personal judgment versus mathematical modeling. The RCAP simulations were also prolonged observations with additional analysis to determine how to

16. The use of simulations in economics and scientific modeling is explored in Morgan 2004 and Maas 2014.

tweak reporting frameworks and how to prescribe and proscribe calculation protocols to narrow modeling choices for the investment banks. The Basel Committee on Banking Supervision intends to use the latter to counter an individual bank's use of optimizing models that minimize the value of its risk-weighted assets in order to minimize the capital it needs to set aside to meet Basel III stipulations.[17]

As with the LSL simulations, the aims of the RCAP's iterative simulations have been to measure inconsistencies and bottlenecks to achieving effective implementation of decision rules and develop specific reporting/decision protocols that entrain desired implementation with low variation in the outcomes. Simulation monitors at both institutions also observed the gaming of the system. They studied ways to ensure that optimization at the system level (e.g., minimizing USAF costs or minimizing risk of a financial crisis) trumped the rational self-interests of individual air bases or investment banks. Implementation rationality at this level was in some ways analogous to avoiding a Nash equilibrium in the prisoner's dilemma by creating a reporting/deciding framework for maximizing benefits for the collective of participants. In both cases the simulations were an iterative, adaptive process with the aim of taming optimizing models, achieving "good-enough" operational rules, and maximizing the effectiveness of the regulations through perfecting data-reporting interfaces and narrowing supervisory personal judgment or modeling choices. Both were attempts to *define* a system.

The RAND Logistics Systems Laboratory and the Basel Committee on Banking Supervision's RCAP simulations occurred in contexts of regulatory or command-and-control systems. It may well be that part of the problem of people gaming a system is a product of the system trying to control the individual. The more compelling story is about the resolution to naturally conflicting optimizations. In some situations, the micro and macro fail to mesh unless a regulatory system with effective information

17. The most obvious evidence of such a practice has come from internal bank e-mail messages revealed in the US Senate investigation of J.P. Morgan's $6 billion "London Whale" loss. These show that quantitative analysts at J.P. Morgan's Chief Investment Office were explicitly "optimizing regulatory capital" to minimize the reported value of capital subject to regulation and to reduce the calculated Value at Risk of trades that the London office persisted in making. The *Financial Times* and Matt Levine at the Dealbreaker blog had good synopses of the RCAP simulations and their relevance to the London Whale incident (see, e.g., dealbreaker.com /2013/01/banks-risk-measurements-rarely-off-by-much-more-than-a-factor-of-ten/, www.ft.com /intl/cms/s/0/6eae8382-6bab-11e2-8c62-00144feab49a.html, ftalphaville.ft.com/2013/04/09 /1450202/ten-times-on-the-board-i-will-not-put-optimizing-regulatory-capital-in-the-subject -line-of-an-email/).

channels is cultivated. The evolution of iterative modeling and solving for rules of action at the LSL and in the RCAP also highlights the advantages of lawmakers giving flexibility to the regulators doing the implementation. The end goals of an efficiently adaptable, stable system as well as the schema of the information-monitoring network are often embodied in the command and control legislation. These experiments in simulation suggest, however, that the explicit narrowing of modeling choices that bind the rationality of the individual units may be best iterated through a process that takes into account the human factor.

Economists at the Logistics Systems Laboratory were searching for a way to implement the optimal policies that matched the organizational objective functions of maximizing alert readiness given resource constraints or minimizing the budget given the operational program. In joining psychology with economics, the LSL came to the conclusion that it had to analyze and synthesize the group as a single organism rather than an aggregation of individuals. A key to growing the organism was to create effective information-processing channels, including feedback loops. Researchers had to allow for learning and adaptation in both the subjects of the experiments and the academic economists and psychologists running the simulations. Interactions with experimental psychologists took RAND economists to another level of detail and complexity. A door opened to nonstandard modeling and an iterative, heuristic specification of economizing rules of action that had a greater chance of implementation.

References

"At RAND: Massed Brains to Meet Air Threat." 1956. *Business Week*, March 3, 86–92.

Basel Committee on Banking Supervision. 2013. "Regulatory Consistency Assessment Programme (RCAP)—Analysis of Risk-Weighted Assets for Market Risk." Basel, Switzerland: Bank for International Settlements.

Baum, Claude. 1981. *The System Builders: The Story of SDC*. Santa Monica, Calif.: System Development Corporation.

Brown, Bernice B., and Murray A. Geisler. 1954. "Analysis of the Demand Patterns for B-47 Airframe Parts at the Air Base Level." RM-1297, RAND Corporation.

Campbell-Kelly, Martin. 2003. *From Airline Reservations to Sonic the Hedgehog: A History of the Software Industry*. Cambridge, Mass.: MIT Press.

Chapman, Robert L. 1958. "Simulation in RAND's System Research Laboratory." In *Report of the System Simulation Symposium*, edited by D. G. Malcolm. Baltimore, Md.: Waverly.

Chapman, Robert L., William C. Biel, John L. Kennedy, and Allen Newell. 1952. "The Systems Research Laboratory and Its Program." RAND Corporation.

Chapman, Robert L., and John L Kennedy. 1955. "The Background and Implications of the Systems Research Laboratory Studies." RAND Corporation.

Chapman, Robert L., John L Kennedy, Allen Newell, and William C. Biel. 1959. "The Systems Research Laboratory's Air Defense Experiments." *Management Science* 5 (3): 250–69.

Crowther-Heyck, Hunter. 2005. *Herbert A. Simon: The Bounds of Reason in Modern America*. Baltimore, Md.: Johns Hopkins University Press.

Driskell, James A., and Beckett Olmstead. 1989. "Psychology and the Military: Research Applications and Trends." *American Psychologist* 44 (1): 43–54.

Erickson, Paul, Judy L. Klein, Lorraine Daston, Rebecca Lemov, Thomas Sturm, and Michael D. Gordin. 2013. *How Reason Almost Lost Its Mind: The Strange Career of Cold War Rationality*. Chicago: University of Chicago Press.

Flanagan, John C., Fillmore H. Sanford, John W. MacMillan, John L. Kennedy, Arthur W. Melton, Frederick W. Williams, Donald E. Baier, and Glen Finch. 1952. *Psychology in the World Emergency*. Pittsburgh: University of Pittsburgh Press.

Gainen, L., H. A. Levine, and W. H. McGlothlin. 1958. "BASELOGS: A Base Logistics Management Game." RM-2086, RAND Corporation.

Geisler, Murray A. 1959. "The Simulation of a Large-Scale Military Activity." *Management Science* 5 (4): 359–68.

———. 1960. "Development of Man-Machine Simulation Techniques." RAND Corporation.

———. 1962. "Appraisal of Laboratory Simulation Experiences." *Management Science* 8 (3): 239–45.

———. 1965. "Reflections on Some Experience with Implementing Logistics Research." P-3066, RAND Corporation.

———. 1986. *A Personal History of Logistics*. Bethesda, Md.: Logistics Management Institute.

Geisler, Murray A., and Allen S. Ginsberg. 1965. "Man-Machine Simulation Experience." P-3214, RAND Corporation.

Geisler, Murray A., William W. Haythorn, and Wilbur A. Steger. 1962. "Simulation and the Logistics Systems Laboratory." RAND Corporation.

Geisler, Murray A., and Herbert W. Karr. 1956. "The Design of Military Supply Tables for Spare Parts. P-799, RAND Corporation.

Goodwin, Richard. 1957. "The System Development Corporation and System Training." *American Psychologist* 12: 524–28.

Hamburger, William. 1956. "MONOPOLOGS: An Inventory Management Game." RM-1579, RAND Corporation.

Haythorn, William W. 1958. "Simulation in RAND's Logistics Systems Laboratory." In *Report of the System Simulation Symposium*, edited by D. G. Malcolm. Baltimore, Md.: Waverly.

Heady, Earl O. 1957. "An Econometric Investigation of the Technology of Agricultural Production Functions." *Econometrica* 25 (2): 249–68.

Huston, James A. 1966. *The Sinews of War: Army Logistics, 1775–1953*. Washington, D.C.: Office of the Chief of Military History United States Army.

Karr, Herbert W., Murray A. Geisler, and Bernice B. Brown. 1955. "A Preferred Method for Designing a Flyaway Kit. RM-1490, RAND Corporation.

Kennedy, John L. 1952. "An Evaluation of Extra-Sensory Perception." *Proceedings of the American Philosophical Society* 96 (5): 513–18.

———. 1953. "Some Practical Problems of the Alertness Indicator." In *Papers Given at the Symposium on Fatigue Held by the Ergonomics Research Society in March, 1952*, edited by W. F. Floyd and A. T. Welford. London: H. R. Lewis.

Klein, Judy L. 2000. "Economics for a Client: The Case of Statistical Quality Control and Sequential Analysis." In *Toward a History of Applied Economics*, edited by R. Backhouse and J. Biddle. *History of Political Economy* 32 (supplement): 27–69.

———. n.d. "Protocols of War and the Mathematical Invasion of Policy Space, 1940–1970." Unpublished paper.

Leonard, Robert. 2010. *Von Neumann, Morgenstern, and the Creation of Game Theory: From Chess to Social Science, 1900–1960*. New York: Cambridge University Press.

Maas, Harro. 2014. *Economic Methodology: A Historical Introduction*. London: Routledge.

Morgan, Mary S. 2004. "Simulation: The Birth of a Technology to Create 'Evidence' in Economics." *Revue d'Histoire des Sciences* 57 (2): 341–77.

Petersen, James W., and Murray A. Geisler. 1955. "The Costs of Alternative Air Base Stocking and Requisitioning Policies." *Naval Research Logistics Quarterly* 2 (1–2): 69–81.

Renshaw, Jean Rehkop, and Annett Heuston. 1957. "The Game MONOPOLOGS." RM-1917-1-PR, RAND Corporation.

Rowan, T. C. 1958. "Simulation in Air Force System Training." In *Report of the System Simulation Symposium*, edited by D. G. Malcolm, 83–87. Baltimore, Md.: Waverly.

Schelling, Thomas C. 1960. "Economic Reasoning and Military Science." *American Economist* 4 (1): 3–13.

Simon, Herbert A. 1952. "Observations and Comments on the Organization Studies of the Systems Research Laboratory." RAND Corporation.

———. 1964. "Rationality." In *Dictionary of the Social Sciences*, edited by J. Gould and W. L. Kolb, 573–74. Glencoe, Ill.: Free Press.

———. 1973. "From Substantive to Procedural Rationality." In *Herbert A. Simon Collection*. Pittsburgh: Carnegie Mellon University.

———. 1976. "From Substantive to Procedural Rationality." In *Method and Appraisal in Economics*, edited by S. J. Latsis, 120–48. New York: Cambridge University Press.

———. 1978a. "On How to Decide What to Do." *Bell Journal of Economics* 9 (2): 494–507.

———. 1978b. "Rationality as Process and as Product of Thought." *American Economic Review* 68 (2): 1–16.

———. 1979. "Rational Decision Making in Business Organizations." *American Economic Review* 69 (4): 493–513.

———. 2000. "Bounded Rationality in Social Science: Today and Tomorrow." *Mind and Society* 1 (1): 25–39.

Vandenberg, General Hoyt S. 1948. "Air Force Letter No. 170-3, Comptroller Project SCOOP." Washington, D.C. Archives, Air Force Historical Research Agency, Maxwell Air Force Base, Alabama.

Voosen, Bernard, J. 1959. "Misslogs: A Game of Missile Logistics." RM-2455, RAND Corporation.

Ware, Willis H. 2008. *RAND and the Information Evolution: A History in Essays and Vignettes.* Santa Monica, Calif.: RAND Corporation.

Wiener, Norbert. 1953. "Harmonic Analysis, Causation, and Operations Research." Paper presented at the Operations Research Society, November 23. Massachusetts Institute of Technology, Norbert Wiener Papers.

Psychology Fails to Trump the Multiyear, Structural Development Plan: Albert Hirschman's Largely Frustrated Efforts to Place the "Ability to Make and Carry Out Development Decisions" at the Center of the Development Economics of the late 1950s and the 1960s

Neil De Marchi

For several decades starting in the early 1950s, the economist Albert Hirschman sought to shift development thinking away from the certainty implied by reasoning of the sort "If structural situation A, then pre-ordained outcome A" and toward more open-ended and historical analyses. This meant greater emphasis on experience with specific projects, as well as an acceptance of uncertainties and possibilities rather than an exclusive focus on the writing of detailed structural plans, with their implicit pretense that those who draw them up are able to allow for eventualities that cannot be known in advance. Among the uncertainties and possibilities was whether administrators of development projects could muster the will to act with alacrity and conviction to overcome inevitable difficulties as they arose. Hirschman's faith that this is possible was bolstered by select contemporary findings in the psychology of human behavior. His urgings were largely ignored.

Below I elaborate by juxtaposing Hirschman's dissenting view against that of a respected contemporary advocate of comprehensive, structural planning: Hollis Chenery. Since Hirschman aligned himself with (select) results from contemporary psychology, I am able to ask whether his failure to persuade Chenery is perhaps an instance of a professional economist being brought face-to-face with psychology but declining to be influ-

Correspondence may be addressed to Neil De Marchi, Duke University, at demarchi@econ.duke.edu.

History of Political Economy 48 (annual suppl.) DOI 10.1215/00182702-3619286

enced by it as superfluous or impossible to reconcile with quantitative, structural modeling. That way of putting the choice does not seem wholly wrong, but it is lacking in nuance.

My reading of the evidence is that leading development economists such as Chenery, and the aid-giving institutions with which they were linked, simply could not grasp the Hirschman alternative. Hirschman identified a weak desire for change and a lack of decision-making capacity as the leading causes of backwardness. To overcome these lacks would have required remaking development policy, to put at its center training programs for the local administrators of development projects (not all-encompassing plans) with the aim of strengthening their confidence that change is possible and unforeseeable difficulties can be overcome. Given the plan-making and related economic expertise in already-*developed* countries, and the concentration of aid-giving programs and international and US governmental institutions in Washington, D.C., and at the United Nations in New York, plus the private foundations in both places, the Hirschman alternative must have seemed impractical, probably more expensive than continuing prevailing practice, and anyway totally unproven.

Not that Hirschman was without exposure to economics or to economic development in particular. Quite the reverse. Economics was part of the studies he began before World War II in the faculty of law at the University of Berlin. Adolf Hitler's rise to power and increasingly virulent anti-Jewish prejudice in Germany led Hirschman to relocate to Paris, where he entered the École des Hautes Études Commerciales de Paris, or HEC. There, for three years, he was schooled in statistics and fairly sophisticated "counting" measures.[1] He moved next to the London School of Economics, where a fellowship permitted him to follow his interests rather than a prescribed degree curriculum. Hirschman also spent time, still prewar, at the Istituto di Statistica of the University of Trieste, applying lessons learned at HEC and drawing on the work of the British demographer George Knibbs, to create more satisfactory measures of Italian demographic change. He received a doctorate from Trieste University in 1938.[2]

The practical portions of Hirschman's training meant that he carried forward into his engagements with development issues a serious and often skeptical interest in the availability and quality of the statistics required for detailed national plans.

1. To hint at his comfort with numbers, Hirschman (1964) anticipated by five years what is commonly known as the Herfindahl concentration index.
2. These and other biographical details are drawn from Adelman 2014.

After the war, Hirschman migrated to the United States and, after working for the Marshall Plan, was initiated into the practical realities of backwardness and development during a four-and-a-half-year stint in Colombia starting in 1952. For the first two years he was economic and financial adviser to the newly formed National Planning Council, thus in the employ of the Colombian government, though the context was an International Bank for Reconstruction and Development (World Bank) development plan for the country, the Bank's first such comprehensive intervention in the region. Hirschman was the Bank's choice for the advisory position. At the end of his contract Hirschman stayed on in a private capacity for an additional two and a half years, traveling throughout the country: endlessly observing, discussing, analyzing.

In 1971, looking back on the way many economists in the early fifties (and, in his judgment, too many still) tended to approach development, Hirschman perceived a strong preference for "dynamic" (multiyear), comprehensive, structural planning. He elaborated on what this meant in *A Bias for Hope*, a selection of his own papers that began with "Economics and Investment Planning: Reflections Based on Experience in Colombia." In this essay Hirschman focused on what he dubbed "aggregative analysis," a designation that covered both structural modeling and time series–based computational analysis.

Among the more prominent US practitioners of structural and computational modeling in the 1960s was Chenery, at that time head of the USAID-funded Project for Quantitative Research in Economic Development at Harvard's Center for International Affairs. Later, from 1972 to 1982, Chenery served as the World Bank's first vice president for development policy.

In 1969 Chenery made available for limited distribution a detailed working paper using computational modeling, with the title "The Process of Industrialisation." I do not know whether Hirschman received a copy of this paper, but he must have acquired it at some point, for he singled it out in the leading essay in *A Bias for Hope*. There he summarized Chenery's approach as the employment of time series of the standard macro-quantities of an economic system—national income, population growth, average and marginal capital/output ratios, and the domestic propensity to save—"to obtain some guidance for the basic economic policies of underdeveloped countries" (Hirschman 1971, 42). He offered two examples.

First, by identifying in national accounting time series for a particular country the likely limits to change within each such series—for growth, implicitly, the probable limit to its *upward* movement—one may infer how much foreign capital might be required to achieve a specific desired rate of growth in per capita income over a chosen period. Second, if a country is already engaged in trade, the income-elasticity of demand for its exports might be combined with assumptions about the probable growth of income in its customer nations and its own propensity to import, along with its desired rate of increase in per capita income, to arrive at a rough notion of the pace of domestic industrialization to aim at.

Hirschman conceded that the guidance an individual country might derive from such aggregative, empirical analysis "is important . . . [and] might in time help shape attitudes towards taxation, foreign investment and a balanced development of industry and agriculture." He added, however, that, at the highest level of aggregation, *there is no special contribution the economist can make!* (Hirschman 1971, 42; italics added).

This was a rather astonishing assertion, but Hirschman went on to show that it is true in a variety of senses. First, there exists already in many developing countries "a whole arsenal of proven monetary, banking, fiscal and foreign exchange techniques," and the task of deploying them well falls to a country's financial adviser rather than the economist per se (43–44).

Second, not only is this so, but there is "very little creative effort" involved in the task of overall development planning. For the main sectors requiring development are quite obvious, so that an economist need only extrapolate the existing pattern of investment while ensuring that there is room in it for adjustments as needed among the obvious priorities (44).

Third, the particular intellectual perspective that economics has to offer, namely, the test of allocative efficiency, amounts to ensuring that the last million pesos of spending on education should have roughly the same impact on GNP growth as the last million devoted to transportation, say, or to public health, or to facilitating access to clean water and electricity, yet this requires just what the economist *cannot* claim to be able to do in the development context. Why not? Because, usually, nothing more precise is known than that *all* the above-named options are "important." Therefore, the decision as to the proper share of investment to be enjoyed by each claimant sector can be made only "intuitively and arbitrarily," within limits set by common sense rather than economics (44–45). This is so because, typically, the means to make choices more objective and precise is lacking. All too often the figures included in a developing country's investment budget are too diverse in quality to permit claims that a program is or is not in fine balance. They will range from pure guesses and extrapolations from the past to projects whose nature is precisely known and financing already assured, and to still others whose nature alone is known. The economist's first task, therefore, prior to committing himself to any one investment pattern, must be to ensure that all his (usually, at that time, "his") numbers for sectoral investment have the same "reality content" (44–45).

Lastly, this difficulty at the *sectoral* level also makes it almost impossible at the specific *project* level for an economist-adviser to spell out in detail more worthy alternatives to one or more that he perhaps considers worthy but not of the highest priority. Yet, without detailed analysis of alternatives, the economist "will not and *should not* be listened to." In this instance the reason is that there exist "not only conceivably better uses for the funds but many worse ones as well, and these are the ones that are surely going to be undertaken if no ready alternative is provided by our objecting economist" (49–50).

Hirschman noted that developing nations experience many false starts before being launched on a secure path of development, partly because of a lack of experts, including economists, who are able to generate truly useful and well-considered plans. Such plans are at a premium and often are all that is left behind from much-vaunted "integrated development programs." Here, drawing on his direct involvement and subsequent observation in Colombia, Hirschman asserted confidently that "in the investment field, the only important achievement of the International Bank's early 'fifties Mission to Colombia was the highway and railroad program, which was also the only one to have been spelled out in fairly concrete terms" (50). Such "truly useful and well-considered plans," he concluded, should go through, if necessary in the face of strictures by the economist-adviser of the "better alternative-uses-of-resources" sort.

Summing up all these reservations and constraints, the best the economist can do is to make sensible suggestions for sector-level programs and to assist other experts in producing well-thought-out and closely specified projects (50–51). This is far from nothing, but acknowledging it ought seriously to constrain the aspirations of a comprehensive, multiyear planner, not least those using diverse and often dubious macro-data series.

As noted, this exposition and sharp criticism of detailed, integrated plans obviously reflected Hirschman's experience in Colombia, but it also had roots in more diverse observations. Thus Hirschman had long since determined that there was a fatal conceptual bias incorporated into much of the discussion of economic development plans, namely, a presupposition that backwardness is owing to certain key obstacles. Remove these once and for all, so the thinking ran, and development will happen. Among these supposed absolute blocks to development was a shortage of domestic savings, sometimes substituted for or paired with inadequate foreign exchange reserves. Building on such diagnoses, there had arisen "one-gap" and "two-gap" theories explaining backwardness. Chenery was of the "gap" persuasion, emphasizing sometimes one, sometimes both, savings and foreign exchange gaps.[3]

Hirschman opposed all such obstacle-based theories, arguing—again based on his familiarity with Colombia, though in this instance also on extensive reading in economic history and the social sciences beyond economics—that it simply is not the case that development is assured provided only that the domestic savings gap or the foreign exchange gap, or any other such putative obstacle, is targeted and removed. Such assurance rests on a complementary false assumption, namely, that funds, if only they are available, will also be invested well, an assumption that cannot be given empirical content, as we have seen, both because of the diverse "reality content" of available statistics and because of a lack of well-conceived and prepared ("ready-to-be-undertaken") projects (Hirschman 1971, 49).

Rather than focus, then, on these two "terminal points"—a shortage of savings or foreign exchange at the origin and ample sound investments at the other end—Hirschman had come to insist, most conspicuously in *The Strategy of Economic Development* ([1958] 1961), that "development is held back primarily by the difficulties of channeling *existing* or potentially existing savings and aid into available productive investment opportunities." Indeed, he had come to think of this in quite other terms: the real difficulty is "a shortage of the ability to make and carry out development decisions" (36). He elaborated further on this lack in the following terms: "The ability to invest is acquired and increased primarily by practice; and the amount of practice depends . . . on the size of the modern sector of the economy. [For] an economy secretes abilities, skills, and attitudes needed for further development roughly in proportion to the size of the sector where these abilities are already required and where these attitudes are being inculcated."

Hirschman listed by way of indirect sustaining evidence a growing awareness among economists that factors other than insufficiency of savings seem to affect developmental prospects. Indeed, increasing numbers of observers had realized that savings and productive investment "are as much a result as a cause of development" ([1958] 1961, 3). For once

3. For a detailed example of gap analysis, see Chenery and Bruno 1962.

development is under way, windfall gains occur at many points. Thus, as development proceeds, consumption versus savings and work versus leisure patterns are readjusted in favor of growth, and time horizons lengthened. The supply of capital, too, is seen to be unexpectedly elastic once profit expectations rise; and even "enterprise," like capital itself, shows signs of being a positive by-product of the very process of development (2–3).

Given such empirical hints that there are in any developing country unutilized possibilities to save, and multiple good investment opportunities—possibilities that come about largely because of the development experience itself—the implication is that, once development has begun, the large task remaining is "to *combine* all these ingredients" (6).

Though in itself not a direct answer to the question of where this multipurpose binding agent might be found, Hirschman noted that at least it represents progress that the emphasis among unbiased observers seemed to have shifted. From husbanding real or imagined scarce resources such as savings and entrepreneurship, attention had moved toward identifying "pressure" points and "inducement mechanisms," and especially what he called "pacing devices," or the ordering of investments in terms of their backward (thus supply-related) and forward (thus demand-generating) linkages. This was a major contribution of *The Strategy of Economic Development*.

Pressure points occur when difficulties arise. These *will* occur, though their form and timing cannot be predicted. They challenge those most directly responsible for implementing investments to act quickly and with resolve; hence Hirschman's stress on the ability and willingness of such persons to take decisions. Inducements in the development context, as Hirschman understood them, are either rewards for behavior that spurs development or penalties for behaviors of the opposite sort. His emphasis in *Strategy* was to encourage and if possible routinize pro-development actions.

To clarify, not all "feedback" effects from development are the same in their impact, and much depends on gradually acquiring a "growth perspective" in the course of growth itself (Hirschman [1958] 1961, 10–11). Hirschman thought of intervening here in terms of inducement mechanisms, though also of "pacing," or the appropriate "sequencing" of investments. At base, it seems, Hirschman's perspective on the difficulties associated with development was that these are difficulties to be resolved, or not, via human action. It followed that a proper grasp of development strategy is not one focused on "villainous obstacles" but one having to do with the mind, with mental attitudes, including "the ability and determination of a nation and its citizens *to organize themselves* for development" (8–11; italics added). The economist, along with others, can contribute by encouraging all manner of reforms and institutional changes to help overcome long-held values that coalesce to the passive acceptance of backwardness as inevitable. But that was a far cry from comprehensive quantitative planning, à la Chenery.

He also dismissed the idea that every attempt to spur development is bound to fail because difficulties will arise along the way. Against such negativism he urged that those administratively responsible can in fact face down such difficulties by acting decisively, quickly, and often if need be.

Such a turnaround in confidence may seem unlikely, but Hirschman held that attitudes can be altered, courage can prevail over fear of failure, and energies be combined in favor of growth. Where did this conviction of his originate? Not surprisingly, given that he identified the chief factor holding nations back as "psychological," and more precisely an "insufficient number and speed of development decisions" (Hirschman [1958] 1961, 20, 25), he found it in the work of select psychologists of individual or social human behavior.

Hirschman was attracted to the work of two psychologists in particular. Both emphasized a positive side to tension. The first was Orval Hobart Mowrer (1907–1982). In *Learning Theory and Personality Dynamics* (1950), Mowrer had reported that subjects with a fear of stress could be taught to face their fear and equally, if not more important, to eschew its opposite, namely, avoiding stress simply by opting not to place themselves in circumstances where they are likely to encounter it. Such avoidance behavior is doubly undermining, since it preserves and even strengthens the inability to cope with stress. Subjects who face their fears, on the other hand, may find that they are able to master it. The relevance of this to Hirschman's focus on decision-making ability as the key ingredient in development is obvious.

The second psychologist whose work appealed to Hirschman was Leon Festinger (1919–1989), originator of the concept of cognitive dissonance. In *A Theory of Cognitive Dissonance* (1957), Festinger discussed how subjects adjust to reduce a discomforting feeling of dissonance. Faced with a reality that does not accord with their prior convictions, such as the failure of the world to end at a date and time specified by a cult leader, some cultists (especially fringe members) might simply leave the cult.

Core cultists, however, will be inclined to search for more complex explanations of the nonoccurrence that even reinforce their original trust in the leader, mispredictions notwithstanding.

It is difficult to see what Hirschman could have taken from Festinger if those who believe development is not possible are the equivalents of his hard-core types. For then the very group needed to face down and successfully address difficulties is the same as that filled with administrators least likely to be flexible enough to acquire for themselves a bias for hope and change their beliefs accordingly.[4]

Although it is just a conjecture, I find it plausible that Hirschman credited Festinger with more than he could, or perhaps wanted to, deliver. Festinger declined an invitation from Hirschman to collaborate, and he seemed equally if not more interested in a quite different aspect of his own investigations: not that some subjects' beliefs might change in the face of reality but with the rationality or irrationality of the choices persons make when various costs and benefits are attached to choices and possible alternatives.

The person who more clearly began helping Hirschman shape his arguments around this time was Nathan Rosenberg, friend and enthusiast for Hirschman's own thinking on development, and increasingly able to back him up based on his own meticulous studies of technology. Rosenberg was a rising star among economic historians of technology, and he applauded Hirschman's emphases in his 1958 *Strategy*, on linkages and, perhaps even more, on inducement mechanisms.

In the late fifties, Hirschman seems to have overlooked the rather limited, if not downright unhelpful, insights he was able to take from Festinger, being satisfied with the result that *some* subjects eliminated cognitive dissonance by altering their beliefs in the face of altered reality and tacitly linking hard-core naysayers with those he hoped to reach by inducement mechanisms. Certainly he wished to challenge the influence, for the development context, of cultural analysts like Max Weber, who had insisted that Protestant beliefs were the necessary precursors of capitalistic behavior and whom Hirschman associated with all who allowed their beliefs to dictate their reality, rather than the other way around. And he wanted to dislodge the "we think the wrong way round" conviction he found among many Latin Americans. That administrators might be the last persons likely to change their thinking seems not to have deterred him.

4. I am grateful to Kevin Hoover, both for general encouragement and for pressing me on this point.

Rosenberg's role in 1958 was probably limited, but by 1969 he was able to express Hirschman's own views, backed by detailed histories of various aspects of technological change. In bold phrasing, this emerged as "new constraints are good for you." And, more circumspectly: "Threats to an established position have often served as inducements to technical change"; and "technological mechanisms share the property of forcefully focusing attention in specific directions. Historically they [have] called attention decisively to the existence of problems the solutions to which were within the capacity of society at the time" (Rosenberg 1969, 19, 21, 23). This last phrase is telling. Translated into Hirschman's own language, it would read something like, yes, difficulties will emerge during the implementation of development projects, but with focus and will they can be faced and overcome. Although later than he might have wished, and outside my own time frame, Hirschman must have been delighted in 1969 to have his friend suggesting in print that a focus on difficulties can at the same time reveal the solution *and* suggest that it is within reach.

From a different perspective, Hirschman found the Mowrer and Festinger findings a refreshing switch from Sigmund Freud. In Hirschman's view, Freud's "pervasive influence" had been quite unhelpful to thinking about development. For it made "pathogenic agents" of "difficulties, conflict and anxiety," rather than, as Hirschman ([1958] 1961, 209n5) would have preferred, seeing in them positive opportunities.

It remains for me to ask how Hirschman fared with orthodox economists in offering these psychological findings as part of what he held up as a more efficacious approach to economic development. It is convenient to invoke Chenery to stand for orthodox skeptics.

Chenery was invited to review for the *American Economic Review* both Hirschman's *Strategy* and a slim training manual by Tinbergen, *The Design of Development*, a guide to planning written at the behest of the Economic Development Institute of the International Bank for Reconstruction and Development.

Chenery's (1959, 1063–65) double review occupied just three printed pages, divided roughly to reflect the relative number of pages in each publication. Beginning as he did with Jan Tinbergen, whose approach had his full approval, Chenery was able to present the thinking behind comprehensive, detailed planning as a model of procedural excellence.

It is striking, then, to find in Tinbergen's *Design* much that resonates with Hirschman's concerns. I have made that argument elsewhere (De Marchi 2016). Granting it, one is led to think that Chenery was unwilling in principle to make some allowance for Hirschman's views. In practice, he simply could not find a place for Hirschman's "psychological" approach in objective obstacle and plan-based development thinking. Chenery comes across in his joint review as simply at a loss to know what to say about Hirschman's dissenting ideas.

I conclude that there was a great gulf of misunderstanding between Hirschman and Chenery. At the same time, there is possible irony in the situation. At the RAND Corporation in Santa Monica, California, in 1950, a request was submitted by one of its leading psychologists for a project to be funded in which psychologists would study how groups of Air Force personnel behave under stress. The proposal was accepted and resulted in the establishment in 1952 of the RAND Systems Research Laboratory, a unit replete with psychologists.

The initial study focused on the speed and accuracy with which spotter crews could detect on their radar screens possible intrusions by Soviet bombers into US air space. Real-world stress in this case was unusually high, the result of actual failure being incalculable. But the pressure even in the laboratory simulation was also intense. The psychologists wanted to capture and understand better what made for improvement in performance, so this study was of a more general class of behavior than decision making alone (for full details of the project, see Klein, this volume); but performance, in the sense of overcoming unpredictable difficulties with development projects in the field, was close enough to decision making to make the RAND study in principle of some relevance to development planners.

The RAND psychologists found improved performance in their spotter crews. Moreover, they discovered something that seemed essential to this gain, namely, that crews (not individual spotters) were treated, along with the very model itself, as forming an organism, which was to be "grown." Essential to this was that crews were treated as teams, not as clusters of individuals. Teams received daily debriefings on their performance relative to expectations, and group feedback and suggestions were encouraged.

The study succeeded beyond expectations: by 1954 a training manual was available, and the US Air Force asked the RAND group to install the Systems Training Program at all 150 of its radar sites. Two years later the RAND study was the subject of an article in *Business Week*.

I suggest that this study came close enough to the stress faced collectively by those in charge of development projects that its outcome was of relevance to the development sphere. Had plan-focused development economists such as Chenery known of the RAND psychologists' success—as they could have by 1959 (when even a full report in published book format appeared)—they might have given more credence to Hirschman's views. At the very least, by 1959 it was not the case that there was no evidence supporting his dissident notions.

Was it not incumbent on East Coast US-based development economists of every stripe to be informed about psychological studies relevant to their concerns?

The implicit negative judgment in that question assumes that the RAND study was not known. It is one thing if it was known but not taken seriously; but even if it was not known, any negative judgment must be muted by the fact that Hirschman spent the summer of 1958 at RAND without, apparently, making it part of his business to seek out anything of possible empirical relevance to his own concerns, even if the study discussed above had long been suspended by that time and Hirschman was busy interacting with his immediate host at RAND, the political theorist Charles Lindblom. The two discussed a range of analytical issues related to development, but not, it seems, or not directly—questions of the sort about to be raised by Chenery.

References

Adelman, Jeremy. 2014. *Worldly Philosopher: A Life of Albert Hirschman*. Princeton, N.J.: Princeton University Press.

Alacevich, Michele. 2012. "Visualizing Uncertainties, or How Albert Hirschman and the World Bank Disagreed on the Project Appraisal and Development Approaches." World Bank Policy Research Working Paper 6260.

Chenery, Hollis B. 1959. Review of *The Design of Development*, by Jan Tinbergen. *American Economic Review* 59: 1063–65.

———. 1969. "The Process of Industrialization." Economic Development Report No. 146, contract no. AID/csd-1543. pdf.gov/_docs/PNAB1355.pdf.

Chenery, Hollis B., and Michel Bruno. 1962. "Development Alternatives for an Open Economy: The Case of Israel." *Economic Journal* 72: 79–103.

De Marchi, Neil. 2016. "Models and Misperceptions: Chenery, Tinbergen, and Hirschman on Development Planning." *Review of the History of Economic Thought and Methodology* (forthcoming).

Festinger, Leon. 1957. *A Theory of Cognitive Dissonance*. Evanston, Ill.: Row Peterson.

Hirschman, Albert O. (1958) 1961. *The Strategy of Economic Development*. New Haven, Conn.: Yale University Press.

———. 1964. "The Paternity of an Index." *American Economic Review* 54: 761–62.

———. 1971. *A Bias for Hope*. New Haven, Conn.: Yale University Press.

Mowrer, Orval Hobart. 1950. *Learning Theory and Personality Dynamics.* New York: Wiley.

Rosenberg, Nathan. 1969. "The Direction of Technological Change: Inducement Mechanisms and Focusing Devices." *Economic Development and Cultural Change* 18: 1–24.

Tinbergen, Jan. 1958. *The Design of Development.* Baltimore, Md.: Johns Hopkins University Press.

Measuring the Economizing Mind in the 1940s and 1950s: The Mosteller-Nogee and Davidson-Suppes-Siegel Experiments to Measure the Utility of Money

Ivan Moscati

This article explores the relationships between economics and psychology in the 1940s and 1950s by investigating the origin, content, and influence on economic analysis of two experiments on individual decision making. Both experiments had the same goal and overall structure: they aimed to measure the utility of money of several individuals on the basis of their preferences in gambles where small amounts of real money were at stake. Both experiments relied on the theory of choices involving risk that in those years was emerging as the dominant one in economics, namely, expected utility theory (EUT), with the utility measures generated by both experiments providing an indirect test of EUT's validity.

The first experiment was performed between 1948 and 1949 at Harvard University by Frederick Mosteller, a statistician who in the late 1940s had become interested in experimental psychology, and Philip Nogee, then a Harvard PhD student in psychology. The Mosteller-Nogee experiment grew directly out of Mosteller's discussions with Milton Friedman and the

Correspondence may be addressed to Ivan Moscati, Department of Economics, University of Insubria, Via Monte Generoso 71, 21100 Varese, Italy; e-mail: ivan.moscati@uninsubria.it. I am grateful to Jeff Biddle, Simon Cook, Catherine Herfeld, and the other participants in the 2015 *HOPE* conference for helpful discussions and suggestions on earlier drafts. This article has also benefited from insightful comments made by Colin Camerer, the participants in a session at the 2015 ASSA meeting, and an anonymous referee. I also thank Fondazione Cariplo and the European Society for the History of Economic Thought for financial support, and Dina Melnichuk for research assistance in Friedman's archives at the Hoover Institution Library. Any errors are mine.

History of Political Economy 48 (annual suppl.) DOI 10.1215/00182702-3619298

statistician Leonard Jimmie Savage. The second experiment was carried out at Stanford University in spring 1954 by Donald Davidson and Patrick Suppes, two analytical philosophers, and Sidney Siegel, who was then completing his PhD in psychology at Stanford with an experimental dissertation on the psychological determinants of authoritarianism. Davidson, Suppes, and Siegel took into account some aspects of the psychology of decision that had been neglected by Mosteller and Nogee in order to neutralize them and thus obtain more reliable utility measures. Both groups of experimenters concluded that their findings supported the experimental measurability of utility as well as EUT.

Although these two experiments do not tell the whole history of the interdisciplinary interaction between economics and psychology in the 1940s and 1950s, they provide a case study that allows us to illuminate a significant part of that interaction. First, the designs of the two experiments exhibit a tension between the economic image of human agency associated with EUT and insights from experimental psychology research carried on since the 1920s. For instance, EUT assumes that individuals' preferences over gambles are fixed and do not fluctuate: if an individual prefers gamble A to gamble B, that individual will not reverse preference if asked to compare the two gambles again. However, experimental psychologists such as Louis Leon Thurstone (1927) had called attention to the fact that, because of judgment errors, distraction, or variation in sensibility, individuals' comparative judgments do fluctuate. Mosteller and Nogee incorporated Thurstone's psychological insight into the design of their experiment. Or, in another example, EUT assumes that individuals do not distort objective probabilities and therefore evaluate the event "heads" in tossing a fair coin as equally likely to the event "tails." Yet experimental psychologists such as Malcolm Preston and Philip Baratta (1948), Richard Griffith (1949), and Ward Edwards (1953, 1954a, 1954b) had shown that in fact individuals do distort objective probabilities, even simple ones. In designing their experiment, Davidson, Suppes, and Siegel took account of this problem and contrived a cunning device to overcome it.

The second reason to focus on the two experiments is sociological. In the 1940s and 1950s, and in fact until recent times, economists typically lacked the expertise to perform experimental research. Therefore economic experiments were often carried out by experimental psychologists and occasionally by other noneconomists. This was also the case with the two experiments under discussion here, and the present article reconstructs how their authors, who were not economists, became interested in measuring an archetypal economic object such as the utility of money using a theory of decision making that was cultivated chiefly by economists. As I show, the relationship between economists and psychologists did not fit a simple model of division of labor, in which the economists supplied the theory and the psychologists provided the experimental technology. The psychologists actively contributed to identifying and also eliminating the "disturbing causes" that could spoil the significance of the experimental measurements of utility.

Third, the limited influence of the two experiments on economics during the late 1950s and 1960s shows, among other things, that economists were not interested in integrating into decision theory the psychological insights contained in the experiments. To do so would clearly have been difficult, and since the two experiments suggested that EUT performed well as a predictor of choice under risk, it could be set aside as nonurgent. Only in the 1970s, when robust experimental evidence against EUT accumulated, were economists compelled to reconsider the psychological phenomena discussed by Mosteller, Nogee, Davidson, Suppes, and Siegel.

1. Setting the Stage

1.1. Thurstone's Probabilistic Method of Measuring Sensations

Since the rise of psychometrics in the second half of the nineteenth century, psychologists have tried to measure sensations and intellectual abilities in an experimental way (Michell 1999). In the 1920s, the American psychologist Louis Leon Thurstone put forward a probabilistic method of measuring sensations known as the "method of comparative judgment." In Thurstone's approach, a single subject is confronted with pairs of stimuli, for example, pairs of lights, and asked to compare them with respect to some dimension, like brightness. Because of judgment errors, distraction, or variation in sensibility, the subject's comparative judgment "is not fixed. It fluctuates" (Thurstone 1927, 274). As a consequence, when confronted more than once with the same pair of stimuli A and B, sometimes the subject will rank A over B, and sometimes B over A. Thurstone used the frequency of the comparative judgments to rank the stimuli: the light perceived as brighter more than 50 percent of the time is taken to be brighter. As I show, Mosteller and Nogee employed Thurstone's probabilistic approach to give an empirical content to the economic notion of indifference.

1.2. Friedman and Wallis's Critique of Thurstone

Since the so-called marginal revolution of the 1870s, the economic theory of decision making has been largely based on the concept of utility. However, the fact that utility cannot be observed and measured in a straightforward way ensured that this concept soon became the subject of controversy (Moscati 2013, 2015). In 1930 Thurstone made a foray into economics, performing a pioneering experiment to measure the indifference curves of an individual (Thurstone 1931; for a discussion, see Moscati 2007). In 1942 Milton Friedman and Allen Wallis, the latter a statistician who had studied at Chicago with Friedman, criticized Thurstone because in his study the experimental subject had to choose from fictional rather than actual commodities: "For a satisfactory experiment it is essential that the subject give actual reactions to actual stimuli. . . . Questionnaires or other devices based on conjectural responses to hypothetical stimuli do not satisfy this requirement" (Wallis and Friedman 1942, 179–80). This criticism influenced the design of the Mosteller-Nogee experiment.

1.3. Measuring Utility through EUT

A new approach to utility measurement was suggested by John von Neumann and Oskar Morgenstern in *Theory of Games and Economic Behavior* (1944). They introduced a set of axioms on the individual's preferences that impose, among other things, the following constraints. First, the individual harbors well-defined preferences over all gambles, independently of whether these gambles are simple or complex; accordingly, for any pair of gambles A and B, the individual prefers A to B or B to A, or judges them indifferent. Second, the individual must understand correctly the objective probabilities of uncertain events, even complicated ones such as 16.67. Third, the individual cannot distort objective probabilities by reinterpreting them according to some subjective disposition. Finally, the individual does not obtain utility from the act of gambling, but only from the gamble's payoffs. Von Neumann and Morgenstern proved that an individual satisfying these and other axioms—an "EUT decision maker"— prefers the gamble associated with the highest expected utility.

Von Neumann and Morgenstern also indicated a handy way in which EUT could be used to measure utility experimentally. If an EUT decision maker is found to be indifferent between, say, a gamble yielding $500 with probability 0.4 and $1,000 with probability 0.6—such a gamble can be written as [$500, 0.4; $1,000, 0.6]—and $600 for sure, then we can infer that for the individual $u(\$600)$ is equal to $0.4 \times u(\$500) + 0.6 \times u(\$1,000)$, where u is the individual's utility function. The EUT axioms also imply that the function u is cardinal in nature, that is, unique up to linearly increasing transformations, so that only two points of it are arbitrary.[1] Thus we can state that $u(\$500) = 0$ and $u(\$1,000) = 1$, and establish that for the EUT decision maker $u(\$600) = 0.4 \times 0 + 0.6 \times 1 = 0.6$.

Beginning in the mid-1940s, the plausibility of von Neumann and Morgenstern's axioms and the validity of EUT became the subject of an intense debate in which Friedman and Savage (1948, 1952), Jacob Marschak (1950, 1951), Paul Samuelson (1950, 1952), Kenneth Arrow (1951), Harry Markowitz (1952), Armen Alchian (1953), Robert Strotz (1953), Maurice Allais (1953), Daniel Ellsberg (1954), and other major economists of the period took part.[2] The Mosteller-Nogee experiment played some role in this debate.

One of the early articles in support of EUT was coauthored by Friedman and Savage (1948). The authors here clarified how EUT can be fruitfully applied to the analysis of gambling and insurance, introduced concepts such as risk aversion that quickly became central to the theory of risky decisions, and suggested how the experimental measures of utility obtained on the basis of EUT could be used to test the validity of EUT. If, to continue the previous numerical example, in a further experiment the EUT decision maker is found to be indifferent between gamble [$10,000, 0.2; $500, 0.8] and $1,000 for sure, then he should also be indifferent between gamble [$10,000, 0.12; $500, 0.88] and $600 for sure.[3] If this is not the case, noted Friedman and Savage (1948, 304), "the supposition that individuals seek to maximize expected utility would be contradicted." The strategy suggested by Friedman and Savage to test EUT was promptly implemented by their friend Mosteller.

---

1. That u is unique up to linearly increasing transformations means that any utility function u' obtained by multiplying u by a positive number α and then adding any number β, that is, any u' such that $u' = \alpha u + \beta$, with $\alpha > 0$, still represents the individual's preferences. The two arbitrary points of a cardinal function reflect the fact that α and β are arbitrary.

2. For reviews of the debate on EUT in economics, see Fishburn 1989, Fishburn and Wakker 1995, Giocoli 2003, Mongin 2009 and 2014, Heukelom 2014, and Moscati 2016a. Although economists investigated and applied EUT more intensively than scholars in other disciplines, the theory was also discussed and used by philosophers, psychologists, mathematicians, and other noneconomists. On the reception of EUT outside economics, see Edwards 1961, Luce and Suppes 1965, Erikson et al. 2013, and Heukelom 2014.

3. If the EUT decision maker is indifferent between [$10,000, 0.2; $500, 0.8] and $1,000 for sure, then $u(\$1,000) = 0.2 \times u(\$10,000) + 0.8 \times u(\$500)$; but $u(\$1,000) = 1$ and $u(\$500) = 0$, and therefore $u(\$10,000) = 1 / 0.2 = 5$. The expected utility of [$10,000, 0.12; $500, 0.88] is $0.12 \times 5 + 0.88 \times 0 = 0.6$, which is exactly the utility of $600 for sure.

2. Friedman, Savage, and the Genesis
of the Mosteller-Nogee Experiment

Mosteller (1916–2006) first studied mathematics and statistics at the Carnegie Institute of Technology and in 1939 began his PhD at Princeton's Department of Mathematics. At a tea in Princeton in 1941, he met Savage, who had studied at the University of Michigan and was spending the academic year 1941–42 at the Institute for Advanced Study, also located in Princeton, as a postdoctoral student and von Neumann's assistant. Savage and Mosteller quickly became buddies and ended up teaching together an undergraduate course in algebra and trigonometry at Princeton University (Mosteller 2010). In 1942, however, Savage left Princeton for Cornell University.

In 1944 Mosteller interrupted his studies and moved to New York to work at the Statistical Research Group (SRG) at Columbia University, a wartime think tank providing statistical analysis for the US Army and directed by Allen Wallis (1980). At SRG, Mosteller found Savage, who had joined the SRG some months earlier. Friedman had been at SRG since March 1943 and had also become acquainted with Savage. At SRG, Mosteller, Savage, and Friedman worked together on various projects: a paper on sequential statistical estimators (Girshick, Mosteller, and Savage 1946), a paper designing a metallurgical experiment to find the alloy that maximizes the time to rupture under a given stress (Friedman and Savage 1947),[4] and a book on acceptance sampling (Freeman et al. 1948).

When the war ended and SRG was dismantled, Mosteller, Savage, and Friedman took different paths. Mosteller returned to Princeton and completed his PhD with a dissertation in statistics. In 1946 he joined the faculty of Harvard's Department of Social Relations, then chaired by the sociologist Talcott Parsons. The department hosted disciplines as diverse as psychology, sociology, and anthropology, and was endowed with a laboratory for psychological experiments. As for Friedman, in 1946 he returned to the University of Chicago, where he began teaching a course in price theory that revived his interest in utility analysis. Savage also joined the University of Chicago in 1946. There, he and Friedman began collaborating on the EUT article mentioned above (Friedman and Savage 1948).

Meanwhile, working in the interdisciplinary environment of Harvard's Department of Social Relations, Mosteller became increasingly involved in psychology. Beginning in 1947–48, he coauthored with some Harvard

---

4. Friedman and Savage did not conduct any actual experiment but only discussed how, based on statistical theory, such an experiment should be carried out.

colleagues various papers measuring visual stimuli, perspective illusions, and pain sensations (Bruner, Postman, and Mosteller 1950; Keats, Beecher, and Mosteller 1950). In 1948–49, Mosteller also taught a course on psychometric methods. Given this background, it is not surprising to find that in late 1947 or early 1948 he conceived an experiment to measure utility: "Von Neumann and Morgenstern's book, *Theory of Games and Economic Behavior*, led to much research on ideas of utility, and I thought it would be worth actually trying to measure utility in real people to see what would happen" (Mosteller 2010, 196).

Beginning in February 1948, Mosteller discussed the experiment design in letters to Friedman and Savage. Wallis also contributed to the discussion, albeit in a minor way.[5] In a letter dated February 27, 1948, and addressed to both Friedman and Savage, Mosteller discussed which payoffs and winning probabilities the gambles in the experiments should have ("I have thought over Jimmy's idea that we should maintain true odds at 1:1 . . . but I don't see where it gets me"), and how to phrase the instructions for the experimental subjects ("One phrase I have considered is 'Try to make as much money as you can'. But this has drawbacks").[6] Friedman and Savage gave prompt feedback to Mosteller and supported his experimental project.[7]

In late February and early March 1948, Mosteller conducted a couple of pilot studies for the experiment, and it is probably at this point that he co-opted into the project Nogee (1916–1980), then a Harvard PhD student in clinical psychology whom Mosteller was supervising. According to Mosteller (2010, 196), Nogee was "very quantitatively inclined and eager to participate in designing and executing such an experiment." In his correspondence with Friedman and Savage, Mosteller did not mention Nogee by name, but, beginning in March 1948, when referring to the experiment, he often used the first-person plural.[8] The hidden figure within Mosteller's "we" was certainly Nogee.

Mosteller and Nogee conducted the actual experiment a year after the pilot study, that is, from February through May 1949, and devoted the

5. See Milton Friedman Papers, box 30, folder 37, and box 39, folder 10.

6. Friedman Papers, box 39, folder 10.

7. See, in particular, Friedman to Mosteller, March 3, 1948, and Savage to Mosteller, March 28, 1948; both letters are in Friedman Papers, box 39, folder 10. On Friedman's stance toward experimental research in the late 1940s and 1950s, see Moscati 2007.

8. Mosteller to Friedman, March 8, 1948: "We have run off one session"; Mosteller to Savage, April 5, 1948: "I think we are closing in pretty sharply on the utility curve with a 5¢." See Friedman Papers, box 39, folder 10.

second part of 1949 and early months of 1950 to analyzing the experimental data. From time to time, Friedman asked Mosteller about the progress of the project.[9] The article was eventually published in October 1951 in the *Journal of Political Economy* under the title "An Experimental Measurement of Utility." By that time, Nogee had left Harvard to become an assistant professor at Boston University.

3. Mosteller and Nogee's Experiment

Mosteller and Nogee (1951, 371–72) presented their article as almost an outgrowth of Friedman and Savage's 1948 paper and addressed two main questions: whether utility can be measured, at least "in a laboratory situation," and whether utility, if measurable, "can be used to predict behavior." I first give an overview of the experiment and its main results, and then discuss the tension between the economic and psychological elements of its design. To appreciate that tension, I present some of the experiment's technical details.

3.1. Overview

Mosteller and Nogee carried out their experiment at the Laboratory of Social Relations at Harvard University. The experimental subjects were ten Harvard undergraduate students and five Massachusetts National Guardsmen. Each had to choose, a number of times, whether to participate in a gamble where they could win or lose small amounts of actual money, or refuse the gamble. Subjects played with one dollar, which they received at the beginning of each experimental session.

The experiment had two parts. In the first, the subjects faced "simple-hands" gambles with the following structure. The experimenters showed a card with five numbers called a "hand," as in the game of poker dice, for example, 66431. The card also indicated an amount of money—call it $M—that a subject would win if, by rolling five dice, he "beat" the displayed "hand," whereby the strength of the hands is calculated as in poker. Thus, for instance, hand 22263 ("three of a kind") beats 66431 ("pair"). The amounts of money ranged from a minimum of 2.5 cents to a maximum of $5.07. If the rolled five dice did not beat the displayed hand, the

9. Friedman to Mosteller, December 13, 1949: "How is the gambling experiment?" Friedman to Mosteller, February 22, 1950: "I am extremely curious how the experiment has been coming out. Does it live up to its premise of last spring? Your paper should be fascinating." See Friedman Papers, box 39, folder 37.

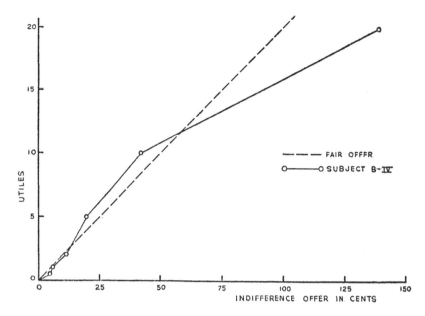

Figure 1. Estimated utility curve for money of experimental subject B-IV. The continuous broken line shows the utility curve for money of subject B-IV. The utility level 101 is not shown. The dotted straight line is the hypothetical utility function of an individual neutral to risk. Source: Mosteller and Nogee 1951, 387

subject lost 5 cents. The subjects were informed about the actual odds for each hand, that is, about the ratio between the probability of winning over that of losing.

By confronting the experimental subjects with different gambles of this form, Mosteller and Nogee (MN) identified a number of monetary amounts $M and odds o for which the experimental subjects were indifferent to participating or not in the gamble. Based on this information and the assumption that $u(\$0) = 0$ and $u(-5\rlap/c) = -1$, MN measured the utility that seven amounts of money had for the experimental subjects. In particular, MN identified the amounts of money corresponding to the utility levels 0.5, 1, 2, 5, 10, 20, and 101, thus identifying seven points of the utility function for money of each subject. By connecting these seven points by straight lines, they drew an approximate graph of the utility curves for money of the subjects. For instance, figure 3b of their article, which is reproduced in figure 1, shows the estimated utility curve for money of experimental subject B-IV.

In the second part of the experiment, Mosteller and Nogee used the utility functions elicited in the first part to predict whether the subjects would accept or reject more complicated gambles called "doublet hands." In a doublet-hand situation, subjects were faced with two hands, such as 66431 and 22263, the odds of beating only the weaker hand (66431), the odds of beating both hands, and the associated winnings. If, by rolling the five dice, the subject did not beat either of the hands, he lost 5 cents.

If the utility function obtained in the first part of the experiment from simple hands could be used to predict the subjects' choices over doublet hands, then EUT and the utility measurements based on it would be validated.

3.2. Findings

In the first part of the experiment, Mosteller and Nogee were able to elicit the utility curves for money of all but one of the experimental subjects.[10] MN's first conclusion was therefore that "it is feasible to measure utility experimentally" (403). In particular, they found that while the Harvard students tended to have concave utility curves for money, that is, to be risk adverse, the Massachusetts National Guardsmen tended to have convex utility curves for money, that is, to be risk seeking.

The findings of the second part of the experiment were less clear-cut, but, nevertheless, Mosteller and Nogee assessed them in a favorable way: predictions of choice behavior over doublet hands based on simple hands "are not so good as might be hoped, but their general direction is correct" (399). Thus, they concluded that "the notion that people behave in such a way as to maximize their expected utility is not unreasonable."

3.3. Design

Many elements in the design of the experiment rely on the economic image of human agency embodied in the EUT decision maker. I begin by discussing these elements (items 1–5), and then move to the parts of the experimental design that were shaped by psychological considerations (items 6–7).

1. *Real Money.* In the psychometric experiments carried out by psychologists, subjects had to respond to stimuli, for example, had to say

---

10. The outlier was a Harvard undergraduate whose behavior was "so erratic that no utility curve at all could be found for him" (Mosteller and Nogee 1951, 385).

which light they perceived as brighter, but did not receive any reward or penalty depending on their responses. In contrast, Mosteller and Nogee introduced actual monetary rewards into the experiment and devoted part of their article to arguing that these rewards represented nontrivial incentives for their subjects (376, 402–3).

Neither in the correspondence between Mosteller, Friedman, Savage, and Wallis that I perused nor in the Mosteller and Nogee article is there any reference to Friedman and Wallis's 1942 critique of Thurstone's experiment (see section 1.2). However, Mosteller and Nogee's commitment to real and nontrivial monetary incentives implicitly agrees with Friedman and Wallis's claim that experiments in which subjects give "conjectural responses to hypothetical stimuli" are of little interest for economists.[11]

2. *Objective Probabilities.* Mosteller and Nogee informed their experimental subjects about the actual statistical odds, that is, about the objective probabilities, of winning and losing. Around the same time, empirical studies on betting behavior carried out by the psychologists Malcolm Preston and Philip Baratta (1948) and Richard Griffith (1949) suggested that bettors harbor "psychological probabilities" that do not coincide with the corresponding mathematical probabilities. In particular, these studies indicated that bettors overvalue low mathematical probabilities and underestimate high ones. The rediscovery of Frank Ramsey's 1926 essay "Truth and Probability" promoted the idea of a subjective approach to probability.

Although Mosteller and Nogee cited Ramsey a number of times and discussed at length whether subjective (or psychological) and objective (or mathematical) probabilities coincide, their experimental design is based on objective probabilities only and, therefore, on the implicit assumption that experimental subjects do not distort objective probabilities.

3. *Complicated Probabilities.* Mosteller and Nogee presented their experimental subjects with gambles having quite complicated odds. The winning odds for the simple hands the subjects faced in the first part of the experiment were 1:0.50, 1:1.01, 1:2.01, 1:5.00, 1:10.17, 1:20.24, and 1:101.32.[12] The winning odds for the doublet hands used in the second

11. The issue of whether monetary incentives are really necessary to motivate experimental subjects is still a subject of controversy between economists, who typically argue that monetary incentives are indeed necessary, and psychologists, who generally do not think so. For recent discussions, see Guala 2005; and Fréchette and Schotter 2015.

12. These winning odds correspond, respectively, to winning probabilities 66.67, 49.75, 33.22, 16.67, 8.95, 4.71, and 0.98.

part of the experiment were even more complicated. Although for an EUT decision maker all probability figures are equally comprehensible, from a psychological viewpoint it is natural to argue that subjects may find it hard to understand odds and probability figures like those used by Mosteller and Nogee.

4. *Gamble versus Sure Outcome.* In the experiment subjects had to choose between a proper gamble, in which they could win $M or lose 5 cents, and the sure outcome associated with the refusal of gambling. In the EUT framework there is no difference between gamble-versus-gamble choices and gamble-versus-sure-outcome choices because EUT rules out the existence of a specific utility or disutility deriving from the very act of gambling. However, if such specific utility for gambling exists—as seems plausible from a psychological viewpoint—such utility would distort utility measures like those obtained by Mosteller and Nogee. A positive utility for gambling would in fact lead to overestimation of the utility of sure amounts of money, while a negative utility for gambling would have the opposite effect.

5. *Different Types of Gambles.* Mosteller and Nogee used the utility measures elicited from choices involving simple hands to predict choices involving doublet hands, which were much more complex. Again, from the economic viewpoint this is perfectly legitimate because an EUT decision maker displays well-defined preferences over all gambles, independently of whether these gambles are simple or complex. From a psychological standpoint, however, using utility measures elicited from simple gambles to predict choices over complex gambles may appear questionable.

Although the above elements of the experimental design rely on the image of human agency associated with EUT, other elements suggest a sensitivity to psychological considerations that EUT rules out.

6. *Understanding Money.* Mosteller and Nogee's utility measurement was based on the identification of monetary amounts $M and odds o such that the experimental subjects were indifferent to participating in a gamble yielding $M with odds o and rejecting it. In principle, the indifferent gamble can be identified in two ways, namely, (1) by fixing $M and adjusting o until the indifference point is reached, or (2) by fixing o and adjusting $M until the indifference point is reached. Within the EUT framework these two methods are equivalent because the EUT decision maker understands amounts of money and odds, that is, probabilities, equally well. However, from a psychological perspective it can be argued that individuals are more familiar with amounts of money than with probabil-

ities and that therefore they are more capable of adjusting the former than the latter. Based on these considerations, method (2) should be preferred. This is in fact Mosteller and Nogee's stance: "The experimenters preferred to . . . search for a [monetary amount] A that would bring a balance [i.e., indifference]. . . . Most people are more familiar with amounts of money than with probabilities" (Mosteller and Nogee 1951, 373).

7. *Probabilistic Indifference.* Although the EUT-based method of measuring utility is grounded on the identifications of indifferent gambles, it is difficult to observe indifference in an actual experimental setting. Experimental subjects typically agree to participation in a gamble or turn the gamble down, but it is not clear what the behavioral correlate of indifference would be: dithering? That the subject dithers for some sufficiently long time?

To circumvent the problem, Mosteller and Nogee resorted to Thurstone's probabilistic approach to comparative judgment and defined a subject indifferent if, when confronted with a gamble more than once, he accepted and rejected it equally often: "When . . . B and D are chosen *equally often*, i.e., each chosen in half of their simultaneous presentations, the individual is said to be indifferent between B and D" (374).

This definition of indifference was accompanied by an explicit criticism of the nonprobabilistic approach to preference built into the EUT axioms. Mosteller and Nogee argued that "subjects are not so consistent about preference and indifference as Von Neumann and Morgenstern postulated" (404). Rather, gradation of preference is the rule, as "the experience of psychologists with psychological tests has shown" (374).

3.4. Summing Up

Mosteller and Nogee were, respectively, a statistician turned experimental psychologist and a psychologist. Nevertheless, their experiment design owes much to the economic image of human agency. Some elements of the design—such as having experimental subjects adjust amounts of money rather than probabilities, or the probabilistic approach to indifference—do rely on psychological insights, but many other elements are tailored to the EUT decision maker. In particular, the design rules out the possibility that actual individuals may distort objective probabilities, misunderstand complicated odds, derive utility from the very act of gambling, or behave differently when faced with different types of gambles. The fact that in the design the tension between the economic understanding of human agency associated with EUT and the psychological insights conflicting with it is resolved very much in favor of the former appears to reflect Friedman and Savage's influence on Mosteller.

4. The Rise of EUT, 1950–54

In 1950 EUT was still only one among many theories of decision under risk on the economists' table (Arrow 1951), but from the early 1950s its fortunes rapidly improved. Marschak (1950) and others provided axiomatizations of EUT more transparent and compelling than that offered by von Neumann and Morgenstern (see Bleichrodt et al. 2016). Marschak (1951) also articulated a normative argument in favor of EUT according to which the theory indicates how rational individuals should choose.

The end of a first phase of the debate on EUT and the rise of the theory as the mainstream economic model for decision making under risk can be associated with an important international conference that took place in Paris in May 1952. At this conference, the opponents of EUT headed by Allais faced a forceful group of supporters of the theory—collectively labeled by Allais as the "American School"—that included Arrow, Friedman, Marschak, Savage, and Samuelson. Samuelson also organized a symposium on EUT that was published in the October 1952 issue of *Econometrica* and collected a number of articles backing EUT.[13] The publication of Savage's *Foundations of Statistics* (1954) reinforced the dominant status of EUT in economics. Building on Ramsey's subjective approach to probability, Savage showed how to extend EUT to the case in which the probabilities of uncertain outcomes are not objectively given but express the decision maker's subjective beliefs about the likelihood of the outcomes.

The Mosteller and Nogee experiment played some role in the rise of EUT. Between 1952 and 1954, advocates of EUT argued that the experiment provided reliable empirical support to the theory (Friedman and Savage 1952; Markowitz 1952; Alchian 1953; Strotz 1953; Marschak 1954; Savage 1954). Critics of EUT, by contrast, claimed that the experiment results were inconclusive or hardly extensible to more realistic situations (Manne 1952; Allais 1953; Ellsberg 1954). At any rate, the experiment showed that EUT has clear empirical implications, can be used to

---

13. On the Paris conference, see Jallais and Pradier 2005; and Mongin 2014. Samuelson was initially a severe critic of EUT, but correspondence and discussion with Savage, Marschak, and Friedman led him to endorse the theory; on Samuelson's conversion to EUT, see Moscati 2016a.

make predictions, and can therefore be falsified by experimental findings. This was not the case for other theories of decision under risk such as Allais's. More importantly, even if inconclusive or hardly extensible to more realistic situations, the results of the Mosteller and Nogee experiment failed to contradict EUT. Therefore, supporters of the theory such as Friedman and Savage (1952, 466) could claim that the experiment justified some "mild optimism" about the validity of EUT.

The rise of EUT as the mainstream economic model for risky choices in the early 1950s explains why Davidson, Suppes, and Siegel, when they entered the economics of decision making from their home disciplines, focused on EUT rather than other theories of choice under risk. But before I turn to their experiment and outline how they embarked on the measurement of utility, a further contextual element should be mentioned.

As illustrated in section 3.3, Mosteller and Nogee had discussed the possibility that subjective and objective probabilities may not coincide. Ward Edwards, another of Mosteller's PhD students in psychology at Harvard, investigated the issue further (on Edwards, see Shanteau, Mellers, and Schum 1999). In his doctoral dissertation and a series of papers derived from it, Edwards (1953, 1954a, 1954b) presented experimental results confirming that bettors harbor subjective probabilities that are at odds with objective probabilities. In particular, Edwards (1953, 363) pointed out that this fact "has serious implications for the utility curves of Mosteller and Nogee and indeed for the whole method of utility measurement proposed by von Neumann and Morgenstern." In fact, if subjective and objective probabilities are different, and the experimenter has no clue about the former, the expected-utility formula presents two unknowns— the utilities of money *and* the subjective probabilities—so that it becomes useless for quantifying the utilities of money in terms of probabilities. In designing their experiment, Davidson, Suppes, and Siegel took account of this problem and contrived a cunning device to overcome it.

5. Suppes, Davidson, Siegel, and the Stanford Value Theory Project

Patrick Suppes (1922–2014) studied physics and meteorology at the University of Chicago (BS 1943) and, after serving in the Army Air Force during the war, in 1947 entered Columbia University as a graduate student in philosophy (Suppes 1979). At Columbia he came under the influence of the philosopher and measurement theorist Ernest Nagel, and also took courses in advanced mathematical topics. Around 1948 he was one of a group of

Columbia PhD students who organized an informal seminar on von Neumann and Morgenstern's *Theory of Games*. He graduated in June 1950 and, in September of the same year, joined the Department of Philosophy at Stanford University, where he remained for the rest of his working life.

Suppes's early publications had little if anything to do with economics, psychology, or the behavioral sciences in general. Rather, Suppes worked on the theory of measurement and the foundations of physics using a strict axiomatic approach. It must be noted, however, that in a footnote in his first article, he (1951, 104n2) criticized von Neumann and Morgenstern's definition of the relation of indifference in *Theory of Games*. This passing criticism shows that from the early stages of his scientific career Suppes had been familiar with von Neumann and Morgenstern's axiomatic approach to utility theory.

Suppes's knowledge of game and decision analysis increased in the early 1950s under the influence of his postdoctoral tutor at Stanford, J. C. C. "Chen" McKinsey (1908–1953), a logician who had worked intensively on game theory at the RAND Corporation, a think tank created by the US Army Air Force in 1946 in Santa Monica, California. In 1951 McKinsey joined Stanford's philosophy department, having being forced to leave RAND because his homosexuality was considered a security risk (Nasar 1998). At the time, he was completing his *Introduction to the Theory of Games* (McKinsey 1952), which became the first textbook in game theory. Suppes's familiarity with game theory and decision analysis was further enhanced by his summer research position in the early 1950s, working with David Blackwell and Meyer A. Girshick while they were writing their book *Theory of Games and Statistical Decisions* (1954), in which the tools of decision and game theory were employed to evaluate statistical procedures.

In 1953 John Goheen, the chair of Stanford's philosophy department, obtained a grant from the Ford Foundation for a study on "value, decision, and rationality." Around the same time, Goheen negotiated contracts with two military agencies, namely, the Office of Naval Research and the Office of Ordnance Research of the US Army, for work on the theory of decisions involving risk. Goheen entrusted McKinsey and Suppes with the project, which was renamed the "Stanford Value Theory Project" (Suppes 1979; Isaac 2013; Moscati 2016b).[14]

---

14. On the reasons why in the 1950s the Ford Foundation and military agencies such as the Office of Naval Research were interested in funding research on decision making, see Pooley and Solovey 2010 and Erikson et al. 2013.

McKinsey and Suppes co-opted into the enterprise Donald Davidson, another philosopher who had joined the philosophy department in January 1951. Davidson (1917–2003) had studied at Harvard University (BA 1939, PhD 1949), where he was influenced by the logician and analytical philosopher W. V. O. Quine. Today, Davidson is best known for his influential work on the philosophy of mind and action, the philosophy of language, and epistemology. However, he published these works only from the early 1960s on. In the 1950s he was still busy with teaching and did not as yet have a clear philosophical project. As he explained in a later interview: "Suppes and McKinsey took me under their wing . . . because they thought this guy [i.e., Davidson] really ought to get some stuff out" (quoted in Lepore 2004, 252). Most of the research connected with the Stanford Value Theory Project was conducted between 1953 and 1955, and appeared in print between 1955 and 1957. However, McKinsey contributed only to the first part of the project because in October 1953 he committed suicide.

The final output of the Stanford Value Theory Project consisted of three articles, which were theoretical in nature,[15] and a book presenting the results of the experiment to measure the utility of money. Davidson and Suppes began thinking about the experiment in November 1953. However, neither had any previous experience in experimental investigation, and they therefore brought Sidney Siegel into the project. Siegel (1916–1961), then completing his PhD in psychology at Stanford, had begun his doctoral studies in 1951, at the age of thirty-five, after having taken a rather singular educational path (Engvall Siegel 1964). In the doctoral dissertation he completed in fall 1953, Siegel (1954) presented a possible measure of authoritarianism based on experimental techniques.

Davidson, Suppes, and Siegel conducted their experiment to measure the utility of money in spring 1954; their experimental subjects were nineteen male students hired through the Stanford University Student Employment Service.[16] They first presented their experimental results in a

15. Davidson, McKinsey, and Suppes (1955) introduced into decision analysis the so-called money pump argument, which shows that an individual with intransitive preferences can be exploited and induced to pay money for nothing. Suppes and his doctoral student Muriel Winet (1955) put forward an axiomatization of cardinal utility based on the notion of utility differences. Davidson and Suppes (1956) developed an axiomatization of subjective EUT in which the set of alternatives over which the individual's preferences are defined is not infinite, as it is in the Ramsey-Savage framework, but finite. See Baccelli and Mongin 2016 for a discussion of the three articles mentioned in this note.

16. Early in 1955, and without Siegel's collaboration, Davidson and Suppes performed a second experiment. This involved seven students in music at Stanford University and aimed at measuring their utility for LP records of classical music on the basis of their choices of gambles,

Stanford Value Theory Project report published in August 1955 (Davidson, Siegel, and Suppes 1955), and two years later in *Decision Making: An Experimental Approach* (1957). As Ellsberg (1958, 1009) noticed in reviewing the book, it is not so much a systematic introduction to decision making as "a long article, dealing fairly technically with problems connected with this particular set of experiments."

On the book's cover, the work is presented as coauthored by Davidson and Suppes "in collaboration with Sidney Siegel," who meanwhile had moved to Pennsylvania State University. In practice, it is difficult to disentangle the individual contributions to the experiment, and therefore in the following I consider it a joint product.

6. The Davidson-Suppes-Siegel Experiment

The primary aim of Davidson, Suppes, and Siegel (henceforth DSS) was "to develop a psychometric technique for measuring utility" in an interval scale, that is, in a cardinal way, within the expected-utility framework (Davidson, Suppes, and Siegel 1957, 25). In particular, they were "originally inspired by the desire to see whether it was possible to improve on the Mosteller and Nogee's results" (20).

As already mentioned, the general structure of the MN and DSS experiments is analogous. However, DSS modified a number of the elements of the MN design in order to make the decision tasks faced by their experimental subjects psychologically more friendly than the tasks faced by the MN subjects. However, and unlike the majority of current behavioral economists, DSS did not exploit their psychological insights to argue that the standard economic theory of decision making was flawed. Rather, they used psychological considerations to avoid confusions or biases in their subjects, thereby generating utility measures as similar as possible to those that would have been obtained if the choices had been made by EUT decision makers. To understand how DSS managed to do this, we have to enter into the technical details of their experimental design.

---

with records as prizes. The significance of this experiment, however, was marred by the high number of intransitive choices observed by Suppes and Davidson. The intransitives, which were probably because most students perceived the LP records as too similar, made it tricky to identify even ordinal utility functions for the records. See Davidson and Suppes 1956; and Davidson, Suppes, and Siegel 1957, 84–103.

6.1. Design

1. *Real Money.* Like MN, DSS used real monetary payoffs. At the beginning of each experimental session, subjects received $2.00 to gamble, and the gambles' payoffs ranged from –35 cents to +50 cents (fractions of cents were not allowed). The use of real money was motivated by philosophical preoccupations very much in accord with the sort of preoccupations expressed by Friedman and Wallis in their critique of Thurstone's experiment. Davidson, Suppes, and Siegel (1957, 7) in fact followed the behaviorist approach to human agency advocated by Bertrand Russell (1921) and Ramsey ([1926] 1950), downplaying the relevance of introspection for decision analysis and arguing that "it is with actual decision-making behavior that decision theory is concerned." Accordingly, DSS required that the decisions made in the experimental situation were "real in the most importance sense," that is, they required that the announcement of preferences between gambles made by a subject was "followed by . . . paying the subject (or collecting from him) the appropriate amount of money" (6–7).

2. *Subjective Probabilities.* While the MN experiment was based on objective probabilities, DSS explicitly advocated a subjective approach to probability and followed the Ramsey-Savage subjective version of EUT. Accordingly, they considered gambles of the form "x cents of dollar if event E occurs, –y cents of dollars if event E does not occur"—for brevity [x¢, E; –y¢, not-E]—whereby each subject was supposed to assign his subjective probabilities $\Pi(E)$ and $\Pi(not-E)$ to the two events. As explained in section 4, however, if subjective probabilities are unknown, the expected-utility formula cannot be used to measure the utility of money.

DSS cited the articles by Preston-Baratta and Edwards showing that individuals often distort objective probabilities and therefore were well aware that the problem could not be solved by choosing events with apparently straightforward objective probabilities, such as "heads" or "tails" in tossing a coin. Moreover, in the pilots of their experiment, Davidson, Suppes, and Siegel (1957, 51) found that their subjects often preferred gamble [x¢, heads; –x¢, tails] to gamble [–x¢, heads; x¢, tails], so showing that they considered "heads" more probable than "tails." DSS eventually solved the problem by constructing special dice with a nonsense syllable, such as ZOJ, on three faces, and another nonsense syllable, such as ZEJ, on the other three faces.[17] If we indicate as ZOJ the event that "the syllable ZOJ comes up when tossing a die" and as ZEJ the event that "the syllable ZEJ comes up," DSS found that their experimental subjects were indifferent between [x¢, ZOJ; –x¢, ZEJ] and [–x¢, ZOJ; x¢, ZEJ], so showing that they actually believed that the mutually exclusive events ZOJ and ZEJ were equally likely, that is, that $\Pi(\text{ZOJ}) = \Pi(\text{ZEJ}) = 0.5$.

3. *Simple Probabilities.* In using the ZEJ and ZOJ events, DSS not only solved the problem associated with the identification of subjective probabilities but also avoided the psychologically tricky odds the MN subjects were presented with. If experimental subjects understand fifty-fifty gambles better than gambles with more complex odds, then the utility measures obtained from choices over ZOJ-ZEJ gambles are more reliable than the measures obtained from choices over the simple and doublets hands used by MN.

4. *Gamble versus Gamble.* In the MN experiment, subjects had to choose between a proper gamble and a sure amount of money corresponding to the status quo. Davidson, Suppes, and Siegel (1957, 23) stressed that if gambling itself has a negative or positive utility for the subject, this approach "would produce the maximum distortion" in the utility measures.

To overcome this problem, in all decision situations but one DSS had their experimental subjects choose between two proper gambles of the form [x¢, ZOJ; –y¢, ZEJ]. In this way, the psychologically plausible utilities for gambling associated with the two bets should cancel out, and therefore the utility measures obtained in the gamble-versus-gamble situation should be more precise than those obtained in the gamble-versus-sure-outcome situation considered by MN.

5. *Same Type of Gambles.* DSS ran a second session of the experiment to check the utility measures obtained in the first session. While MN performed this test by using the utility functions elicited from choices involving simple hands to predict choices involving doublet hands, DSS considered choices over the same type of gambles. Specifically, DSS ran a second experimental session that took place at some period—varying

17. According to Alberta Engvall Siegel (1964, 9), Siegel's second wife, it was Siegel who came up with the idea of the ZOJ-ZEJ dice: "A central problem [in the DSS experiment] was identifying an event which had subjective probability .50 for the subject, and Sid devised a zero-association nonsense-syllable die to serve as this event." I have found no evidence confirming or disconfirming this claim. In their autobiographies, Davidson (1999) and Suppes (1979) tend to downplay Siegel's role in the experiment (Davidson does not even mention Siegel), but do not discuss the paternity of the ZOJ-ZEJ dice.

from a few days to several weeks—after the first one. In this second session they reelicited the utility curves for money of their experimental subjects from choices between [x¢, ZOJ; –y¢, ZEJ] gambles analogous to those used in the first session. Finally, DSS checked whether the utility curves elicited in the second experimental session were like those elicited in the first.

6. *Understanding Money*. In the DSS experiment, the payoffs of all gambles had the same probability, namely, 0.5. Accordingly, the identification of indifferent gambles was necessarily based on modification of the monetary payoff at stake in the gambles. In this respect, the DSS experiment was similar to the MN one. In particular, DSS (1957, 7–9) ruled out fractions of cents, which are knotty from a psychological viewpoint, and considered only payoffs consisting of integer amounts of cents.

7. *Approximate Indifference*. Like MN, DSS faced the problem of identifying an empirical correlate of the notion of "indifference." They could not follow MN and use Thurstone's probabilistic definition of indifference because their subjects did not change their minds when confronted more than once with the same pair of gambles. For DSS, this outcome was chiefly because their gambles were simpler than those used by MN. "Once they [the experimental subjects] chose a given option over another, they consistently held to this choice. . . . The primary reason for this kind of response is no doubt the relative simplicity of the offers. Mosteller and Nogee, using the more complicated game of poker dice to generate chance events, did get a distribution of responses" (Davidson, Suppes, and Siegel 1957, 41).

DSS adopted a definition of indifference according to which two gambles A and B are indifferent if A is preferred to B, but, by adding one single cent to one of B's payoffs, the new gamble B′ is preferred to A. For instance, if a subject prefers A = [15¢, ZOJ; –12¢, ZEJ] to B = [11¢, ZOJ; –9¢, ZEJ] but prefers B′ = [12¢, ZOJ; –9¢, ZEJ] to A, then A and B are said to be "indifferent." This is an approximate definition of indifference in the sense that it only allows the statement that there exists some amount of money z included between 11 cents and 12 cents such that [z¢, ZOJ; –9¢, ZEJ] is indifferent to A.

DSS assigned utility values –1 and +1 to amounts of money $a = -4$¢ and $b = 6$¢. Then, for each subject, they looked for four monetary amounts c, d, f, g such that $u(c) = -3$, $u(d) = +3$, $u(f) = -5$ and $u(g) = +5$. For the reason explained above, however, DSS could determine c, d, f, and g only by approximation, and therefore were able to elicit only the bounds of the subjects' utility curves rather than the utility curves themselves.[18]

6.2. Findings

In the first part of their experiment, DSS managed to elicit the bounds of the utility curves of fifteen of their nineteen experimental subjects. The subjects' utility curves were presented in graphs like the one reproduced in figure 2 below, which refers to Subject 1.

Regarding the fifteen subjects for whom it was possible to elicit utility curves, the main experimental findings obtained by DSS (1957, 62–72) can be summarized as follows:

1. The utility curves of ten subjects displayed a trend similar to the curve of Subject 1's, i.e., convex for wins (love for risk) and concave for losses (risk aversion);
2. The utility curves of two subjects displayed the opposite trend: they were concave for wins and convex for losses;
3. The utility curves of the remaining three subjects were fundamentally linear through their length, suggesting that they were risk neutral.

DSS compared these findings with those obtained by MN from choices over simple hands and argued that, despite the differences between the two experiments, the degree of similarity between their results was "fairly striking" (75).

In the second session of the experiment, DSS reelicited the utility curves of ten of the original fifteen experimental subjects and found that, for nine of the ten subjects, the utility curves elicited in the two sessions were in fact very similar.[19] Thus, like MN, DSS concluded their experimental study in an optimistic way, that is, by arguing that measuring utility experimentally appears feasible: "The chief experimental result may be interpreted as showing that for some individuals and under appropriate circumstances it is possible to measure utility in an interval scale [i.e., in a cardinal way]" (19). This result, in turn, supported the thesis that "an indi-

18. For instance, DSS found that, for Subject 1, the sum c corresponding to utility level -3 lies between $-11¢$ and $-10¢$; the sum d corresponding to utility level $+3$ lies between $11¢$ and $12¢$; the sum f corresponding to utility level -5 lies between $-18¢$ and $-15¢$; and the sum g corresponding to utility level $+5$ lies between $14¢$ and $18¢$.

19. The behavior of the remaining subject was explained by the fact that he was a foreign student with some language difficulty (Davidson, Suppes, and Siegel 1957, 69).

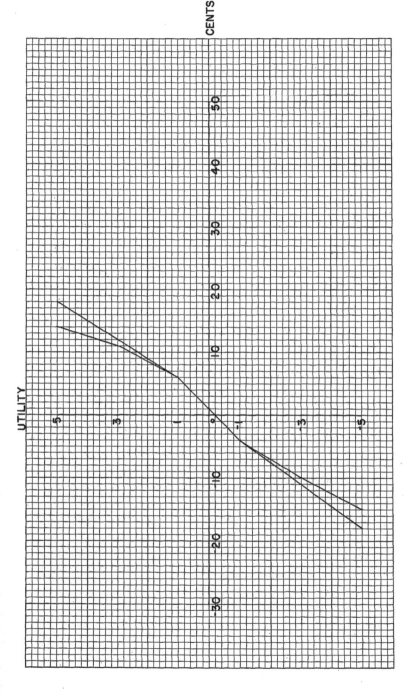

Figure 2. Bounds for Subject 1's utility curve of money. The two continuous lines are the bounds within which the "true" utility curve lies. The bounds are drawn for the utility values −5, −3, −1, +1, +3, +5, which are connected by straight lines. Source: Davidson, Suppes, and Siegel1957, 63

vidual makes choices among alternatives involving risk as if he were trying to maximize expected utility" (26).

6.3. Summing Up

In designing their experiment, DSS took into account a number of psychological phenomena that MN had neglected, such as the fact that actual individuals may distort objective probabilities or get confused when facing gambles with complicated odds. If considered from the viewpoint of EUT, these phenomena may be seen as "disturbing causes" that jeopardize the validity of the theory and spoil the significance of the experimental measurements of utility. The very fact of discussing these psychological phenomena in a book addressed not only to psychologists but also, and primarily, to economists was certainly pioneering.

However, DSS took those aspects of the psychology of decision making into account mostly in order to neutralize them. One may say that they took into consideration the psychology of decision making only to have their experimental subjects behave like brave EUT decision makers. It is therefore not surprising that DSS concluded that utility is measurable and EUT validated.

7. Influence in Economics

In the economic literature of the decade 1955–65, the MN and DSS experiments were cited in connection with issues about the measurability of utility and the probabilistic theory of choice. However, their overall impact on the economic analysis of the period was limited.

The most comprehensive discussion of the significance of the utility measurements carried out by MN and DSS can be found in Duncan Luce and Howard Raiffa's *Games and Decisions*, a book that after its publication in 1957 quickly became a key reference point for economists working in decision analysis. Luce and Raiffa summarized the methods used by MN and DSS to measure utility, praised the DSS experiment as "the most elegant in the area" (35), but pointed out that the MN and DSS utility measures do not appear replicable or applicable outside the laboratory. Despite this limitation, which today we would call an "external validity problem," Luce and Raiffa argued that laboratory attempts to measure utility are worth undertaking "to see if under any conditions, however limited, the postulates of the model can be confirmed" (37).

Other commentators, such as Ellsberg (1958) and Arrow (1958), made a similar external-validity point: the utility measurements carried out by MN and DSS appeared hardly extendable to situations different from the specific ones designed by MN or DSS, for example, to situations involving larger amounts of money.

Suppes was well aware of this issue. In a paper presented at a conference on game theory held at Princeton in 1961, he acknowledged that experimental studies of utility measurement were as "yet entirely too fragile in relation to the massive claims sometimes made for utility theory" (Suppes 1962, 62). In particular, he stressed the necessity of measuring utility in situations in which individuals "are making weighty and significant decisions" (62). Suppes even predicted that operations-research people in government and industry were on the verge of undertaking these kind of studies.

This prediction, however, was not fulfilled. In the 1960s economists lost interest in the experimental measurement of utility. Marschak was one of the few who in collaboration with the psychologist Gordon Becker and the statistician Morris DeGroot, made a further attempt to measure experimentally the utility of money (Becker, DeGroot, and Marschak 1964).[20] However, at that point of his career Marschak was far from being a typical economist. Since the mid-1950s, his research interests had moved away from traditional mathematical economics toward psychology and, more generally, the behavioral sciences (Cherrier 2010). Indeed, the Becker-DeGroot-Marschak article was not published in an economics journal but in the interdisciplinary review *Behavioral Science*.

Marschak and associates presented their experiment as an evolution of the MN experiment and did not cite DSS. In particular, like MN and unlike DSS, Becker, DeGroot, and Marschak assumed that the two Yale students who were their experimental subjects understood well, and did not distort, objective probabilities. Marschak and associates asked the students to state their minimum selling prices for wagers the payoffs of which ranged from 0¢ to +100¢ and, based on EUT, used the selling prices to elicit the students' utility curves for money. The authors concluded that, as the students became more familiar with the experimental task, they behaved more consistently with the EUT model.

More than in the Becker-DeGroot-Marschak study, the psychological insights embodied in the MN and DSS experiments found application in the probabilistic theory of choice, which was advanced in the mid-1950s

20. Another experiment to measure the utility of money was performed by F. Trenery Doldbear (1963) as part of his PhD dissertation at Yale University.

by Marschak (again) and other economists. The theory is based on a Thurstonian definition of preference—a subject prefers alternative A to alternative B if the probability that he chooses A over B is at least one-half—and its proponents often referred to MN's definition of indifference as a pioneering use of the probabilistic approach in economics (Marschak 1955; Quandt 1956; Debreu 1958; Luce 1959). In association with David-son (Davidson and Marschak 1959), as well as with Becker and DeGroot (Becker, DeGroot, and Marschak 1963), Marschak also ran experiments to test the probabilistic theory of choice. To circumvent subjective distortions of objective probabilities, he and his coauthors used the ZOJ-ZEJ dice introduced by DSS. However, by the mid-1960s the probabilistic approach to choice was substantially abandoned in economics, possibly because its implications for demand and equilibrium analysis were unclear.

With the vanishing of the economists' interest in both the probabilistic theory of choice and the experimental measurement of utility, the psychological phenomena discussed by MN and DSS disappeared from the purview of the mainstream economic theory of decision. Integrating them into decision theory would clearly have been a difficult task, and since the MN, DSS, and even the Becker-DeGroot-Marschak experiments suggested that EUT was an acceptable predictor of choice under risk, the difficult task could be set aside as nonurgent.

It was only in the 1970s, when robust experimental evidence against EUT accumulated and theories alternative to EUT began to be advanced, that the psychology of decision regained importance for economists. Thus it does not appear merely accidental that, in the celebrated article in which Daniel Kahneman and Amos Tversky (1979, 276) put forward their prospect theory, they cited the MN and DSS experiments.[21] For Kahneman, Tversky, and other non-EUT theorists, however, psychological phenomena such as those discussed by MN and DSS ceased to be disturbing causes to be removed and became fundamental causes to be investigated.

8. Summary and Conclusions

This article has explored a part of the interdisciplinary interaction between economics and psychology in the 1940s and 1950s by studying the origin, content, and impact of two experiments to measure the utility of money. Both experiments were performed by psychologists and other noneconomists, and their design contained elements that responded to psychological

21. On prospect theory, see Staddon, this volume.

insights rather than the economic image of human agency associated with EUT. Between 1955 and 1965, these psychological insights found some application in the short-lived theory of probabilistic choice, but were quickly forgotten.

The story told in this article, therefore, can be framed as an actual encounter between economics and psychology or, more specifically, between the mainstream economic theory of decision under risk represented by EUT and the experimental tradition in psychology associated with psychometrics. In this meeting, the psychologists not only provided the technology to perform the experiments but also identified certain aspects of the psychology of decision that could spoil the significance of the experiments and suggested how to deal with those aspects.

This meeting, however, remained at a superficial level and did not initiate any substantial modification in the body of economic analysis. The main reason for this outcome appears to have been the difficulty of incorporating the psychological insights contained in the two experiments into EUT without making the latter knotty and unmanageable. Only in the 1970s was economics compelled to reconsider its relationship with psychology and the psychological phenomena discussed by Mosteller, Nogee, Davidson, Suppes, and Siegel.

References

Alchian, A. 1953. "The Meaning of Utility Measurement." *American Economic Review* 43: 26–50.

Allais, M. 1953. "Le comportement de l'homme rationnel devant le risque: Critique des postulats et axiomes de l'ecole americaine." *Econometrica* 21:503–46.

Arrow, K. J. 1951. "Alternative Approaches to the Theory of Choice in Risk-Taking Situations." *Econometrica* 19: 404–37.

———. 1958. "Utilities, Attitudes, Choices: A Review Note." *Econometrica* 26: 1–23.

Baccelli, J., and P. Mongin. 2016. "Choice-Based Cardinal Utility: A Tribute to Patrick Suppes." *Journal of Economic Methodology* 23.

Becker, G. M., M. H. DeGroot, and J. Marschak. 1963. "An Experimental Study of Some Stochastic Models for Wagers." *Behavioral Science* 8: 199–202.

———. 1964. "Measuring Utility by a Single-Response Sequential Method." *Behavioral Science* 9: 226–32.

Blackwell, D., and M. A. Girshick. 1954. *Theory of Games and Statistical Decisions.* New York: Wiley.

Bruner, J. S., L. Postman, and F. Mosteller. 1950. "A Note on the Measurement of Reversals of Perspective." *Psychometrika* 15: 63–72.

Bleichrodt, H., L. Chen, I. Moscati, and P. P. Wakker. 2016. "Nash Was a First to Axiomatize Expected Utility." *Theory and Decision* 81.

Cherrier, B. 2010. "Rationalizing Human Organization in an Uncertain World: Jacob Marschak, from Ukrainian Prisons to Behavioral Science Laboratories." *History of Political Economy* 42: 443–67.

Davidson, D. 1999. "Intellectual Autobiography." In *The Philosophy of Donald Davidson*, edited by L. E. Hahn, 3–70. Chicago: Open Court.

Davidson, D., and J. Marschak. 1959. "Experimental Tests of a Stochastic Decision Theory." In *Measurement: Definitions and Theories*, edited by C. W. Churchman and P. Ratoosh, 233–69. New York: Wiley.

Davidson, D., J. C. C. McKinsey, and P. Suppes. 1955. "Outlines of a Formal Theory of Value, I." *Philosophy of Science* 22: 140–60.

Davidson, D., S. Siegel, and P. Suppes. 1955. "Some Experiments and Related Theory on the Measurement of Utility and Subjective Probability." Technical Report No. 1, August 15, 1955. Stanford University.

Davidson, D., and P. Suppes. 1956. "A Finitistic Axiomatization of Subjective Probability and Utility." *Econometrica* 24: 264–75.

Davidson, D., P. Suppes, and S. Siegel. 1957. *Decision Making: An Experimental Approach*. Stanford, Calif.: Stanford University Press.

Debreu, G. 1958. "Stochastic Choice and Cardinal Utility." *Econometrica* 26: 440–44.

Dolbear, F. T. 1963. "Individual Choice under Uncertainty: An Experimental Study." *Yale Economic Essays* 3: 419–69.

Edwards, W. 1953. "Probability-Preferences in Gambling." *American Journal of Psychology* 66: 349–64.

———. 1954a. "Probability-Preferences among Bets with Differing Expected Values." *American Journal of Psychology* 67: 56–67.

———. 1954b. "The Reliability of Probability-Preferences." *American Journal of Psychology* 67: 68–95.

———. 1961. "Behavioral Decision Theory." *Annual Review of Psychology* 12: 473–98.

Ellsberg, D. 1954. "Classic and Current Notions of 'Measurable Utility.'" *Economic Journal* 64: 528–56.

———. 1958. Review of *Decision Making*, by D. Davidson, P. Suppes, and S. Siegel. *American Economic Review* 48: 1009–11.

Engvall Siegel, A. 1964. "Sidney Siegel: A Memoir." In *Decision and Choice: Contributions of Sidney Siegel*, edited by S. Messick and A. H. Brayfield, 1–24. New York: McGraw-Hill.

Erikson, P., et al. 2013. *How Reason Almost Lost Its Mind*. Chicago: University of Chicago Press.

Fishburn, P. C. 1989. "Retrospective on the Utility Theory of von Neumann and Morgenstern." *Journal of Risk and Uncertainty* 2: 127–58.

Fishburn, P. C., and P. Wakker. 1995. "The Invention of the Independence Condition for Preferences." *Management Science* 41: 1130–44.

Freeman, H. A., M. Friedman, F. Mosteller, and W. A. Wallis, eds. 1948. *Sampling Inspection*. New York: McGraw-Hill.

Fréchette, G. R., and A. Schotter. 2015. *Handbook of Experimental Economic Methodology*. New York: Oxford University Press.

Friedman, M. Papers. Hoover Institution Archives. Hoover Institution, Stanford University.

Friedman, M., and L. J. Savage. 1947. "Planning Experiments Seeking Maxima." In *Techniques of Statistical Analysis*, edited by C. Eisenhart, M. W. Hastay, and W. A. Wallis, 363–72. New York: McGraw-Hill.

———. 1948. "The Utility Analysis of Choices Involving Risk." *Journal of Political Economy* 56: 279–304.

———. 1952. "The Expected-Utility Hypothesis and the Measurability of Utility." *Journal of Political Economy* 60: 463–74.

Giocoli, N. 2003. *Modeling Rational Agents*. Cheltenham, U.K.: Elgar.

Girshick, M. A., F. Mosteller, and L. J. Savage. 1946. "Unbiased Estimates for Certain Binomial Sampling Problems with Applications." *Annals of Mathematical Statistics* 17: 13–23.

Griffith, R. M. 1949. "Odds Adjustments by American Horse-Race Bettors." *American Journal of Psychology* 62: 290–94.

Guala, F. 2005. *The Methodology of Experimental Economics*. Cambridge: Cambridge University Press.

Heukelom, F. 2014. *Behavioral Economics: A History*. New York: Cambridge University Press.

Isaac, J. 2013. "Donald Davidson and the Analytic Revolution in American Philosophy, 1940–1970." *Historical Journal* 56: 757–79.

Jallais, S., and P.-C. Pradier. 2005. "The Allais Paradox and Its Immediate Consequences for Expected Utility Theory." In *The Experiment in the History of Economics*, edited by P. Fontaine and R. Leonard, 25–49. New York: Routledge.

Kahneman, D., and A. Tversky. 1979. "Prospect Theory: An Analysis of Decision under Risk." *Econometrica* 47: 263–92.

Keats, A. S., H. K. Beecher, and F. Mosteller. 1950. "Measurement of Pathological Pain in Distinction to Experimental Pain." *Journal of Applied Physiology* 3: 35–44.

Lepore, E. 2004. "Interview with Donald Davidson." In *Problems of Rationality*, by D. Davidson, 231–66. Oxford: Oxford University Press.

Luce, R. D. 1959. *Individual Choice Behavior*. New York: Wiley.

Luce, R. D., and H. Raiffa. 1957. *Games and Decisions*. New York: Wiley.

Luce, R. D., and P. Suppes. 1965. "Preference, Utility, and Subjective Probability." In vol. 3 of *Handbook of Mathematical Psychology*, edited by R. D. Luce, R. R. Bush, and E. Galanter, 249–410. New York: Wiley.

Manne, A. S. 1952. "The Strong Independence Assumption—Gasoline Blends and Probability Mixtures." *Econometrica* 20: 665–68.

Markowitz, H. 1952. "The Utility of Wealth." *Journal of Political Economy* 60:151–58.

Marschak, J. 1950. "Rational Behavior, Uncertain Prospects, and Measurable Utility." *Econometrica* 18: 111–41.

———. 1951. "Why Should Statisticians and Businessmen Maximize Moral Expectation?" In *Proceedings of the Second Berkeley Symposium on Mathematical Statistics and Probability*, edited by J. Neyman, 493–506. Berkeley: University of California Press.

————. 1954. "Probability in the Social Sciences." In *Mathematical Thinking in the Social Sciences*, edited by P. F. Lazarsfeld, 166–215. Glencoe: Free Press.

————. 1955. "Norms and Habits of Decision Making under Certainty." In *Mathematical Models of Human Behavior*, 45–53. Stamford, Conn.: Dunlap and Associates.

McKinsey, J. C. C. 1952. *Introduction to the Theory of Games*. New York: McGraw-Hill.

Michell, J. 1999. *Measurement in Psychology*. Cambridge: Cambridge University Press.

Mongin, P. 2009. "Duhemian Themes in Expected Utility Theory." In *French Studies in the Philosophy of Science*, edited by A. Brenner and J. Gayon, 303–57. Springer: New York.

————. 2014. Le paradoxe d'Allais: Comment lui rendre sa signification perdue. *Revue économique* 65: 743–79.

Moscati, I. 2007. "Early Experiments in Consumer Demand Theory: 1930–1970." *History of Political Economy* 39: 359–401.

————. 2013. "Were Jevons, Menger, and Walras Really Cardinalists? On the Notion of Measurement in Utility Theory, Psychology, Mathematics, and Other Disciplines, 1870–1910." *History of Political Economy* 45: 373–414.

————. 2015. "Austrian Debates on Utility Measurement, from Menger to Hayek." In *Hayek: A Collaborative Biography, Part IV*, edited by R. Leeson, 137–79. New York: Palgrave Macmillan.

————. 2016a. "How Economists Came to Accept Expected Utility Theory: The Case of Samuelson and Savage." *Journal of Economic Perspectives* 30: 219–36.

————. 2016b. "Measurement Theory and Utility Analysis in Suppes' Early Work, 1951–1958." *Journal of Economic Methodology* 23.

Mosteller, F. 2010. *The Pleasures of Statistics*. New York: Springer.

Mosteller, F., and P. Nogee. 1951. "An Experimental Measurement of Utility." *Journal of Political Economy* 59: 371–404.

Nasar, S. 1998. *A Beautiful Mind*. New York: Simon and Schuster.

Pooley, J., and M. Solovey. 2010. "Marginal to the Revolution: The Curious Relationship between Economics and the Behavioral Sciences Movement in Mid-Twentieth-Century America." *History of Political Economy* 42 (supplement): 199–233.

Preston, M. G., and P. Baratta. 1948. "An Experimental Study of the Auction-Value of an Uncertain Outcome." *American Journal of Psychology* 61: 183–93.

Quandt, R. E. 1956. "A Probabilistic Theory of Consumer Behavior." *Quarterly Journal of Economics* 70: 507–36.

Ramsey, F. P. (1926) 1950. "Truth and Probability." In *Foundations of Mathematics and Other Logical Essays*, edited by R. B. Braithwaite, 156–98. New York: Humanities.

Russell, B. 1921. *The Analysis of Mind*. London: Allen and Unwin.

Samuelson, P. A. 1950. "Probability and the Attempts to Measure Utility." *Economic Review (Keizai Kenkyu)* 1: 167–73.

————. 1952. "Probability, Utility, and the Independence Axiom." *Econometrica* 20: 670–78.

Savage, L. J. 1954. *The Foundations of Statistics*. New York: Dover.

Shanteau, J., B. A. Mellers, and D. A. Schum, eds. 1999. *Decision Science and Technology: Reflections on the Contributions of Ward Edwards*. Boston: Kluwer.

Siegel, S. 1954. "Certain Determinants and Correlates of Authoritarianism." *Genetic Psychology Monographs* 49: 187–254.

Strotz, R. H. 1953. "Cardinal Utility." *American Economic Review, Papers and Proceedings* 43: 384–97.

Suppes, P. 1951. "A Set of Independent Axioms for Extensive Quantities." *Portugaliae Mathematica* 10: 163–72.

———. 1962. "Recent Developments in Utility Theory." In *Recent Advances in Game Theory*, edited by O. Morgenstern and A. W. Tucker, 61–72. Princeton, N.J.: Princeton University Press.

———. 1979. "Self-profile." In *Patrick Suppes*, edited by R. J. Bogdan, 3–56. Dordrecht: Reidel.

Suppes, P., and M. Winet. 1955. "An Axiomatization of Utility Based on the Notion of Utility Differences." *Management Science* 1: 259–70.

Thurstone, L. L. 1927. "A Law of Comparative Judgment." *Psychological Review* 34: 273–86.

———. 1931. "The Indifference Function." *Journal of Social Psychology* 2: 139–67.

Von Neumann, J., and O. Morgenstern. 1944. *Theory of Games and Economic Behavior*. Princeton, N.J.: Princeton University Press.

Wallis, W. A. 1980. "The Statistical Research Group, 1942–1945." *Journal of the American Statistical Association* 75: 320–30.

Wallis, W. A., and M. Friedman. 1942. "The Empirical Derivation of Indifference Functions." In *Studies in Mathematical Economics and Econometrics*, edited by O. Lange, F. McIntyre, and T. O. Yntema, 175–89. Chicago: University of Chicago Press.

The Sidney Siegel Tradition: The Divergence of Behavioral and Experimental Economics at the End of the 1980s

Andrej Svorenčík

Vernon Smith once asked Amos Tversky whatever happened to the tradition of Sidney Siegel in psychology. "You are it," Tversky replied. "That was not a compliment," Smith explained. "That was a touché. He was putting me down. 'You are it. You continued a bad tradition'" (Svorenčík and Maas 2015, 88).[1]

It was during a two-day conference, held in 1988, when this brief and at first sight innocuous, if not jocular, exchange took place. Even if we have to rely solely on Smith's memory—Tversky died two decades ago—this exchange is far from being merely a cute anecdote. Rather, it is symptomatic of an unease growing at that time between experimental economists,

Correspondence may be addressed to Andrej Svorenčík, Department of Economics, University of Manheim, L7 3-5, 68163 Mannheim, Germany; e-mail: svorencik@uni-mannheim.de. I would like to thank the participants of the HES session "Histories of Behavioral Economics" at the 2015 AEA/ASSA meetings in Boston, Colin Camerer in particular; the 2015 *HOPE* conference attendees, Ivan Moscati in particular; as well as an anonymous referee and Vernon Smith for their helpful comments on the manuscript. My gratitude goes equally to all my interview subjects listed in the references. Research of the Russell Sage Archive located at the Rockefeller Archive Center has been supported by a grant-in-aid from the center. This support is gratefully acknowledged. All errors are mine.

1. The recollection of this conversation appears several times in Smith's writings, but in all instances the circumstances, such as when the encounter took place, are not preserved. It first appeared as a cryptic note in E. Roy Weintraub's history of game theory volume in 1992. A decade later it can be found in a special issue on the relationship of psychology and economics. And it has also a prominent place in Smith's autobiography. See Smith 2008, 200; Hertwig and Ortmann 2001, 442; and Smith 1992, 247.

History of Political Economy 48 (annual suppl.) DOI 10.1215/00182702-3619310

including Smith, and a group of economists and cognitive psychologists soon to be referred to as behavioral economists.

Indeed, the conference was plainly titled "Experimental Economics and Psychology"; in 1988, when it took place, economists following the work of Tversky and Daniel Kahneman, two cognitive psychologists, had not yet claimed the label behavioral economics. But the label, itself with a distinguished history (Sent 2004; Augier 2005; Heukelom 2010), was in the air again. The Russell Sage Foundation revived it through its Behavioral Economics Program that ran between 1986 and 1992, as did the Alfred P. Sloan Foundation with a similar program between 1984 and 1989. The link between these two programs was Eric Wanner, who served first as a program officer and vice president at the latter, then as a trustee and president of the former institution. Unsurprisingly, Wanner attended this conference. In fact, the Sage Foundation funded the meeting.

It might have been the warm California weather that was the reason for selecting February as the time for this intimate gathering. Historical weather records confirm that for most of the one dozen participants, February 12–13, 1988, on the West Coast was a welcome respite from the harsh Midwest and East Coast weather.[2] But the location was certainly not accidental. The campus of the California Institute of Technology was chosen because of Caltech's position at the forefront of experimental economics research. Most important, unlike Smith's University of Arizona, the other leading center of experimental economics in the United States at the time, it housed experimentalists also doing research on individual choice—a topic near and dear to psychologists.

In a seminal paper on preference reversals, the Caltech economists David Grether and Charles Plott had attempted a decade earlier to remedy what they considered the flaws of psychologists' experimental design. Two of the thirteen reasons that they entertained as possible explanations for this phenomenon stand out. One was that the experimenters in the

2. The attendees were Eric Wanner, Colin Camerer (Pennsylvania), Donald Coursey (Washington), Robyn Dawes (Carnegie-Mellon), John Kagel (Houston), Daniel Kahneman (UC Berkeley), Charles Plott (California Institute of Technology), Alvin Roth (Pittsburgh), Vernon Smith (Arizona), Shyam Sunder (Minnesota), Richard Thaler (Cornell), and Amos Tversky (Stanford). The psychologists are Dawes, Kahneman, Tversky, and Wanner. The rest are economists. Camerer is a special case. He received a doctorate in decision theory. When asked about how he would describe himself in the 1980s, he answered, "I started as an experimental judgment researcher and quickly began to do experimental economics in my first faculty job. But, for example, my dissertation research was about the psychology of judgment, and it did have some experiments in it, but it wasn't closely tied to economics" (interview with Colin Camerer, September 6, 2011, California Institute of Technology).

previous studies were psychologists. Having the reputation for deceiving subjects and subjects second-guessing psychologists' experiments, Grether and Plott (1979, 629) "felt that the experimental setting should be removed from psychology" in order to give the results additional credibility. Thus the critical point was not the involvement of particular psychologists per se but how deception and reputation for deceiving corrodes experimental control. The other reason that stands out is what Grether and Plott called misspecified incentives. Most prior studies focused on hypothetical, unmotivated choice and did not incorporate performance-based monetary payments for experimental subjects. Despite the great lengths that Grether and Plott took to prevent preference reversal from occurring, ultimately they failed in their attempt to disprove the psychologists' findings.[3]

The no-deception rule and insistence on paying subjects are the hallmarks of experimental economics research, and the latter is being traced back by experimental economists to none other than Sidney Siegel, a psychologist briefly active in the 1950s and early 1960s. These precepts only partly explain Tversky's rejoinder to Smith's question about Siegel's legacy in psychology. Tversky, a meticulous experimenter himself, was aware of the pitfalls of deception and proper motivation for maintaining experimental control. Yet during the 1970s, as Floris Heukelom (2011a) argues, the types of experiments run jointly by Tversky and Kahneman while developing their research program of heuristics and biases shifted toward questionnaires with hypothetical choices.[4]

There was also something other than the contrast between hypothetical choices and subject payments that motivated Tversky's response. Siegel, as Smith has frequently argued (see footnote 2 for details), was seen by Tversky

> as part of the Skinner animal behaviorist tradition in psychology, a tradition that approached decision behavior as an objectivist "black box" study of the choices made by animals and people under various controlled experimental conditions. It eschewed the idea of studying decision in humans as part of cognitive processes using introspection, surveys, and subject oral and written reports, which are then interpreted by the scientist in terms of models of cognition. Skinner had rejected this

---

3. A similar case is Grether's replication of Kahneman and Tversky's experiments from the 1970s on the violation of Bayes' rule that led them to the "representativeness heuristic." For details and references for Kahneman and Tversky's papers, see Grether 1980.

4. Heukelom (2011a, 820) referred to this as a shift to "more relaxed standards of the experimental method."

methodology as unreliably subjectivist. Cognitive psychologists in turn rejected Skinner's behaviorism as devoid of all attempts to understand mental thought processes. This is typical academic maneuvering: They are both right (and wrong). (Smith 2008, 200)

Thus the brief conversation between Smith and Tversky is a window into a complex relationship between experimental economists and contemporary behavioral economists. Francesco Guala (2008, 156) refers to this relationship as marked by "a persistent low-intensity conflict at the methodological and theoretical level." In this article I place the historical beginning of this "low-intensity" conflict at the 1988 Caltech meeting.

The historical understanding of the emergence of contemporary behavioral economics has been greatly enhanced by the groundbreaking work of Heukelom (2014). In particular, the patronage of the Sloan and Sage Foundations played a crucial role in the rapid ascent of behavioral economics (Heukelom 2012). Experimental economists were involved in the Behavioral Economics Program from early on, as well. There was even a working group on decision making and experimental economics created. Its first meeting was the conference at Caltech, where the exchange between Tversky and Smith took place. More important, the meeting was also the last gathering of the working group, and what emerged from it sheds light on the separation of experimental and behavioral economics at the end of the 1980s.

The remainder of the article is divided into four sections. The first one focuses on the meaning and emergence of the "Siegel tradition." In the second section, I focus on the Caltech meeting and its significance within Sage Behavioral Economics Program. The penultimate section deals with the divergence between market experimental economists and behavioral economists. The last section ties the threads of this article together and relates them to the rest of this volume.

1. Sidney Siegel and "His" Tradition

> The thing that got me really, deeply interested in heavy experimental gaming was Sidney Siegel. And to me, it was a true tragedy that he died so young.
> —Interview with Martin Shubik, June 30, 2010

For Shubik, Siegel's premature death was not just a missed research opportunity; "Sid's" death was also a personal calamity. Their friendship started under the most unlikely circumstances. While spending the academic year 1955–56 at the Center for Advanced Study in the Behavioral Sciences (hereafter CASBS), a recently established institution for the study of human behavior overlooking Stanford University's campus, Shubik went camping with Martin J. Beckmann, a mathematical economist at the Cowles Foundation at Yale, to Yosemite National Park. In the evening at a public campground fireplace at the Tuolumne Meadows surrounded by other nature explorers, instead of reflecting on the day's trek and the beauty around them, the two men explored a different type of beauty, namely, the axiomatization of utility theory. There was somebody on the other side of the fireplace who was obviously listening to their conversation. "Finally," Shubik recalls, "he could not stand it any longer, and so he came around the fireplace to where Beckmann and I were seated and sort of immediately joined the discussion and introduced himself." It was Siegel, an assistant professor of psychology at Pennsylvania State University.[5]

By 1955 Siegel had had by any measure an unconventional academic career. In 1951, at the mature age of thirty-five, he obtained his bachelor's degree from San Jose State College. By 1954 he had obtained a PhD in social psychology from Stanford University and embarked on a mainly experimental project "to measure subjective probability *behavioristically* on the basis of empirically determined utilities" (Davidson, Suppes, and Siegel 1957, 25; emphasis mine).[6] Siegel's interest in both utility theory and experimental measurement remained unabated after he joined Penn State in the summer of 1954.

Being on different coasts was not ideal for collaboration even though Shubik and Siegel "immediately took a complete liking and complete understanding to each other."[7] Siegel helped Shubik get an adjunct appointment at Pennsylvania State University from 1957 to 1959, although Siegel spent the academic year 1957–58 at the CASBS.[8] The last hurdle preventing their collaboration was Siegel's prior commitment to a joint project with Lawrence E. Fouraker, an economist at Penn State who later became dean of the Harvard Business School. During the winter of 1958,

5. Interview with Martin Shubik, June 30, 2010, Shubik's home, New Haven, Conn. See also Smith 1992, 250.

6. The coauthors were two young, Stanford-based philosophers, Donald Davidson and Patrick Suppes. A preliminary report of their work appeared already in 1955 as Davidson, Suppes, and Siegel 1955.

7. Interview with Martin Shubik, June 30, 2010; referring to the campfire conversation.

8. At the CASBS, Siegel was attracted to the work of the economists who were spending a year at the center, namely, Kenneth J. Arrow, Milton Friedman, Robert M. Solow, and George Stigler.

Siegel and Fouraker conducted experiments in bilateral monopoly leading to a book, now a classic in experimental economics (Siegel and Fouraker 1960). Finally in 1959, a few years after their fortuitous meeting, Shubik, together with Siegel and Fouraker, ran additional oligopoly experiments exploring quantity adjustment models (Fouraker, Shubik, and Siegel 1961). Siegel and Shubik planned to embark on a major experimental research project.[9] Their correspondence reveals Shubik as the driving force behind the plans, who was often urging Siegel to devote more time to their ambitious endeavor: "Siegel, we are growing old and there is work to be done."[10]

1.1. Probability Matching Experiments

Siegel's approach is well represented by his work on so-called probability matching. William Estes (1950), an eminent experimental psychologist, conducted experiments in the early 1950s that studied his own learning theory, in which learning was represented as a converging stochastic process.[11] In his experiments, Estes let two lights flash on and off repeatedly, with one light being more likely to be turned on. Then he asked participants to predict which light would go on next in a series of 120 trials, with no rewards for correct or penalties for incorrect guesses. He concluded that subjects simulated the frequencies of the lights turning on—hence probability matching. This result appeared in the proceedings of the 1952 Santa Monica conference and drew a lot of attention from the conference participants, as it contradicted the simple game-theoretic prediction that subjects should always choose the more frequent light (Estes 1954; Flood 1954; see also Smith 1992, 260–70 for an insightful discussion).

Siegel got interested as well and hypothesized that since subjects had to perform so many repeated guesses, the observed matching behavior was caused by the absence of any incentives to guess correctly as well as boredom. He then modeled both factors within the expected utility framework, with utilities associated with correct predictions and variability of the decision situation. The lack of financial incentives made guessing

---

9. See, for instance, a letter to Sidney Siegel from Martin Shubik, dated July 5, 1960, which elaborates on sixteen open issues that could be addressed experimentally (box 8, Martin Shubik Papers).

10. Martin Shubik to Sidney Siegel, February 15, 1960, box 8, Martin Shubik Papers.

11. Estes was a graduate student under Skinner's direction, but in the 1950s, to Skinner's disappointment, he drifted more toward mathematical modeling of mental processes. For more on Estes, see Association for Psychological Science 2011.

costless. In his experiments therefore Siegel introduced two new varia-tions. In addition to providing no monetary incentives for correct guesses, in one new treatment he paid subjects for the number of times they were correct and in another included both rewards and a penalty for being incorrect. He also devised a set of ingenious techniques to relieve the tediousness of long sequences of binary choices. In the original Estes design, subjects adhering to the game-theoretic rational prediction would be required to choose one light—either the one on their left or on their right side. To prevent what Siegel called kinesthetic monotony, subjects were seated in a swivel chair and randomly asked to turn right or left. On one side there was a panel with the two electric lights, and on the other side there was a mirror reflecting those two lights. Hence if a subject wanted to choose the same light again and again, he did not have to choose "right" repeatedly, but depending which side he was randomly asked to turn, he would vary between "right" and "left." The net result of monetary incentives and the swivel chair was that the students did not simulate the frequency but picked the optimal pure strategy against the flashing lights (Siegel and Goldstein 1959; Siegel 1961).

1.2. Birth of a Tradition

Siegel died suddenly on November 29, 1961, from a fatal heart attack in his office at the CASBS. During his second residence at the center, he had planned to complete a book that would combine experimental tests and mathematical modeling of repeated choice such as those just described (Siegel 1964, vii).

The incomplete elements of the joint work with Shubik became part of the posthumously written book by Fouraker, a sequel to their volume of 1960 (Fouraker and Siegel 1963). Both volumes have become classics in experimental economics. That happened not because of the lasting sig-nificance of the experimental investigation of bilateral monopolies and oligopoly. On the contrary, that topic had become something of a dead end by the early 1970s.[12] Rather, its lasting importance lies in the way Siegel employed the experimental method as well as the way these two volumes were integrated and interpreted by subsequent experimentalists, Vernon

---

12. Charles Plott and James Friedman at the Witness Seminar, quoted in Svorenčík and Maas 2015.

Smith and his associates in particular, as the origin of proper methodology for experimenting in economics.[13]

Shubik was not the only one whose research plans were thwarted by Siegel's premature death. So too were those of Smith. He was spending the academic year 1961–62 at Stanford as a visiting associate. At a dinner organized by Marc Nerlove, an econometrician and agricultural economist as well as the 1969 Clark medalist,[14] Smith and Siegel met only to discover that they had both been doing experimental research for some years (Smith 2008, 198). Within a few weeks of their meeting, Siegel died. Nevertheless, the brief encounter had a profound impact on Smith. Even four decades later, when receiving the 2002 Nobel Prize in Economics, he expressly thanked Siegel for influencing his experimental career.

None of Siegel's psychology doctoral students continued his experimental economics research, and Fouraker soon became a full-time administrator. Shubik, in part lacking Siegel's experimental guidance, immersed himself in simulations research and experimental gaming—the type of open-ended experimental work that Siegel did not pursue (Engvall Siegel 1964, 17). In contrast, Smith clearly is an intellectual disciple of Siegel. The first of his experimental papers was published in the spring of 1962. In it, Smith referenced Siegel in only one footnote, and that was a late addition, since they had become aware of each other's work just prior to Siegel's death (Smith 1962, 111n2). The reported experiments were done without monetary payments, though another footnote reported Siegel's completed and future experiments with monetary incentives (Smith 1962, 121n9).

Siegel was not the first to note the importance of monetary payments in economic experiments as a way to exercise better control over subjects' motivations.[15] But he was the first to systematically apply it in a series of experiments, notably in those that experimental economists include in their bibliographies. In the mid-1980s Caltech with Plott and Arizona with Smith were the largest and most influential centers of experimental

13. It was Siegel, not Fouraker or Shubik, who brought in the experimental know-how to their collaboration.

14. Nerlove was also Grether's adviser. During Smith's stay at Stanford he taught for one term the graduate microeconomics sequence, and he presented some of his market experiments. Grether was one of the attendees. Interview with David Grether, November 29, 2009, California Institute of Technology.

15. It seems that Wallis and Friedman (1942) were the first to point out the significance of experimental payments. Mosteller and Nogee (1951) used payments as well. For details, see Moscati, this volume.

economics research in North America (Svorenčík 2015). Both Plott and Smith maintained a comprehensive library of all works relevant for experimental economics, which were the go-to repositories for local experimentalists at Caltech and Arizona until papers could be easily retrieved online. The library catalogs from the time shortly after the 1988 Caltech conference reveal a specific picture of reception of Siegel's work. What is included is a small fraction of the twenty-eight publications that Siegel wrote during his brief career (Engvall Siegel 1964, 22–23). The "U of Arizona Bibliography" from January 22, 1990, lists only the two books by Fouraker and Siegel. Plott's "Inventory Experimental Lab Bibliography" from October 9, 1989, has in addition the two papers mentioned in the context of the probability matching experiments—the one coauthored with Donald Goldstein and the 1961 paper on decision making and learning, as well as Siegel's last book, *Choice, Strategy, and Utility*, from 1964. Most of Siegel's work in psychology journals is absent from both bibliographies. That is not because experimental economists were avoiding such outlets. The Arizona bibliography has over one hundred articles in psychology journals, and the Caltech one has just over fifty articles in psychology journals. Similarly, a bibliography of experimental research compiled by Elinor Ostrom from 1984 lists only the two books by Fouraker and Siegel. A comparison of these inventories with an online bibliography made a decade later by Charles Holt at the University of Virginia at the end of the 1990s reveals an almost identical picture with the Caltech inventory.[16]

To understand Siegel's position on monetary payments, it is instructive to read a longer quote from the book that Siegel was working on at the time of his death, and which was later completed by Siegel's wife assisted by one of his graduate students:

> Siegel was quite convinced that hypothetical choices were unreliable and that experimental subjects had to be rewarded in order to be adequately motivated. On this matter, Siegel departed from psychologists' standard approach: "Because of our belief in the central importance of employing payoffs which are meaningful to subjects, rewards which in

16. This *does not* mean that experimental economists were ignorant of other work by Siegel. This is evidenced, for instance, in Smith's extensive discussion of Siegel's work in his reflections on game theory and experimental economics in the 1992 *History of Political Economy* supplemental issue on game theory. Rather, Siegel's other work was considered less relevant for experimental economics. NB: All three inventories are in the Charles Plott Papers at the California Institute of Technology.

fact they covet, we have little confidence in experiments in which the 'payoffs' are points, credits, or tokens. Or perhaps it would be more accurate to say that we have little confidence in the use of the term payoff to label such trivia. The relevance of such experiments to any theoretical notions about reward, payoff, or utility seems to be dubious." (Siegel 1964, 148)

Siegel, unlike many of his contemporaries, was against the use of deception in experimental research. In general, deception in experiments occurs when the actual purpose of an experiment differs from the purpose announced to the test subjects. In a discussion about the timing of subject payments, he warned that "college students are by now so familiar with the notion of an experimental 'hoax,' with experimenters who employ deception in the service of their experiments, that they might not believe an experimenter who told them he was going to pay them at the conclusion of their trials" in probability matching experiments (Siegel 1964, 152). Put differently, deception in Siegel's view undermined the relationship between the experimenter and the subjects, who, in consequence, are often too preoccupied with the true agenda of the experiment or doubt the announced relation between actions and rewards, which therefore ultimately jeopardizes experimental control.[17]

Both opposition to deception and performance-based payments have been stressed in Smith's work ever since he met Siegel and were adopted as standard precepts by experimental economists (Smith 1976, 1982; Plott 1982; Wilde 1981; Guala 2005).[18] When Don Coursey applied to the Sage Foundation for a grant to organize a working group on experimental economics that eventually led to the Caltech meeting, he wrote that "although the exact origin of experimental economics techniques is hard to pinpoint, most economists working in the area would attribute a large share of the development credit to Sidney Siegel and Lawrence Fouraker's work in the late 1950s."[19] Indeed, Siegel's premature death allowed experimental

17. According to Siegel's wife, for him it was primarily an unethical malpractice. See Engvall Siegel 1964.

18. The above-mentioned memoir by Siegel's wife also lists clear procedures: no deception, closeness to data, and closeness to theory as other core themes of Siegel's research (Engvall Siegel 1964, 16–21).

19. Don Coursey to Eric Wanner, February 26, 1987, subgroup 2, box 193, folder 1424, Russell Sage Archives, Rockefeller Foundation Archives, Rockefeller Archive Center, Sleepy Hollow, New York. More than two decades later, the participants of the Witness Seminar on the history of the experiment in economics also singled out Siegel in the very same fashion (Svorenčík and Maas 2015).

economists who have continued to work on market experiments to appropriate him as the intellectual and historical source of procedural standards of experimental economics research, thereby creating a tradition that Smith in his question to Tversky concisely labeled as the Siegel tradition.

2. Russell Sage's Experimental Economics Working Group

The major catalyst of Kahneman and Tversky's work in economics that led to contemporary behavioral economics was the Behavioral Economics Program of the Sloan and Sage Foundations (Heukelom 2014). This program, the brainchild of Wanner, was run by Sloan from 1984 to 1989. After being promoted to vice president of the Sloan Foundation in the summer of 1985, Wanner was appointed as a trustee and president of the Russell Sage Foundation in the summer of 1986. The Behavioral Economics Program at the Sage Foundation ran from then until 1992. Under Wanner's leadership both foundations provided the necessary support for behavioral economics and created "a sense of mission" (Heukelom 2012).

In 1986 Wanner wanted to create working groups focused on particular topics. Besides a group on intertemporal choice headed by George Loewenstein and Jon Elster and a behavioral approaches to financial markets group headed by Richard Thaler and Robert Shiller, the Advisory Committee of the Behavioral Economics Program approved a third working group, one on experimental economics. From the very start, one of the catchment areas of the Sloan program "experiments with simulated markets designed to examine the market consequences of individual and social psychological processes."[20] Hence it was natural to start a working group on experimental economics. The initial idea was that a senior experimentalist such as Plott, together with one senior cognitive psychologist such as Kahneman, should be in charge. Eventually Coursey, who graduated in 1982 from Arizona under Smith's supervision, and recipient of a grant from the Sloan Foundation, took the lead and submitted a proposal motivated by some of the very same considerations I discussed in the previous section:

20. Russell Sage Foundation Board of Trustees Docket, June 1988, subgroup 2, box 194, folder 1433, Russell Sage Archives, Rockefeller Foundation Archives, Rockefeller Archive Center, Sleepy Hollow, New York.

It has become clear that certain experimental economics environments produce behavior which can only be fully understood through the use of cognitive psychology. In particular, economists must often reconcile the role of pecuniary motives with the role of non-pecuniary motives in describing individual behavior. Additionally, standard economic theory has often been observed to do a better job explaining the behavior of individuals in latter, rather than initial, segments of experiments. Individuals often converge to the predictions of economic theory, but the process through which they learn or adapt to this end is a puzzle.[21]

The 1988 meeting of the working group at Caltech did not have a fixed agenda. The first day was dedicated to the different approaches and priors that economists and cognitive psychologists bring to the laboratory. To stimulate and guide the discussion, two papers were circulated. One was an early draft of Smith's paper "Theory, Experiment, and Economics" that appeared in 1989 in the *Journal of Economic Perspectives*. The other paper comprised notes by Kahneman written for the meeting, with the title "Experimental Economics from a Psychologist's Perspective." A visit to Plott's recently established experimental economics laboratory at Caltech and a demonstration of market experiments using the multiple double auction software took place in the afternoon.[22]

The second day was left for discussion of current research projects of the participants (for their list, see footnote 2). Thaler talked about endowment effect experiments and preference reversal; Alvin Roth discussed sequential bargaining such as in ultimatum games; Plott discussed prospect theory tests; John Kagel outlined his latest behaviorist animal experimental research on Giffen goods and the violation of the matching law; Colin Camerer talked about the hindsight bias; Coursey addressed the prisoner's dilemma and public goods; and Shyam Sunder discussed salient payments.[23] It is a shared recollection of the participants that the meeting

21. Don Coursey to Eric Wanner, February 26, 1987, subgroup 2, box 193, folder 1424, Russell Sage Archives, Rockefeller Foundation Archives, Rockefeller Archive Center, Sleepy Hollow, New York.

22. For details about the history of Plott's laboratory and the MUDA software, see Svorenčík 2015.

23. Wanner's handwritten notes from the meeting, subgroup 2, box 193, folder 1424, Russell Sage Archives, Rockefeller Foundation Archives, Rockefeller Archive Center, Sleepy Hollow, New York.

was lively and revealing of the different nature and role of experimentation in economics and cognitive psychology.[24]

Two years after the meeting, Wanner reflected that it "resulted in something of a *donnybrook* between the experimental economist and psychologists present."[25] The heated argument focused on three issues covered in Smith's and Kahneman's accompanying papers: (1) inclusion of data gained from hypothetical questions for which there is no economic incentive to give any particular answer; (2) focus on (market) equilibrium as a result of repeated experience versus focus on one-shot experiments without the opportunity for learning; and (3) experiments with deception. In regard to allowing deception and hypothetical choices in economic experiments, experimental economists wanted to maintain Siegel's dictum of always avoiding deception and always paying subjects based on their performance, while cognitive psychologists and Thaler, unsurprisingly, did not.[26] In regard to the second issue, as Heukelom (2012, 279) succinctly puts it, "Smith and Plott wanted to concentrate on the question how the market eventually steers individual behavior towards rational equilibrium, and what the equilibrium exactly looks like. Wanner, Kahneman, Thaler, and the advisory committee, on the other hand, were more interested in how initial individual behavior deviates from the theoretically defined equilibrium, irrespective of whether it exists or not. In addition, Wanner, Kahneman, and Thaler questioned how often economic markets are allowed the time to mature towards."

These different approaches were not discussed on an abstract level only; they framed, for instance, the discussion about the empirical validity of the theoretical claim that the willingness to pay for an object equals the willingness to accept. In line with the prospect theory, it was proposed that the

24. Interviews with Colin Camerer, September 6, 2011, California Institute of Technology; David Grether, November 29, 2009, California Institute of Technology; John Kagel, September 22, 2009, Ohio State University; John Ledyard, January 12, 2015, California Institute of Technology; Charles Plott, November 25, 2009, California Institute of Technology; Vernon Smith, November 17, 2009, Chapman University; Richard Thaler, June 16, 2014, University of Chicago; and Eric Wanner, April 15, 2015, New York City. Both Grether and Ledyard attended the meeting, as they were based at Caltech, but are not listed as official attendees.

25. Board Meeting memo, February 27, 1990, subgroup 2, box 7, folders 69, Russell Sage Archives, Rockefeller Foundation Archives, Rockefeller Archive Center, Sleepy Hollow, New York; my emphasis.

26. When asked about the meeting, Thaler recalled: "It's clear that psychologists and economists had very different views about what was a proper experiment. One difference still exists today which is economists have this taboo about deception" (interview with Richard Thaler, June 16, 2014, University of Chicago).

observed difference, first established through answers to hypothetical questions, between the two quantities can be explained by the so-called endowment effect—once you own something, you value it more. In a series of articles in the second half of the 1980s, it was discussed whether real incentives, repeated interaction, and involvement of markets reveal both quantities to be equal (Knetsch and Sinden 1984; Kahneman, Knetsch, and Thaler 1986a, 1986b, 1990; Knetsch 1989). Kahneman et al. 1990 in particular was a result of discussion between Smith and Kahneman and Thaler at a conference organized by Roth (1987) in May 1985. Smith's position was that "these results were suspect until they were demonstrated in a market context with monetary incentives and opportunities for learning."[27] The discussion has not been settled and continues to fill the pages of leading journals such as the *American Economic Review* (Plott and Zeiler 2005, 2007, 2011; Isoni et al. 2011; Cason and Plott 2014), though Kahneman, Knetsch, and Thaler are not active in this line of inquiry anymore.[28]

When Smith asked Tversky about the fate of the Siegel tradition in psychology, he did not have only subject payments versus hypothetical choices and the no-deception rule in mind. There are two other things that can be reconstructed from Smith's writings evaluating psychologists and behavioral economists from the time shortly after the Caltech conference.

First, in 1991 he published an article, "Rational Choice: The Contrast between Economics and Psychology," in the Chicago-based *Journal of Political Economy*. It was a review and fierce criticism of *The Behavioral Foundations of Economic Theory*, which was based on a conference that took place in 1986 at the University of Chicago (Hogarth and Reder 1987). This conference is often viewed as the first real test of the new behavioral economics program, since it met such resistance from many proponents of rational expectations theory (Heukelom 2014, 158).[29] Smith (1991, 893) argued that "psychologists since Siegel have not attempted to apply their perspective and questions to market experiments of the kind studied by experimental economists." Smith not only defended experimental economics from the various criticisms raised against it in the volume but was highly critical of the work of Kahneman, Tversky, and Thaler because it had turned away from Siegel.

27. Thaler's Proposal to the Behavioral Economics Program February 1988, subgroup 2, box 172, folder 1222, Russell Sage Archives, Rockefeller Foundation Archives, Rockefeller Archive Center, Sleepy Hollow, New York.

28. Their last involvement was Knetsch, Tang, and Thaler 2001.

29. Interview with Richard Thaler, June 16, 2014, among others.

Second, this turning away from Siegel was not just on the level of experimental technique but also on a conceptual level: how to modify economic theory in light of rigorous behavioral-experimental evidence not matching it. For Smith, Siegel's probability matching experiments discussed in detail above are "exemplary in showing what psychology can contribute to economics by modifying decision theory in the light of rigorous experiment. In contrast, "many psychologists today who study decision making emphasize the predictive failures of 'rational' theory" (Smith 1992, 268). In experiments without sufficient motivation and excessive tedium, it was rational for subjects not to be "rational." Once these factors were accounted for theoretically, Siegel studied them experimentally. Smith argued, and many experimentalists at the meeting such as Plott and Sunder shared his view, that research on anomalies including the one on endowment effect and the difference between willingness to pay and willingness to accept should follow in Siegel's footsteps. Yet embracing the Siegel tradition does not exclude cognitive psychology. Reflecting on the exchange with Tversky, Smith summarized this position: "Obviously you use all the instruments at your disposal, recognizing the hazards of subjectivism and the dead-end extreme of the behaviorist's unwillingness to delve into that 'black box' called the brain" (Smith 2008, 200).

2.1. Behavioral Game Theory Working Group

After the conference meeting at Caltech, the working group on experimental economics never convened again.[30] Instead, the remainder of its appropriated funds was later spent on a conference organized by Camerer on behavioral game theory at the University of Pennsylvania in 1990. Given its success, later a new working group with the same name was established.[31] The goal was to bring experimenters and theorists together "to share experimental evidence of bounded rationality and speculate about

30. Coursey, Plott, and Tversky apparently formed a committee, but no evidence of output has been found (Coursey to Eric Wanner, February 17, 1988, subgroup 2, box 198, folder 1463, Russell Sage Archives, Rockefeller Foundation Archives, Rockefeller Archive Center, Sleepy Hollow, New York).

31. Richard Thaler to Eric Wanner: "I think this meeting is an example of the behavioral economics program at its finest" (May 27, 1992; Participant Evaluations 1992, subgroup 2, box 196, folder 1442, Russell Sage Archives, Rockefeller Foundation Archives, Rockefeller Archive Center, Sleepy Hollow, New York).

how such evidence might be used to build new theory."[32] Three issues were involved—how much rationality is necessary for players to determine equilibrium strategies; the role of fairness in bargaining outcomes; and whether learning from experience leads to equilibrium choices.[33]

Camerer's friendly takeover of the moribund experimental economics working group, refocusing it on experimental game theory along the goals mentioned above, was exactly within the purview of the Behavioral Economics Program. This move bypassed the issue of how "anomalies" fare in reward-driven markets, and experimentation of a different type than market experiments gained a foothold in the program.[34] Although the program closed soon after establishing the working group, it provided the seed for Camerer's (2003) acclaimed book on this topic.

In a paper published in 1990, Camerer elaborated on the bones of contention at the Caltech meeting, namely, whether markets correct biases, and probability judgment in particular.

The point of experiments like these is to establish empirically what kinds of irrationality persist under the experience, incentives, institutional structure, and learning opportunities that are present in markets. Representativeness does seem to persist in one set of experiments (though it is eroded by experience); other irrationalities may vanish

32. Russell Sage Foundation Meeting of the Board of Trustees, Appendix D, February 27, 1990, subgroup 2, box 7, folder 67, Russell Sage Archives, Rockefeller Foundation Archives, Rockefeller Archive Center, Sleepy Hollow, New York.

33. The attendees included twenty-four experimenters and theorists: James Andreoni, University of Wisconsin; Robert Aumann, Hebrew University; Kenneth Binmore, University of Michigan; Russell Cooper, University of Iowa; Robyn Dawes, Carnegie-Mellon University; Robert Forsythe, University of Iowa; Charles Holt, University of Virginia; Eric Johnson, University of Pennsylvania; Ehud Kalai, Northwestern University; Dave Kreps, Stanford University; George Mailath, University of Pennsylvania; Paul Milgrom, Stanford University; Andy Postlewaite, University of Pennsylvania; Amnon Rapoport, University of Arizona; Al Roth, University of Pittsburgh; Ariel Rubinstein, Tel-Aviv University; Andy Schotter, New York University; Reinhard Selten, University of Bonn; Hugo Sonnenschein, University of Pennsylvania; Richard Thaler, Cornell University; Amos Tversky, Stanford University; John van Huyck, Texas A&M; Keith Weigelt, University of Pennsylvania.

34. The transition was facilitated by Camerer's high regards in both communities. He obtained a PhD in behavioral decision science from Chicago, supervised by experimental psychologists. He had been involved in the Behavioral Economics Program from early on. And his first encounter with economics experiments was through Plott. Plott spent the winter term 1980 in Chicago and gave a graduate course on experimental methods. Only a handful of students attended, and Plott, as he always does in such a course, required them to devise an individual experimental project. Camerer and Sunder are two attendees of the Caltech conference who credit the beginning of their experimental career to Plott's Chicago course.

quickly. For instance, it is easy to extinguish "probability matching" and induce maximizing in subjects. An empirical understanding of what irrationalities persist, and under what conditions, could lay the foundation for an economic theory that uses evidence of systematic irrationality to make better predictions, rather than invoking the tired argument that markets always correct irrationality. (Camerer 1990, 169)

The reference to probability matching is important. Imagine Siegel had not turned his attention to probability matching but to another "irrationality" that is harder, if not impossible, to eliminate with the introduction of performance-based payments and proper motivation control. The magnitude of that decision for the future of experimental economics only equals the perennial thought of what would have happened if Siegel had not died at such a young age.[35]

3. The Aftermath

In the spring of 1992, when the decision to discontinue the Behavioral Economics Program was pending, Wanner approached everyone previously involved with the program.[36] In a lengthy response to Wanner, Vernon Smith strongly criticized both the organization of the program and the research on which it had focused. He was the only critical voice out of the thirty-eight letters received. In particular, he was "still puzzled by these rejections, and the similar experience, I understand, of other experimental economists."[37] Indeed, several experimental proposals were rejected: Mark Isaac and James Walker's on public goods provision; Shyam Sunder's on bounded rationality modeling of individual behavior in market setting; Raymond Battalio's on duopoly markets; Ronald Harstad's on a behavioral approach to normative economic analysis; John van Huyck's on coordination failures; Amnon Rapoport's on voluntary provision of step-level public goods; Camerer's on bubbles and fads in asset prices as well

35. This gives a new quality to the review of Siegel's last book written by Ward Edwards (1967, 293): "We cannot know what Siegel might have done. But this book is a deeply impressive record of what he did do. Even with 20 more years than Siegel had, how many of us can aspire to do so much?"

36. In fact, the Behavioral Economics Program was closed in the summer of 1992.

37. Smith to Eric Wanner, May 15, 1992, box 16, Vernon Smith Papers, David M. Rubenstein Rare Book and Manuscript Library, Duke University.

as a renewal grant for Smith and Isaac.[38] With the exception of Camerer's proposal, which was rejected in the fall of 1987, all these projects were declined a few months after the Caltech meeting in May 1988.[39] Smith's subsequent two resubmissions were rejected as well.

If the program were to be continued, Smith intimated, "you need to address the issue of why experimental economics was not more prominent in the program."[40] The fact that the significance of experimentation for behavioral economics decreased is an important historical question (Heukelom 2011a, 2011b). In the late 1970s, once Thaler acquainted himself with the work of Kahneman and Tversky as well as experimentalists like Smith and Plott, he believed that behavioral economics would become primarily an experimental enterprise.[41] However, once it became apparent that experimental market economists in their proposals were unable, at least in the eyes of the Advisory Committee of the Behavioral Economics Program, to make a "sufficiently clear connection between behavioral principles and experimental market predictions to impress the Committee favorably," their projects were not supported.[42]

---

38. Smith and Isaac held a Sloan grant for a project to conduct research in experimental economics on market anomalies, computerized matching markets, and public goods provisions. In 1986–87 a renewal proposal was rejected.

39. Advisory Committee Meeting, May 17, 1988, subgroup 2, box 194, folder 1433, Russell Sage Archives, Rockefeller Foundation Archives, Rockefeller Archive Center, Sleepy Hollow, New York. The archival records containing the assessment of individual projects are restricted indefinitely, preventing the historian from reconstructing the particular reasons why these proposals were not funded.

40. "In [Wanner's] list of Grantees there are only about 7 in 45, and I believe these were largely funded under the Sloan round before Sage took over" (Smith to Eric Wanner, May 15, 1992, box 16, Vernon Smith Papers).

41. Interview with Richard Thaler, June 16, 2014.

42. In full, the Advisory Committee concluded at its meeting in May 1988 that "although there were a number of competent proposals for *market experimentation*, one involving cooperative behavior in duopolies, another on public goods provision, and a third on aftermarkets, none of these projects developed a sufficiently clear connection between behavioral principles and experimental market predictions to impress the Committee favorably. . . . The lean yield from this exercise provides additional evidence (whether needed or not) that the interdisciplinary territory we are attempting to occupy in the behavioral economics program is thinly populated. Theorists confine themselves to theory, *experimentalists to market experiments*, and ethnographers to descriptive work. It is difficult to find individuals willing to cross traditional lines and *look at naturally occurring decision problems in a way that is guided by, and relevant to, behaviorally grounded theories of economic decision making*" (Advisory Committee Meeting, May 17, 1988, subgroup 2, box 194, folder 1433, Russell Sage Archives, Rockefeller Foundation Archives, Rockefeller Archive Center, Sleepy Hollow, New York; my emphasis).

It did not imply at all that any proposal with an experimental component was automatically rejected. Alvin Roth received a small grant for a new edition of his book on axiomatic models of bargaining that explicitly aimed to incorporate experimental evidence.[43] Even more interestingly, John Kagel's work on the winner's curse was repeatedly funded by both foundations in the years 1986–91. For both Thaler and Wanner, Kagel's combination of theoretical, field, and experimental research is a prime example of behavioral economics.[44]

After the Sloan Foundation closed its Behavioral Economics Program in 1989, the trustees of the Sage Foundation placed their program on hold, resulting in halving the available budget (Heukelom 2012). This funding restriction translated into fewer grants, and those who were funded were more attuned to the program's goals; the Advisory Committee was more risk averse in its decision making, and its preference as to what behavioral economics should look like became more recognizable. In 1990, when it was not clear that the program would close as soon as 1992, Kahneman joined the Advisory Committee, a sign for market experimental economists of revealed preference about the future of behavioral economics and its single most important patron.

Last but not least, the Caltech conference made the depth of divide between both camps clear. As Kahneman, Tversky, and Thaler's approach to experimentation diverged from that of Smith, Plott, and other experimental economists invested in market experiments, the emerging behavioral economics became less and less reliant on experimentation and was equally embracing other empirical as well as modeling approaches. This move to a less experimentally driven behavioral economics was facilitated by the absence of a formal institutional umbrella with explicit membership rules; there was no flag hoisted and no territory clearly demarcated. Unlike experimental economists and the Economic Science Association established in 1986, there was only the Behavioral Economics Program and no society of behavioral economics that would group

---

43. The second edition did not appear, because when Roth "began to prepare the material I discovered that the experiments on strategic models weren't yet comprehensive enough to reliably draw conclusions addressed to the theory, and so I set out to fill some of the gaps, including gaps in the theory." Instead, one theoretical and two experimental papers were published (Alvin Roth to Eric Wanner, May 22, 1992, subgroup 2, box 155, folder 1114, Russell Sage Archives, Rockefeller Foundation Archives, Rockefeller Archive Center, Sleepy Hollow, New York).

44. Interviews with Richard Thaler, June 16, 2014, and Eric Wanner, April 15, 2015.

economists involved in the program.[45] Consideration for financial support was initially by invitation only, and a group of carefully selected open-minded economists and psychologists was approached.[46] The program's executive body was the Advisory Committee, with four to six members equally split between economists and psychologists, and it served as a gatekeeper. In 1992 when the program closed, it was replaced by the Behavioral Economics Roundtable, which has kept the gatekeeper role. Former recipients of behavioral economics grants were consulted, and ten of them with the most votes were installed. Only one of them, Camerer, can be classified as an experimental economist.[47] On the one hand, by not formally separating behavioral economics from the rest of the profession, it allowed behavioral economics to easily fuse with the rest of the profession and thus avoided the marginalization that befell Simon's behavioral economics two decades earlier. On the other hand, by maintaining the program semiclosed and seeking out young talents and high-profile scholars, it fostered a behavioral economics identity and guaranteed its self-replication. It afforded behavioral economics with increased focus, giving the group "a sense of mission" as well as allowing behavioral economics to gain a foothold in top economics departments.

4. Conclusions

Over two days in February 1988 several key experimental economists and cognitive psychologists met to explore the possibilities of joint research promoted by the Sloan and Russell Sage Foundations under the rubric behavioral economics. Wanner's original vision that the meeting could open a line of inquiry to study the growing body of behavioral "anomalies" and their robustness in market setting proved naive. The divide between both camps was too big to bridge given the fundamentally different approaches to experimentation. One promoted by Kahneman, Tversky,

45. This is not to say that behavioral economists are a homogeneous group. From the early 1980s, there has been the Society for the Advancement of Behavioral Economics, whose membership does not overlap with members of the Behavioral Economics Roundtable. From the early 1990s Gerd Gigerenzer has been a vocal opponent of Kahneman and Tversky's research on heuristics and biases.

46. In no small part this was due to the size of available resources. An open call would impose too much of a burden on the Advisory Committee and would likely lead to increased disappointment, as only a small fraction of submitted grants could be supported.

47. The initial ten were George Akerlof, Alan Blinder, Camerer, Elster, Kahneman, Loewenstein, Thomas Schelling, Shiller, Thaler, and Tversky.

and Thaler had its origins in cognitive psychology; the other, by Smith, Plott, and other market experimental economists, had its foundations in Sidney Siegel's experimental practice. In terms of tools and techniques, the former group advocated allowing deception and hypothetical choices in economic experiments; the latter avoided such experiments. In terms of conceptual frames, economic equilibrium in particular, the former group was more interested in how initial individual behavior deviates from the theoretically defined equilibrium, irrespective of whether it exists or not. Instead of a radical vision of abandoning neoclassical economics, the goal was to adjust it using various observations, data, and insights from cognitive psychology. Experimental economists, on the other hand, at that time wanted to concentrate on how the market steers individual behavior toward rational equilibrium and what the equilibrium exactly looks like. Furthermore, they had spent considerable resources—laboratories with the latest computer technology and custom-made software—to study these research questions. Their aim was not to protect neoclassical economics but to produce rigorous data that theory and theorists need to take seriously.

I have argued elsewhere that the second half of the 1980s and early 1990s was pivotal for what I label the experimental turn in economics—turning economics into an experimental discipline. During this period the experimental economics community institutionalized itself through the Economic Science Association established in 1986, the number of computerized laboratories exploded, leading journals were steadily publishing experimental research, an important internal dispute was played out openly in front of the economics profession, and ultimately increasing trustworthiness of experimental economics broke out shortly after the 1988 Caltech meeting (Svorenčík 2015). The emerging divide between nascent behavioral economists and experimentalists is an integral part of the experimental turn not only because the divergence coincides with these changes but also because it relates to the turn's underlying issue—the reconceptualization of the relationship between economic theory and rigorous experimental data. The differences between both groups—both on the methodological level of how to conduct experiments and what their role is and on the conceptual level of how to modify theory in light of countervailing evidence and what is considered such evidence—became common knowledge thanks to the meeting at Caltech. Thus the Behavioral Economic Program moved away from resolving these differences that the experimental economics working group was supposed to examine to being focused on supporting projects of developing economic models on the basis of "behavioral principles."[48] The end of Sloan's support of the program in 1989 only reinforced this move. While experimental market economists such as Smith and Plott were effectively excluded and felt so, other experimental projects such as Kagel's on the winner's curse, Roth's on bargaining, and Camerer's on behavioral game theory were supported. During the 1990s, experimental economists grew as a community in its size and in the diversity of its members' research interests. Although the proportion of experimental market economists declined, the experimental economics community has retained the basic procedural standards that it claimed and cultivated from Sidney Siegel.

References

Association for Psychological Science. 2011. *Remembering William K. Estes*. www .psychologicalscience.org/index.php/publications/observer/2011/november-11 /remembering-william-k-estes.html. Accessed April 9, 2015.

Augier, M. 2005. "Behavioral Economics: The Carnegie School." In vol. 1 of *Encyclopedia of Social Measurement*, edited by K. Leonard Kempf. Boston: Elsevier/ Academic.

Camerer, C. 1990. "Do Markets Correct Biases in Probability Judgment? Evidence from Market Experiments." In *Advances in Behavioral Economics*, edited by L. Green and J. H. Kagel, 126–72. Norwood, N.J.: Ablex Publishing Corporation.

———. 2003. *Behavioral Game Theory: Experiments in Strategic Interaction*. New York: Russell Sage Foundation.

Cason, T. N., and C. R. Plott. 2014. "Misconceptions and Game Form Recognition: Challenges to Theories of Revealed Preference and Framing." *California Institute of Technology Social Science Working Paper* 1363.

Davidson, D., P. Suppes, and S. Siegel. 1955. "Some Experiments and Related Theory on the Measurement of Utility and Subjective Probability." Technical Report No. 1, August 15, 1955. Stanford University.

———. 1957. *Decision Making: An Experimental Approach*. Stanford, Calif.: Stanford University Press.

Edwards, W. 1967. "Review: Decision and Choice: Contributions of Sidney Siegel." *Journal of the American Statistical Association* 62: 291–93.

Engvall Siegel, A. 1964. "Sidney Siegel: A Memoir." In *Decision and Choice: Contributions of Sidney Siegel*, edited by S. Messick and A. H. Brayfield. New York: McGraw-Hill.

Estes, W. K. 1950. "Toward a Statistical Theory of Learning." *Psychological Review* 57: 94–107.

---

48. See footnote 42 for details and Staddon, this volume, for a criticism of behavioral economics.

————. 1954. "Individual Behavior in Uncertain Situations: An Interpretation in Terms of Statistical Association Theory." In *Decision Processes*, edited by R. M. Thrall, C. H. Coombs, and R. L. Davis. New York: Wiley.

Flood, M. M. 1954. "On Game-Learning Theory: and Some Decision-Making Experiments." In *Decision Processes*, edited by R. M. Thrall, C. H. Coombs, and R. L. Davis. New York: Wiley.

Fouraker, L. E., M. Shubik, and S. Siegel. 1961. *Oligopoly Bargaining: The Quantity Adjuster Models*. Research Bulletin 20. Pennsylvania State University, Department of Psychology.

Fouraker, L. E., and S. Siegel. 1963. *Bargaining Behavior*. New York: McGraw-Hill.

Grether, D. M. 1980. "Bayes Rule as a Descriptive Model: The Representativeness Heuristic." *Quarterly Journal of Economics* 95: 537–57.

Grether, D. M., and C. R. Plott. 1979. "Economic Theory of Choice and the Preference Reversal Phenomenon." *American Economic Review* 69: 623–38.

Guala, F. 2005. *The Methodology of Experimental Economics*. Cambridge: Cambridge University Press.

————. 2008. "Experimental Economics, History of." In *The New Palgrave Dictionary of Economics*, edited by S. Durlauf and L. Blume. 2nd ed. London: Palgrave-Macmillan.

Hertwig, R., and A. Ortmann. 2001. "Experimental Practices in Economics: A Methodological Challenge for Psychologists?" *Behavioral and Brain Sciences* 24: 383–403.

Heukelom, F. 2010. "Measurement and Decision Making at the University of Michigan in the 1950s and 1960s." *Journal of the History of the Behavioral Sciences* 46: 189–207.

————. 2011a. "Three Explanations for the Kahneman-Tversky Programme of the 1970s." *European Journal of the History of Economic Thought* 19: 797–828.

————. 2011b. "What to Conclude from Psychological Experiments: The Contrasting Cases of Experimental and Behavioral Economics." *History of Political Economy* 43: 649–81.

————. 2012. "A Sense of Mission: The Alfred P. Sloan and Russell Sage Foundations' Behavioral Economics Program, 1984–1992." *Science in Context* 25: 263–86.

————. 2014. *Behavioral Economics: A History*. New York: Cambridge University Press.

Hogarth, R. M., and M. W. Reder. 1987. *Rational Choice: The Contrast between Economics and Psychology*. Chicago: University of Chicago Press.

Isoni, A., G. Loomes, and R. Sugden. 2011. "The Willingness to Pay—Willingness to Accept Gap, the 'Endowment Effect,' Subject Misconceptions, and Experimental Procedures for Eliciting Valuations: Comment." *American Economic Review* 101: 991–1011.

Kahneman, D., J. L. Knetsch, and R. Thaler. 1986a. "Fairness as a Constraint on Profit Seeking: Entitlements in the Market." *American Economic Review* 76: 447–64.

———. 1986b. "Fairness and the Assumptions of Economics." *Journal of Business* 59: S285–S300.

———. 1990. "Experimental Tests of the Endowment Effect and the Coase Theorem." *Journal of Political Economy* 98: 1325–48.

Knetsch, J. L. 1989. "The Endowment Effect and Evidence of Nonreversible Indifference Curves." *American Economic Review* 79: 1277–84.

Knetsch, J. L., and J. A. Sinden. 1984. "Willingness to Pay and Compensation Demanded: Experimental Evidence of an Unexpected Disparity in Measures of Value." *Quarterly Journal of Economics* 99: 507–21.

Knetsch, J. L., F.-F. Tang, and R. H. Thaler. 2001. "The Endowment Effect and Repeated Market Trials: Is the Vickrey Auction Demand Revealing?" *Experimental Economics* 4: 257–69.

Mosteller, F., and P. Nogee. 1951. "An Experimental Measurement of Utility." *Journal of Political Economy* 59: 371–404.

Plott, C. R. 1982. "Industrial Organization Theory and Experimental Economics." *Journal of Economic Literature* 20: 1485–527.

Plott, C. R., and K. Zeiler. 2005. "The Willingness to Pay—Willingness to Accept Gap, the 'Endowment Effect,' Subject Misconceptions, and Experimental Procedures for Eliciting Valuations." *American Economic Review* 95: 530–45.

———. 2007. "Exchange Asymmetries Incorrectly Interpreted as Evidence of Endowment Effect Theory and Prospect Theory?" *American Economic Review* 97: 1449–66.

———. 2011. "The Willingness to Pay—Willingness to Accept Gap, the 'Endowment Effect,' Subject Misconceptions, and Experimental Procedures for Eliciting Valuations: Reply." *American Economic Review* 101: 1012–28.

Roth, A. E., ed. 1987. *Laboratory Experimentation in Economics: Six Points of View.* Cambridge: Cambridge University Press.

Sent, E. M. 2004. "Behavioral Economics: How Psychology Made Its (Limited) Way Back into Economics." *History of Political Economy* 36: 735.

Shubik, Martin. Papers. David M. Rubenstein Rare Book and Manuscript Library, Duke University.

Siegel, S. 1961. "Decision Making and Learning under Varying Conditions of Reinforcement." *Annals of the New York Academy of Sciences* 89: 766–83.

———. 1964. *Choice, Strategy, and Utility.* New York: McGraw-Hill.

Siegel, S., and L. E. Fouraker. 1960. *Bargaining and Group Decision Making: Experiments in Bilateral Monopoly.* New York: McGraw-Hill.

Siegel, S., and D. A. Goldstein. 1959. "Decision-Making Behavior in a Two-Choice Uncertain Outcome Situation." *Journal of Experimental Psychology* 57: 37–42.

Smith, V. L. 1962. "An Experimental Study of Competitive Market Behavior." *Journal of Political Economy* 70: 111–37.

———. 1976. "Experimental Economics: Induced Value Theory." *American Economic Review, Papers and Proceedings of the Eighty-Eighth Annual Meeting of the American Economic Association* 66: 274–79.

————. 1982. "Microeconomic Systems as an Experimental Science." *American Economic Review* 72: 923–55.

————. 1989. "Theory, Experiment, and Economics." *Journal of Economic Perspectives* 3: 151–69.

————. 1991. "Rational Choice: The Contrast between Economics and Psychology." *Journal of Political Economy* 99: 877–97.

————. 1992. "Game Theory and Experimental Economics: Beginnings and Early Influences." In *Toward a History of Game Theory*, edited by E. R. Weintraub. *History of Political Economy* 24 (supplement): 241–82.

————. 2008. *Discovery: A Memoir*. Bloomington, Ind.: AuthorHouse.

Svorenčík, A. 2015. "The Experimental Turn: A History of Experimental Economics." PhD thesis, University of Utrecht.

Svorenčík, A., and H. Maas. 2015. *The Making of Experimental Economics: Witness Seminar on the Emergence of a Field*. Heidelberg: Springer.

Wallis, W. A., and M. Friedman. 1942. "The Empirical Derivation of Indifference Functions." In *Studies in Mathematical Economics and Econometrics in Memory of Henry Schultz*, edited by O. Lange, F. McIntyre, and T. Yntema. Chicago: University of Chicago Press.

Wilde, L. L. 1981. "On the Use of Laboratory Experiments in Economics." In *Philosophy in Economics*, edited by J. C. Pitt. Amsterdam: Reidel.

The Economics of Motivations:
Tibor Scitovsky and Daniel Berlyne

Marina Bianchi

In 1996 *Critical Review* published a special issue of papers written for a symposium held in honor of Tibor Scitovsky, twenty years after the first edition of *The Joyless Economy*. In answer to some of the issues that a group of scholars had raised in the symposium,[1] Scitovsky (1996, 595) began: "I am overwhelmed by all the praise, statistical confirmation, constructive criticism, and wealth of highly relevant new ideas sparked . . . by my book, which originally received scant recognition and poor sales."[2] Indeed, it was true: Scitovsky's book, which, over the years gathered a large appreciative audience, was initially received coolly and elicited mainly skepticism.

Most of the book reviews offered two major points of criticism.[3] The first had to do with what Scitovsky had been arguing, in previous works as well, about American consumption practices.[4] As he saw it, puritanism,

Correspondence may be addressed to Marina Bianchi, Department of Economics and Law, University of Cassino, Via S. Angelo, 03043 Cassino, Italy; e-mail: marina.bianchi@unicas.it.

1. The participants in the symposium were Michael Benedikt, Jeffrey Friedman, Albert Hirschman, Ronald Inglehart, Adam McCabe, Juliet Schor, and Amartya Sen.

2. Scitovsky (1996) himself wrote a paper titled "My Own Criticism of *The Joyless Economy*," where he addressed a topic that much occupied his later years, namely, the boredom of the idle and the idle poor, a problem that, he said, he had wrongly neglected in *The Joyless Economy*, where the focus was on the boredom of the idle rich.

3. See Aufhauser 1976; Peacock 1976; Zikmund 1977; and Ballard 1978.

4. See, e.g., Scitovsky and Scitovsky 1959, where, in discussing the problem of productivity changes and the use of time, he anticipates several of the themes developed further in *The Joyless Economy* (see Bianchi 2003).

History of Political Economy 48 (annual suppl.) DOI 10.1215/00182702-3619322
Copyright 2016 by Duke University Press

with its work ethic and profitable business pursuits, had bent American society toward increasing material comforts at the expense of those more pleasure-inducing cultural and social activities that characterized continental Europe's consumers. Understandably upsetting for many Anglo-Saxon economists, Scitovsky's positions were criticized as too sweeping, comprising generalizations with no institutional or historical basis, and, worse, being value-laden.

It is, however, the second point of criticism that interests me here.

Scitovsky's point of departure in his new theoretical analysis was the (rational) theory of consumer choice. He questioned the tacit assumption in this theory that choices and preferences coincide, an assumption that left the analysis of their possible mismatch and its potential causes quite unexplored. He therefore proposed that economists need to look at other disciplines, in particular the recent literature in experimental psychology, for the beginnings of an answer.

Reviewers of the book found Scitovsky's position legitimate but also questionable. According to them, economics had already filled many of the gaps that Scitovsky exposed and resolved some of the flaws that he imputed to rational choice theory. And, they added, this progress was achieved without changing the underlying analytical apparatus and with no recourse to psychology. The psychology that occupied so central a position in Scitovsky's own book was either bypassed by these critics or represented in paradoxical ways.[5]

In the preface to the first edition of *The Joyless Economy*, Scitovsky (1976, xi) did indeed lament not only his lack of success in getting financial support for the completion of his work but also the "unbroken string of negative reactions" that accompanied the book when he first presented some of its parts to economists (this part of the preface was deleted in the 1992 revised edition).

Twenty years later things had changed markedly. The experimental findings and progress of behavioral economics had partly legitimized the use of experimental psychology in economics and had emphasized as well the several suspensions of rationality that limited the use of individual maximization procedures. Happiness studies, for their part, had further

5. Particularly sarcastic was Alan Peacock's review that, besides making fun of Scitovsky's representation of the American lifestyle, accused him of wanting to amend a theory that had already amended itself. This had been done through the use of expanded individual welfare functions that incorporated as arguments many of the elements that Scitovsky had found missing in traditional utility maximization. The only review that was more appreciative was the one by W. G. Zikmund in the *Journal of Marketing* (1977).

progressed and identified many of the components of the satisfying life, a task that, for Scitovsky, was one of the goals of his book. As the discussion among the participants in the symposium made clear, Scitovsky's quest for a "joyful" economy had entered economists' discourse, and its analytical consequences in terms of rationality, freedom, and well-being had become a matter of serious debate.

After twenty years, then, Scitovsky's approach was less distant from the economic community and its use of psychology considered more acceptable. Yet his effort to study the determinants of individual choice and how they relate to individual and social well-being remains a unique economic endeavor. The reason for this is mainly related, as we shall see, to what he had to say on the motivational background of choices and to what he had discovered in a branch of experimental psychology that is still rather alien in today's economics.

1. A Psychology of Motivations

Scitovsky has discussed several times why he turned to psychology in his search for the possible sources of individual satisfaction and well-being. Some of his colleagues, he recalls, were shocked by this change of focus and considered it a possible sign of incipient senility, but to him it was simply a natural extension of his long-standing interests (Scitovsky 1991a, 234; see also 1992). Much of his work had been on the economics of welfare, so it seemed logical, he said, to inquire into the motivations of behavior that affected individual welfare. He had also tried, in earlier publications, to relax the assumption of economic rationality, stressing the effects of incomplete and asymmetric knowledge on the functioning of the market (see Scitovsky [1951] 1971, 1990). In that context, too, it seemed logical to explore the welfare implications of the individual's incomplete knowledge of the sources of his or her satisfaction.

The new turn to psychological findings dates from the two years Scitovsky spent in Paris (1968–69) at the development center of the Organisation for Economic Co-operation and Development. It was there that he realized with ever-greater conviction that "the enjoyment of life had no less to do with consumption skills than with income" (Scitovsky, n.d., 105a).[6]

---

6. See also Scitovsky 1999. For biographical details based on Scitovsky's own memoirs, see Bianchi 2012. For an accurate analysis of Scitovsky's work, as well as of its internal connections and developments, see Earl 1992.

This conviction, he says, challenged the standard economic tenets that more is preferable to less and income is a satisfactory measure of well-being (105a). Yet once he started to question these assumptions and the notion that all we can know about preferences is inferable from actual choices, Scitovsky discovered that he himself, as an economist, in fact had no knowledge of what makes life enjoyable. Early suggestions toward a richer approach came to him from the lesser-known writings of Cambridge economists: those of Alfred Marshall, John Maynard Keynes, Roy Harrod, and in particular of Ralph Hawtrey (1926), whose distinction between defensive and creative goods he found especially helpful.

But a real turning point came when Scitovsky was introduced to recent experimental research in psychology and early neurophysiology. The suggestion to explore this literature came in 1970 from a psychologist at the medical school at Stanford, the university to which Scitovsky had returned after his years in Paris. This colleague and friend drew his attention to some fresh studies on motivation made by a group of physiological psychologists (Scitovsky, n.d., 105a). As Scitovsky recalled:

> Some of them were a revelation to me. They answered all my questions; fitted in with introspection into my own feelings and behavior; and seemed to verify and provide a scientific explanation also of the remarkable insights of Plato and Hawtrey. I was thrilled to learn how animal experiments and scientific research on the workings of the central nervous system accorded with my own feelings and actions, and how well some of the data I was able to collect fitted in with the psychologists' findings. (106)

The fact that here Scitovsky refers to Plato is not accidental. In a 1985 paper entitled "How to bring joy into economics," a previous and shorter version of which was (revealingly) entitled "How to Bring Psychology Back into Economics" (1985, 183n), he tells us that it was from the classical Greek philosophers and their acute insights into human psychology that, he suggested, the Cambridge economists, with their classical education, probably had learned their psychology.

Plato in book 9 of *The Republic* had distinguished between two sources of pleasurable feelings: those that come from the relief of pain and discomfort and lead to a situation of absence of both pain and pleasure, and those that *do not* depend on any antecedent of pain or discomfort. He called the former feelings illusory in that, though often they are acute, they are also transitory. The feelings that do not depend on the relief of pain, though they may be less intense, are also more enduring. These, Plato said, generate real or pure pleasure.

This distinction, which plays a decisive role in *The Joyless Economy*, was present, though also unexplored, according to Scitovsky, in some of the writings of those Cambridge economists he found especially inspiring. Marshall, for example, distinguished between satiable wants, which are satisfied through market goods and activities, and those activities pursued for their own sake and with the sole desire of achieving excellence and dexterity. The desire for these pursuits, though noneconomic, Marshall thought was in fact responsible for the development of the sciences and the arts and had a substantial positive impact on the growth of an economy. Keynes, for his part, by introducing the notion of animal spirits, the spontaneous urge to action rather than inaction, recognized the human psychological need to engage in activities for their own sake, for the very excitement of creating something new and constructive (Scitovsky 1985, 189).

It was Hawtrey, however, who came closest to the analysis of those purely creative activities pursued uniquely for the positive gratification they provided. Hawtrey also put forward an argument that Scitovsky later developed further, namely, that to pursue and enjoy creative activities—and move beyond the defensive satisfaction of our wants—skills, imagination, and knowledge are required.

These insights from an earlier generation of economic thinkers turned out, in Scitovsky's view, to be theoretically more productive and to have a greater interpretive power when cast within the findings of the recent psychophysiological experimental research he had discovered. The most important and decisive of these findings were those of Daniel Berlyne (1960, 1971a), whose studies of the motivational underpinnings of human action came to form the basis of *The Joyless Economy* and shaped the direction of Scitovsky's own further research.

The first piece of this new "jigsaw puzzle," according to Scitovsky (1985, 184), was the concept of arousal. Neurophysiologists such as Donald Hebb (1949) and Berlyne (1960) had shown that feelings of pain and pleasure occur in different areas of the brain: one that avoids stimulation, called the aversion or punishment system, and two other areas where stimulation was sought and experienced as pleasant. These two areas identified what was called the primary and secondary pleasure or reward system (Scitovsky [1976] 1992, 59). The arousal or activation of the primary system generated feelings of pure pleasure; the activation of the secondary system instead generated a pleasure associated with "de-arousing," that is to say, with counteracting the pain caused by the activation of the aversion system. The existence of these separate systems in the brain confirmed for Scitovsky our introspective feeling that pleasure is something different from the absence of pain and discomfort and offered a rationale for why we might experience pain and pleasure at the same time (60). It also showed that pain and pleasure do not belong to a unidimensional scale that runs from misery to bliss (61) and, importantly, that pain is not a pre-condition for the feeling of pleasure (62).[7]

It was against this "broad canvas" of new psychophysiological studies that Scitovsky (1976, 80) reentered economics. He started to do so by distinguishing, as had Hawtrey, two different sources of human satisfactions, those arising from comfort, the avoidance of pain, and those arising from stimulating activities pursued for their own sake. In so doing, Scitovsky's aim was to enlarge the scope of economics to include all those life activities and forms of consumption that are not strictly economic yet contribute most to social welfare.

Before analyzing the various steps and developments of Scitovsky's conjunction of these two disciplines, I shall devote some attention to the main source of inspiration of his new insights, the works of Berlyne. He brought to the fore in psychology the role that motivations, and in particular exploration and interest, play in human behavior.[8]

2. Berlyne's Collative Motivation

Berlyne's psychological experimental research dates back to the late 1940s and early 1950s and was initially focused on the study of exploratory behavior and curiosity.[9] The first findings of this research stressed

7. "We must abandon the old fashioned notion that pain and pleasure are the negative and positive segments of a one-dimensional scale, something like a hedonic gauge, calibrated from utter misery to supreme bliss, on which a person's hedonic state registers the higher the better off he is" (Scitovsky [1976] 1992, 61).

8. And it was Berlyne whom Scitovsky (1976, xi) thanked in the preface of *The Joyless Economy*, "for much help and inspiration."

9. Daniel Berlyne was born in England in 1924. He received his BA in 1947 and MA in 1949 at Cambridge University. In 1951 he went to Yale University, where he obtained a PhD. After having held academic positions at various universities (the University of Aberdeen, Scotland; the University of California, Berkeley; and Boston University), he moved to the University of Toronto in 1962, where in the following year he became professor of psychology and where he remained until his death in 1976. During his career Berlyne wrote or coedited seven books and about 150 articles and chapters. For biographical notes on Berlyne's studies, research, and academic appointments (and personality), see Day 1977 and Konecni 1978. His saying that his first

the existence, both in animals and in humans, of forms of behavior pursued without any biological basis that would explain why they are chosen or should prove gratifying.

These findings were not new. Already in the 1920s and 1930s, American students of animal behavior had found that animals showed forms of behavior whose only function was to expose sense organs to stimulation. In some experiments rats were found to wander around alternative routes of a maze even if they did not lead to the reward of food or water; in others, they would even suffer a shock on crossing an electrified grid to enter another maze that was filled with objects of various sorts new to them (see Hebb 1955; and Hunt 1965a, 1965b).[10] What was interesting in these earlier experiments was that this exploratory behavior started not as a response to some external stimulation, as a Pavlovian stimulus-response explanation would dictate. In the instances mentioned, the very opposite was true, since stimulation occurred simply as a result of exploration having been undertaken (Berlyne 1978, 120).

Experimental research on exploratory behavior revived in the 1950s, and many of the previous findings were confirmed and extended. Eventually it grew to a point where its results became difficult to ignore and to be accommodated into prevailing psychological theories of behavior. These findings represented a challenge both to theories cast in terms of minimal stimulation, or drive reduction (as espoused, for example, by Hull 1952), and to those who explained behavior as motivated either directly or indirectly by biological needs (see Berlyne 1967 and 1978, 124).[11]

To account for these apparently odd forms of behavior, psychologists reverted to different named drives such as exploratory and manipulative, or boredom and curiosity. Yet these supposed behavioral drives did not really provide an explanation or account for all exploratory behavior, since

---

interest was interest (see Day 1981) was matched by a variety of accomplishments and passions in his own life. Fluent in six or seven languages and an accomplished pianist, he was versed in philosophy, art history, and the general history of ideas, and "an avid collector—of books, of paintings, of jokes, of subways (one of his many goals being to ride on every subway in the world)" (Konecni 1978, 136; see also Furedy and Furedy 1981).

10. Some experiments, for example, showed that monkeys would engage in solving puzzles, even in the absence of external incentives and for the intrinsic reward of doing it. Other monkeys instead, when confined in a box, would repeatedly open a heavily sprung door to observe what was going on in the outside room (Harlow 1950; Butler 1953). On the other side, some experiments studied how sensory deprivation affected human behavior and cognitive processes (Bexton, Heron, and Scott 1954).

11. Berlyne's view of behaviorism, its limits, but also its merits, can be found in Berlyne 1975.

changes in stimulation can apparently be rewarding even in the absence of boredom (Berlyne 1978, 142). As Hebb (1955, 246) observed, commenting on these findings, "The human brain is built to be active, and . . . as long as it is supplied with adequate nutrition will continue to be active." What they all confirmed was that organisms do not become quiescent when stimulation is reduced to a minimum (Hunt 1965b, 84).[12]

But why do organisms engage in exploratory behavior? What is the reward value of this kind of activity? That answers to these questions were still lacking was due, according to Berlyne, to the fact that investigators in psychology "have been content to confine their consideration to agents of proven positive hedonic value, such as food, water, relief from pain, and money. So they have been led away from the question of what events have reward value or utility and why" (Berlyne and Madsen 1973, 11).

The answer that Berlyne found was straightforward. All the extensive experimental studies with both animals and humans just referred to contained a common feature: that the probability, intensity, and direction of such exploratory activities depended on specific stimulus properties, all of them linked to variables such as novelty, complexity, "surprisingness," conflict, and uncertainty. These, then, were properties that, for Berlyne, accounted for the hedonic value of such activities.

For these stimulus properties, Berlyne coined the term *collative* variables. They measured the ease with which an incoming stimulus could be compared (collated) with previously experienced stimuli. They were also meant to be distinguished from those classes of stimuli that were more commonly the object of psychological studies, namely, the "psychophysical" variables—those associated with levels of sensory stimuli such as brightness or loudness—and from the "ecological" ones, those associated with reward and punishment (Berlyne 1971a, 81).

All collative variables were deemed dimensions of arousal potential, having the ability to affect the intensity of arousal. The concept of arousal, which was meant to represent the activation system based in the brain, had supplanted the previous notion of drive that was considered too general and unable to distinguish between learned and unlearned stimulating factors. For Berlyne, however, the reward value of an activity rested not on the *levels* of arousal, as it was commonly assumed in optimal arousal

---

12. Donald Fiske and Salvatore Maddi (1961) studied the relation between behavioral development and restricted stimulation as well as the role played by variation seeking and exploration. See also Maddi et al.1962. This experimental literature was well known to Scitovsky, who discusses it in particular in chapter 2 of *The Joyless Economy*.

theories, but on its *fluctuations* and changes, or on what he called the arousal potential.

How changes in arousal affected the hedonic value of an activity could be assessed experimentally through verbal ratings;[13] through psychophysiological measures, such as EEG and GSR (galvanic skin response) measures; or through behavioral measures, such as the length of exploration time (Berlyne 1974, 13).

The results of these experimental assessments showed that both low and high levels of arousal potential were perceived by organisms as aversive. This condition prompted a reaction either to decrease the arousal potential if it is perceived as being too high—as was indeed the case with biological needs—or by increasing it if it is perceived as being too low and not stimulating, as was the case with explorative behavior.

It was in references to these two classes of concepts—the collative variables and the arousal model of reward—that Berlyne introduced the distinction, later to become the reference point of all studies on exploration, curiosity, and interest, between diversive and specific investigation (see Berlyne 1960, 1965). The former is an exploratory response to situations of low arousal potential and corresponds to looking for entertainment, relief from boredom, or new experiences that might come from sources of different kinds (Berlyne 1960, 80). The latter is the exploration that corresponds to situations of high arousal potential, those perceived as unsettlingly complex and uncertain. Curiosity, for Berlyne (1978, 143–44), belongs to this second kind of situation, one that requires the specific, focused exploration that might reduce this state of tension.[14]

When matched against collative variability, the hedonic value of exploration can be described by a curvilinear relationship taking the form of an inverted U curve, where pleasure is maximal at moderate levels of collation, that is, for levels of uncertainty, complexity, surprise, and novelty that are neither too high nor too low (Day 1982, 20–21; see also 1971, 1981).

This collative-motivation model (Konecni 1978) was subsequently applied by Berlyne to the study of aesthetics. The first experimental studies of what could be regarded as motivational aesthetics had been made by Gustav Fechner (1871). Following Fechner, Berlyne was well aware that

13. Such as Osgood's seven-point rating scale used to measure the pleasingness-interestingness of a stimulus (later increased through descriptive scales, evaluative scales, internal state scales, stylistic scales).

14. Additionally, Berlyne (1960, 79) distinguished between extrinsic exploration—exploration whose aim is instrumental to some other goal—and intrinsic exploration, of a sort that is sufficient in itself, independently of its practical value.

the word *aesthetics*, though usually associated with the arts, was much more encompassing. Aesthetics was the study of the pleasing and displeasing, and dealt with the properties of stimulus patterns that might affect judgment indicative of pleasure or its opposite (Berlyne 1978, 103).

Aesthetic appreciation and preferences reflected the hedonic effects that collative variables were able to determine. Following the same functional relation described by the inverted U curve used in the model of curiosity, for Berlyne (1971a, 1974), the enjoyment of works of art was the result of the arousing or de-arousing devices that these set in motion.[15]

For example, playing on novelty and complexity, increasing dishabituation and contrast (of colors, words, sounds), or introducing surprise and incongruity were all devices that, by increasing stimulation when this was felt to be too low, had positive hedonic effects. But also pleasurable could be all those devices aimed at reducing stimulation when this was felt to be too high and threatening. In this case, playing on familiarity, recognizability, and repetition become instances of pleasing devices used in art. In his studies of aesthetics, Berlyne, however, distinguished between the feelings of pleasantness found to be associated with variables such as novelty and surprise, and the feelings of interest that seem to respond more to complexity.

Berlyne's approach remained influential even after his premature death in 1976, though somewhat weakened by the abandonment in psychological research of the concept of arousal (see Silvia 2006; Litman 2005; and Petri and Govern 2004). Several experimental results (Zuckerman 1979; Neiss 1988) showed that arousal is too broad and undifferentiated a physiological construct to be able to distinguish among different psychobiological states, such as fear, anxiety, anger, surprise, joy, and sadness.[16] The study of human responses to these discrete emotions—this was what the critics of arousal stressed—should therefore include affect and cognition as well as physiology.

Berlyne (1971b, 192) was aware of these difficulties, and, while hoping that future research would clarify the role of arousal potential, he himself

15. Berlyne's inverted U curve is similar to the one drawn by Wilhelm Wundt (1874). But there is an important difference between the two in the variables measured along the horizontal axis. Whereas Wundt measures the *levels* of stimulus, Berlyne measures *changes* in the stimulus. The consequence of this is that the old idea of an "optimal level" of stimulus has to be rethought.

16. For example, Zuckerman 1979 had shown that with sensory deprivation different indexes of arousal—EEG, behavioral, or GSR—all follow different patterns of response over time. Therefore there seems to exist no one-dimensional continuum of arousal. For further analyses of Berlyne's approach, see also Konecni 1996.

suggested that collative variables motivate exploration in individuals even without reference to arousal.

If Berlyne's use of arousal has been questioned, his work nevertheless remains highly influential at the level of the foundations of the psychology of art and experimental aesthetics. Many recent experimental studies have confirmed that collative variables such as novelty, complexity, and uncertainty do indeed affect our aesthetic preferences and feelings of interest and enjoyment (Silvia 2005). The same studies, however, also reveal that the contextual frame of appraising collation—not just the events themselves but the evaluation and judgment of them as well—is relevant for understanding aesthetic emotions (Lazarus 2001).

Even without the mediation of the concept of arousal, then, the core of Berlyne's research, the discovery of collative variables and their motivational relation to exploration, interest, and curiosity, remains a central reference point in various research fields, from the psychology of emotion to the analysis of aesthetic responses to learning and education.[17]

3. Scitovsky: Comfort and Pleasure

It comes as no surprise that Scitovsky (1973, 16) felt great excitement when he stumbled on these new experimental studies that addressed exactly the problem of the different types of motivations and forms of satisfactions that accompany active behavior. He must have thought not much differently from what Berlyne had observed in relation to psychology, that in economics, too, investigators had been content to focus their attention on forms of behavior of proven hedonic value, such as those connected to biological needs, forgetting more complex and challenging activities. And particularly revealing to Scitovsky must have been the discovery that what was challenging in these activities were variables linked to change, to variety, novelty, and uncertainty, variables mostly outside the realm of economic investigation. After an introductory chapter, three whole chapters (2, 3, and 4) of *The Joyless Economy* (both editions) were devoted to analyzing this new experimental psychophysiological research and how its findings could be relevant for the understanding of both economic and noneconomic choices.[18]

17. For an overview of these recent findings and an analysis of their relevance for our understanding of preferences, see Bianchi 2014a, 2014b.

18. In particular, his references are to Hebb 1949, 1955; Fiske and Maddi 1961; Hunt 1965a; and Berlyne 1960, 1967, 1971a. He also refers to the studies on personality based on the concept of arousal made by Eysenck 1967.

For Scitovsky, these findings revealed that there were two different sources of pleasure and satisfaction and that these could be associated with two different kinds of goods and activities: those aimed at *reducing* stimulation/arousal from an unpleasantly high level and those intended to *increase* it from an unpleasantly low level.

The former include all the activities connected with the satisfaction of our bodily needs and the relief of bother, discomfort, pain, and the unknown. These situations correspond to states of heightened arousal, the lowering of which is experienced as pleasurable. The latter, instead, are all the activities that increase stimulation by playing on novelty, variety, and the other collative variables when arousal levels are felt to be unpleasantly low. This distinction for Scitovsky seemed to perfectly agree, as we have seen, with what he had learned from the Cambridge economists he read, in particular Hawtrey's distinction between defensive and creative activities, between activities that are pursued mainly for instrumental reasons and those that are self-rewarding. Scitovsky called the former sorts of satisfaction comforts and the second simply pleasing stimulations or pleasure.

According to him, only the former among the sources of satisfaction had been studied by economists: the pleasure that comes from the satisfaction of bodily needs up to satiation, a situation where there is no pain or pleasure. Yet for Scitovsky (1973, 16–17), this was a "lopsided psychological theory," one that considered this unstimulated condition the height of bliss and simply left unexplained the major sources of an enjoyable life. Activities such as the arts, sports, travel, as well as work, scientific creation, and, importantly, mutual company and social intercourse, were all activities that expressed our desire for actions that are, as Plato had anticipated, intrinsically rewarding.[19]

This missing part, however, was difficult to fit in the economist's utility function, because the "pleasures of stimulation, unlike those of want satisfaction, are not eliminated by their too persistent and too continuous pursuit" (Scitovsky 1976, 77–78). Activated by novelty and uncertainty, there is no resting point for these forms of pleasures (on this point, see note 27).

Yet pleasure-seeking and comfort-seeking activities were not only different, for Scitovsky, but also alternative forces that compete for our time, attention, and effort, a competition that can become a source of conflict.

---

19. There are other recent strands of psychology that, starting in the early seventies, focused on the importance of intrinsic motivations: Edward Deci and Richard Ryan (1985), who related them to the growth of individual autonomy and competence, and Teresa Amabile, who connected them to individual and social creativity (see Amabile and Pillemer 2012).

In Berlyne's model, as I have shown, pleasure is the result of changes in arousal levels. Analogously, for Scitovsky, comfort is pleasurable only as long as its satisfaction implies a change from a situation felt as uncomfortable to one less so. But once reached, comfort, as the absence of pleasure or pain, corresponds to a state of no change. Maintaining this state (the equilibrium position of economic theory) corresponds to a situation that is inevitably inimical to experiencing pleasure. To obtain pleasure, concluded Scitovsky, one must give up comfort.[20]

But comfort, once gained, is not easy to abandon. If the gain in comfort is obvious and instantaneous, the loss of pleasure that accompanies its continuous pursuit will be recognized only gradually. When this happens, and comfort reveals itself to be less pleasurable than it promised, it may be too late, for by then comfort has become a habit (Scitovsky [1976] 1992, 71–72). The original motivation, the satisfaction of comfort, is now replaced by the new and different desire to avoid the pain of giving up the habit one has become accustomed to.

The formation of habits (and addictions), which are easy to learn and acquire but costly to abandon, opened up for Scitovsky the possibility of a second source of conflict, that between choice and preferences, between what people choose and what is best for them.[21]

This conflict, which anticipated what behavioral economists later analyzed and modeled in terms of intertemporal inconsistencies, was also at the basis of Scitovsky's criticism of the economist's assumption of rational behavior, a criticism that was, in fact, the starting point for the analysis in *The Joyless Economy* (see Sen 1996).[22]

20. This is what Scitovsky (1972b, 65–66) was already writing: "Such seeking of comfort and safety is very different from the active pursuit of pleasure the leisure classes of the past engaged in. . . . We shall never be affluent enough to afford both pleasure and comfort, because pleasure depends on the assimilation of novelty, the relief of strain, the resolution of conflict, the understanding of complexity; and one cannot have the pleasure without accepting into the bargain the facing up first to the initial shock. A predictable happy ending or too simple a piece of music is that much the less enjoyable; too great ease or explicit-ness turns much potential pleasure into mere defense against boredom. The old leisure classes fully understood this and were adventurous enough to take the risks and make that investment of time and effort in the development of mind and body, senses and spirit, so essential for the enjoyment of the good things of life." See also Scitovsky 1974.

21. The problem of a conflict between choice and preferences is a recurrent theme in Scitovsky's analysis and one strictly linked to his analysis of social welfare. Already in 1962 he discussed the possible other-directedness of people's tastes because of producers' willingness to play safe and cater only to the demand of the less informed, less innovative, but more numerous, part of the population (see also Scitovsky 1972a, 1972b).

22. In reviewing Robert Frank's book *Passions within Reason* (1988), Scitovsky (1991b) analyzed different models of intertemporal choices in order to explore the affinity that might

These conflicts were exacerbated for Scitovsky by the increased affluence of modern society (and of American society, in particular), for affluence prizes especially the economy of time and effort, thus making comfort the ultimate goal of economic growth. This happens also through an
education system that privileges production skills at the expense of consumption skills, whose existence instead is vital for a more balanced life
between comfort and pleasure (see also Scitovsky 1972a). Only a cultural
education that equips people to enjoy the more difficult-to-learn creative
activities can in fact redress the balance in their favor.[23] As he put it:

> The remedy is culture. We must acquire the consumption skills that
> will give us access to society's accumulated stock of past novelty and so
> enable us to supplement at will and almost without limit the currently
> available flow of novelty as a source of stimulation. Different skills of
> consumption open up different sources of stimulation, and each gives
> us greatly enhanced freedom to choose what we personally find the
> most enjoyable and stimulating, holding out the prospect of a large res-
> ervoir of novelty and years of enjoyment. Music, painting, literature,
> and history are the obvious examples. (Scitovsky 1976, 235)

Yet Scitovsky was rather skeptical about this possibility being realized
in the near future. The Puritan ethic, a biased education system that does
not pay attention to forming consumption skills, as well as the uniformity
and sameness of mass production, all seemed to conspire to make our life
both too good and too dull.

Some evidence for this could be found for Scitovsky by looking at the
figures that measure the monetary increase of national income and those
that measure the population's self-reported well-being. Though satisfaction and happiness cannot be measured, still Scitovsky could refer to Richard Easterlin's studies of time series of self-reported well-being as the
available data on how people rank their happiness.[24] These studies revealed

---

exist between a rationality that involves also willpower to resist temptations, and honesty,
which involves a similar commitment. He does this in discussing the question posed by Frank
whether a rational person is closer to an honest person and vice versa (82), and to stress what he
had already argued in *The Joyless Economy*, namely, that the concept of rationality is more
complex and subtle than the one assumed by economists.

23. For an analysis of these three forms of conflict—between preferences and choices,
between comfort and pleasure, and between production and consumption skills—see Bianchi
2003.

24. Scitovsky, as is well known, was among the first to bring Easterlin's studies to the attention of economists.

a low correlation between individual happiness and the secular rise of income and seemed to confirm that other measures apart from income needed to be analyzed and included in the study of social well-being (see Easterlin 1974, 1995).[25] If Easterlin pointed out the importance of rank and status in the income hierarchy as a possible explanation of this gap, Scitovsky (1976, 137) highlighted additionally not only the importance of work satisfaction but also, coherently with his analysis, the stimulation of novelty and the role of addiction in anchoring one's own behavior to the routines of comforts.

4. The Economic Implications of the Psychology of Motivations

Scitovsky, in his quest for what makes life enjoyable, used his psychological references and discoveries to stress how the dynamic of motivations pulled individual choices in opposite directions. In Scitovsky's hands, Berlyne's dual hedonic process of arousal-moderating and arousal-heightening devices becomes the distinction between comfort and stimulation, defensive and creative activities as two different sources of enjoyment. This is a distinction that becomes a conflict when, because of the bewitching and addictive nature of comfort, we end up overindulging in comfort at the expense of pleasure. With no skills to overcome this imbalance, all the economy of time and effort that the organization of our large-scale economy produces ends up wasted in residual, unplanned activities that do not improve individual enjoyment or social well-being. Worse, the desire for stimulation, once so unfed and unsatisfied, can be channeled toward unsocial activities, such as aggression and violence.[26]

By entering into and developing Berlyne's motivational model as one interpretive key of modern economic society or, as he says in the preface to the first edition, by placing economic activity and welfare into the much larger framework of psychologists, Scitovsky actually went many steps beyond that model.

25. Thanks to the large literature that in recent years has explored the so-called happiness paradox, it is this particular aspect of Scitovsky's analysis that is most familiar to researchers (see Pugno 2014a).

26. In his 1930 essay "Economic Possibilities for Our Grandchildren," John Maynard Keynes (1972, 328) had argued along similar lines, in cautioning against the formidable difficulties that future generations might encounter in cultivating the "art of life itself" once, in a not-so-distant future, the struggle for subsistence and absolute needs would be solved.

In Berlyne there is no empirical justification that allows us to identify a conflict or a dichotomy between arousing and de-arousing activities. Nor is there any hierarchy between them or between higher and lower desires, as Scitovsky (1973, 17) sometimes labels pleasure and comfort.

These two processes act concomitantly in what Berlyne deemed to be the source of pleasure. Then, too, in his analysis of exploratory activity and curiosity, diversive and specific exploration are two dimensions of the same process and correspond to what we can identify as problem-finding and problem-solving activities. As he suggested, and as recent experimental research in both aesthetic preferences and curiosity has confirmed, novelty is always a relative concept that must be accompanied by a certain degree of familiarity, of knowledge and experience, to be processed and understood. It is always bounded novelty, a novelty that mixes the challenges of the new with the reassurance of the known.

What is true, however, is that any position of rest, of minimum stimulation, of what economists had long defined as the equilibrium position of choice, is not supported by the findings of the experimental studies we have analyzed. These systematically showed that disequilibrating activities are as important as equilibrating ones.[27] This condition of unrest that they have highlighted, the desire of acting for the pure challenge it represents, is also a condition of human freedom, as Scitovsky ([1976] 1992, 78) underlined when he stated that there is greater scope for free and rational choice because of the pleasure we derive from actions pursued for their own sake.

Finally, we have seen that Scitovsky's argument rests on a motivational framework that makes significant use of the physiological concept of arousal. After the criticism that this concept has suffered, Scitovsky's framework might seem to stand on a too generic empirical ground. Still, as noted, Berlyne's discovery of collative variables, when accompanied by the specification of the cognitive processes involved in their perception, appears to be crucial in explaining exploratory behavior and aesthetic preferences, even without the intermediation of the concept of arousal.

Within this enlarged set of psychological findings, Scitovsky's contribution remains fundamental on two counts: for having highlighted the importance of those stimulating activities that need not have any antecedent of pain in order for us to want to pursue them and for having tried to answer *why* these activities are self-rewarding and thus a source of intrin-

27. This crucial point shows that to interpret Scitovsky in terms of optimal arousal theories (as Angner and Loewenstein 2012 do, for example) is not correct.

sic pleasure. As was true of the original motivational Berlyne model, and holds for the new experimental aesthetic, these pleasurable activities are high in collative variables, and dynamically so. Such sorts of activity, thanks to their complexity and combinatory potential, lend themselves to being constantly renewed and changed, thus becoming a self-sustaining source of positive engagement and interest.

Within this motivational framework, the contrast that Scitovsky draws between comfort and pleasure loses its weight. So too does his view that a culture of material comfort must be regarded as responsible for the negativities of economic growth. The contribution that matters most for economics is the economic recognition of those activities that are self-renewing and engaging, that stimulate exploration, curiosity, and the formation of interests and that, for these very reasons, are self-rewarding. These are not only a source of renewed well-being but also a condition of individual freedom.

5. Concluding Remarks

Scitovsky's attempt to bring joy into economics did not have much immediate impact on mainstream economic thinking. Nevertheless, twenty years after his initial discussion of them, many of his central insights had become subjects of independent research, and some of the questions he posed were then, and remain, a matter of debate in economics. This is the case in particular with the problem of negative addictions, and the personally and socially destructive behaviors associated with them, and, conversely, with the positive determinants of individual and social well-being. Equally relevant are the methodological issues that discussing them involves, namely, the role of rationality in choice and the freedom of choice.

Interestingly, however, whereas after twenty years Scitovsky's critical analysis of stimulating activities, as well as his contribution to the study of the nonmonetary components of economic welfare, had come to enjoy some acceptance, this happened without engagement on the part of economists of the empirical psychological support that Scitovsky himself so happily appropriated. In the 1996 *Critical Review* symposium, only Michael Benedikt, a professor of architecture, explored that literature in any detail.

The psychology that has most fully entered economics was not the motivational theory that inspired Scitovsky but the neobehavioral psychology of Daniel Kahneman and Amos Tversky. As John Staddon, however, in this volume shows, they focused on the limits that systematic errors may impose on the rationality of choices, especially those related to loss aversion and intertemporal inconsistencies, not on what motivates such choices.[28]

In that neglect we have lost the question of *why* the stimulating activities studied by Scitovsky are self-rewarding and a source of pleasure. The dynamics of motivations and their implications for economics in terms of creative endeavor and positive enjoyment remain outside the mainstream concerns of economists. Inquiry into them has again been left to other disciplines, such as the social psychology of creativity and the experimental analysis of aesthetic preferences and interest, with no curiosity yet on the part of the average economist to discover what they might add to our understanding of economic choice.

References

Amabile, T. M., and J. Pillemer. 2012. "Perspectives on the Social Psychology of Creativity." *Journal of Creative Behavior* 46 (1): 3–15.

Angner, E., and G. Loewenstein. 2012. "Behavioral Economics." In *Philosophy of Economics*, edited by U. Mäki, 641–89. Kidlington: North Holland.

Aufhauser, K. 1976. Review of *The Joyless Economy*, by Tibor Scitovsky. *Economic Journal* 86 (344): 911–13.

Ballard, R. J. 1978. Review of *The Joyless Economy*, by Tibor Scitovsky. *Southern Economic Journal* 45 (1): 301–2.

Benedikt, M. 1996. "Complexity, Value, and the Psychological Postulates of Economics." *Critical Review* 10 (4): 551–94.

Berlyne, D. E. 1960. *Conflict, Arousal, and Curiosity.* New York: McGraw-Hill.

———. 1965. *Structure and Direction in Thinking.* New York: Wiley.

———. 1967. "Arousal and Reinforcement." In vol. 15 of *Nebraska Symposium on Motivation*, edited by D. Levine, 1–110. Lincoln: University of Nebraska Press.

———. 1971a. *Aesthetics and Psychobiology.* New York: Appleton Century Crofts.

———. 1971b. "What's Next? Concluding Summary." In Day et al. 1971: 186–96.

———, ed. 1974. *Studies in the New Experimental Aesthetics: Steps toward an Objective Psychology of Aesthetic Appreciation.* Washington, D.C.: Hemisphere.

———. D. E. 1975. "Behaviorism? Cognitive Theory? Humanistic Psychology? To Hull with Them All!" *Canadian Psychological Review* 16 (2): 69–80.

———. 1978. "Curiosity and Learning." *Motivation and Emotion* 2 (2): 97–175.

Berlyne, D. E., and K. B. Madsen, eds. 1973. *Pleasure, Reward, Preference.* New York: Academic Press.

---

28. For an analysis of the differences between the two psychological approaches in relation to Scitovsky's analysis, see Pugno 2014b. On Scitovsky's approach beyond behavioral economics, see Di Giovinazzo 2012.

Bexton, W. H., W. Heron, and T. H. Scott. 1954. "Effects of Decreased Variation in the Sensory Environment." *Canadian Journal of Psychology / Revue Canadienne de Psychologie* 8 (2): 70–76.

Bianchi, M. 2003. "A Questioning Economist: Tibor Scitovsky's Attempt to Bring Joy into Economics." *Journal of Economic Psychology* 24: 391–407.

———. 2012. "A Joyful Economist: Scitovsky's Memoirs." *History of Economic Thought and Policy*, no. 2: 57–73.

———. 2014a. "The Allure of Novelty and Uncertainty in Art Consumption." In *Risk and Uncertainty in the Art World*, edited by A. Dempster, 145–62. London: Bloomsbury.

———. 2014b. "The Magic of Storytelling: How Curiosity and Aesthetic Preferences Work." "Economics, Psychology and Choice Theory," special issue, *Economics*, no. 8: 1–31. www.economics-ejournal.org/economics/journalarticles/2014-44.

Butler, R. A. 1953. "Discrimination Learning by Rhesus Monkeys to Visual-Exploration Motivation." *Journal of Comparative and Physiological Psychology* 46 (2): 95–98.

Day, H. I. 1971. "The Measurement of Specific Curiosity." In Day et al. 1971: 99–112.

———. 1977. "In Memoriam: Daniel Ellis Berlyne (1924–1976)." *Motivation and Emotion* 1 (4): 377–83.

———, ed. 1981. *Advances in Intrinsic Motivation and Aesthetics*. New York: Plenum.

———. 1982. "Curiosity and the Interested Explorer." *NSPI Journal*, May, 19–22.

Day, H. I., D. E. Berlyne, and D. E. Hunt, eds. 1971. *Intrinsic Motivation: A New Direction in Education*. New York: Holt, Rinehart and Winston.

Deci, E. L., and R. M. Ryan. 1985. *Intrinsic Motivation and Self-Determination in Human Behavior*. New York: Plenum.

Di Giovinazzo, V. 2012. "Memories of a Long-standing Friendship: Janos Kornai Reports on Tibor Scitovsky." *History of Economic Ideas* 20 (3): 193–202.

Earl, P. E. 1992. "Tibor Scitovsky." In *New Horizons in Economic Thought: An Appraisal of Ten Leading Economists*, edited by W. J. Samuels, 265–93. Aldershot, U.K.: Edward Elgar.

Easterlin, R. 1974. "Does Economic Growth Improve the Human Lot? Some Empirical Evidence." In *Nations and Households in Economic Growth: Essays in Honor of Moses Abramovitz*, edited by D. A. David and M. W. Reder. New York: Academic Press.

———. 1995. "Will Raising the Incomes of All Increase the Happiness of All?" *Journal of Economic Behavior and Organization* 27: 35–48.

Eysenck, H. J. 1967. *The Biological Basis of Personality*. Springfield, Ill.: Thomas.

Fechner, G. T. 1871. *Zur Experimentalen Aesthetik*. Leipzig: S. Hirzel.

Fiske, D. W., and S. R. Maddi, eds. 1961. *Functions of Varied Experience*. Oxford: Dorsey.

Frank, R. H. 1988. *Passions within Reason: The Strategic Role of the Emotions*. New York: Norton.

Furedy, J. J., and C. P. Furedy. 1981. "My First Interest Is Interest: Berlyne as an Exemplar of the Curiosity Drive." In Day 1981: 1–18.

Harlow, H. F. 1950. "Learning and Satiation of Response in Intrinsically Motivated Complex Puzzle Performance by Monkeys." *Journal of Comparative and Physiological Psychology* 43 (4): 289–94.

Hawtrey, R. G. 1926. *The Economic Problem*. London: Longmans, Green.

Hebb, D. O. 1949. *The Organization of Behavior*. New York: Wiley.

———. 1955. "Drives and the C.N.S. (Conceptual Nervous System)." *Psychological Review* 62: 243–54.

Hull, C. L. 1952. *A Behavior System*. New Haven, Conn.: Yale University Press.

Hunt, J. McV. 1965a. "Intrinsic Motivation and Its Role in Psychological Development." In vol. 13 of *Nebraska Symposium on Motivation*, edited by D. Levine, 221–24. Lincoln: University of Nebraska Press.

———. 1965b. "Traditional Personality Theory in the Light of Recent Experience." *American Scientist* 53 (1): 80–96.

Keynes, J. M. 1972. "Economic Possibilities for Our Grandchildren." In *Essays in Persuasion*, vol. 9 of *The Collected Writings of John Maynard Keynes*, 321–32. London: Macmillan for the Royal Economic Society.

Konecni, V. J. 1978. "Daniel E. Berlyne: 1924–1976." *American Journal of Psychology* 91 (1): 133–37.

———. 1996. "Daniel E. Berlyne (1924–1976): Two Decades Later." *Empirical Studies of the Arts* 14 (2): 129–42.

Lazarus, R. S. 2001. "Relational Meaning and Discrete Emotions." In *Appraisal Processes in Emotion: Theory, Methods, Research*, edited by K. R. Scherer, A. Schorr, and T. Johnstone, 37–67. New York: Oxford University Press.

Litman, J. A. 2005. "Curiosity and the Pleasures of Learning: Wanting and Liking New Information." *Cognition and Emotion* 19 (6): 793–814.

Maddi, S. R., A. M. Charlens, D. A. Maddi, and A. J. Smith. 1962. "Effects of Monotony and Novelty on Imaginative Productions." *Journal of Personality* 30 (4): 513–27.

Neiss, Rob. 1988. "Reconceptualizing Arousal: Psychobiological States in Motor Performance." *Psychological Bulletin* 103 (3): 345–66.

Peacock, A. 1976. Review of *The Joyless Economy*, by Tibor Scitovsky. *Journal of Economic Literature* 14 (4): 1278–80.

Petri, H. L., and J. M. Govern. 2004. *Motivation: Theory, Research, and Applications*, 15th ed. Belmont, Calif.: Thomson/Wadsworth.

Pugno, M. 2014a. "Scitovsky's The Joyless Economy and the Economics of Happiness." *European Journal of the History of Economic Thought* 21 (1): 278–303.

———. 2014b. "Scitovsky, Behavioural Economics, and Beyond." *Economics: The Open-Access, Open-Assessment E-Journal* 8: 2014–24.

Scitovsky, T. n.d. "Memoirs." Undated typescript. Tibor Scitovsky Papers, David M. Rubenstein Rare Book and Manuscript Library, Duke University.

———. (1951) 1971. *Welfare and Competition*. Rev. ed. Chicago: Irwin.

———. 1962. "On the Principle of Consumer Sovereignty." *American Economic Review, Papers and Proceedings* 52 (2): 262–68.

———. 1972a. "Notes on the Producer Society." In Scitovsky 1986: 47–69.

———. 1972b. "What's Wrong with the Arts Is What's Wrong with Society." *American Economic Review* 62 (1–2): 62–69.

———. 1973. "The Place of Economic Welfare in Human Welfare." In Scitovsky 1986: 13–25.

———. 1974. "Are Men Rational or Economists Wrong?" In Scitovsky 1986: 70–82.

———. 1976. *The Joyless Economy: The Psychology of Human Satisfaction.* Oxford: Oxford University Press.

———. (1976) 1992. *The Joyless Economy: The Psychology of Human Satisfaction.* Rev. ed. Oxford: Oxford University Press.

———. 1981. "The Desire for Excitement in Modern Society." In Scitovsky 1986: 128–35.

———. 1985. "How to Bring Joy into Economics." In Scitovsky 1986: 183–203.

———. 1986. *Human Desires and Economic Satisfaction: Essays on the Frontiers of Economics.* New York: New York University Press.

———. 1990. "The Benefits of Asymmetric Markets." *Journal of Economic Perspectives* 4 (1): 135–48.

———. 1991a. "Hindsight Economics." In Scitovsky 1995: 223–38.

———. 1991b. "Moral Sentiments and Welfare of Nations: A Review of Robert H. Frank's *Passions within Reason.*" In Scitovsky 1995: 72–85.

———. 1992. "My Search for Welfare." In *The Life Philosophy of Eminent American Economists,* edited by M. Szemberg, 248–60. Cambridge: Cambridge University Press.

———. 1995. *Economic Theory and Reality: Selected Essays on Their Disparities and Reconciliation.* Aldershot, U.K.: Elgar.

———. 1996. "My Own Criticism of *The Joyless Economy.*" *Critical Review* 10 (4): 595–606.

———. 1999. "A Proud Hungarian: Excerpts from a Memoir." *Hungarian Quarterly* 40 (155): 33–53 (pt. 1); 40 (156): 24–43 (pt. 2).

Scitovsky, T., and A. Scitovsky. 1959. "What Price Economic Progress." *Yale Review* 49: 95–110.

Sen, A. K. 1996. "Rationality, Joy, and Freedom." *Critical Review* 10 (4): 481–93.

Silvia, P. J. 2005. "Emotional Responses to Art: From Collation and Arousal to Cognition and Emotion." *Review of General Psychology* 9 (4): 342–57.

———. 2006. *Exploring the Psychology of Interest.* New York: Oxford University Press.

Wundt, W. 1874. *Grundzüge der physiologischen psychologie.* Leipzig: Engelmann.

Zikmund, W. G. 1977. Review of *The Joyless Economy: An Inquiry into Human Satisfaction and Consumer Dissatisfaction,* by Tibor Scitovsky. *Journal of Marketing* 41 (2): 137–38.

Zuckerman, M. 1979. *Sensation Seeking: Beyond the Optimal Level of Arousal.* Hillsdale, N.J.: Erlbaum.

Theoretical Behaviorism, Economic Theory, and Choice

John Staddon

Psychology is not a single science. There are—alas—many psychologies. Behaviorism is one of them, and "theoretical" is one kind of behaviorism.[1] Economics also is far from unified. To understand the relation between psychology and economics, it might be best to begin with one psychology and one economics, rather than attempt a review of two highly various fields. I compare two ways to look at choice behavior: *theoretical behaviorism* and *prospect theory*, a popular approach to behavioral economics as it has been presented in Daniel Kahneman and Amos Tversky's seminal 1979 paper and later writings.

What is *choice*? Charles Darwin wrote copious notes, two months before his engagement to his cousin Emma Wedgwood, listing the pros and cons of marriage.[2] A sample:

> *Marry* [pros]:
> Children—(if it Please God)—Constant companion,
> (& friend in old age) who will feel interested in one,—

Correspondence may be addressed to John Staddon, Department of Psychology and Neuroscience, 242 Soc/Psych Building, Duke University, Durham, NC 27708; e-mail: jers@duke.edu. Many thanks to Neal De Marchi and Marina Bianchi for the opportunity to participate in this conference.

1. For a review of the behaviorisms, see Staddon 2014a. For one attempt to apply theoretical behaviorism to the financial system, see Staddon 2012. An early effort to bring together psychology, biology, and economics is a collection of papers in Staddon 1980.

2. See www.darwinproject.ac.uk/darwins-notes-on-marriage.

History of Political Economy 48 (annual suppl.) DOI 10.1215/00182702-3619334

object to be beloved & played with.—better than a
dog anyhow.—Home, & someone to take care of
house—Charms of music & female chit-chat.—These
things good for one's health.—but *terrible loss of
time* . . .
Not Marry [cons]: Freedom to go where one liked—choice of Society
& little of it.—Conversation of clever men at clubs—
Not forced to visit relatives, & to bend in every
trifle.—to have the expense & anxiety of children—
perhaps quarrelling—Loss of time.—cannot read in
the Evenings—fatness & idleness . . .

There is much more, but you get the idea. This is choice indeed! No one
would imagine that animals choose like this. Indeed, they do not, and for
the most part, people do not either. So, I begin with the simplest possible
choice situation. The two-armed bandit is popular not just in Las Vegas
but among operant conditioners, those who study learned instrumental
behavior. The subjects are usually animals—more easily, and ethically,
subjected to experimental conditions than human beings and probably
easier to understand. Pigeons and rats often seem to follow elementary
economics. They are *rational*, in the sense that they maximize the rate of
reward. For example, a hungry pigeon in a Skinner box randomly paid off
on average for one in every ten pecks (termed a *random-ratio* schedule)
on a response key on the left and on average for one in every five pecks for
pecking on the right—such a pigeon will soon peck only on the right. It
maximizes.

Indeed, optimality theory can explain many characteristics of the operant behavior of animals, of the ways they adapt to different kinds of *reinforcement schedules*. But animals also fail to act rationally, even in some
strikingly simple situations.[3] The failures are more interesting than the
successes. Sticking with ratio schedules, consider a *fixed*-ratio schedule
that requires exactly one hundred pecks for each food reward. A pigeon
will soon learn to get food this way. But he will always wait a second or
two after each reward before beginning to peck, thus delaying food delivery unnecessarily. Fatigue? No; on a comparable *random* ratio, he will
respond steadily, not waiting after food.

3. See, e.g., Staddon 2007 and references therein. For a comprehensive treatment, see Staddon 2016.

The reason he waits is that he has a built-in, automatic timing mechanism that responds to the minimum time between food deliveries enforced by the fixed (but not the random) ratio by pausing after each food. It is easy to show this by comparing two kinds of time-based schedules. Suppose you start a sixty-second timer after each food delivery and do not reward a peck until sixty seconds have passed (a fixed-interval schedule). As you might expect, once the animal has learned, he waits perhaps thirty seconds after each reward before beginning to peck. If his time sense were perfect, no variability, he would presumably wait exactly sixty seconds so as not to waste pecks. The pigeon's timing is a bit variable, so he usually starts early. Perfectly rational: do not waste pecks, but do not delay food unnecessarily. Now suppose you modify the procedure slightly by starting the sixty-second timer only after the first peck. The rational adaptation is simple: respond immediately after food, and then wait as before. But animals do not do this. If the interval duration is T seconds and the typical wait time is $T/2$, then on this response-initiated-delay schedule they will wait not $T/2$ but T seconds, delaying reward quite unnecessarily.

The message: optimality theory is of limited use in understanding what these animals are doing. Animals never, and humans almost never, are *explicit maximizers*, computing marginals and choosing accordingly, as in some interpretations of rationality. They adapt via built-in processes, like timing, that sometimes yield "rational" behavior and sometimes do not. Behavioral ecologists call them "rules of thumb" or (a familiar term to decision theorists) heuristics.

The time dimension adds complexity, and the way in which time is incorporated into learned behavior is still not perfectly understood. So, let us stick with random-ratio schedules, where time is irrelevant. A choice situation where there is no rational strategy or, to put it a little differently, all strategies are rational is choice between two *identical* random ratios. What do pigeons do and how might theoretical behaviorism explain it? The explanation follows the Darwinian consensus: instrumental learning is selection and variation. There is a repertoire of response tendencies—candidates. Candidates could be simple responses, heuristics, or what Gerd Gigerenzer calls an "adaptive toolbox" (Gigerenzer and Selten 2001). But only one response occurs at a time. In the example I am about to give, these candidates compete in a nonlinear, winner-take-all way, so that only the strongest tendency, the *active* response occurs. The other responses are *silent*—like recessive genes. The active response is either strengthened (if it is followed by reward) or diminished in strength (if there is no reward). Notice that the variation-selection approach allows for individual differences. Different people will come to a given situation with different repertoires and different active responses.

Many dynamic processes have been proposed to describe how response strength increases after reward and decreases after nonreward. The one we have found that best combines simplicity and generality incorporates the organism's history of both reward and responding. It is not the last word.[4] Nevertheless, it shows how a simple moment-by-moment process can yield complex and often adaptive behavior. I show later that prospect theory, although not a theory in the same sense as the CE model—it is classification of the data, not a predictive model—nevertheless implies a similar underlying framework.

The assumptions of the *cumulative effects (CE) model* are as follows:

1. In a given choice situation, there is a repertoire of *candidates* (responses).
2. Each response has a certain *strength*, which is given by the following, equation 1:

$$X_i = \frac{\Sigma R_i + R_i(0)}{\Sigma x_i + x_i(0)}$$

where X_i is the strength of response i, R_i, and x_i are the rewards received and i-responses made; $R_i(0)$ and $x_i(0)$ are initial conditions. In words, the strength of each response tendency is just the cumulated payoff probability for that response, biased by prior reward and response totals. The learning rule is very simple: a response not followed by reward increases the denominator and thus reduces X_i; a reward increments the numerator proportionately more than the denominator and thus increases X_i.

3. Response tendencies compete to become active in winner-take-all fashion.

This simple model behaves rationally in choosing between two options that pay off with different probabilities: it will eventually fixate on the higher-probability choice.

More surprising is that it can duplicate pigeons' performance on successive-reversal learning (Davis et al. 1993; Staddon 2014b). In these

---

4. For one thing, it is deterministic, not stochastic. The randomness in my example is provided by the schedule. On fixed-ratio schedules, the result is usually indifference, which is probably not correct—although the necessary experiment does not seem to have been done.

experiments the pigeon chooses between two keys, as in the previous example. On day 1, pecks on the left key (say) are paid off randomly with probability 1/8; the right key is not paid off. On day 2, this is reversed: right p(reward) = 1/8, left p(reward) = 0.

And so on for many days: left and right rewarded on alternate days.

Unsurprisingly perhaps, pigeons improve over days, switching their preference faster and faster each day. This is called "reversal learning set," and many cognitive explanations have been offered for it. But the CE model can duplicate the effect because, over successive reversal days, the X values of the two choices get closer and closer so that switching from one to the other (because of the winner-take-all rule) gets faster and faster. No need to postulate a "set" or anything beyond simple learning.[5] The same model also predicts, correctly, that reversal performance will improve less if reversals take place every four days rather than every day.

So what does the CE model (and many models like it) predict should happen when the animal must choose between two *identical* ratio schedules? Maximization makes no prediction because the animal's choice has no effect on payoff. A version of H. A. Simon's satisficing[6] might predict random fixation on one side, given that switching entails some small cost, but that is not what happens.

Figure 1 shows a simulation of the CE model in this situation and some data (Horner and Staddon 1987).[7] The model predicts, and the data show, that the animal's behavior depends on the absolute value of the payoff probability. If it is high, the animal tends to fixate (randomly) on one or other choice; if it is low, it tends toward indifference.

Gordon Tullock (1971), who was one of the first economists to look at biological problems from an economic viewpoint, proposed something like this in his nifty little note "The Coal Tit as a Careful Shopper": "Assume that the bird, like any other food-consuming animal, explores a number of different food sources [pine cones with grubs, in this case], and then settles on the one which provides the most food with the least energy expended. Since it would tend to exhaust the food supplies in that particular area, it should be 'programmed' in such a way that it periodically investigates different areas." The CE model adds dynamics plus the prediction that the bird turns sooner to "periodical investigation" when it pecks a

---

5. Pigeons never show *spontaneous reversal*—switching on the first response each day. They always require a few unsuccessful responses to yesterday's "hot" key before switching.

6. See en.wikipedia.org/wiki/Satisficing.

7. For an extensive theoretical analysis of this and related situations, see Staddon 1988.

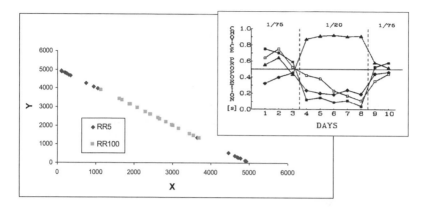

Figure 1. The pattern of choice between identical schedules as a function of absolute reinforcement rate. *Note*: CE model simulation: Two identical random ratios, 5 and 100. Preferences after twenty runs each of 4,993 time steps. Graph plots total responses: X vs. Y for two ratios: 5 and 100. Exclusive choice is favored at the smaller ratio (diamonds), indifference at the large value (squares). Initial values in Equation 1: $R_L = R_R = 5$, $x = y = 10$. Data: The figure plots the proportion of choices of the right-hand alternative across daily sessions for each of four pigeons for two equal-random-ratio conditions, $p = 1/75$ and $p = 1/20$, in ABA sequence (Horner and Staddon 1987, fig. 1). In both simulation and data, exclusive choice is favored at the high probability, indifference at the low.

relatively grub-free pine cone. This in outline is how one theoretical school of psychology thinks about the processes that underlie choice. How does prospect theory treat problems like this?

Human Choice

Animals must actually experience the different payoffs to arrive at a stable preference. Not so for people: you can just ask them (Kahneman 2011).[8] Consequently, the study of human choice behavior has developed along very different lines from the study of choice in animals. Nevertheless, I show that both can be conceived in a similar way.

---

8. But of course what they do when they actually experience outcomes may be very different from what they say in advance they will do. See, e.g., Ludvig, Madan, and Spetch 2014. Portions of this section, by the way, appear in Staddon 2016.

The study of human choice differs from animal choice in four main ways:
1. People begin with a stock of *wealth*. There is no real equivalent in animal experiments.[9]
2. There is no animal equivalent to *loss*.
3. Individual differences: *There is rarely unanimity in choice experiments with people.* Even when there is a statistically significant preference, 30–40 percent of subjects may deviate from the majority choice. In most animal choice experiments the effects are reversible (see figure 1), so the result can be replicated with the same subjects and no statistics are required. In practice, close to 100 percent of subjects give the same result.
4. Human choice patterns can be changed by experience: risk aversion can be changed to risk seeking by appropriate training or prompting,[10] for example. In most animal studies, choice is stable.

Because people will give immediate answers to many hypothetical choice questions, and because their decisions can often be accurately anticipated, hypotheses can be tested quickly. This strategy was adopted by two of the leaders in this field, Daniel Kahneman and the late Amos Tversky. They posed questions to themselves, and based on their own answers (which were later checked with groups of human subjects), they quickly found flaws in *utility theory*, the standard explanation in economics.

Prospect Theory

Daniel Bernoulli in the eighteenth century pointed out that the utility of a given increment in wealth is inversely related to the amount of wealth you already have. A hundred dollars is worth much more to a pauper (net wealth: $5) than to a millionaire.[11] Anticipating a now well-known principle in psychophysics, the Weber-Fechner law, Bernoulli proposed that the relationship between wealth and utility is logarithmic, so that equal

9. One experiment has tried, with some success, to induce monkeys to treat a stock of tokens as wealth: see Lakshminarayanan, Chen, and Santos 2011. This effect fits in with the more general analysis I present here, but it does suggest that monkeys are smarter than pigeons.

10. Experienced traders show fewer biases than novices; for example, see Kahneman 2011.

11. Comparing utility between individuals is epistemologically flawed, of course, even though it is the basis for the idea of social justice. We can verify that person A prefers X to Y and person B the reverse. We cannot say whether A values X more than B does. After all, the millionaire may be one just because he values a dollar, any dollar, more than does the pauper. Bernoulli's assumption is verifiable for individual utility but not for interpersonal comparison.

ratios correspond to equal value. A pay raise of $1,000 is worth as much to an employee whose base pay is $10,000 as a raise of $10,000 to one who makes $100,000.

The standard utility function is negatively accelerated, which means diminishing marginal utility. Because each increment of value adds a smaller increment of utility, people will generally be *risk averse* with respect to gains because doubling a reward less than doubles its utility. For example, in a typical experiment (Problem 3 in Kahneman and Tversky 1979),[12] ninety-five people were asked to choose between two outcomes: 4,000 with probability 0.8, versus 3,000 for sure. Eighty percent chose the sure thing, even though it is less than the expected value of the gamble: 3,000 < 3,200. Apparently, 0.8 times the utility of 4,000 is less than the utility of 3,000, $0.8 \times U(4,000) < U(3,000)$, because the utility function is negatively accelerated.

Yet expected value alone explains Problem 4, where 65 percent of the same ninety-five people preferred a 0.2 chance of 4,000 to a 0.25 chance of 3,000: in expected values, 800 was now preferred to 750—no sign of diminishing returns there. Evidently *certainty* has an effect that goes beyond the probability of one.

There is another way to look at Problem 3. The "3,000 for sure" option is guaranteed. It increments your current state of wealth, *unless* you choose the risky option, in which case, with probability 0.2 (the chance you *do not* win the 4,000), your wealth could go down by 3,000, a *loss*. So the issue becomes the following: is $|0.2 \times U(-3,000)| > U(4,000 - 3,000)$, that is, is 0.2 times the cost of losing 3,000 (i.e., actual expected value 600), greater than the benefit of a net gain of 1,000? And the answer is yes if the origin of the utility curve is shifted up by 3,000 on the utility axis (i.e., 3,000 is subtracted from each utility). In this case the disutility of a loss of 600 is greater than the utility of a gain of 1,000. But such a shift requires a further assumption about how people *perceive* a choice situation. The shift of origin is not really required for Problem 3, since the all-positive utility curve works as well, but it is necessary to account for other results.

Data like these led Kahneman and Tversky to propose *prospect theory* as a replacement for standard utility theory. Prospect theory is a

---

12. The example is Problem 3; amounts are in Israeli currency. This version of prospect theory was elaborated in Tversky and Kahneman 1992, and there is a vast secondary literature. See also Kahneman's readable book *Thinking Fast and Slow* (2011) and his Nobel Prize address: www.nobelprize.org/mediaplayer/?id=531.

hybrid. The "front end" is what they term *editing*: "Prospect theory distinguishes two phases in the choice process: an early phase of editing and a subsequent phase of evaluation" (Kahneman and Tversky 1979, 274). Editing is their name for cognitive processes that set up the problem for the *evaluation* part of the theory. Editing is a process, but it is not defined in any calculable way. Terms such as framing, combination, segregation, isolation, coalescing, and cancellation have been used to label operations that the decision maker can use to simplify and structure the choice problem so that it can be evaluated. Exactly when these processes are invoked and precisely how they work are not specified by any economic theory.

The core of prospect theory is the second phase: *evaluation*, which is a modified version of expected utility theory. Evaluation is a teleological/ functional theory; it describes an outcome but not the process the system uses to achieve it. Evaluation, according to prospect theory, modifies utility theory in three ways:

1. The idea of a *reference point* or adaptation level, which is set by the subject's current state of wealth.[13] The reference point moves the origin of the utility curve to a point representing the subject's current wealth. A choice option that yields a state of wealth less than the reference point is perceived as a loss. The idea that people are sensitive to changes rather than absolute values is a core principle of perceptual psychology.

2. Thus, the upper-right quadrant of the utility graph is the same as before. But the lower left part is modified, to deal with the following results involving losses. There are three steps; the last two require changes in the standard form. First, most people will choose a 50 percent chance of losing $100 only if the other possibility is a win of $200 or more: "People tend to be risk averse in the domain of gains and risk seeking in the domain of losses" (Kahneman 2011, 344). Thus, the first part of the southwest quadrant must be steeper than the first part of the northeast. This requires no big change in the shape of the standard Bernoulli utility graph, which gets steeper as it approaches the origin.

But, second, 65 percent of subjects preferred a 0.2 chance of winning 4,000 over a 0.25 chance to win 3,000 (expected values: 800 > 750;

---

13. See also Markowitz 1952.

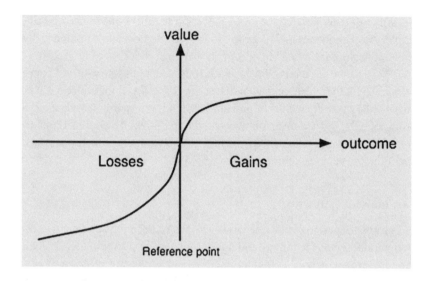

Figure 2. Prospect theory utility function

Problem 4), that is, they were in line with expected value theory and not risk averse. So the curve must straighten out at intermediate probabilities. And finally, 86 percent of people preferred a 0.9 chance to win 3,000 over a 0.45 chance to win 6,000 (Problem 7), even though both gambles have the same expected value. Now subjects showed risk aversion. Hence the curve in the southwest quadrant must begin steep, then straighten, and then flatten out. This is the iconic prospect theory utility graph (see figure 2: Kahneman and Tversky 1979, fig. 3).
3. Gambles at extreme odds do not fit even this modified utility graph. For example, 73 percent of people prefer a .001 chance to win 6,000 over a .002 chance to win 3,000 (Problem 8), even though the expected values are the same, that is, back to risk seeking.

Another exception is provided by something called probabilistic insurance. Suppose that you are indifferent about whether or not to insure your house against earthquakes. A creative salesman then makes you this offer: we are willing to insure you for just 45 percent of the original premium if we are allowed to toss a coin after an incident to decide whether we pay you or just refund your premium. Obviously this is a better deal than the original one, which you were on the point of accepting. Yet people will usually reject it. Not that they are against probabilistic insurance on principle. As Kahneman and Tversky point out, the decision to quit a risky habit like smoking is a form of probabilistic insurance.

These problems cannot be solved through changes in the utility curve alone. To fix them, Kahneman and Tversky (1979, fig. 4) introduce a somewhat untidy transformation of probabilities ("π is not well-behaved near the end-points"), termed *decision weights*, that parallels Bernoulli's transformation of value. Evidently both the utility curve and the probabilities must be transformed to accommodate data.

A Common Framework

Attempts to quantify all these modifications require four or even five fitted parameters.[14] That is just too many for a useful scientific theory. John von Neumann, genius, computer pioneer, and coinventor of game theory, famously remarked: "With four parameters I can fit an elephant, and with five I can make him wiggle his trunk." Prospect theory has evolved into a set of descriptions, not a predictive system. Nevertheless, as I will show, the underlying concepts can be related in an interesting way to choice in nonhuman animals.

Human choice behavior is affected by many things: not just the numbers you are presented with but your state of wealth; your experience, both recent and historical; the kind of goods on offer—money or things, for example—the context in which the task is presented; and your willingness to think through the options.

Kahneman and Tversky tackle this complexity by pointing out that prospect theory deals only with decisions that are made quickly. They distinguish between fast and slow cognitive processing,[15] what Kahneman calls System 1 (fast, thoughtless) and System 2 (slow, reflective). Presumably, the rapid process is simpler to understand than the slow one.

Their scheme is not as different from the analysis of animal choice behavior that I presented earlier as you might think. Consider three aspects of prospect theory: the role of consciousness, framing, and the fast-slow distinction.

---

14. See, e.g., Wilkinson and Klaes 2012, 163.

15. I think that the fast-slow distinction is actually due to Kahneman, but because Tversky would probably have agreed had he lived, and because prospect theory is identified with both of them, I use both names.

Prospect theory is usually considered a cognitive, as opposed to a behavioristic, system. Yet the role of consciousness, especially in the fast system, is minimal: "The mental work that produces impressions, intuitions, and many decisions goes on in silence in our mind"; and "Studies of priming effects have yielded discoveries that threaten our self-image as conscious and autonomous authors of our judgments and our choices" (Kahneman 2011, 4, 55). Compare this with the following comment by a behaviorist: "Astrophysicists now tell us that more than 80 percent of the matter in the universe, so-called *dark matter*, cannot be observed. The unconscious is the dark matter of psychology. Its processes are responsible for all creative activity and most recollection" (Staddon 2014a, 9). The autonomy of the unconscious is not even a very new idea. Well before Sigmund Freud, the eccentric genius Samuel Butler (1835–1902) referred frequently to the unconscious in his posthumously published novel *The Way of All Flesh*, which is in effect an autobiographical study of his own psychological development.

Cognitive psychologists are admittedly more interested than behaviorists in consciousness. But the contemporary view, like Butler's, is that consciousness is not an active agent but something like a workspace, which "allows the novel combination of material" (Baddeley 2007). Let us agree, therefore, that cognitivists and behaviorists no longer differ greatly on the role of the unconscious.

Framing is the term Kahneman and Tversky give to the effect of context and the way a problem is presented on the response that is made. The term does not occur in the 1979 paper but, with a number of other labels such as nonlinear preference and source dependence, was made necessary by new data that did not fit the original formulation. An example of framing is "The statement that 'the odds of survival one month after surgery are 90%' is more reassuring than the equivalent statement that 'mortality within one month of surgery is 10%.' Similarly, cold cuts described as '90% fat-free' are more attractive than when they are described as '10% fat.' The equivalence of the alternative formulations is transparent, but an individual normally sees only one formulation, and what she sees is all there is" (Kahneman 2011, 88). The way in which a question is asked (this is also sometimes termed *choice architecture*) can have a huge effect on the subject's response.

There is a counterpart to framing in animal choice. It grows out of the consensus that learning in animals is best conceived as a process of variation and selection, that is, selection by consequences, and variation constrained by the situation:

> For example, Pavlovian conditioning, which allows a neutral stimulus to acquire signal properties, will itself give rise to a repertoire of reinforcer-related activities from which operant reinforcement can then select. A stimulus associated with food, or food by itself, will induce a wide range of food-related activities in a hungry animal—activities from which operant contingencies can select. Pigeons peck, chickens peck and scratch, raccoons manipulate. Pavlovian conditioning, with (say) a food US [unconditioned stimulus], in effect frames or *labels* the context as food-related. The label then limits the emitted behavior to a food-related repertoire, which is defined partly by past history but also by the organism's evolutionary history. (Staddon 2014a, 92)

The situation-induced behavioral repertoire of animals is constrained—framed—in much the same way as human choice behavior. Sometimes "Pavlovian framing" will facilitate learning—if the desired response is within the induced repertoire; but sometimes it will not—as when the induced behavior interferes with the trainer's target behavior (so-called instinctive drift).

Note that framing in this sense means that all rewards are not equivalent—as most economists seem to assume. The repertoire induced by money will be different from the repertoire induced by love of ideas or a wish to cure patients. Consequently, paying teachers or doctors more will not necessarily produce better teaching or medical care.

Finally, let us look at Kahneman's fast-slow distinction. He contrasts the quick answers he and Tversky got to their choice questions—answers that were often "irrational" in the sense that they did not maximize gain—with the slower and more "correct" answer that most people arrive at after deliberation. The quick system responds with answers that are more "available" or "accessible" than other responses that may in fact be better. Kahneman (2011, 415) also tells his readers to "remember that the two systems do not really exist in the brain or anywhere else." They are ways to talk about the fact that people may respond one way at first and another way after given some time for reflection.

But there is no difference between Kahneman's System 1 and System 2 and what I earlier called "active" and "silent" responses. The active response is the first thing to occur in a given situation. But if the consequences are unsatisfactory, the active response is eventually supplanted by another response from the "silent" repertoire—Kahneman's "slow" system. Individual differences reflect available response repertoires of different individuals—differences that reflect different histories and propensities. Human responses are more complex than key pecks, of course. They are heuristics, rules of thumb and analytic strategies, the "adaptive toolbox." But there is no reason to doubt that they are emitted and selected by consequences, just like the simpler response of pigeons.

The economic approach has been looking for utility functions and decision weights that best fit a set of quite variable choice data. Since these data usually depend on historical factors that are not part of the analysis, this is likely to be an endless quest. A symptom of the difficulties this causes is that many very clever people have puzzled over the fact that human behavior often violates logical axioms such as transitivity and independence.

Transitivity is simple: if A is preferred to B and B to C, then logic says that A must be preferred to C—but often people disagree.

Independence is a bit more complicated. Look at table 1, which shows two pairs of gambles, A versus B and C versus D (Kahneman and Tversky 1979, Problem 1). Boldface shows which one of each pair is generally preferred (again, there are always individual differences): B over A, but C over D. There are two things to notice about this pattern: first, people pick the (slightly) lower expected value in the first pair but the (slightly) higher EV in the second. Second, the only difference between these two pairs of gambles is that the payoff .66*2400 (italics) has been added to both choices in A and B. Otherwise, the choice between A and B is the same as between C and D. Thus, most people's choices violate the independence assumption. The prospect theory explanation is the primacy of the certain outcome (Gamble B), which describes the result but does not explain it.

But why on earth should violations of logical axioms like this be worrisome and consume so much mental energy? Behavior is not physics or predicate calculus. Even human beings rarely maximize in an explicit way, following all the rules of optimality theory—especially when they must decide quickly. They do not consider all the options in an unbiased, neutral, and history-independent way, and then compute the costs and benefits and choose accordingly. There is therefore *no reason whatever* that human (and animal) choice should fit any set of simple axioms.

Table 1 Violation of the Independence Assumption **Preferences**
Change When a Constant Is Added to Each Choice

		Probability		Expected Value
Gamble	0.33	0.01	0.66	
A	2500	0	2400	2409
B	2400	2400	2400	2400
C	2500	0	0	825
D	2400	2400	0	816

Conclusion

The problem these examples illustrate goes beyond prospect theory. It is a fundamental problem for any outcome-based theory like expected utility. EUT is a functional/optimality theory and not a mechanism. It says that behavior will adjust so that marginal utilities are matched (or whatever), but provides no causal account for how this is accomplished. But there must be a causal account, a mechanism, and that mechanism will fail to optimize—to "act rationally"—under some conditions. Hence EUT will also fail sometimes—as Kahneman and Tversky eventually recognized. They did not, I think, understand the causal-functional distinction. They thought prospect theory was what I call a real (i.e., causal) theory and so were surprised when they had to keep adding kludges to make it work with a wider range of data.

Functional—mechanism-free—theories are not without value, but they will always run up against limits. Theoretical behaviorism, based on the simpler problems posed by learning in animals, suggests that it may be more profitable to look at the historical factors that determine people's response repertoire. Rather than rely on some form of utility theory as the ultimate explanation for economic behavior, future research might better examine the historical and cultural—*causal*—factors that explain why a particular question format drives people to frame a problem in a certain way, a way that allows them to pick "best in repertoire" even if it is not optimal.

Exactly what are the "editing" processes that cause people to perceive logically identical problems quite differently? What kind of training affects how decision makers perceive different kinds of problems? The optimality approach—marginal utility theory—can help us understand a particular choice problem. It will never tell us how people actually choose.

References

Baddeley, A. 2007. *Working Memory, Thought, and Action.* www.oxfordscholarship
.com/view/10.1093/acprof:oso/9780198528012.001.0001/acprof-9780198528012
-chapter-1.

Davis, D. G. S., J. E. R. Staddon, A. Machado, and R. G. Palmer. 1993. "The Process
of Recurrent Choice." *Psychological Review* 100: 320–41.

Gigerenzer, G., and R. Selten, eds., 2001. *Bounded Rationality: The Adaptive Toolbox.* Cambridge, Mass.: MIT Press.

Horner, J. M., and J. E. R. Staddon. 1987. "Probabilistic Choice: A Simple Invari-
ance." *Behavioural Processes* 15: 59–92.

Kahneman, D. 2011. *Thinking Fast and Slow.* New York: Farrar, Straus and Giroux.

Kahneman, D., and A. Tversky. 1979. "Prospect Theory: An Analysis of Decision
under Risk." *Econometrica* 47 (2): 263–91.

Lakshminarayanan, Venkat R., M. Keith Chen, and Laurie R. Santos. 2011. "The
Evolution of Decision-Making under Risk: Framing Effects in Monkey Risk Preferences." *Journal of Experimental Social Psychology* 47: 689–93.

Ludvig, E. A., C. R. Madan, and M. L. Spetch. 2014. "Priming Memories of Past
Wins Induces Risk Seeking." Online first publication, December 22. doi:10.1037
/xge0000046.

Markowitz, H. 1952. "The Utility of Wealth." *Journal of Political Economy* 60: 151–58.

Staddon, J. E. R., ed. 1980. *Limits to Action: The Allocation of Individual Behavior.*
New York: Academic Press.

———. 1988. "Quasi-dynamic Choice Models: Melioration and Ratio-Invariance.
Journal of the Experimental Analysis of Behavior 49: 303–20.

———. 2007. "Is Animal Learning Optimal?" In *Constructal Theory of Social Dynamics*, edited by A. Bejan and G. W. Merkx, 161–67. New York: Springer Verlag.

———. 2012. *The Malign Hand of the Markets: The Insidious Forces on Wall Street
That Are Destroying Financial Markets—and What We Can Do about It.* New
York: McGraw-Hill.

———. 2014a. *The New Behaviorism.* 2nd ed. Philadelphia: Psychology Press.

———. 2014b. "On Choice and the Law of Effect." *International Journal of Comparative Psychology* 27 (4): 569–84.

———. 2016. *Adaptive Behavior and Learning.* 2nd ed. New York: Cambridge University Press.

Tullock, Gordon. 1971. "The Coal Tit as a Careful Shopper." *American Naturalist*
105: 77–80.

Tversky, A., and D. Kahneman. 1992. "Advances in Prospect Theory: Cumulative
Representation of Uncertainty." *Journal of Risk and Uncertainty* 5: 297–323.

Wilkinson, N., and M. A. Klaes. 2012. *Introduction to Behavioural Economics.* 2nd
ed. Basingstoke, U.K.: Palgrave Macmillan.

Contributors

Marina Bianchi is professor of economics at the University of Cassino, Department of Economics and Law, where she teaches industrial economics and a course on creative economy and entrepreneurship. She has written on topics related to the theory of the firm and consumer theory, with a specific focus on the problems of change, learning, and the emergence of social rules. In a number of articles and two edited books (*The Active Consumer: Novelty and Surprise in Consumer Choice* [1998], and *The Evolution of Consumption: Theories and Practices* [2007]) she has analyzed the characteristics of creative goods and the limits of the traditional economic framework in explaining choices concerning goods and activities of this type. She has tried to provide an alternative account of the motivations that can explain apparent paradoxes of behavior ranging from addiction to collecting to fashion and the social dimension of consumption. More recently, her interests have focused on the role of curiosity and exploratory behavior in shaping aesthetic preferences and self-rewarding actions.

Simon J. Cook is an independent scholar, residing in Luzit, Israel. After publishing his 2009 monograph on Alfred Marshall, he directed his research away from the history of economic thought. After his archival discovery of a hitherto unknown essay on world history by the young Marshall, Simon's research has increasingly focused on the broad history of English historical thought in the late nineteenth and early twentieth centuries. Recent publications include "The Making of the English: English History, British Identity, Aryan Villages, 1870–1914" (2014); "Squaring the Shield: William Ridgeway's Two Models of Early Greece" (2014); "The Peace of Frodo: On the Origin of an English Mythology" (2015); and "The Tragedy of Cambridge Anthropology" (2016).

History of Political Economy 48 (annual suppl.) DOI 10.1215/0018270? 3688118
Copyright 2016 by Duke University Press

Neil De Marchi is emeritus professor of economics at Duke University. His research has involved analytical and historical studies of art markets, and he is working on two projects: a paper on James Christie's business model for a volume celebrating the auction house Christies 250th anniversary, in December 2016; and a study of how paintings from communities with no Western or Eastern aesthetic have been curated, looking specifically at Australian Aboriginal paintings.

José Edwards is assistant professor of economics at the School of Government of the Universidad Adolfo Ibáñez (Chile). His research focuses on the production and analysis of subjective data by economists and psychologists and, more generally, on the history and methodology of recent economics.

Tiziana Foresti (PhD in history of economic thought, University of Florence) is currently junior researcher at the Baffi-Carefin Centre for Applied Research on International Markets, Banking, Finance and Regulation, Bocconi University, Milan. In recent years she has researched the quantitative measurement of the value to Italian firms of early political connections with the Fascist regime during Benito Mussolini's rise to power. This research was awarded with an Inet grant in both 2014 and 2015. She was previously a postdoctoral fellow in the Department of Statistics at the University of Rome, La Sapienza, and has been the recipient of research grants from the Deutscher Akademischer Austausch Dienst. Her research interests include the problem of the stabilization of financial markets in historical perspective and the dissemination of economic ideas from Europe to the United States between the 1860s and the 1930s.

Craufurd D. Goodwin is James B. Duke Professor Emeritus at Duke University and a former editor of this journal. His most recent publication is *Walter Lippmann: Public Economist* (2014).

Judy L. Klein is professor of economics, emerita, at Mary Baldwin College in Virginia. She is the author of *Statistical Visions in Time: A History of Time Series Analysis, 1662–1938* (1997), coeditor of *The Age of Economic Measurement* (2001), and coauthor of *How Reason Almost Lost Its Mind: The Strange Career of Cold War Rationality* (2013). She is completing a book on how US military needs during World War II and the Cold War steered applied mathematicians to an economic way of thinking about scarce resources, including limited computational resources, and how economists incorporated the resultant modeling strategies into their models.

Harro Maas is a professor in history and methodology of economics at the Walras-Pareto Center for the History of Economic and Political Thought at the University of Lausanne. His research interests are in research practices of (political) economists and the interactions between economists, policy agents, and the public. His contribution to this volume fits into his wider interest in a shifting discourse in which rational conduct in an uncertain world came no longer to be seen in terms of moral perfectibility but in terms of choices between probabilistic events. His recent publications include *Economic Methodology: A Historical Introduction* (2014) and, with

Andrej Svorenčík, *The Making of Experimental Economics: Witness Seminar on the Emergence of a Field* (2016).

Ivan Moscati is an associate professor of economics at Insubria University, Varese, Italy, and teaches history of economics at Bocconi University, Milan. His research focuses on the history and methodology of microeconomics, with special attention to choice and utility theory. He is an associate editor of the *Journal of Economic Methodology*, and the work has appeared in the *Journal of Economic Perspectives*, the *Journal of Behavioral and Experimental Economics*, *Theory and Decision*, *History of Political Economy*, *European Journal of the History of Economic Thought*, *Journal of the History of Economic Thought*, and *Journal of Economic Methodology*. He is working on a book on the history of utility measurement, under contract with Oxford University Press.

John Staddon is James B. Duke Professor of Psychology, and Professor of Biology Emeritus, at Duke University. He obtained his PhD in experimental psychology at Harvard University and also did research at the MIT Systems Lab. He has taught at the University of Toronto and done research at Oxford University (UK), the University of São Paulo at Riberão Preto, the University of Mexico, the Ruhr Universität, Universität Konstanz, and the University of Western Australia, and is an honorary visiting professor at the University of York (UK). He is a past editor of the journals *Behavioural Processes* and *Behavior & Philosophy* and a fellow of several scientific organizations, including the AAAS and the Society of Experimental Psychologists. He has a Docteur, *Honoris Causa*, from the Université Charles de Gaulle, Lille 3, France. His research is on the evolution and mechanisms of learning in humans and animals and the history and philosophy of psychology biology, and economics. His laboratory has studied optimality analysis and behavior, mechanisms of choice behavior and interval timing in animals, and choice behavior in human beings. He is the author of more than 250 research papers and several books: *Limits to Action: The Allocation of Individual Behavior* (1980); *Adaptive Dynamics: The Theoretical Analysis of Behavior* (2001); *The Malign Hand of the Markets: The Insidious Forces on Wall Street That Are Destroying Financial Markets—and What We Can Do about It* (2012); *The New Behaviorism: Mind, Mechanism, and Society*, 2nd ed. (2014); *Unlucky Strike: Private Health and the Science, Law, and Politics of Smoking* (2014); and *Adaptive Behavior and Learning* (1983, new edition 2016).

Andrej Svorenčík is a postdoctoral scholar at the Department of Economics, University of Mannheim, where he manages the local experimental economics laboratory. The overarching theme of his research is the emergence, diffusion, and reception of scientific communities, their related ideas and practices that make these epistemic groups distinct. His current book project is on the history of experimental economics. With Harro Maas he has edited *The Making of Experimental Economics: Witness Seminar on the Emergence of a Field* (2016).

Index

Accounting practices
  and cognitive theory, 18, 37,
    39–40
  as mental deliberation, 17–19,
    40–41
  and morality, 19, 21, 31–34
    (*See also* moral algebra)
  and the self, 24–26, 31
  Victorian domestic, 18–19, 21, 25
Adams, Henry, 144–46
Allais, Maurice, 7, 243, 252–53
Almanacs, 22, 24–25
American consumption, 295–96, 306
American exceptionalism, 73
American identity, 141–43
American psyche, 5, 73, 143–44, 160
Anderson Jr., B. M., 87–88
Angell, Norman, 109–11
Arousal
  and collative variables, 302–6
  and pleasure, 299, 306–7
  and satisfaction, 306
  Scitovsky's use of, 309–10
  weakness of, 304

Backwardness, 9–10, 227–28, 230–31
Bain, Alexander
  decision making, theory of, 34–35
  influence on Eliot, 35–36, 38
  influence on Jevons, 2, 18, 35–36
  mind, theories of, 32–33
  and moral algebra, 33, 35, 36–40
Bankruptcy, 19, 31
Bartlett, Sir Frederic C.
  and Cambridge psychology, 47
  cultural diffusion work, 44–46,
    62–65
  early career, 47, 50
  and evolution, 63
  and instincts, 50–51, 63
  as Rivers's protégé, 50
  social psychology of, 62–67
Behavior
  as accounting practice, 18
  conceptions of, 190, 192
  control of, 170–72, 177–78, 180
  experimentally controlling,
    187–88
  human, 326, 329

History of Political Economy 48 (annual suppl.) DOI 10.1215/00182702-3619446
Copyright 2016 by Duke University Press

Behavior (*continued*)
  irrational, 114–17, 285–86, 317–18,
    328–29
  Skinnerian control of, 183–84
Behavioral Economics Roundtable,
    289
Behaviorism (psychology)
  and consumer choice theory, 175
  and consumer demand theory,
    189–90
  and control, 170–72, 178
  critiques of, 93–95
  in economics (*See* economics,
    behaviorist)
and functionalism, 179
  history of, 171, 174, 180
  and institutionalism, 170, 191–92
  and Knight, 136–38
  McDougall's influence, 94
  and Mitchell, 191
  and neoclassical economics, 174
  and operationism, 188
  and ordinalism, 171–72, 184–85
  Skinnerian, 182–84
  theoretical, 318–20, 330
  turn in economics, 172
  and Watson, 93–94, 178, 180–82
  Watson's attack on, 173–74
Bentham, Jeremy
  critiques of, 3, 121–22
  and the economic man, 160
  influence of, 77
  influence on Jevons, 3, 18, 36
  and marginal economists, 74–75
  Mitchell, influence on, 126
Berlyne, David. *See also* Collative
    variables
  arousal research, 302–3, 305
  asethetics research, 303–5
  early research, 300–2
  exploration, studies of, 303, 310
  legacy, 305
  life of, 300n9

motivation model, 300–5, 309
  Scitovsky, influence on, 11, 299,
    305, 309
Biel, William C., 207, 212
Bernays, Edward L., 111–12
Biological determinism, 52, 59, 60,
    82, 151
Bloomsbury group, 155–157, 159
Bridgman, Percy, 171, 184–85, 187–89
Brown, Bernice B., 205
Business studies, 149–150

Caltech conference (1988), 271
Cambridge psychological model, 3,
    48, 51, 53–55, 65
Camerer, Colin, 271n2, 281, 284–85
Capital, human, 78–79
Carnegie, Andrew, 115, 142–43
Carver, Thomas N., 132
Center for Advanced Study in the
    Behavioral Sciences
    (CASBS), 274, 276
Chadwick, H. M., 62–63, 65
Chapman, Robert L., 207
Chenery, Hollis, 228–29, 231, 235–36
Childs, Harwood L., 113–14
Choice. *See also* behaviorism
    (psychology), theoretical;
    Cumulative effects (CE)
    model; Prospect theory;
    Rational choice theory
  architects, 192
  and control, 172
  definition of, 316–17
  equilibrium, 285, 310
  human, 14, 74, 321–22, 326
  hypothetical, 272, 278, 282–83,
    290, 322
  individual, 97, 297
  influences on, 326
  modeling, 220–22
  preference, conflicts with, 307
  probabilistic theory of, 263–64

rational theory of, 17–18, 72,
    74–75, 89, 296
Sherwood on, 80–82
and theoretical behaviorism, 320–21
Clark, John B., 115–16
Clark, John M., 128–31, 190
Cleveland, Alfred A., 79–80
Cognitive dissonance, 233–34
Cognitive psychology, 188–89,
    281–82, 284, 327
Collative variables, 302, 304–5, 310
Comparative philology, 57
Consciousness, 327
Consumer choice theory, 175, 296
Consumer cooperation, 112
Consumer demand theory, 170–72,
    184, 189–90
Consumption
    American, 295–96, 308
    of comforts, 11
    and economic development, 83–84
    and rationality, 119
    Victorian morality of, 21
Consumption skills, 297, 308
Copeland, Morris A., 92, 100, 131,
    140, 191
Coursey, Donald, 271n2, 279–81,
    284n30
Creel, George, 109–10
Cultural diffusion, 44–46, 62–65
Cumulative effects (CE) model,
    11–12, 319–21

Daily planners. *See* diaries
Darwin, Charles, 34, 37, 51, 88, 152,
    317–18
Davenport, Herbert L., 132–3
Davidson, Donald, 255
Davidson-Suppes-Siegel experiment
    (DSS). *See also* Mosteller-
    Nogee experiment (MN)
    background, 240, 253
    critiques of, 262–63

design, 257–60
findings, 260–62
goal of, 256
impact, 241, 262–64
money, use in, 257
origins of, 255
psychological considerations,
    256, 262, 265
timeline, 255–56
Deception, 7, 14, 272, 279, 282–83,
    290
Decision making, rational, 17,
    34–35, 37
Deduction, in economics, 74–77,
    82, 119, 159
DeGroot, Morris, 263–5
Dewey, John N., 75, 105, 180,
    187–88
Diaries
    and almanacs, 22
    Bain's use of, 34–35
    for decision making, 2, 34
    and domestic accounting, 21,
        23, 25–26
    Eliot's use of, 26–28
    Jevons's use of, 28–31
    and moral algebra, 34–35, 39
    and moral economy, 24–26
    and self-improvement, 23–24
    varieties of, 23
Diffusion, cultural, 45, 62–65
Disciplinary history, 46–47
Doob, Leonard, 112
Douglas, Paul H., 100, 131

Easterlin, Richard A., 176
Economic development
    Hirschman's views on, 9–10,
        229–233
    as similar to RAND Systems
        Training Program,
        236–37
Economic pathology, 106

Economic Science Association
(ESA), 290
Economics
aspriations to science, 73–74
behavioral (*See* economics,
behavioral)
classical, 75
deductive methods, use of, 74, 76,
159
as deductive science, 77–78
early history of, 72–77
evolutionary, 56–57, 60
foundations in history, 16
as fundamental science, 80, 83
historical methods, use of, 74,
76
instinct psychology, applied to,
104–7
instinct theory, use of, 92–93
institutional, 75, 77
neoclassical (*See* neoclassical
economics)
normative, 199
Patten's perspectives on, 83–84
research methods, 74–75
Sherwood's perspectives on,
80–82
subfields, division into, 148
utilitarianism, basis in, 72
Ward's psychological approach to,
78–79
Economics, behavioral
and experimental economics, 14,
270–71, 273, 288, 290
goals of, 192
misunderstandings in, 177
myth of, 177–78
and "nudging," 6, 192–93
origins of, 172–3, 177, 273, 280,
289
revival, 11, 271
and subjective outcomes, 175–76

Economics, experimental
and behavioral economics, 14,
270–71, 273, 288, 290
methods, 13–14, 272, 290
origins of, 290
Edie, Lionel D., 87
Edwards, Ward, 253
Eliot, George
Bain, influence of, 35–36
Middelmarch, 2, 35–36, 38–39
Spinoza, influence of, 32
use of diaries, 26–28
Estes, William, 275–76
Evans, Mary Anne. *See* Eliot,
George
Evolutionary economics, 56–57, 60
Expected utility theory. *See also*
Davidson-Suppes-Siegel
experiment (DSS); Mosteller-
Nogee experiment (MN)
assumptions of, 240
decision makers, 248, 250–51,
256, 262
critiques of, 251, 330
debates over, 243, 252
decline of, 264
failures, 330
and gambling, 243, 250
history of, 252–53
and meausuring utility, 242–3,
248, 251
model decision makers, 242–43,
248, 250–51
rise of, 252–53
subjective, 255n15, 257
testing, 6–7, 239, 263 (*See also*
Davidson-Suppes-Siegel
experiment; Mosteller-Nogee
experiment (MN))
validation of, 240
von Neumann and Morgenstern's
axioms, 242–43

Experimental Economics and
    Psychology conference, 271
Explicit maximizers, 318
Exploratory behavior, 301–2

Fast-slow distinction, 328
Festinger, Leon, 10, 233–35
Fixed-ration schedules, 317
Florence, Alix S., 155–57
Fouraker, Lawrence E., 274–79
Framing, 327–28
Franklin, Benjamin, 2, 22, 33–34.
    See also Moral algebra
Freud, Sigmund. *See also*
    psychoanalysis
  and art, 158–59
  Bloomsbury group, influence on,
    156–57
  Hirschman's critique of, 235
  Lippmann, influence on, 152–55
  Tugwell on, 100
Friedman, Milton
  background, 244
  on EUT, 243
  and Mosteller-Nogee experiment
    (MN), 245
  Thurstone, critique of, 242
Fry, Roger, 157–59
Functionalist psychology, 179–81,
    180n5, 191n19, 193

Gambling, 240
Game simulation, 206, 213–16
Game theory, 207n8, 254, 284–85
Games and Decisions, 262
Games and human interaction, 79–80
Geisler, Murray, 201, 203–4
Giddings, Franklin H., 77–78, 142
Gigerenzer, Gerd, 18, 34, 41, 289n45
Great Depression, The, 146, 148
Great War, The, 101–2, 106, 109,
    114, 116–17

Grether, David, 271–72, 277n14,
    282n24
Grote, the Reverend John, 47, 52–53,
    55, 57
Group learning, 208–12
Group stress, 211–12

Habit, theories of
  Marshall, 49, 51, 53
  McDougall, 59
  Veblen, 4, 51–52, 58–60, 98
Hadley, Arthur T., 86
Hall, G. Stanley, 150–51
Hobbes, Thomas, 72, 74, 77, 124
Hobson, John R., 97–98
Hapgood, Norman, 117–18
Happiness, 308–9
Hedonic value, 302–3, 305
Hedonism
  and collative variables, 304, 309
  concept, defense of, 132–34
  critiques of, 121–22, 300n7
  and evolution, 77
  as motivation, 97
Hirschman, Albert
  aggregative analysis, 228
  on backwardness, 227, 230–31
  career, 227–28
  on economic development, 9–10,
    229–33
  Festinger, influence of, 10 233–34
  on Freud, 235
  goals of, 234
  on investmenting, 232
  Mowrer, influence of, 10, 233
  on productive investment, 231–32
  and RAND, 236–37
  reactions to, 227, 235–36
  Rosenberg, influence of, 234–35
  structural planning, critiques of,
    226, 228
Human capital, 78–79

Human-machine interaction, 208
Human nervous system, 48–49
Huxley, Thomas H., 32, 88
Hypothetical choices, 278, 282, 290,
    322

Implementation rationality, 8, 200–1,
    203–6, 211, 218
Inducement mechanisms, 232, 235
Induction, 13, 74–75, 159, 214
Information processing, 208–9
Instinct psychology
    Bartlett, 4, 50–51, 63
    Clark, 129–30
    Cleveland, 79
    failures of, 131–32
    James, 89
    Link, 91–92
    Marshall, 4, 53
    McDougall, 49–50, 52, 54, 59,
        89–90
    Mitchell, 123–24, 191
    Parker, 105–6
    Rivers, 4, 49–51, 67
    Taussig, 126–28
    Tead, 149
    Veblen, 4, 51–52, 58–61, 67, 96
    Wallas, 93, 123
Instincts
    and behaviorism, 94–95
    conflicting, 50–51, 63, 67
    perversion of, 106
    social, 66
Institutionalism
    American, 160, 170–71
    and behavioral control, 190–93
    behaviorist, 191–92
    critique of ordinalism, 178
    defense of, 140
    and empiricism, 77
    failure of, 131

history of, 75, 100, 147
    and marginalism, 118
    and the New Deal, 75
    and psychic conditions, 117
    and social control, 139
    and social psychology, 118
Institutions, social, 67, 81, 84, 98,
    120
Instrumental learning, 318
Intellectual revolution (1880s), 57
Introduction to Social Psychology,
    49, 51n7, 52, 67, 90
Irrational behavior, 114–17, 285–86,
    317–18, 328–29

Jackson, Hughlings, 3, 48
James, William
    influence on McDougall, 52
    influence on Veblen, 4, 51
    instincts, theory of, 89, 126
    psychology, influence on, 74–76
Jevons, William Stanley
    Bain, influence of, 2, 35–36
    diaries, use of, 2, 28–31
    equivocation of reason and
        emotion, 38–40
    life history, 28, 30
    and moral algebra, 2, 36–37
    on pleasure and pain, 36–37, 40
    The Theory of Political Economy,
        18
    as Victorian prude, 160
Johnson, Alvin, 87
*Joyless Economy: The Psychology
    of Human Satisfaction*
    American consumption, 295–96
    Berlyne, influence of, 299, 305
    goals of, 297
    and Plato, 298–99
    rational choice, critique of, 296
    reception, 10–11, 13, 295–97, 311

Kagel, John, 271n2, 281, 288, 291
Kahneman, Daniel
  as experimental economist, 8, 12
  influence of, 271
  prospect theory, 14, 262, 326–27
Karr, Herbert, 205
Kennedy, John L., 207–8, 212
Keynes, John Maynard
  education, early, 155
  Freud, influence of, 155, 157
  on happiness, 309n26
  and psychoanalysis, 151
Knight, Frank, 100, 136–40, 148,
  151

Labor market, 101, 103, 108
Labor movement, 102
Lamarck, Jean-Baptiste, 90
Lapouge, Vacher de, 57–58
Layard, Richard, 174, 176–77
Leisure class, 61
Letts, John, 22
Lewes, George Henry, 23, 28, 32, 36
Link, Henry C., 91–92
Lippmann, Walter, 103, 111, 151–54
Logistics, 199, 203
LSL (RAND Logistics Systems
    Laboratory)
  board games by, 214, 216n14
  economists in, 214, 219
  findings, overall, 218–20, 222
  game simulations, use of, 206,
    213–18
  goals, 199
  history of, 8, 201, 212
  psychologists in, 219, 222
  research methods of, 199

Macroeconomics, 111, 114, 151
Malthus, Thomas Robert, 77–78
Marginal protection kits, 204–5

Marginal revolution, the, 5, 72, 74,
  134, 160, 173, 242
Marginal utility
  criticism of, 88, 95, 98–99, 121–22,
    130–31
  defenses of, 132–34, 136
  economics, 75, 81
  theory of, 88–89, 132–33, 136,
    330
Marginalism
  American, 58n16
  critiques of, 88–89
  growth of, 75
  reactions against, 88, 99, 132
  Sherwood's theory of, 80–81
Market theory, 72, 130
Markets, 73, 96, 104, 285–86
Marschak, Jacob, 243, 252, 263–64
Marshall, Alfred
  at Cambridge, 53–54
  early work of, 46, 52
  and economics, 55–56, 74, 160
  and evolution, 53, 55, 60
  habits, theory of, 49, 51, 53
  instincts, theory of, 50n6, 53
  mind, model of, 52–56, 66
  nervous system, model of, 48–50
  primitive-modern divide (theory),
    55, 57, 66
  Principles of Economics, 49, 53,
    58n16
  self-consciousness, theory of,
    52–53
  Veblen, differences from, 51,
    57–60, 67
Marshall, Leon, 117
Mayo, Elton, 116–17
McDougall, William
  critiques of, 91–92
  on economics, 89–91
  habit, theory of, 59

influence on behaviorism, 94
influence on Veblen, 52
instincts, theory of, 49–50, 52, 54,
    59, 89–90
Introduction to Social Psychology,
    49, 51n7, 52, 67, 90
James, influence of, 52
Mitchell, influence on, 4, 118–19
Parker, influence on, 104–5
McKinsey, J. C. C., 254–55
Middlemarch (Eliot), 2, 35–36, 38–39
Mill, John Stuart, 18, 37, 48, 54, 74
Miller, Peter, 19
Mind
    accumulative model of, 49
    Marshall's model, 52–56, 66
    primitive *vs.* modern, 55, 57, 66
    as untrustworthy, 36–37
    Veblen's model of, 47
Mitchell, Wesley C.
    and behaviorism, 191
    Bentham, critiques of, 3, 121,
        126
    consumer demand theory,
        critique of, 190–91
    economics, critiques of, 119–22,
        125, 190
    human nature, improving, 122–23,
        125–26
    instincts, theory of, 123–24
    as institutionalist, 3–4, 119, 126
    Lippmann, influence of, 125
    McDougall, influence of, 118–9,
        122, 191
    and psychology, 118–9, 122, 125
    and rationality, 119
    Tugwell, influence on, 99
    and Veblen, 124
    and Wallas, 123–24, 126
Moral accounting. *See* accounting
    practices, moral

Moral algebra
    and Bain, 33, 35, 36–40
    and diaries, 39
    and Franklin, 2, 18, 33–34,
        36–37, 39
    in *Middlemarch,* 38–39
    reinterpretation by Jevons,
        36–37
Moral economy, 17, 21, 24
Moral philosophy, 4, 73, 146
Morgenstern, Oskar, 242–43, 245,
    251–54
Mosteller, Frederick, 239, 244–45
Mosteller-Nogee experiment
    (MN). *See also* Davidson-
        Suppes-Siegel experiment
    critiques of, 251–53, 262–63
    design, 248–51
    findings, 248, 253
    impact, 241, 252–53, 262–64
    money, use in, 249
    origins, 239–40, 244–45
    overview, 245–48
    and psychology, 251–52, 265
    research questions, 246
Mowrer, Orval Hobart, 10, 233, 235
Myers, C. S., 54, 62, 65, 66n26

Neoclassical economics, 56–57, 96,
    174
von Neumann, John
    critiques of, 251, 253
    *Theory of Games and Economic
        Behavior,* 242–43, 245, 254
    utility research, 242–43
Newell, Allen, 207, 212
"Night-mind," 116–17
Nogee, Philip, 239, 245. *See also*
    Mosteller-Nogee experiment
    (MN)
"Nudgers," 192–93

Operationalism, 185–87
Operationism, 188–89
Optimality theory, 317–18, 329–30
Ordinalism, 171–72, 178, 184–85
Ordinalist revolution, 170
Organism (concept), 208
Organizations, growing, 209

Pain and pleasure, 18, 33, 36–38, 40,
    77, 298–300
Parker, Carleton, 103–7, 151, 160
Patten, Simon N.
    critiques of other disciplines,
        84–85
    economics, perspectives on, 83–84
    psychology, perceived use to
        economics, 83–85, 88
    responses to, 85–88
    social sciences as equals, 83
Payments, experimental, 277–78
Philology, comparative, 57
Plato, 298–99, 306
Pleasure economy, 83, 85, 87
Plott, Charles, 8, 271–72
Preferences
    Bernays's theory of, 111–12
    Doob's theory of changing, 112
    manipulation of, 109, 111
    stability of, 110
    as variables, 113
Price theory, 96, 100, 126, 129, 148
Probabilistic insurance, 325–26
Probabilistic theory of choice,
    263–64
Probability distortion, 7
Project for Research and
    Development (RAND). See
    RAND (Project for Research
    and Development)
Propaganda, 109–14
Prospect theory, 14, 322–27, 329–30

Psyche, American, 5, 73, 143–44, 160
Psychoanalysis, 100, 150–1, 157–58.
    See also Freud, Sigmund
Psychology
    aspirations to science, 73–75
    associationist, 18, 32
    behaviorist, Behaviorism
        (psychology)
    Cambridge school, 46–47
    cognitive, 188–89, 289–90
    deductive economics, threat to, 82
    early history of, 72–77
    as eclectic, 75–76
    in economic subfields, 148–9
    and evolution theory, 72
    experimental, 76
    functional, 171, 178–80, 180n5,
        190, 191n19
    as fundamental science, 77–78
    gestalt, 185–6, 188, 189n17
    histories of, 173, 178–80, 187–9
    industrial, 16, 65
    instinct (See Instinct psychology)
    military, 206–7
    research methods, 74–76, 159
    social (See Social psychology)
    struggle for recognition, 76
    worker, 102–3
Public opinion. See Propaganda

RAND (Project for Research and
    Development). See also LSL;
    SCOOP; SRL
    history of, 199
    logistics department, 203–6
    simulations, use of, 8, 206, 208
    System Training Program, 212,
        236
    Systems Development
        Corporation, 212
    uniqueness of, 13

Ratio schedules, 317–18, 320
Rational actor theory
  and Bloomsbury group, 156–57
  crtiqiues of, 88, 95–96, 121
  and instinct theory, 89
  loss of, 132
  McDougall's critique, 90–91
  Whitaker's defense of, 134
Rational choice theory, 17–18, 72,
    74–75, 89, 296
Rational decision making, 17,
    34–35, 37
Rationality
  conditions enabling, 117
  economic, 115, 317
  and education, 115
  implementation, 200–1, 203–6,
    211, 218
  procedural, 200, 211
  substantive, 200, 211
Regulatory Consistency Assessment
    Programme (RCAP), 220–22
Reinforcement schedules, 317
Responses, 318–19, 328–29. See also
    Cumulative effects (CE)
    model
Reversal learning, 319–20
Rivers, W. H. R.
  and instincts, 49–51
  McDougall, as influenced by, 67
  model of human nervous system,
    48
  and the unconscious, 49–50
Robinson, Edward S., 112–13
Rosenberg, Nathan, 234–5
Roth, Avlin, 271n2, 281, 283,
    285n33, 288
Russell Sage Foundation
  behavioral economics program, 8,
    271, 273, 280, 288, 290–91
  experimental economics group,
    280–3, 285, 287

Samuelson, Paul
  and Expected Utility Theory
    (EUT), 252
  and gestalt psychology, 185–86
  as non-behaviorist, 177, 185, 187
  as ordinalist, 171–72
  revealed preferences project,
    185–6
"Satisficing," 200, 216, 318
Savage, L. J., 239, 243–45, 252
Scitovsky, Tibor. See also Joyless
    Economy: The Psychology of
    Human Satisfaction
  affluence, problems of, 308, 311
  on American consumption, 295–
    96, 308
  and arousal, 310
  Berlyne, influence of, 11, 299,
    305, 309
  and Cambridge economists,
    298–99, 306
  comfort and pleasure, 306–9,
    311–2
  contribution of, 310–11
  and Greek philosophy, 298
  psychology, turn to, 297–98
  rational choice, critique of, 296,
    298, 307
  and satisfaction, 299–300
SCOOP (Project for the Scientific
    Computation of Optimum
    Programs), 201–3
Seager, Henry R., 85–86
Sen, Amartya, 175, 177
Sherwood, Sidney, 80–82
Shubik, Martin, 273–77
Siegel, Sidney. See also Davidson-
    Suppes-Siegel experiment
  death of, 273–74, 276
  deception, experimental, 279
  education, 255–56, 274
  experimental payments, 276–79

legacy, 276–80, 286, 290
probability matching experiments, 275–76
and Shubik, 274–76
Smith, influence on, 277
Tversky's views on, 270, 272–73
Simon, Herbert, 200, 209–11
Simulations, 202, 208, 211–13, 220
Skinner, B.F.
   behaviorism, 171, 182–85, 272–73
   and conditioning, 6, 317
   as operationist, 188–89
Sloan foundation, 8, 273, 280, 286–87, 290–91
Smith, Adam, 72, 77, 82, 100, 108, 126–127
Smith, Vernon L.
   goals of, 8
   Siegel, defense of, 283–84
   Siegel, influence of, 270, 272–73, 277, 279, 283
Social institutions, 67, 81, 84, 98, 120
Social psychology. See also McDougall, William
   Bartlett, 62–66
   habits and sociality, 51
   and institutional change, 52
   of Parker, 104–6
   Sherwood's claim as economic, 80
   solving economic crises, use in, 101–2
Social sciences, the, 57, 73, 77–78, 80
Spencer, Herbert, 3, 48–49, 53, 147
Spinoza, Baruch, 32
SRL (RAND Systems Research Laboratory)
   ADDC model, 208–9
   creation of, 208
   System Training Program, 212
   work of, 9, 208–12

Stanford Value Theory Project, 254–55. See also Davidson-Suppes-Siegel experiment (DSS)
Strachey, Alix S., 155–57
Strachey, James, 155–57
Strachey, Lytton, 155–57
Sunder, Shyam, 271n2, 281, 284–5
Suppes, Patrick, 253–54, 263. See also Davidson-Suppes-Siegel experiment
Systems Development Corporation, 9, 212

Tannenbaum, Frank, 102–3, 107, 132
Taussig, Frank, 104, 126–28
Tead, Ordway, 149–50
Thackeray, William Makepeace, 16, 23–24
Thaler, Richard
   on behavioral economics, 287–88
   career, 271n2, 280–81
   on mental accounting, 17–18
   Nudge, 192
Theory of Games and Economic Behavior, 242–43, 245, 254
Thrift, 111, 142
Thurstone, Louis Leon, 241–42, 251
Tinbergen, Jan, 235–6
Todd, Peter M., 18, 34
Tolman, Edward C., 171, 178, 182–83 188–89
Truth and Probability, 249
Tugwell, Rexford, 99–100, 135, 148
Tversky, Amos
   as experimental economist, 7–8
   influence of, 271
   mental accounting, theory of, 17–18
   prospect theory, 14, 264, 272, 326–27
   on Siegel, 270, 272–73

Unconscious, the, 4, 49, 150, 327
United States of America, The
    Adams's perception of, 145–46
    cultural identity of, 141–143
    exceptionalism, 73, 143–44, 160
    psychology, perceptions of, 143
Utilitarianism, 72–74, 75
Utility. *See also* Davidson-Suppes-
        Siegel experiment; Expected
        utility theory; Marginal
        utility; Mosteller-Nogee
        experiment (MN)
    limits of, 306
    measurement of, 240, 242–43,
        250–51, 263–64
    and rationality, 136

Vanderlip, Frank A., 114–15
Veblen, Thorstein
    economics, critiques of, 96–98
    education of, 146–47
    and evolutionary economics,
        56–57, 60
    habits, theory of, 4, 51–52, 58–60,
        98
    individuals, theory of, 58
    instincts, theory of, 51–52, 58–61,
        67, 96
    institutions, theory of, 52, 60–61,
        124
    James, influence of, 4, 51
    on leisure class, 61
    Marshall, differences from, 4, 51,
        57–60, 67
    McDougall, as influenced by, 52,
        59–60

    mind, model of, 47
    neoclassical economics,
        challenges to, 56–57
        as obtuse, 95–96, 98
    Paker, influence on, 105
    rational actor, critique of, 95–96
    and social evolution, 60–61
Viner, Jacob, 135–36

Wallas, Graham, 93, 123–24
Wallis, Allen, 242, 244–5, 249, 257
Wanner, Eric, 271, 280, 286, 288,
        289
War
    avoiding, 115
    propaganda, 109–14
    as psychological problem,
        116–17
Ward, James, 47, 62n19, 77
Ward, Lester, 78–79
Watson, John B., 93–94, 178,
        180–82, 187
Weber, Max, 16–18, 22, 40
Weber-Fechner Law, 16, 322–23
Whitaker, A. C., 133–34
Wolfe, A. B., 100–1
Wolman, Leo, 102, 107–9
Women, as domestic accountants,
        21
Woolf, Virginia, 156–57
Worker psychology, 102–3
World War 1, 101–2, 106, 109, 114,
        116–17
Wright, H. W., 92

Young, Allyn, 140